Emerging Metropolis

New York Jews in the Age of
Immigration, 1840–1920

CITY OF PROMISES was made possible in part through the generosity of a number of individuals and foundations. Their thoughtful support will help ensure that this work is affordable to schools, libraries, and other not-for-profit institutions.

The Lucius N. Littauer Foundation made a leadership gift before a word of CITY OF PROMISES had been written, a gift that set this project on its way. Hugo Barreca, The Marian B. and Jacob K. Javits Foundation, Mr. and Mrs. Peter Malkin, David P. Solomon, and a donor who wishes to remain anonymous helped ensure that it never lost momentum. We are deeply grateful.

CITY OF PROMISES

A HISTORY OF THE JEWS OF NEW YORK

GENERAL EDITOR: DEBORAH DASH MOORE

VOLUME 1

Haven of Liberty

New York Jews in the
New World, 1654–1865

HOWARD B. ROCK

VOLUME 2

Emerging Metropolis

New York Jews in the
Age of Immigration, 1840–1920

ANNIE POLLAND AND

DANIEL SOYER

VOLUME 3

Jews in Gotham

New York Jews in a
Changing City, 1920–2010

JEFFREY S. GUROCK

Advisory Board:
Hasia Diner (New York University)
Leo Hershkowitz (Queens College)
Ira Katznelson (Columbia University)
Thomas Kessner (CUNY Graduate Center)
Tony Michels (University of Wisconsin,
 Madison)
Judith C. Siegel (Center for Jewish History)
Jenna Weissman-Joselit (Princeton University)
Beth Wenger (University of Pennsylvania)

CITY OF PROMISES

A HISTORY OF THE JEWS OF NEW YORK

EMERGING

METROPOLIS

NEW YORK JEWS IN THE AGE OF
IMMIGRATION, 1840–1920

ANNIE POLLAND AND
DANIEL SOYER

WITH A FOREWORD BY

DEBORAH DASH MOORE

AND WITH A VISUAL ESSAY BY

DIANA L. LINDEN

NEW YORK UNIVERSITY PRESS ■ NEW YORK AND LONDON

NEW YORK UNIVERSITY PRESS
New York and London
www.nyupress.org

References to Internet websites (URLs) were accurate at the time of writing.
Neither the author nor New York University Press is responsible for URLs that
may have expired or changed since the manuscript was prepared.

Library of Congress Cataloging-in-Publication Data
City of promises : a history of the Jews of New York / general editor, Deborah Dash Moore.
v.   cm.
Includes bibliographical references and index.
Contents: v. 1. Haven of liberty: New York Jews in the New World, 1654–1865 / Howard B.
Rock — v. 2. Emerging metropolis: New York Jews in the age of immigration, 1840–1920 /
Annie Polland and Daniel Soyer — v. 3. Jews in Gotham: New York Jews in a changing city,
1920–2010.
ISBN 978-0-8147-7632-2 (cl : alk. paper) — ISBN 978-0-8147-4521-2 (ebook) —
ISBN 978-0-8147-7692-6 (ebook) — ISBN 978-0-8147-1731-8 (boxed set : alk. paper) —
ISBN 978-0-8147-2932-8 (e-set)
1. Jews—New York (State)—New York. 2. New York (N.Y.)—Ethnic relations.   I. Moore,
Deborah Dash, 1946– II. Rock, Howard B., 1944–
F128.9.J5C64 2012
305.892'40747—dc23   2012003246

New York University Press books are printed on acid-free paper,
and their binding materials are chosen for strength and durability.
We strive to use environmentally responsible suppliers and materials
to the greatest extent possible in publishing our books.

Manufactured in the United States of America

10   9   8   7   6   5   4   3   2   1

To Mike and Lily (AP)
and
To the Soyer, Futterman, Chassner, and Wilson
families—Jewish New Yorkers in three centuries (DS)

CONTENTS

"[O]f all the big cities," Sergeant Milton Lehman of the *Stars and Stripes* affirmed in 1945, "New York is still the promised land."[1] As a returning Jewish GI, Lehman compared New York with European cities. Other Jews also knew what New York offered that made it so desirable, even if they had not served overseas. First and foremost, security: Jews could live without fear in New York. Yes, they faced discrimination, but in this city of almost eight million residents, many members of its ethnic and religious groups encountered prejudice. Jews contended with anti-Semitism in the twentieth century more than German Protestants or Irish Catholics dealt with bias, perhaps; but the Irish had endured a lot in the nineteenth century, and Jews suffered less than African Americans, Latinos, and Asian New Yorkers. And New York provided more than security: Jews could live freely as Jews. The presence of a diverse population of close to two million New York Jews contributed to their sense that "everyone was Jewish."[2] New York Jews understood that there were many ways to be Jewish. The city welcomed Jews in all their variety. New York Jews saw the city as a place where they, too, could flourish and express themselves. As a result, they came to identify with the city, absorbing its ethos even as they helped to shape its urban characteristics. When World War II ended in Europe with victory over Nazi Germany, New York's promises glowed more brightly still.

New York's multiethnic diversity, shaped in vital dimensions by its large Jewish population, shimmered as a showplace of American democratic distinctiveness, especially vis-à-vis Europe. In contrast to a continent that had become a vast slaughterhouse, where millions of European Jews had been ruthlessly murdered with industrial efficiency, New York glistened as a city Jews could and did call their home in America. The famous skyline had defined urban cosmopolitanism in the years after World War I. Now the city's thriving ethnic neighborhoods—Jewish and Catholic, African American and Puerto Rican, Italian and Irish—came to represent modern urban culture. New York's economy responded robustly to demands of war production. By the end of hostilities, its per capita income exceeded the national average by 14 percent.

But as a poster city for immigration, with a majority population composed of immigrants and their children, the city had to contend with negative perceptions. Considered undesirable by many Americans, Jews and other foreigners in the city contributed to impressions that New York seemed less American than other cities with large percentages of native-born residents.[3]

As the city flourished during and after the war, it maintained its political commitments to generous social welfare benefits to help its poorest residents. Jews advocated for these policies, supporting efforts to establish a liberal urban legacy. In modeling a progressive and prosperous multiethnic twentieth-century American city, New York demonstrated what its Jews valued. Versions of Jewish urbanism played not just on the political stage but also on the streets of the city's neighborhoods. Its expressions could be found as well in New York's centers of cultural production.

By the middle of the twentieth century, no city offered Jews more than New York. It nourished both celebration and critique. New York gave Jews visibility as individuals and as a group. It provided employment and education, inspiration and freedom, fellowship and community. Jews reciprocated by falling in love with the city, its buildings' hard angles and perspectives, its grimy streets and harried pace. But by the 1960s and '70s, Jews' love affair with the city soured. For many of the second generation who grew up on New York's sidewalks, immersed in its babel of languages and cultural syncretism, prosperity dimmed their affection for the working-class urban world of their youth. Many of them aspired to suburban pleasures of home ownership, grass and trees that did not have to be shared with others in public parks. Yet New York City remained the wellspring of Jewish American culture for much of the century, a resource of Jewishness even for those living thousands of miles west of the Hudson River.

Jews had not always felt free to imagine the city as their special place. Indeed, not until mass immigration from Europe piled up their numbers, from the tens of thousands to the hundreds of thousands, had Jews laid claim to New York and influenced its politics and culture. Its Jewish population soared from five hundred thousand at the turn of the twentieth century to 1.1 million before the start of World War I. On the eve of World War II, Jews, over a quarter of New York's residents, ranked as the largest ethnic group.[4] Demography both encouraged many outsiders to perceive New York as a Jewish city and underwrote local cultural productions, such as a thriving theater scene, a flourishing popular music business, and extensive publishing in several languages. Jews were used to living as a minority in Europe and the Middle East. New York offered life without a majority population—without one single ethnic group dominating urban society. Now Jews could go about their business, much of it taking place within ethnic niches, as if they were the city's predominant group.

When and in what sense did New York become a city of promises for Jews? Certainly not in the colonial era. During that period, seeds for future promises were planted, most importantly political, economic, and religious rights. While New York's few hundred Jews lived in the shadow of far more prosperous Jewish communities in London and Amsterdam, New York Jewish men enjoyed citizenship rights and responsibilities that their peers in London could only envy. These rights gradually led New York Jews to emerge from a closed synagogue society and to participate with enthusiasm in revolutionary currents sweeping the colonies. Jews in New York absorbed formative ideas regarding human rights; they tasted freedom and put their lives on the line for it during the Revolution. In the decades that followed, they incorporated ideals of the American Enlightenment into their Jewish lives.

Sometime during the nineteenth century, these changes attracted increasing attention from European Jews. New York began to acquire a reputation as a destination in itself. Arriving from Europe at Castle Garden, increasing numbers of Jewish immigrants decided to stay. New York's bustling streets enticed them, so they put off riding west or south to peddle or settle. Sometimes, older brothers made that choice, as did Jonas and Louis Strauss, who sent their younger brother Levi to the West Coast via steamship in 1853 to open a branch of their New York City dry-goods firm. Levi Strauss did better, perhaps, than they expected when he went into manufacturing copper-riveted denim work pants after the Civil War.[5] But such a move into garment manufacturing from selling dry goods and, especially, used clothing had already taken root in New York prior to the war. It formed the basis of an industry that became the city's largest, and more than any other, it made New York the city of promises.

In 1962, the historian Moses Rischin published his pioneering book, *The Promised City: New York's Jews, 1870–1914*. Rischin aimed to "identify those currents of human and institutional vitality central to the American urban experience that converged on the Lower East Side in the era of the great Jewish migration just as New York emerged as the nation's and the world's most dynamic metropolis."[6] The interlocking themes of Jewish immigration from eastern Europe and the rise of New York as a "city of ambition" led Rischin to cast his account as a "revolutionary transformation" not only in American urban history but also in Jewish history.[7] Rischin saw a universal paradigm of modernization unfolding in the very particularistic experiences of New York Jews. His vision of democratic urban community remains relevant to contemporary scholars.

What did the city promise? First, a job. Close to half of all immigrants sewed clothing in hundreds of small-scale sweatshops that disguised an ever-burgeoning industry that soon became one of the nation's most important. Second, a place to live. True, the overcrowded Lower East Side bulged with residents, even its modern tenements straining to accommodate a density of Jewish population that rivaled Bombay. Yet by the early twentieth century, bridges to Brooklyn and rapid transit to Harlem and the Bronx promised improvements: fresh air, hot and cold running water, even a private toilet and bathroom. Third, food. Jewish immigrants had not starved in Europe, but New York's abundance changed their diets and attitudes toward food and its simple pleasures. In New York, a center of the nation's baking industry, Jews could enjoy a fresh roll and coffee each morning for pennies. Fourth, clothing. It did not take long, especially laboring in the garment industry, for Jews to trade their old-world clothes for the latest ready-made styles. Thus properly attired, they looked and felt like modern men and women, able and willing to make their way.[8]

Such promises might be quotidian, but they opened Jews' eyes to other more important ones. Young Jewish immigrants embraced the city's promise of free public education, from elementary school to secondary school, all the way through college. Only a handful of Jewish immigrants in the nineteenth century and years before World War I ever managed to take advantage of such a magnificent offer. Although a family economy that privileged sons over daughters when decisions about post-elementary education had to be made and costs of forgoing income from teenaged children often required Jews to go to work and not attend school, increasingly Jews flocked to the city's free schools. Some immigrants, especially women, thought the city promised freedom to choose a spouse, though matchmakers also migrated across the ocean. Still others rejoiced in what they imagined was a promise of uncensored language: written and spoken, published and on stage, in Yiddish, Hebrew,

German, Ladino, and English. Some conceived of the city's rough democracy as holding a promise of solidarity among working men and women, while a significant number demanded extension of civil and voting rights to women.

Then there were more ambiguous promises. Did New York offer Jews a chance to live without a formal, legally constituted Jewish community? Did it suggest that Jews no longer needed to practice Jewish rituals or observe the Sabbath? Some Jewish immigrants thought they could leave behind old-world ways of thinking and acting; they secularized their Jewish lives, often starting the process in Europe even before they emigrated. Others fashioned ways of being Jewish, both secular and religious, in tune with New York's evolving cultures. Both groups identified their own visions of what it meant to be Jewish in America with New York itself.

That New York City bloomed with such promises would have been hard to anticipate in 1654. Then the ragged seaport only reluctantly welcomed its first contingent of miserable Jewish migrants. In fact, not receiving permission to settle, Jews had to petition to stay, to live and work in the outpost. They agreed to practice their religion in private even as they participated in civic culture. When the British turned New Amsterdam into New York, they accepted these arrangements, giving Jews unprecedented legal rights. Here lay hints of future promises. Gradually the British increased opportunities for public religious expression and extended to Jewish men civil rights, including citizenship, the right to vote, and the right to hold office. When Jews founded their first congregation, they called it Shearith Israel (Remnant of Israel), an apt name for the handful living in a colonial town far from European centers of Jewish life. Yet during the eighteenth century, Jews integrated into the fabric of New York life. They faced challenges of identifying as Jews within a free society. As the first to enjoy such political freedoms, they struggled to balance assimilation with Jewish distinctiveness. By the time of the Revolution, many New York Jews felt deeply connected to their city and fellow American patriots, enough to flee the British occupation for Philadelphia. The end of the war marked a new democratic consciousness among New York Jews who returned to rebuild their city and community.

A democratic ethos pervaded Jewish urban life in the new republic, opening possibilities for individual and collective ambition as well as cooperation. This republicanism changed how Jews organized themselves religiously and how they imagined their opportunities. Shearith Israel incorporated and drafted its own constitution, modeled on the federal example. Republicanism animated women, inspiring them to establish charities to help succor the poor. Once Jewish immigration brought sufficient ethnic and economic diversity to New York in the 1830s and 1840s, Jews started to build a different type of community. They forged bonds based on intimacy, gender, shared backgrounds, common aspirations, and urgent necessities. Jewish religious life became increasingly diverse, competitive, and strident. Democracy without an established religion fostered creativity and experimentation. Congregations multiplied in the city, but most Jews chose not to join one, despite variety ranging from Orthodox to Reform. The city saw a fierce battle between proponents of orthodoxy and advocates of reform. These debates engaged Jews deeply but did not lead the majority to affiliate. Still, increasingly synagogue buildings formed part of the cityscape, an indication of Jewish presence. Democratic freedoms permitted a new type of urban Jewish life to emerge. Lacking formal communal structures, Jews innovated and turned to other forms of organization as alternatives. They established fraternal orders and literary societies, seeking a means to craft connections in a rapidly growing and bewildering city. Yet soon they multiplied these activities as well. Pleas for charity and education, hospitals and libraries, mobilized Jewish New Yorkers.

With the extension of the franchise, more Jewish men acquired the right to vote, irrespective of their economic situation, encouraging them to enter political debates with enthusiasm. They paid attention to events overseas affecting fellow Jews, especially examples of anti-Semitism, and tried to convince the president to help. New York Jews mastered the arts of petition and protest. They took sides as individuals in election cycles, first between Federalists and Jeffersonians, later between Democrats and Whigs, and finally between Democrats and Republicans. Domestic issues divided Jews; even the question of slavery found supporters and opponents. Rabbis debated the subject in pulpit and press until the Civil War ended their polemics and both sides rallied to the Union cause. Politics necessarily pushed Jews into public consciousness; non-Jews noticed them. Prejudice began to appear in social life, and stereotypes started to circulate in the press. Yet Jewish New Yorkers were hardly the retiring sort, and many gave as good as they got.

Jewish immigrants readily found employment, entering the city's expanding economic marketplace as they carefully tested its promises of personal fulfillment. Although the Panics of 1857 and 1873 threw thousands out of work, during normal times, Jews coped with capitalist volatilities. Many gravitated to small-scale commerce and craft production. Men and women both worked and drew on family resources, especially the labor of their children, to help make ends meet. Jews saved regularly to withstand seasonal swings in employment. Within the city's diversifying economy, they located ethnic niches that became occupational ladders of advancement for many. Some of the merchants trading in old clothes around Chatham Street initiated manufacturing of cheap goods. A garment industry took shape; it received a big boost with demand for uniforms in the Civil War. As the industry grew, its need for workers increased steadily, employing an ever-greater proportion of Jewish immigrants to the city. Small shops and a competitive contracting system continued to dominate the industry. Despite miserable conditions, the system tempted many workers with a promise of self-employment. Taking a risk, some immigrants borrowed money, often from relatives and fellow immigrants from the same European town, to supplement meager savings. Then they plunged into contracting, trying with a new design idea to secure prosperity. As often as not, they failed, falling back into the laboring class. But success stories trumped failures; they stood as reminders that the city had fulfilled its promise.

Merchants and peddlers, who occupied another popular Jewish economic niche, viewed the rise of department stores as an urban achievement. These commercial emporiums proffered a magical array of goods under one roof and represented the pinnacle of success for local hardware-store owners or dry-goods shopkeepers. Retail establishments proliferated around the city as it grew; Jewish entrepreneurship flourished on local shopping streets in the Bronx and Brooklyn. Pitkin Avenue in Brownsville and Fordham Road in the Bronx could not rival Manhattan's Fifth Avenue or even Fourteenth Street. But they provided a measure of prosperity and independence to Jewish merchants, enough so that they could enjoy some of the perquisites of middle-class living, such as sending one's sons and even one's daughters to high school and college. Mobility came in many forms, and often immigrant Jews achieved economic and social mobility first through business and then through education.

New York's explosive growth at the turn of the twentieth century produced radical social movements based on class struggle and politics. For many Jewish immigrants, becoming a small manufacturer paled beside a larger vision of a just society, one without workers living in overcrowded, filthy tenements, exposed to disease, and wracked by despair. Hedging their bets, they dreamed of becoming capitalists even as they sought in socialism better living conditions, fair wages, and reasonable working hours. Socialism as a utopian ideal promised equality, an economic system that took from each according to his or her ability and returned to everybody whatever he or she needed. Even some Jewish capitalists subscribed to such an ideal. But on a pragmatic level, socialism appealed to Jewish workers for its alternatives to unrestrained capitalist exploitation. Paths to socialism led through union organizing, the polling booth, fraternalism, and even cooperative housing. Jewish immigrants embraced them all. They forged vibrant garment-workers unions, as well as unions of bakers and plumbers, teachers and pharmacists. They voted for Socialist candidates, sending Meyer London in 1914 to represent the Lower East Side in Congress. They organized the Workmen's Circle, initially in 1892 as a mutual-aid society and then in 1900 as a multibranch fraternal order in which they could socialize with fellow workers and receive health and social welfare benefits not provided by a wealthy but stingy city government. And after World War I ended, New York Jews pushed for legislation that would allow them to build cooperative housing projects, so that they could enjoy living in decent apartments together with other Jewish workers. These examples of democratic community radically reshaped the city and contributed to its progressive commitments even as Jewish struggles for social justice empowered them both individually and as a group.

For several centuries, until the beginning of the twentieth, most New York Jews lived in Lower Manhattan, with smaller numbers residing in Williamsburg and Bedford, in the city of Brooklyn. The consolidation of New York with Brooklyn and the creation of a city of five boroughs, including the Bronx, Queens, and Staten Island, stimulated construction of subways and bridges which expanded opportunities for Jewish immigrants to leave the constricted quarters of the Lower East Side. Once they started to move, only the Great Depression, discrimination, and wartime constraints made Jews pause. New neighborhoods held out hopes of fresh beginnings. Adjusting to the strangeness of a neighborhood invited ways to reimagine one's relationship to New York City. Jews adopted different perspectives on themselves and their city as they exchanged views out kitchen windows. Modern tenements, with steam heat, hot and cold running water in the kitchen sink, and an icebox, proclaimed a sense of accomplishment worth the pain of dislocation produced by immigration. Modern apartment buildings with parquet floors, windows in every room, and the latest conveniences announced a form of success. It did not matter that these apartments were rented; home ownership did not rank high on Jewish New Yorkers' requirements for either the good life or economic security—better to be able to catch the express train and in ten minutes travel two stops on the subway to reach the Midtown garment district than to own a house in the suburbs with a commute of an hour to work each day. And renting let Jews move as their finances fluctuated, freeing funds for other purposes.

New York Jews committed themselves to a wide array of neighborhoods, reflecting different desires. Did one wish for a neighborhood filled with modern synagogues and kosher butcher shops, bakeries, and delicatessens? There was a range of choices based on how much rent one was willing to pay. Did one seek a lively center of radicalism where socialism was considered "right wing" in comparison to "left wing" communism, an area filled with union activities, cultural events, and places to debate politics? A slightly narrower number of neighborhoods fit the bill. Did one yearn to speak Yiddish or German or Ladino or Russian, to find traces of the old home in familiar styles of shopping and praying? Neighborhoods, not just a block or two but a cluster of them, catered to those who yearned for what they had left behind in Europe or the Middle East. Did one seek a yeshiva for sons and eventually for daughters, as well as intimate congregations for daily study and prayer? New York made room for these as well. In all of them, Jews had neighbors who were not Jewish, but that mattered less than the neighbors who were Jewish. Jews lived next door to other white ethnics, as well as to African Americans, and, after World War II, Puerto Ricans. While most Jews tolerated their non-Jewish neighbors, economic competition, national and international politics, and religious prejudice ignited conflict. An uneasy coexistence among neighbors characterized many New York neighborhoods. Despite this diversity of residential neighborhoods, Jews stayed in an area usually only for a generation. New neighborhoods beckoned constantly; children moved away from parents; parents lost money or made money. Primarily renters, unlike other groups, Jews did not remain committed for long to a neighborhood. They were ready to move elsewhere in the city, to try something different. Such was New York's promise of community for Jews.

New York Jews began to leave their city in the 1960s, a process that continued for the rest of the century. The largest decline in Jewish population occurred in the 1970s when the city's fiscal crisis arrived, just in time to welcome

Abe Beame, New York's first Jewish mayor. As Jews departed, African Americans and Puerto Ricans moved into the city in ever-greater numbers. By the mid-1950s, a million African Americans lived in New York. After liberalization of immigration laws in 1965, an increasingly diverse array of immigrants from Asia, especially China, and also from the Caribbean, Latin America, and Africa arrived in New York. Jewish immigrants figured among them, most prominently from the Soviet Union; these new immigrants brought some of the same drive and energy that had made New York a city of promises a hundred years earlier.

At the start of the twenty-first century, New York still lacked a majority population. In contemporary ethnic calculus, Jews made up a significant percentage of white New Yorkers. But whites constituted a minority in the city, hence Jews' overall percentage of the population declined. Most Jews were college educated; many had advanced degrees. Having overcome occupational discrimination that endured into the 1960s, Jews held jobs in real estate, finance, publishing, education, law, and medicine in this postindustrial city. They still congregated in neighborhoods, but Queens attracted more Jews than the Bronx did. They still worked in commerce, usually as managers of large stores rather than as owners of small ones. New York Jews still debated how to observe Jewish rituals and holidays. Most declined to join a congregation, yet many retained a consciousness of being Jewish. Often awareness of Jewish differences grew out of family bonds; for some, their sense of Jewishness flowed from work or neighborhood or culture or politics. A visible minority rigorously observed the strictures of Judaism, and their presence gave other Jews a kind of yardstick by which to judge themselves. Despite Jews' greatly reduced numbers, the city still honored Jewish holy days by adjusting its mundane rhythms. New York Jews knew they lived in American Jews' capital city; the cluster of national Jewish organizations announced this fact. These organizations, able to mobilize effective protests or to advocate for a cause, focused on problems facing Jews throughout the world. Jewish cultural creativity also endured along with effervescent, experimental, multiethnic commitments to new forms of democratic urban community.

City of Promises portrays the history of Jews in New York City from 1654 to the present. Its three volumes articulate perspectives of four historians. In the first volume, Howard Rock argues that the first two centuries of Jewish presence in the city proved critical to the development of New York Jews. He sees an influential template in communal structures created by colonial Jews and elaborated in the nineteenth century by Jewish immigrants from central Europe. Rock emphasizes the political freedom and economic strength of colonial and republican Jews in New York. He shows that democratic religious and ethnic community represented an unusual experiment for Jews. Using American political models, Jews in New York innovated. They developed an expansive role for an English-language Jewish press as a vehicle for collective consciousness; they introduced fraternal societies that secularized religious fellowship; they crafted independent philanthropic organizations along gendered lines; they discussed the pros and cons of reforming Judaism; and they passionately debated politics. They were the first American Jews to demonstrate how political and economic freedoms were integral to Jewish communal life. Although many of them arrived as immigrants themselves, they also pointed a path for future migrants who confronted the city's intoxicating and bewildering modern world. In so doing, these eighteenth- and early nineteenth-century Jews laid the foundations for the development of a robust American Jewish community in New York.

In the second volume, Annie Polland and Daniel Soyer describe the process by which New York emerged as a Jewish city, produced by a century of mass migration of Jews from central and eastern Europe as well as from the Middle East. Focusing on the urban Jewish built environment—its tenements and banks, its communal buildings and synagogues, its department stores and settlement houses—the authors convey the extraordinary complexity of Jewish immigrant society in New York. The theme of urban community runs like a thread through a century of mass migration beginning in 1840. Polland and Soyer revise classic accounts of immigration, paying attention to Jewish interactions in economic, social, religious, and cultural activities. Jews repeatedly seek to repair fissures in their individual and collective lives caused by dislocation. Their efforts to build connections through family and neighborhood networks across barriers of class and gender generated a staggering array of ethnic organizations, philanthropic initiatives, and political and religious movements. Despite enormous hardship and repeated failures, Jewish immigrants in New York developed sufficient institutional resilience to articulate a political vision of social solidarity and reform. New York Jews also stepped forward into national leadership positions by establishing organizations that effectively rallied American Jews on behalf of those still suffering in Europe.

New York City became the capital of American Jews in these years and the largest Jewish city in history.

In telling the story of twentieth-century New York Jews in the third volume of the series, Jeffrey S. Gurock looks to the neighborhood, the locale of community and the place where most Jews lived their lives. Jews liked their local community and appreciated its familiar warmth. But New York Jews also faced demands for political action on behalf of a transnational Jewish world. During the crucial decade from 1938 to 1948, New York Jews debated what course of action they should take. How should they balance domestic needs with those of European Jews? World War II and the Holocaust demonstrated the contrasts between Jews in New York and Jews in Europe. Gurock shows how Jewish neighborhoods spread across the boroughs. He describes Jewish settlement in Queens after World War II, illuminating processes of urban change. Ethnic-group conflict and racial antagonism left deep scars despite efforts to overcome prejudice and discrimination. New York Jews were found on both sides of the barricades; each decade produced a fresh conflagration. Yet Jewish New Yorkers never ceased to lead movements for social change, supporting women's rights as well as freedom for Soviet Jewry. New York City retained its preeminence as the capital of American Jews because of deep roots in local worlds. These urban neighborhoods, Gurock argues, nourish creative and unselfconscious forms of Jewishness.

Each volume contains a visual essay by art historian Diana L. Linden. These essays interpret Jewish experiences. Linden examines diverse objects, images, and artifacts. She suggests alternative narratives drawn from a record of cultural production. Artists and craftspeople, ordinary citizens and commercial firms provide multiple perspectives on the history of Jews in New York. Her view runs as a counterpoint and complement to the historical accounts. Each visual presentation can be read separately or in conjunction with the history. The combination of historical analysis and visual representation enriches the story of Jews in New York City. In the first essay, Linden emphasizes the foreignness and loneliness of being Jewish in the colonial and republican periods, even as Jews integrated themselves into Christian society. They were the first to create a new identity as "American Jews." The second visual essay chronicles the challenges of navigating a rapidly expanding city. It explores contrasts of rich and poor. Jews in immigrant New York fashioned new charitable, educational, and cultural institutions as they established the city as the capital of the

American Jewish world. The third visual essay takes as its theme New York Jews in popular American imagination. It presents many meanings and identities of "New York Jew" over the course of the twentieth century and the beginning years of the twenty-first century.

These different viewpoints on Jews in New York City situate their history within intersecting themes of urban growth, international migration, political change, economic mobility, religious innovation, organizational complexity, cultural creativity, and democratic community. Jews participated in building the Empire City by casting their lot with urbanism, even as they struggled to make New York a better place to live, work, and raise a family. Their aspirations changed New York and helped to transform it into a city of promises, some fulfilled, some pending, some beckoning new generations.

DEBORAH DASH MOORE

GENERAL EDITOR'S ACKNOWLEDGMENTS

All books are collaborative projects, but perhaps none more than this three-volume history of Jews in New York City. The eminent historians directly involved in the project, Jeffrey S. Gurock, Annie Polland, Howard Rock, Daniel Soyer, and art historian Diana L. Linden, have devoted their considerable skills not only to their own volumes but also to evaluating and enhancing each other's work. Editorial board members helped to guide the project and served as crucial resources. City of Promises began during my term as Chair of the Academic Council of the American Jewish Historical Society, and I owe a debt of gratitude to David P. Solomon for making a match between Jennifer Hammer of New York University Press and the Academic Council.

Good ideas have legs, but they require the devotion and support of influential men and women. City of Promises fortunately found both in William Frost z"l of the Lucius N. Littauer Foundation and Jennifer Hammer of NYU Press. Bill Frost generously underwrote the project when it was just an idea, and I think that he would have treasured this history of a city he loved. Jennifer Hammer worked prodigiously to turn vision into reality, never faltering in her critically engaged commitment despite inevitable obstacles. I am indebted to both of them for staying the course, and I greatly appreciate the opportunity to work with Jennifer, an excellent, flexible, and insightful editor.

City of Promises received additional important financial support from individuals and foundations. I want to thank the Malkin Fund, The Marian B. and Jacob K. Javits Foundation, Hugo Barreca, David P. Solomon, and an anonymous foundation donor for significant support, as well as several other individuals including Judd and Karen Aronowitz, David and Phyllis Grossman, Irving and Phyllis Levitt, Irwin and Debi Ungar, and Rabbi Marc Strauss-Cohen of Temple Emanuel, Winston-Salem, North Carolina. All recognized the importance of this project through timely contributions. I appreciate their generosity.

Several students at the University of Michigan provided assistance that helped to keep the volumes on track. Alexandra Maron and Katherine Rosenblatt did valuable research, and I am grateful for their aid.

These volumes are dedicated to my family of New York Jews. Without their steadfast encouragement, and especially that of my husband, MacDonald Moore, City of Promises would not have appeared.

Dedicated to my grandchildren,
Elijah Axt, Zoe Bella Moore, and Rose Alexa Moore,
authors of future chapters

DEBORAH DASH MOORE

AUTHORS' ACKNOWLEDGMENTS

Thanks are due, first of all, to our colleagues on the City of Promises team: Deborah Dash Moore, Howard Rock, Jeffrey Gurock, Diana Linden, and, of course, Jennifer Hammer of NYU Press. All helped keep the project on track and gave valuable advice on the manuscript. Without the research assistance of Katie Rosenblatt, Diane De Fazio, Shoshana Olidort, and Elizabeth Stack this book could not have been written so quickly. Roberta Newman's expert services as a photo researcher helped give the book added depth and attractiveness. In addition to the City of Promises team, Andrew Dolkart, Rebecca Kobrin, David Mikics, and Peter Eisenstadt made helpful comments on the manuscript, as did two anonymous readers for the press.

The book could not have been written without the collections of a number of libraries and archives, or the assistance of their staffs. Thanks to the New York Public Library, the YIVO Institute for Jewish Research, American Jewish Historical Society (Susan Malbin), the New York City Municipal Archives, Central Synagogue Archives (Anne Minenberg), Museum at Eldridge Street (Amy Milford), and Fordham University.

Finally, thanks to our families, Michael and Lily Smrtic, and Moses Cohen-Soyer (fifth- or sixth-generation New Yorker, depending on how you count) for putting up with us while we wrote this book.

ANNIE POLLAND AND DANIEL SOYER

Emerging Metropolis

New York Jews in the Age of
Immigration, 1840–1920

The premier Jewish immigrant aid organization, the Hebrew Sheltering and Immigrant Aid Society (HIAS), established a kosher kitchen on Ellis Island in 1911. It also took charge of the Passover seders that had been occurring since the beginning of the century. (Archives of the YIVO Institute for Jewish Research, New York)

Introduction: The Emerging Jewish Metropolis

On April 10, 1906, 160 detained eastern European Jewish immigrants gathered in the Great Hall of the immigration center at Ellis Island for a Passover seder, the traditional ceremonial meal that commemorates the flight of the children of Israel from Egyptian slavery. Alexander Harkavy, a member of a delegation of immigrant communal leaders, welcomed the detainees by drawing parallels between the Israelites of the Exodus and the Jews of Ellis Island: whether fleeing the oppression of Pharaoh's Egypt or Tsarist Russia, both groups sought freedom in a Promised Land. A few days later, Yiddish journalist Yakov Pfeffer described the moving seder, proclaiming that the poor, bedraggled immigrants—no longer fearful of blood-libel accusations or pogroms—had celebrated the Passover holiday as *bene horin*, children of freedom. In addition to linking these Ellis Island immigrants to the Haggadah's ancient Israelites, Pfeffer argued that the contemporary immigrants merited their own mention in the chronicle of Jewish history: "When the future historian tells the story of the freedom of the Jewish people, when that person has the good fortune to tell not only of the sorrows but also the joys of the Jewish nation, . . . he will need to tell of the Seder night on Ellis Island."[1]

The Jews who celebrated the seder on Ellis Island in 1906 arrived in the United States at the crest of a century-long wave of Jewish immigration from Europe. Beginning in the 1820s, economic change in their European homelands drove many Jews out of their accustomed trades and, along with political and religious persecution, sent them in search of new livelihoods. By contrast, the burgeoning United States needed workers and offered unparalleled political freedom. Early on, most Jewish immigrants came from central Europe, particularly the German lands. By the end of the nineteenth century, eastern European Jews predominated. One-third of eastern Europe's Jews uprooted themselves. The vast majority headed for the United States.

Most of these immigrants entered the country through New York Harbor, which by the second decade of the nineteenth century had overtaken Philadelphia as North America's busiest port. New York's rise was conditioned by its natural advantages, which included access to a large hinterland via the Hudson River and Long Island Sound; deep channels; and a well-protected harbor. But innovative business practices and government support also played an important role. The introduction of regularly scheduled transatlantic departures in 1818 and the opening of the Erie Canal in 1825 drew shipping to the city. New York's status as the country's largest port made it the most important textile and financial center, as well as the main point of entry for European news and fashion. The port of New York became the dominant entry point for people as well as goods. Three-quarters of the thirty-three million immigrants who entered the United States between 1815 and 1915 came through New York. Many supplied the cheap labor that enabled the city to grow into a major manufacturing center. New York's streets led from the docks to the garment shops that produced most of the country's ready-made clothing.[2]

In 1855, faced with an ever-increasing influx and almost complete lack of oversight by the federal government, New York State established an immigrant processing center at Castle Garden off the southern tip of Manhattan. Castle Garden had a varied history, each stage of which left a mark on the building's unusual shape. Built on an artificial rocky island some one hundred yards off shore, its original round masonry walls and twenty-eight guns formed part of the harbor's defense system. In 1823, it was decommissioned and turned into a "resort, theater, and restaurant." In 1845, a domed roof was added, along with additional tiers of galleries, transforming Castle Garden into a popular concert hall. By the time the state took it over for an immigration station, landfill had moved the shoreline closer to the Garden, and soon Battery Park completely surrounded the old fort. To placate respectable local residents, who feared that placing the immigration station in Castle Garden would cause disagreeable immigrants to overrun the Battery, a twelve-foot

NO ADMITTANCE
Ginzung verboten.

NO ADMITTANCE FOR BOARDING HOUSE KEEPERS

ARRIVAL AT CASTLE GARDEN

Between 1855 and 1890, the state of New York operated an immigration station at Castle Garden, offering immigrants information on jobs and housing in an attempt to help them avoid the "runners," "scalpers," and "loafers" who took advantage of vulnerable newcomers. (Prints and Photographs Division, Library of Congress, Washington, DC)

fence was erected around the building. A number of smaller structures completed the complex.[3]

For the next three and a half decades, this odd structure—like a "huge reservoir or gas-holder" in appearance—was the first American building encountered up close by millions of immigrants. By establishing the station, the state aimed to protect immigrants from the "runners," "scalpers," "loafers," and prostitutes who frequently robbed and cheated them while offering to find them work, transport, or lodging.[4] At Castle Garden, immigrants could receive reliable information about jobs and housing, exchange money at official rates, acquire railroad tickets without exorbitant surcharges, receive decent medical care, buy food at reasonable prices, and even take a bath. The centralization of services also allowed the state to collect comprehensive data on immigration for the first time. Some of the newcomers stayed overnight at Castle Garden, preparing coffee on coal stoves from the piped-in Croton water and

In 1892, the newly built federal facility at Ellis Island assumed control of immigrant processing. The strenuous inspection process there engendered fear among immigrants that they might be returned to their point of origin. But after the turn of the century, dozens of ethnic and religious aid associations established posts on the island, helping newcomers navigate entrance into their new country. (Prints and Photographs Division, Library of Congress, Washington, DC)

exchanging intelligence on the economic situation in the city. Castle Garden closed in 1890, but so ingrained had it become in the immigrant consciousness that Jewish immigrants referred to New York's subsequent immigration station as "Castle Garden" for years thereafter.

A massive new federal installation opened on Ellis Island in 1892, replacing Castle Garden. The Ellis Island station's original wood-frame structures, "wretched barns" that were "monuments to ugliness," burned down in 1897, replaced in 1900 by the buildings that have become iconic in the collective memory of American immigration. The fireproof new main building, constructed in French Renaissance style, sported a steel frame trimmed with brick and limestone, and four hundred-foot domed towers. The giant central "registry room," where new arrivals lined up to be processed, was surrounded by offices, hearing rooms, dining rooms, and dormitories. Eventually, a total of thirty-three structures dotted the island, which had been expanded to meet the needs of the station. Ellis Island ironically became practically synonymous with the giant wave of (mainly) European immigration of the end of the nineteenth century and beginning of the twentieth, despite its role in enforcing a growing number of regulations aimed as much at keeping certain kinds of people out as admitting them in.[5]

Ellis Island became known to Jews as the "Island of Tears," a place from which arrivals judged deficient would be returned to the countries they had hoped to escape. In truth, most people's experience of the island was not nearly so bad. True, immigrants endured intrusive (and quick) medical examinations and oral questioning that might concern their intended destinations and livelihoods, mental state, family situation, and politics. But although treatment fluctuated with government policy, officials, many of them multilingual, were generally polite and efficient. They were assisted—and watched—by representatives of ethnic aid organizations such as the Hebrew Immigrant Aid Society (HIAS) and the National Council of Jewish Women. As Aaron Domnitz, an immigrant from Belarus later recalled, the first impression was not necessarily a bad one:

> My first contact with my new country was the short conversation between me and the immigration officials. We were put into short lines as we entered the large buildings at Ellis Island. Each line had to go by a small table next to which officials sat who questioned each immigrant in his language. The new immigrant felt right at home. My line spoke Yiddish. Hence, a big, strange country recognized my language that I had brought here with me from abroad as an official language. In Russia and Germany, I did not receive any such privilege.
>
> One official asked me what I would do in America. I told him that until then I had been a Hebrew teacher. He smiled, "A *rebbe*?"
>
> "No," I said, "A teacher!"
>
> A second official called out, "What's the difference?" I explained that a "rebbe" is hasidic. They laughed at me. "Go, go," they said, "you'll be a great rebbe in America," and pushed me aside. I looked around. Here I am on the other side of the railing, among those who have been let in. But why did they laugh at me? It's nothing. People are good-natured here and they were joking. I liked the reception.[6]

Arriving from Warsaw, Minnie Goldstein had a different experience. When her relatives failed to pick her up at the station, she was left behind, "along with the people who were being sent back home": "When I saw them wringing their hands and crying, I was overcome with fear." This fear of being among the 2 percent who were rejected gave Ellis Island its dubious reputation. But most, like Goldstein and Domnitz, found themselves "on the other side of the railing" within eight hours of arrival.[7]

Tens of millions of people flowed through Castle Garden, Ellis Island, and New York on their way to other cities, towns, and rural settlements. But most Jews stayed in their port of entry, joining a population that consisted largely of immigrants from Ireland, Germany, England, the Russian and Austro-Hungarian Empires, and Italy, along with their children. If the Passover detainees conformed to the general pattern among Jewish arrivals, approximately 40 of them (25 percent) traveled to other U.S. cities, while 120 of them (75 percent) followed Harkavy and Pfeffer back to New York's immigrant neighborhoods, where they started the process of adjustment to American life.

Jewish immigrants wove a dense network of formal and informal support systems in their new neighborhoods. Often, in fact, they found their way *to* the neighborhoods with the help of relatives, friends, and communal organizations. HIAS helped Domnitz find his cousin in Brownsville. His cousin helped him find a job. Ben Reisman's brother-in-law was late in picking him up, so the immigrant from Galicia found his way to his sister's apartment with the aid of strangers:

> [An immigration official] told them to show me where the ferry was and they took me and showed me. I took my suitcase and went out. I saw many people going to the ferry. I followed them. On the ferry I recognized a Jew and asked him how to get to Eldridge Street. He told me that he would put me on the right streetcar himself and wrote on a piece of paper for me to show the conductor. The conductor let me off at Grand Street and showed me which way to go.

There followed a whirl of activity, as relatives and people from the same hometown came to hear reports of "the old home" and to give the newcomer advice on life in the new country. Buying the "greenhorn" a new suit of American clothes was a common important symbolic first step in the adjustment process. Getting him or her a job and housing were important material steps.[8]

People seldom remained in their first work and living arrangements for long. New York promised mobility—social and residential, the two often coupled. Even by 1881, when Harkavy arrived in the vanguard of the eastern European wave, most of the central European Jews who had lived in Lower Manhattan's Five Points and Kleindeutschland neighborhoods as glaziers and tailors had resettled in Upper Manhattan as merchants and professionals. A few had even become spectacularly wealthy, as the owners of major department stores such as Macy's or as financiers. By 1906, when the Ellis Island seder took place, even many of the early eastern European arrivals had moved uptown or to neighborhoods in Brooklyn and the Bronx, since 1898 joined with Manhattan in the consolidated city of Greater New York. New York City rapidly became a patchwork of Jewish neighborhoods ranging from areas of first immigrant settlement, such as the Lower East Side in Manhattan, Brownsville and Williamsburg in Brooklyn, and the East Bronx, to upper-middle-class and even upper-class sections such as the Upper West Side, the Bronx's Grand Concourse, and Brooklyn's Eastern Parkway.

New York also promised freedom. But from what? Of what? Pfeffer folded the American immigrant experience into the broader scope of Jewish history and argued that the new immigrants stationed at Ellis Island, "the border between the land of *goles* [exile] and the land of freedom," would soon leave the shadow of exile for the safety and security of America. To Pfeffer, precisely this safety and freedom from violence and persecution represented a new chapter in Jewish history. Sheer numbers introduced another new factor in Jewish life. In 1840, there were perhaps seven thousand Jews in New York City. By 1920, there were over a million and a half. Along with the conditions of relative security noted by Pfeffer and the loosening of traditional communal constraints, which he did not mention, their numbers gave New York Jews freedom to hammer out a staggering variety of expressions of Jewish identity —religious and secular. New York became the capital of the Jewish world, providing leadership to American Jewry and relief to Jews abroad in periods of calm and crisis.

Over the course of this century, the majority of New York's Jews were immigrants and working class. Even as many Jews ascended a ladder of economic and social mobility, the city continued to attract Jewish newcomers, replenishing the ranks of its working class. Sometimes, there was interclass cooperation, as more established members of the community assumed obligations to aid those less fortunate. But often conflict erupted: eastern Europeans founded parallel institutions that they thought could serve them better than those formed by the earlier arrivals; largely Jewish unions struggled against mainly Jewish employers in predominantly Jewish trades; ideologues with differing views of what it meant to be Jewish and what the Jewish future should hold clashed over the shape that the Jewish community should take.

The struggle of a largely immigrant and working-class community to define itself and work out its place in American culture and society produced a tremendous amount of creativity. In this period, Jews began to carve out prominent places in the arts that they later occupied so conspicuously. They produced theater and literature in German, Yiddish, English, and other languages. They wrote hit popular songs and helped introduce modernism into the American visual arts. Some of these artistic expressions focused on Jewish subjects, some did not. Some were in Jewish languages and intended for Jewish audiences, but some were not. Taken together, Jews helped to make New York the American cultural capital, just as the city introduced them to modern urban life. Similarly, Jews promoted a political style that emphasized social solidarity and justice and became associated in particular with New York.

This volume explores the central European and eastern European Jews' encounter with New York City, tracing immigrants' economic, social, religious, political, and cultural adaptation between 1840 and 1920. By looking at New York's department stores, sweatshops, settlement houses, newspaper buildings, banks, synagogues, schools, and streets, it shows how Jews wove their ambitions and aspirations—for freedom, security, and material prosperity—into the very fabric of the city. Each chapter explores the mark left by immigrant and native-born Jews on the streets of New York, examining the commercial activity, political protest, consumer unrest, and religious devotion that characterized their engagement with the city. Despite their numbers, Jews never became a majority in New York City. A history of Jewish New York therefore necessarily includes other people, non-Jews, with whom Jews interacted, sometimes harmoniously and sometimes in conflict. New York promised its Jews the ability to integrate into society and at the same time to maintain a vigorous independent existence. The New York Jewish story is therefore one of both Jewish distinctiveness and Jewish absorption into the city as a whole. It is the story of how New York became the greatest Jewish metropolis of all time.

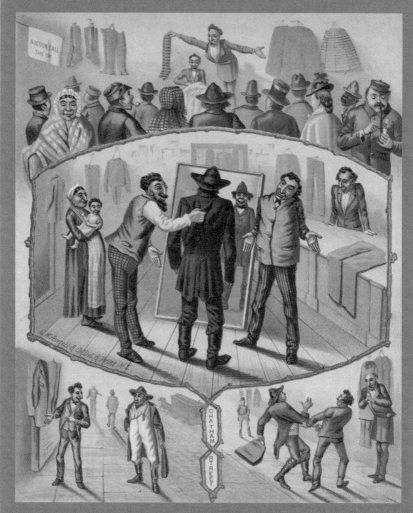

In this 1878 drawing, hook-nosed Jewish merchants manipulate unsuspecting Americans into purchasing ill-fitting used clothing. Caricatures of immigrant groups—whether simian Irish or beer-drinking Germans—commonly appeared in the nineteenth-century press and theater. (New York Public Library, New York)

CHAPTER 1

Neighborhood Networks

In the middle of the nineteenth century, European and American visitors to New York knew to stop by Chatham Street, a commercial district just to the northeast of City Hall, at the base of the Bowery. So characteristic of New York with its commercial hustle and bustle, Chatham Street's ramshackle storefronts and frenzied merchants almost begged for inclusion in travel accounts. In their colorful depictions, pants and shirts hanging off signs and rustling in the wind seemed designed to ensnare unwary passersby; once so detained, the hapless marks were susceptible to the "gentle" yet persistent enticements of "natty, blackbearded, fiercely mustached" Jewish merchants, who had a beguiling way of selling a fellow clothes that did not fit. The accounts' descriptions of the flapping layers of fabric, the waist-length beards, and the devious mannerisms not so subtly marked these businessmen as ethically and even racially suspect. One observer declared that a "Yankee shopkeeper" would have no hope of succeeding on Chatham Street; his presence was a "physical impossibility." Yet another observer suggested that P. T. Barnum create a museum or circus out of the activity there. Jewish writers, too, often preferred to dissociate themselves from the area; Rabbi Isaac Mayer Wise's memoirs summarily dismissed Jewish Chatham as "a disgrace."[1]

Indeed, Wise's distaste for Chatham Street was indicative of his dislike of New York in general when he arrived in 1846 from Radnitz, Bohemia. Wise surveyed Broadway all the way to Canal Street, reporting, "The whole city appeared to me like a large shop where every one buys or sells, cheats or is cheated. I had never before seen a city so bare of all art and of every trace of good taste; likewise I had never witnessed anywhere such rushing, hurrying, chasing, running."[2] Chatham Street thus exemplified a business current that pulsed through all of Manhattan. A contemporary observer, Cornelius Mathews, disparaged Chatham commerce but suggested that this very competitive spirit was after all part and parcel of New York's history and future and that the terrain itself inspired a competitive spirit among its inhabitants: "This street, reader, was in the old times of this Island, a warpath of Manhattan Indians to the west; civilization hath not affected it greatly. The old red men scalped their enemies, the Chatham Clo'men skin theirs. So little difference have two-hundred years in changing the character of mankind!"[3] Whether or not one accepts Mathews's suggestion that Chatham Street's soil fostered this fierce competitive drive, his account leaves no doubt that Jews' commercial ambitions had made them a highly visible part of New York life.

While Cornelius Mathews returned home and Isaac Mayer Wise journeyed on to Albany and then Cincinnati, those who were most engaged with the Chatham Square street scene remained to live and work there. The clothing business was not a literary curiosity for them but rather the means through which they could stitch together a new life in America. From the mid-1820s to the 1880s, the area around Chatham Street, especially the south side, remained a touchstone for immigrant Jews arriving in New York. There they found housing, work, and community. Although many of these Jews moved on to other neighborhoods to the east and north within a few years, a continuous influx of immigrants maintained a constant Jewish presence. Those who settled learned to navigate the neighborhood. Jewish residents of Chatham Street interacted with its diverse populations yet also created sites of Jewish interest. The twists and turns of Mott, Mulberry, and Orange Streets introduced them to a vast array of New Yorkers—Irish carpenters, African American laborers, and German brewers—as well as to Henry L. Goldberg, who in 1852 is listed in the New York City directory as a "scriber of the Pentateuchs" at 63 Mott Street. Unflustered by flapping merchandise or peddlers' entreaties, Jewish immigrants soon learned that the handsome three-story New York Dispensary on the corner of Centre and White not only offered medical attention but also housed temporarily several congregations, including Shearith Israel, Anshe Chesed, Shaarey Zedek, and Beth Israel.[4] A Bayard Street tenement's staircase led to Gittel Natelson, who sold wigs to married Jewish women and arranged matches for those yet unmarried.[5] Jews discovered that a saloon's rear room might be a meeting place of a B'nai B'rith lodge or that Newman Cowen's Canal Street glass warehouse doubled as a charitable distribution site at the beginning of each Jewish month.[6] More important, this neighborhood provided opportunities to pioneer—to find occupations, to forge partnerships, and to start congregations. In seeking advice and finding companionship, newly arrived immigrants also received the impression that in a few years' time, they too might be in a position to help the next wave of newcomers.

In the vanguard of a century of migration that eventually brought nearly three million central and eastern European Jews to the United States, Chatham Jews by the end of the nineteenth century had created the neighborhood and industrial web of associations that made New York a magnet for immigrant Jews and made Jews garment manufacturers for the nation. Upon arrival, mid-nineteenth-century immigrant Jews tended to settle around Chatham Street, in the so-called Five Points. By the 1850s, Jews also formed a "conspicuous" segment of the German-speaking immigrants in Kleindeutschland, or Little Germany, located to the east of the Bowery, in an area later known as the Lower East Side.[7] In the first few decades of the century of migration, many immigrants continued the journey west, but enough remained to make New York home to approximately forty thousand Jews, 25 percent of the United States' Jewry by 1860 and approximately 5 percent of New York's population.[8] By 1880, New York Jews numbered close to eighty thousand, and many of them were firmly established in the middle class and living uptown.

They ascended by carving out their own place in the city's "niche economy." Jews from Bavaria, Prussia, Bohemia, and Poland came with experience in trade and peddling.[9] In New York, they applied this experience wholeheartedly to dry goods and the used-clothing trade. They then parlayed their foothold in the used-clothing business into a pioneering role in the ready-made garment industry, both as manufacturers and as marketers, guiding Americans to what was then a novelty—ready-made clothing for middle-class and even upper-class people. By the end of the century, they thus left an unmistakable imprint on the city's economy and in so doing also set a pattern for future Jewish immigrants' relationship to the city.[10] The needle trades were New York's largest manufacturing sector, employing large numbers of more recent Jewish immigrants from eastern Europe, who provided the industry with the cheap labor necessary for its rapid growth.[11]

■ Neighborhood Beginnings

From the colonial period until the beginning of the nineteenth century, most Jews, like most New Yorkers, lived and worked in the area to the south of City Hall. The Jewish community's sole synagogue, Shearith Israel, had been located on Mill Street since the early eighteenth century. By the late 1810s, the more prominent Jews had already moved farther north, to the west of Broadway, on the "quiet, tree-shaded blocks" of upper Greenwich, Laight, Charlton, Greene, and Wooster Streets. From there, New York's wealthier families could still walk to their businesses and their places of worship.[12] Poorer Jews from England and central Europe had begun to settle to the north of the synagogue as well, though they followed other newcomers to the east of Broadway, on Broome, Houston, Lispenard, Canal, and Franklin Streets. But while the Protestants could choose among an array of churches, many reflecting class, denominational, and ethnic differences, all Jewish New Yorkers, regardless of wealth or neighborhood, headed to Shearith Israel.

Much more than simply a place of worship, Shearith Israel was also the Jewish communal center, providing access to kosher meat, Passover matzos (unleavened bread), and education. A hazan, or prayer leader, led services in Hebrew, and men and women sat separately, according to traditional custom. Early leaders of the congregation had instituted the Sephardic rite, emanating from Spain, whose pronunciation of Hebrew and order of prayers differed from those of the Ashkenazi, or central and eastern European, rite. Though the majority of New York Jews were of Ashkenazi descent by 1728, Shearith Israel maintained what had become a New York Sephardi rite. Despite these traditional elements, however, changes in Jewish life reflected New York's environment of relative freedom and openness. Whereas traditional Jewish communities in Europe could exert force over the population through the threat of *herem*, or excommunication, America's more tolerant environment diminished this threat. In the absence of sanctions, many members of Shearith Israel led less than fully observant lifestyles outside the synagogue. More recent immigrants tended to follow the law more scrupulously than did older members. Moreover, to the ears of these more observant Ashkenazi newcomers, the Sephardic pronunciation of Hebrew seemed strange. But Ashkenazi Jews seeking changes encountered entrenched opposition.

Tensions came to a head in April 1825, when the English-born Barrow E.

Cohen refused to make a traditional charitable contribution for the honor of reading the Torah. Shearith Israel's leaders deliberated over their course of action, ultimately forgoing the imposition of a fine in favor of a milder reprimand. Unsatisfied, Cohen and the newer, traditionalist Ashkenazi immigrants seized an opportunity to demand the right to conduct a separate morning service within the congregation, one requiring more stringent Sabbath observance by its leaders. While the Shearith Israel elite was willing to discard the fees for participation in the service, it rejected these signs of independence. The leadership feared that separate services would breach the unity of the congregation and sensed that the growing numbers of newcomers threatened longstanding rituals and traditions and, more pointedly, its authority. The venerable Shearith Israel could no longer contain the diversity of its congregation, and a contingent separated to form B'nai Jeshurun, thereby setting in motion a pattern of splintering and diversity that characterized New York Jewish congregational life for the next two centuries.[13]

Contemporary observers blamed the breakup of Shearith Israel on the growing geographic spread of the Jewish population. Edmund Blunt's 1828 *Picture of New York* attributed the split from Shearith Israel to the fact that "the increase of the city has left few families in that neighborhood [where Shearith Israel was located], and this, with the great increase, and the continued arrivals from the continent of Europe, rendered it necessary to erect a new temple."[14] The seceders themselves cited "the distance at which many lived from the Spanish and Portuguese house of worship."[15]

Neighborhoods reflected variations in class, occupations, and points of origin, which often led to different modes of daily life. While the more established Shearith Israel leaders who lived to the west of Broadway might have used oil lamps, coal stoves, and ice boxes, those on the eastern side inhabited dilapidated and hastily subdivided wooden homes and depended on candles, oil lamps, and found wood. Clearly, those who lived to the west of Broadway and constituted the leadership of Shearith Israel could more easily afford the twenty-five-cent dues for Torah honors than could newly arrived immigrants living to the east. This class division reflected broader trends in New York City religious congregations—in Protestant churches, newcomers protested pew rentals that they could ill afford.[16]

Eventually, the Ashkenazi Jews who created B'nai Jeshurun rented a former church on the corner of Canal and Elm, in the very heart of Five Points,

New York's immigrant working-class neighborhood. And by 1833, Shearith Israel had rebuilt its synagogue on Crosby Street, closer to its more established members. Though B'nai Jeshurun and Shearith Israel cultivated a working relationship, this division marked a turning point in New York Jewish communal life.

Until the 1820s, New York's five hundred Jews united fairly easily as a minority, and the congregational unit could contain and foster community. But increasing numbers of immigrants diversified the Jewish population and its institutions. A more pronounced upper class and a growing working-class population emerged, as the varied hometowns of the new immigrants and their desires for more stringent observance of Jewish law sparked additional differences. American democracy and freedom encouraged individual Jews to aspire to leadership positions within the synagogue. No single institution could contain these variations, as the earlier congregation had done. Neither could one congregation accommodate all the would-be leaders, who over a thirty-year period called into being twenty-seven congregations.

When Jews did go to synagogue, they went to pray and to socialize. But, increasingly, New York Jews found alternative places not only to socialize but also to buy kosher meat and to engage in acts of charity. New York Jews spent more time beyond the confines of the synagogues—in tenements, on the streets, and in the market. They interacted with non-Jewish New Yorkers on a daily basis, forming relationships that influenced synagogue life and encouraged new patterns of Jewish association. New York synagogue-goers adapted what they learned from New York politics, business, and society to introduce such new trends within the synagogue as elected officers and Jewish ministers able to represent the congregation in ecumenical gatherings and to deliver English-language sermons. But daily life in New York also inspired the formation of new, more secular forms of Jewish community—including Jewish newspapers, social clubs, libraries, hospitals, lectures, and charities. Thus, the story of New York synagogues and their various divisions, while telling, is not *the* story of Jewish New York. Rather, we can find the story of Jewish New York in the markets, tailor shops, saloons, and butcher stores where Jews formed an ethnic economy and forged neighborhood networks. These more informal networks in turn influenced synagogue structure and shaped new forms of associational life for New York Jews.

Raphael Cowen was one of the new immigrants who built the diversified

Jewish community in New York. In the mid-1840s, Cowen left his hometown of Graetz in Prussia to seek work as a tailor's apprentice. He first made his way to Janowicz, Posen, where he met and married Julia Manasseh. The Cowens journeyed to Manchester, England, in search of economic opportunity but soon left for New York. They joined a migration of 150,000 Jews from central Europe to the United States between 1820 and 1880. As central Europe transitioned from a society of estates, in which Jews served as middlemen between peasants and nobles, to an industrial society, many Jews faced dismal economic prospects. Matrikel laws, restricting Jewish marriages in Bavaria and elsewhere, made it all but impossible for young Jews to establish households. While the slightly better-off went to larger cities in search of work, poor young Jews migrated to the United States. Migration accelerated in the 1850s. Letters home and newspaper articles heralded economic opportunities and spoke of helping hands extended by fellow Jews.

Jewish immigrants thus joined a great migration streaming out of various regions of Germany. Indeed, Jews tended to emigrate in larger proportions than did their non-Jewish neighbors, who were also leaving in large numbers. For example, while Jews made up 1.5 percent of the Bavarian population, they composed 5 percent of the Bavarian migration to the United States. Whereas most Germans who emigrated tended to be slightly better-off peasants, coming as family units, Jews arrived with little money and often in groups of single men and women. Most important, whereas the majority of German emigrants sought farmland, Jews opted for towns and cities.[17]

Whether young immigrant Jews left Prussia, Bavaria, or Bohemia, they shared characteristics: lack of formal education, little money, and hardly any knowledge of English. Like all immigrants to New York, they desired communities in neighborhoods that could help them adapt to their new surroundings. When the Cowens arrived in 1849, they "sought that section of the city that was then the destination of German Jewish immigrants. . . . Finding countrymen they knew, [they] located near them on Mott Street, and [Raphael] set out as a boss tailor." Julia gave birth to Nathan soon after their arrival in March 1849, and their son Philip was born in 1853, when they had moved a few blocks to the corner of Canal and Mulberry.[18]

The Cowens passed their first years in Five Points, where difficult living conditions were offset by familial and communal ties. Five Points, so called due to the five-cornered intersection of Anthony, Orange, and Cross Streets (now Baxter, Park, Worth), was bounded by Centre Street on the west, the Bowery on the east, Canal Street to the north, and Chatham and Pearl Streets to the south. The neighborhood became lodged in collective memory as a place of crime, prostitution, and disorder; but it primarily served as a home and workplace for a struggling but burgeoning working-class population. By mid-nineteenth century, Irish immigrants and their children—the largest immigrant group in New York City—constituted 75 percent of Five Points' population. German-speaking immigrants composed the second-largest group (approximately 20 percent), and of these, approximately half were Jewish.[19] Like the Cowens, approximately 70 percent of the Jews living in Five Points came from Posen, Polish territory then governed by Prussia.

Built over an improperly drained pond, Five Points' two-and-a-half-story wooden structures regularly flooded. Yet the neighborhood's stables, workshops, and factories provided a convenient combination of work and residence, making it a prime destination for the tens of thousands of immigrants who sought affordable rent in housing close to work. As a result, the dilapidated wooden homes contained far more inhabitants than one might expect. The first floors often housed stores, and backyards had additional sheds and work stations. Soon, the great demand for homes and work in this neighborhood led property owners to tear down the old wooden structures in order to build brick tenements. But the tenements' crowdedness, dark interior spaces, and cellars made for miserable housing.[20]

Various immigrant groups clustered in specific industries and occupations. Initially, the movement into specific occupations reflected skills and experience that the immigrants brought with them. Irish immigrants arrived extremely poor, with only agricultural experience, and they thus entered the laboring jobs. By mid-nineteenth century, they composed the majority of laborers in New York City—longshoremen, shipyard workers, warehousemen, quarrymen, and construction workers. Germans possessed more money. They had experience in trades such as carpentry, tailoring, shoemaking, tanning, pottery making, bricklaying, and weaving.[21]

Just as other ethnic groups specialized in certain occupations within the city's economy, so did immigrant Jews find their niche in peddling and selling used clothing. German Jews applied their old-country experience in these areas to their new situation, supplying demand in the city and countryside. As many as 50 percent of Jewish new arrivals took up peddling. Others worked as tailors or shoemakers, also using skills they had learned in their country of origin. These Jews joined their fellow German immigrants who worked in similar trades.[22]

As immigrant Jews took root in Five Points, they, like other ethnic groups, settled on specific blocks and even in specific tenement buildings. Baxter Street, below the Five Points intersection, hosted many Jewish stores; similarly, Mott Street, between Bayard and Canal, had a higher-than-average Jewish population. But even blocks that had a high proportion of a certain immigrant group still retained a heterogeneous population. In other words, just because a block attracted more Jews did not mean that all the shops or all the residences were necessarily Jewish. For example, the "Jewish" block on Mott Street had Jewish residents in only three of the seventeen buildings; the remaining buildings held large numbers of Christian Germans and Irish immigrants. And 56 Mott, the most "Jewish" of the buildings, still had two Irish families living among twelve Jewish households. Even when immigrants lived on more "Jewish blocks," they formed a diverse mix of residence, commerce, and communal associations created by people of all backgrounds.[23]

A closer look at the buildings through the 1860 U.S. Census demonstrates this point: 91 Mulberry had a typically diverse mix of residents who, nevertheless, shared commonalities. Most important, the Irish, German-Jewish, and Russian-Jewish heads of households—John Purcell, Samuel Lesser, Isaac Jacobs, Moses Davis, and Mary McFay—all worked as peddlers. Though the Jacobs family originated in Russia and the Lesser family started out in Germany, both stopped along the way in London, as indicated by the fact that both families had middle children born there.[24] In the spring of 1858, Jacobs applied for free Passover matzo from a Jewish congregational consortium, and he might have seen Myer and Sarah Levy, who lived at 56 Mulberry, in line as well. Myer, a twenty-four-year-old secondhand clothier, and his wife, Mary, came from Russia and found a home on the "Jewish" block of Mulberry.[25] However, they appear to have been the only Jewish family in that particular building, living among Irish tailors, milk dealers, and laborers.

All the residents of 33 Mulberry Street, by contrast, appear to have been Jewish, and looking at the census allows us to speculate as to how the Cohens, Colanders, Inspecks, Isaacses, Levys, and Schuls moved beyond past identities as residents of various regions in Germany or Poland to forge New York Jewish bonds of support and community. Julius Isaacs, a storekeeper from

Russia-Poland, was perhaps the most established. The 1860 census recorded his personal estate of $500, most likely his store merchandise, perhaps located on the first floor of 33 Mulberry. Augusta Isaac, who appears to have been his daughter, was twenty-six and also born in Russia-Poland, and Isador Isaac, his oldest son at fourteen, was born in New York, suggesting that the family immigrated between 1834 and 1846. Least established, Poline Tichner, a forty-year-old widow from Russia-Poland, worked as a peddler and boarded with the Inspecks from Germany. Most households included older children born in their respective home countries and younger siblings born in New York. Of the six heads of households, two identified as peddlers, two as cap makers, one as a tailor, and one as a storekeeper. Additionally, Charles Cohen, one of the cap makers, had a seventeen-year-old son named Marx, who is listed in the 1859 city directory as a glazier at 33 Mulberry. Both Poline Tichner and Marx Cohen also appear on an 1858 charity list for free matzos sponsored by the Jewish community.[26] It is hard to know if Poline told Charles about the matzo distribution or whether any of the residents knew each other from Europe or even if Abram Schul, twenty-seven, met Charles Cohen, fifty-seven, through their shared work as cap makers in New York.[27]

Unmarried women—whether widows or daughters—often worked as peddlers, washerwomen, and tailors, while many married women kept house. In Five Points, 48 percent of employed women worked in the needle trades, 25 percent as domestic servants, 8 percent as laundresses, and 13 percent as boardinghouse keepers. While some seamstresses labored in workshops, many worked in their apartments, taking home sewing. Whether employed outside the home or not, most women kept house. Whether through wage work or house work, shared occupations and responsibilities of the Five Points Jews created informal but vital neighborhood networks. When Mary Wasserzug's family arrived in the mid-1870s, they lived in a series of Five Points homes in which the water pump was either in the first-floor hallway or the courtyard, necessitating many trips up and down stairs with pails and much social interaction with neighbors: This arrangement provided a first-floor neighbor with an opportunity to court Mary: "Louis would watch for Mary, and would take the pail away from her, pump it full, and carry it up for her." Most women lacked suitors to handle this work, but one can imagine the countless ways in which housework and shared spaces nurtured neighborhood relationships.[28]

Indeed, in immigrant neighborhoods, newcomers often relied on ethnic ties to gain a foothold. Employers, conversely, looked to members of their own ethnic groups as workers on whom they could rely and with whom they could easily communicate.[29] Once settled, Raphael and Julia Cowen helped relatives who arrived in New York after them, both those passing through and those, like Newman Cowen, a cousin from Russia-Poland, who settled down. Newman reciprocated years later when he gave Raphael and Julia's American-born son Philip a job in his glass business at 207 Canal Street. Though Philip was uninterested in his cousin's glass business and intent on preparing for a career in printing and journalism, he marveled at the communal support Newman provided to less fortunate Jewish immigrants: "His store was the rallying place for nearly every Jew from Russian Poland who came here. He was in very truth their guide, philosopher and friend. To him they went with their troubles, for advice, to be set up in business, or to entrust their funds. . . . He started the newcomer with a box of glass on condition that he took a territory not already covered."[30] Neighborhoods like Five Points offered not only jobs but also Jewish community networks. Networks helped newcomers directly even as more established Jews used them to create an American Jewish identity that involved caring for coreligionists in need. Philip Cowen noted in his memoir that Newman's work anticipated both the United Hebrew Charities (1873) and the Industrial Removal Office (1901), suggesting how informal neighborhood networks developed fundamental elements of more formalized charitable organizations as the community grew.

Newman Cowen's assistance represented more than simple charity. By offering a bundle of glass to a newcomer and earmarking new territory, Cowen not only gave an immigrant a chance but also furthered his own business, expanding its market. Cowen required new peddlers to cover new territory to protect the more established peddlers' routes and to avoid duplication. If an immigrant succeeded in selling that first box of glass, doubtless he would return to Cowen for more boxes: "These people returned to the city every Friday to be with their families over the Sabbath, and called Sunday mornings to pay their debts and get additional stock."[31] In Five Points, people relied on those they knew, often those of shared hometown and family, to get started, and this help also often benefited the giver. Such work propelled individuals forward, even as it knit together a tight ethnic economy.

Thus, while Jews might bicker in the synagogue, they forged ties with one another in the streets. They helped each other find jobs, expand business networks, and form community in shops and on street corners. Over time, this community even survived the dispersal of its members. Within five years, Raphael and Julia Cowen moved uptown to Third Avenue and Thirtieth Street, where Raphael opened a clothing store, joined a new synagogue, Beth El, and had six more children. But the Cowens returned to Five Points to visit the old synagogue, to patronize Jewish book dealers, and to buy Passover groceries and matzo. Thus, though the Cowens had moved to a more pleasant neighborhood, they relied on Five Points for jobs for their children and for social ties for themselves. The Jewish ethnic economy's stores and services also served a social role as a source for New York Jewish identity, even when they were no longer geographically convenient. Just as these neighborhood networks could transcend the neighborhood, they could also cultivate strong ties that could compete with family bonds. Cowen recalled Rachel Weinstock, "a woman of large stature and kindly feeling," who "made a comfortable living selling walking sticks on the corner of Broadway and Canal." Even though her grown sons had established themselves on the West Coast and wanted her to join them, she stood her ground in Five Points: "Her life, she said, was with the people with whom she had been brought up." Though Cowen remembered Weinstock citing the importance of shared hometown origins, she was clearly specifying those from her hometown with whom she had reconnected in Five Points, as well as new ties she forged selling walking sticks on a daily basis in her neighborhood.[32]

Upon arriving in New York City in 1846, Isaac Mayer Wise recalled finding "a number of young fellow-countrymen of culture transformed into factory hands, cigar makers, and peddlers." Wise had loftier ambitions, as he hoped to become a congregational leader and intellectual, and so became disgruntled when the acquaintances he called on consistently advised him to peddle or learn a trade. But conversations he had with several professors led him to an understanding: "a few drops of water and a confession of Christianity would open for me the way to all hearts"—and, one presumes, professions.[33] As a Jew, he faced a choice, it seemed, to peddle or convert. While Wise rejected both and became a leading rabbi and writer, the majority of immigrants arriving in the 1830s, 1840s, and 1850s became peddlers. But like Wise, they associated peddling with the humble conditions of basement-dwelling young fellow countrymen, and many of the peddlers assiduously worked to ascend the socioeconomic ladder that led from peddler to dry-goods merchant.

In the 1840s and 1850s, approximately one-third of New York's Jewish wage earners earned a living through peddling.[34] Peddlers hoped one day to open their own store on Chatham Street, then within a few years to relocate to Grand Street or the Bowery, and then, ultimately, to form a larger concern on William or Fulton Street. A letter in the *Asmonean*, New York's first Jewish weekly, detailed this process:

> When the newly arrived Israelite asks what he shall do to make a living, he is most commonly advised to go and peddle. Accordingly a basket is hastily fixed up, and he is hurried into the country. The country merchants . . . receive them [*sic*] coolly and oppose them step by step. An acrimonious feeling takes hold of the pedlar's heart—he is disappointed and discouraged, and yet he goes on from day to day, changes the basket for the bundle, the bundle for the horse and wagon peddling, and finally emerges a sleek, thrifty merchant. Have the history of one of these men and you have the history of them all.[35]

The myth of ascent appealed to many immigrants, but some entrepreneurs preferred the security of the ethnic neighborhood. In this way, if one went out of business, one was more likely to find employment through local ethnic networks.[36]

Many peddlers expanded their businesses by developing ties with Jews elsewhere in the country. By 1860, the majority of the sixteen thousand peddlers in the United States were Jewish, and this enabled New York Jewish merchants to take advantage of new regional and even national markets. In establishing business connections with communities throughout the country, Jewish peddlers thus also facilitated the growth of New York suppliers. For example, Joseph and James Seligman operated a dry-goods store on William Street but also sent clothing to a brother, William, in St. Louis and to connections in California. Likewise, Levi Strauss made headway in the West in part through his close business connections with his brothers, Jonas and Louis, who had opened J. Strauss & Co., a wholesale dry-goods business in New York. When Levi arrived from Bavaria in 1847, he first stayed in New York and worked for his brothers, learning from them but also recalling his father's experience as a dry-goods peddler in Germany. Six years later, Levi went to San Francisco, buoyed by the steady stream of credit and goods from his brothers. Subsidiary wholesale and manufacturing centers such as Cincinnati emerged, led by transplants from the shops and warehouses of New York.[37]

Jewish peddlers often specialized in the sale of secondhand clothing. In the first two-thirds of the nineteenth century, ready-made clothing was marginal—intended for sailors, miners, or slaves. Most Americans made clothes at home, had clothes sewn by a custom tailor, or bought reconditioned used garments. While some custom tailors were Jews, such as Raphael Cowen, most were non-Jewish Irish, Germans, and native-born Anglo-Americans. Most Jews' clothing businesses concentrated on the secondhand trade. Settling on Chatham Street, Jewish secondhand-clothing merchants took in, cleaned, and renovated old clothing, preparing it for both retail and wholesale markets. Jewish secondhand traders actually "renovated" the traffic, incorporating innovative commercial ideas as well as experimenting with the production of new clothes on the side. Contemporary observers credited Jewish peddlers with introducing the installment plan (selling on "time"), direct selling, and lower prices, made possible by a willingness to maintain a smaller profit margin. One visitor from Chicago noted, "There are quite a number of time peddlers in New York, and they are most useful members of the community. They are all Hebrews, and sell everything on the installment plan." Jews placed eighteen out of twenty advertisements in the *New York Herald* for used clothing for sale in New York, as well as in the southern and western markets.[38]

The secondhand-clothing trade was often "an object of ridicule and contempt," but it allowed Jews to make significant contributions to the emerging garment industry, despite the fact that they played no role in technological advances such as the invention of the sewing machine. Jewish merchants experimented in both marketing and manufacturing. At first, they dabbled in the production of cheap clothing—"slops"—which they sold to miners and workers. A dry-goods merchant with cloth in stock risked little by hiring workers to produce inexpensive ready-made clothes, a process that transformed him from a merchant into a small manufacturer.[39]

■ In Congregations and Societies

Five Points Jews formed the city's third, fourth, and fifth congregations; indeed, for a time prior to the Civil War, more Jews prayed in Five Points than anywhere else in New York. When Raphael Cowen arrived in 1849, he immediately joined a newly established congregation, Bikur Cholim.[40] Perhaps the same countrymen who helped him find a home helped him locate the congregation, otherwise unrecognizable as a synagogue as it was housed in the New York Dispensary. The bonds he forged there must have been strong, because he stayed with the congregation as it moved to 56 Chrystie. Even after the Cowens moved uptown, where Raphael joined the newly formed Beth El, the family continued to attend services fairly regularly at the Chrystie Street synagogue.

Jewish religious life reflected the city's reach into newer neighborhoods, its competitiveness, and its increasing role as a magnet for Europeans in search of new homes. Jewish congregations, lacking resources to purchase their own buildings, rented a variety of spaces typical of the heterogeneous and evolving neighborhood, including basements, saloons, storefronts, workshops, and old Protestant churches. Even when Jews possessed the means to build a new synagogue, as in the case of Shearith Israel, they often needed to rent during construction. The New York Dispensary, a stately structure on the corner of Centre and Walker, rented its second floor to a revolving array of congregations. Humbler secular sites also harbored congregations: Matt Brennan's saloon, at Centre and Pearl, hosted several congregations in the 1840s and 1850s. Once Beth Hamedrash Hagadol, the nation's first Russian congregation (1852), secured the funds and members to move out of a Bayard Street garret, they found themselves below a carpentry shop. Their next stop, a year later, situated them above a saloon.[41] Their frequent moves demonstrated their members' mobility and energy.

While geographic mobility certainly shaped congregations in the mid-nineteenth century, so did increasing numbers. In forming B'nai Jeshurun in 1825, Five Points Jews set a pattern that proved more lasting than the founding of the second synagogue. After that initial division from one congregation into two, New York Jews grew into a linguistically, religiously, and socially diverse community. Their differences found expression in the creation of ever more congregations. For example, in 1828 some discontented members of B'nai Jeshurun left to form Anshe Chesed. In 1839, both B'nai Jeshurun and Anshe Chesed lost members to the newly formed Shaarey Zedek, and Anshe Chesed also lost members to Shaarey Shamayim. In each case, the original congregation survived, attracting incoming immigrants to replace those who had shifted allegiance. In some cases, the new congregations formed due to variations in ritual that can be attributed to hometown customs. Thus, when a critical mass of immigrants from a particular region settled, they formed their own congregation; while in the 1820s the first Ashkenazi congregation included English, Dutch, and German together, by the 1840s new congregations reflected English, Dutch, Polish, German, and Bohemian divisions.

Sometimes arguments over procedure and Jewish law sparked a split. In the case of Ohabey Zedek, a contingent left when the leadership refused to allow a member to officiate at a wedding; in the case of Shaarey Zedek, divisions occurred when a member wished to have a non-Jewish wife converted. Other contentious congregational factions debated over fees. Power struggles underlay many of the disputes. Indeed, in 1845, the leadership of B'nai Jeshurun, which had originally broken from Shearith Israel over their lack of influence as newcomers, now feared that new arrivals jeopardized their own power. Abandoning B'nai Jeshurun, they strove to secure their control by forming Shaarey Tefilah and specifically safeguarded the founders' power. In this way, the congregations' competitive drive mirrored the business spirit that shaped immigrants' daily lives.[42]

While the competitiveness, and sometimes pettiness, that fostered the multiplication of New York's synagogues diminished hopes for a united Jewish community, this dynamic also highlighted the loyalty that individual Jews possessed for their own congregations and traditions. Had they not cared how a congregation should be led or services orchestrated, they would not have devoted considerable time and energy to establishing new congregations. Congregations encouraged individuals and communities to blend affection for prayers and melodies from their European hometown with a new style of American governance. In Bohemia, Germany, or Poland, these Jews would most likely have had little say in synagogue governance. In New York, however, they could vote and debate, and they found ultimate recourse in challenging authority by walking away and forming a new congregation.

Mutual aid associations at first took shape within synagogues. But by the middle of the nineteenth century, these societies opened possibilities of Jewish affiliation outside the synagogue. A turning point came in 1845, when B'nai Jeshurun's Hebrah Gmilut Hassed, or Hebrew Mutual Benefit Society, remained intact even as B'nai Jeshurun itself lost a contingent of members to Shaarey Tefilah. To maintain the integrity of the mutual aid association, which now drew on members from both the original B'nai Jeshurun and the new Shaarey Tefilah, the leadership decided to make membership to the mutual aid association available to any New York synagogue member. Now New York had an organization extending beyond a single synagogue. In the 1850s, the Hebrew Mutual Benefit Society and other mutual aid societies began to purchase their own cemeteries, thereby weakening the synagogue's hold on those who joined to secure a proper Jewish burial. While many society members retained synagogue memberships, this status was no longer a given, and a New York Jew could live—and be buried—as a Jew without synagogue membership.[43]

Just as mutual aid associations came into their own, thereby diminishing the centrality of the synagogue in Jewish life, so too did kosher slaughterers and Passover matzo bakers move beyond the synagogue's purview. Changes in the distribution and sale of kosher meat in New York point to a transition from the synagogue as the center of Jewish community to the neighborhoods. In the first few decades of the nineteenth century, congregations hired their *shohetim* (kosher slaughterers) directly, and Jews bought their kosher meat from the synagogue. By the 1840s, however, butchers began to hire *shohetim* on their own. While several congregations maintained their *shohetim*, both Jewish and non-Jewish butchers who hired their *shohetim* directly gained a much larger share of the kosher-meat market. In the 1850s, the sale of matzo at Passover, paralleled this transition from the synagogue community to the open market.[44] The fact that Christian butchers and bakers found it profitable to offer kosher meat and unleavened bread indicates significant demand. While we cannot dismiss the criticisms of various rabbis and leaders, such as Rabbi Max Lilienthal, who accused the purportedly kosher butchers of mixing kosher meat with nonkosher meat, we should appreciate the continued demand for kosher meat. Those who purchased kosher meat undoubtedly thought that the meat advertised and priced as kosher was indeed kosher; otherwise, they would have simply purchased less expensive nonkosher meat.

The commercial streets of Lower Manhattan's immigrant neighborhoods, with their Jewish groceries and butcher shops, allowed Jews to maintain a Jewish lifestyle in New York outside the synagogue. Ethnic stores sold food and other items that appealed to members of particular immigrant groups. Store owners established the loyalty of consumers not only by offering certain goods but also by doing business in the old language. Stores became social centers where people exchanged news of the old country and the new neighborhood. Any Jewish-owned dry-goods or grocery store could become a place for Jewish immigrants to gather, to read letters from home, to exchange gossip or business tips, and in the process, to foster familial and business relationships.

Of course, local commerce also offered opportunities for entrepreneurship catering to a Jewish clientele.

Women played a particularly active role in the identity-building function of the neighborhood streets. While welcome to attend synagogue services with their husbands or fathers, women could not be active or leading members of congregations. Yet, as consumers, Jewish women, like other housewives in New York, dominated street commerce. The preference for kosher food gave shopping religious overtones for Jews and made grocery stores and, especially, butcher shops venues for women to express their Jewish identities.[45]

Mid-nineteenth-century Jewish leaders acknowledged the importance of Jewish commerce as a gauge of the Jewish community and population. When asked to approximate the Jewish population in New York, contemporary leaders and historians increasingly depended on Passover matzo purchases for the answer. In 1855, the leader of Shearith Israel, Jacques Judah Lyons, estimated the Jewish population of New York based on matzo consumption. Samuel Myers Isaacs, the leader of congregation Shaarey Tefilah and the editor of the *Jewish Messenger*, the leading Jewish New York weekly in the 1850s and 1860s, noted in 1864 that the Passover holiday provided an important potential gauge on population statistics: "It is a pity we have no statistics of the number of Israelites in our city. That they are rapidly increasing is evident from the scarcity of matzos on the eve of the late festival, although the bakers assured us that all of them had supplied themselves with quantities in excess of former years."[46] The fact that by mid-nineteenth century communal leaders increasingly linked population statistics to the consumption of matzo, as opposed to synagogue membership and seating, affirms the importance of neighborhood networks and shopping, suggesting that Jewish ritual practice could exist independently of and in addition to the synagogue.

Advertisements for kosher meat and groceries in the *Jewish Messenger* reveal (1) movement from neighborhood to neighborhood, (2) continued allegiance to a former neighborhood, and (3) the ongoing importance of kosher goods. Kosher butcher stores and groceries advertising in the English-language Jewish press followed the Jewish population from Five Points east to Kleindeutschland and then uptown; these advertisements also suggest that even the Five Points stores that remained in place adjusted to the movement of Jews away from the neighborhood by offering delivery services. In 1860, Lyons and Guion, a store in Five Points at 132 Chatham Street, advertised its wares and promised that "orders thankfully received from the Israelitish community" would be "promptly sent to any part of the city." This advertisement suggests, too, that even those who moved beyond the immigrant neighborhood continued to desire kosher groceries and value Five Points ties. Phillip Friedman kept one store in Five Points, at 131 Elizabeth Street, but added one at number 9 in the Essex Street Market, in the heart of Kleindeutschland. Friedman supplied kosher meat to individuals and organizations. His advertisement in an 1850 issue of the *Asmonean* read, "Societies, Festivals, Dinner Parties, and Balls Contracted for, at a low rate and executed in the best manner." In September 1855, perhaps in response to increased movement to Kleindeutschland, Friedman announced that he had moved his Elizabeth Street store to 134 Rivington and maintained his store at the Essex Market. From Kleindeutschland, he was prepared to send kosher meat to the West Indies as well. Another Five Points store, McGowan and Hart, had moved to Grand Street, a major Kleindeutschland artery, by 1860. Its advertisement referred explicitly to kosher "English and Dutch Cheese" among a list including "Family and Fancy Groceries," not identified as kosher.[47]

By 1860, Jews in search of kosher beef and poultry could venture further uptown to a new kosher meat market at 669 Eighth Avenue, between Forty-Sixth and Forty-Seventh Streets, with the assurance that this meat market had downtown approval. C. Willmot assured *Jewish Messenger* readers that his *shohet*, Rev. Isaac Marks, was recommended by rabbis in England and certified by Rev. Samuel Myers Isaacs of Shaarey Tefilah, Dr. Morris Raphall of B'nai Jeshurun, and the officials at Beth Hamedrash and "therefore solicits the patronage of those families who depend upon a proper place for getting real kosher meat." Here shopkeepers advertised their allegiance to standards, showing that rabbis and shopkeepers were not the only arbiters of Jewish law but that customers also had a role in determining communal standards through their patronage. Willmot also promised "to deliver to any part of the city free of charge," indicating that Jews in search of kosher meat were not located in one specific neighborhood.[48]

Although the Five Points neighborhood remained a center of Jewish immigrant life through the turn of the twentieth century (in 1890, Jews composed 18 percent of the population there), Jews had started to move east of the Bowery as early as the 1840s and '50s. A ribbon of Jewish settlement headed east from Mott and Baxter Streets along East Broadway and then north to

Broome and Houston and still further east to Attorney and Ridge Streets. In many ways, Kleindeutschland resembled Five Points—both were decidedly working-class immigrant neighborhoods that housed and employed its resident laborers. However, the population here was more German than Irish, and the German language dominated. In fact, Kleindeutschland was the first massive foreign-language urban enclave in American history. Manhattan and Brooklyn constituted the world's third-largest German-speaking city after Berlin and Vienna, and Kleindeutschland itself ranked as the fifth-largest German-speaking city. In many ways, this city-within-a-city proved profitable for immigrant entrepreneurs—they catered to their fellow countrymen and established grocery stores, saloons, and dry-good stores, as well as breweries and cigar factories. Tailors, shoemakers, and furniture makers set up shop in Kleindeutschland's "maze of alleyways . . . [with] internal courtyards crowded with industrial workshops."[49]

Kleindeutschland nurtured an ethnic economy that catered to German-speaking immigrants, both Jewish and non-Jewish. Grocers, delicatessen owners, and cigar manufacturers depended on the immigrant community for their customers.[50] Yet at the same time, the immigrants formed the labor pool on which the broader city depended; though a distinct quarter, these immigrants were fundamentally part of New York City. They could establish German societies, and they could reconstitute Catholic parishes or build Lutheran churches, but their children would learn English. Even their German-language newspapers, while leaving space to follow events in the homeland, focused primarily on New York politics and events. Similarly, the Jewish immigrants of Kleindeutschland often lived and labored side by side with their German-speaking Christian neighbors but at the same time maintained distinctive congregations and associations.

Census records indicate that German Jews lived in buildings that often had at least one other Jewish family, as well as several non-Jewish families. For example, in 1860, Mayer Stern, a shoemaker, lived with his family at 220 Second Street with nine other families. Of the ten households, all parents were born in Germany (Baden, Bavaria, Prussia), and three families out of the ten (including the Sterns) appear to have been Jewish. At 129 Willett Street, Baden-born Jacob Abraham, who worked at an exchange office in 1860 but had worked as a baker in 1859, and his Bavarian-born wife, Fanny, lived with their five children, all born in New York. They shared the building with three other families. Their neighbors Herman, a shoemaker, and Barbara Meyer, from Wurtemburg and Bavaria, raised their own New York–born children, Meyer and Mary, and appear to have been Jewish; the other two families both hailed from Darmstadt and do not appear to have been Jewish.[51]

Jews formed one of Kleindeutschland's many regionally or religiously defined ethnic subgroups.[52] Within the German community as a whole, class distinctions became more important over time, reshuffling former regional affiliations in favor of shared socioeconomic status. German-speaking Jews followed a similar pattern in some respects, though not in others. Within Kleindeutschland, they married other German-speaking Jews (irrespective of region) and lived in specific areas. Their institutional affiliations gradually came to emphasize their Jewishness over their Germanness. By the late 1850s, however, more-successful German-Jewish immigrants had moved beyond Kleindeutschland, while the working classes remained. An 1858 list of Jews who applied for free Passover matzo showed distinct clusterings around Ridge and Attorney Streets.

One way that Jews continued to mark their separate identity as Jews was by forming congregations. New congregations sprouted in rented spaces in Kleindeutschland: Shaarey Shamayim (1839) and Rodeph Shalom (1842), the sixth and seventh congregations in New York, started on Attorney Street. Bohemian Jews formed Ahawath Chesed (later Central Synagogue) in rented quarters on Ludlow Street in 1844. In 1852, Jews from Poland and Germany formed Beth El on Thirty-Third Street, the first "uptown" congregation. Beth Hamedrash, the Russian congregation that had moved from garret to carpenter shop to saloon, excitedly jumped at the opportunity to purchase an old Welsh church on Allen Street in 1856. Years later, the congregation remembered this site as "a good spiritual and physical situation."[53] In addition to Shaarey Hashamayim and Rodeph Shalom, Temple Emanu-El (1845), Bikur Cholim (1849), Shaarey Rachamim (1849), and Beth Elohim (1853) were founded in Kleindeutschland. Other congregations followed individuals out of Five Points and often into Kleindeutschland. Though in 1850, B'nai Jeshurun, the original Five Points congregation, bypassed Kleindeutschland and built a new synagogue on Greene Street and Houston, Anshe Chesed, the second congregation formed in Five Points, installed its congregation in an impressive Gothic synagogue on Norfolk and Houston. Temple Emanu-El, born in Kleindeutschland, spearheaded the radical changes in Jewish ritual and thought that led to the Reform movement in Judaism.

Despite the importance of religious congregations, however, the majority of immigrants devoted much of their time and energy to secular associations and clubs. In this respect, Jews resembled their non-Jewish neighbors. The German community, in particular, included many free thinkers who did not attend church of any kind. The *Staats-Zeitung*, the city's major German-language newspaper, noted in 1860 that 50 percent of the Kleindeutschland community lacked church affiliation; in another article, the newspaper claimed that only one out of five German immigrants could be considered a "regular church-goer." Jews also strayed from strict religious practice. In the 1840s and 1850s congregational participation diminished in two ways. Newspapers noted the increasing numbers of the unaffiliated. Additionally, those who did affiliate with congregations neglected religious obligations. By the 1840s, congregational leaders realized that they could not depend on ten members to attend prayer services to make the requisite ten-man quorum, or minyan, and so hired "minyan men" to attend services.[54]

In place of church, German immigrants became known as inveterate creators and joiners of voluntary associations, or *Vereine*.[55] While some *Vereine* represented particular hometowns, others promoted a certain trade or occupation, political interest, or leisure pursuit. Many German immigrants had been members of voluntary associations in Germany, so this form of organizing was familiar. Voluntary, democratic gathering meshed well with American social trends. American fraternalism flourished in the second half of the nineteenth century. Beginning with the Masons and Odd Fellows, millions of American men and hundreds of thousands of women subjected themselves to elaborate initiation rituals to become "brothers" and "sisters" of a myriad of secret societies and fraternal orders. Fraternal orders claimed one out of five American men; many joined several societies.[56]

Both the "fraternals" and the *Vereine* offered material benefits. Although the oldest order, the Masons, relied mostly on an informal system of mutual aid, most of the newer orders formalized the benefits they provided. Most paid a "death benefit" to the survivors of a brother who died. Many also supplied medical care to the sick and burial. At a time when there was little government-provided social insurance, or even privately sponsored pensions, these benefits offered a modicum of security to working- and middle-class men and women.

Germans found that one could join a fraternal organization and further both German identity and integration into American culture at the same time. The Independent Order of Red Men, for example, translated the pseudo-Indian lore of an American order into German.[57] Likewise, Jews often joined German fraternal orders yet preserved their religious identity. Jews assumed leadership of lodges of such German fraternal orders as the German Order of the Harugari, the Orden der Hermanns Soehne (Order of the Sons of Hermann), the Independent Order of Red Men, and the Improved Order, Knights of Pythias (the last two were breakaways from mainstream English-speaking orders). Sometimes, Jews joined predominantly Jewish lodges of these German orders.

On October 13, 1843, a group of German-speaking Jews, some with experience as Masons and Odd Fellows, some with active synagogue memberships, gathered at Sinsheimer's saloon on Essex Street and created a wholly new Jewish association: B'nai B'rith, Sons of the Covenant. This organization derived its identity both from the daily aspects and structures of Kleindeutschland and from Jewish values and rituals. The founding's very setting—a saloon—shows the influence of Kleindeutschland social norms. The lager beer saloon served as the quintessential living room of Kleindeutschland, whose Tenth Ward alone hosted 526 of them in 1865.[58] As evidenced by notices in the German-language newspaper the *Staats-Zeitung*, hundreds of chapters of the Masons, Odd Fellows, and International Order of Red Men gathered in the rear rooms of saloons. Still, the dozen founders of B'nai B'rith, of whom 25 percent were members of prominent German fraternals, chose to gather at a saloon owned by a fellow Jew, and they chose to organize a distinctly Jewish fraternal.

Why form a distinctly Jewish secular association when one could join a preexisting secular association such as the Masons? Or, for that matter, a synagogue? To some extent, strains of anti-Semitism or discomfort within the general fraternal orders could have motivated the twelve men. But in their own preamble to their constitution, they stated that they formed a new association precisely because they felt that the synagogues had failed to capture the attention of the Jewish youth: "to speak plainly, a youth would rather not be recognized as a Jew, and never thinks of visiting a synagogue, it becomes necessary for us to try at least to remedy this evil and show the beauties of our Holy Religion."[59] Even as they established a secular institution that mimicked the rituals and forms of standard fraternal organization, they infused those forms with Jewish content and used it to fulfill a goal of Jewish unity and fellowship.

Like most fraternal associations, B'nai B'rith supported "its members in the event of illness and other untoward events" and also helped support "the widow and the orphan." The founders also emphasized that B'nai B'rith strove to unite Jews in the interests of humanity, promoting "science and art" and "developing and elevating the mental and moral character of the people of [the Jewish] faith."[60] But beyond simply supporting fellow Jews and pursuing an interest in broader civilization, it aimed to redress a void in Jewish life. Even as it looked forward to the creation of a new, vital Jewish association, B'nai B'rith founders acknowledged a void left in New York by the synagogue's fading hold. Henry Jones, usually accorded pride of place among the order's twelve founders, conflated Jewish and fraternal symbols and practices as he explained how Jewish fraternalism would rescue Judaism from the hidebound traditions increasingly rejected by modern youth. Jones, born Heinrich Jonas in Hamburg, was a thirty-two-year-old mechanic when the meeting at Sinsheimer's took place. Dark haired and bespectacled, with a prominent nose and cleft chin framed by a fringe of beard, Jones was secretary of congregation Anshe Chesed and "a born organizer." He averred,

> The Jewish religion has many observances and customs corresponding to the secret societies known to us. The synagogue, for instance, might be compared to a lodge room. It used to be open twice a day; for a Jew desiring to find a friend, he had but to go there and make himself known by certain signs and tokens; he was sure to find assistance. The sign consisted of a grip given with a full hand and the magical words *Sholem Alechem*. The *Mesussah* on the door-post was the countersign. The *Arbacanphoth* represented the regalia. *Shema Israel* was the password. But now, since the synagogue is open but once a week, since the *Mesussah* is to be found at very few doorposts, since the regalia, the *Arbacanphot*, has almost disappeared from the breasts of our coreligionists, since the pass-word is not given twice a day as it used to be, and therefore has lost its magical power.[61]

Jones appeared to yearn for the power of a traditional Jewish lifestyle—its rites and customs—to shape the texture of daily life and form community, and he attempted to graft Judaism's symbols onto *Vereine* culture. While the synagogue had, to Jones's mind, failed, the thriving *Vereine* and fraternal culture of

Kleindeutschland could perhaps strengthen Jewish customs and community, making them a visible part of daily life for American Jews.

Rooted in a particular Kleindeutschland saloon, and conditioned by a structure of mutual aid that coursed through the German immigrant quarter and American society, B'nai B'rith spoke to a fundamental desire of immigrant Jews: to adapt their Jewish identity to new American formats. By 1852, the order had more than seven hundred members in New York City, in addition to lodges in Baltimore and Cincinnati. That year, the New York lodges dedicated Covenant Hall, at 56 Orchard Street, containing meeting rooms, a large assembly hall, and a library, as well as a private restaurant run by an order member. New York's B'nai B'rith enrolled nearly one thousand members by 1856; by 1861, every state in the country had a B'nai B'rith lodge. Beginning in New York, this novel mode of Jewish identification spread throughout the United States. In every city and town in which it took root, B'nai B'rith offered a means for Jews of various hometowns and levels of religious observance to unite around a shared Jewish identity. It created a whole new way of affiliating with the Jewish community that was fully compatible with contemporary American culture. The trend of establishing Jewish organizations outside the synagogue escalated in ensuing decades. By 1860, New York had twenty-seven synagogues but forty-four charitable and benevolent societies.

At least sixteen additional national Jewish fraternal orders arose between the 1840s and the 1910s. They had names like Independent Order Free Sons of Israel, Kesher shel Barzel, Order Ahavas Israel, Order Brith Abraham, and Independent Order Brith Sholom. All offered material benefits and combined Judaic symbols with fraternal elements. Membership overlapped and rituals diffused throughout the community as joiners accumulated fraternal experience. Hirsh Heinemann, for example, one of the founders of B'nai B'rith, subsequently served as first Grand Master of the Free Sons of Israel, which once included a whole lodge of former members of the Harugari. Among the founders of Order Ahavas Israel were several Masons, Odd Fellows, and members of Sons of Benjamin and Independent Order Brith Abraham (IOBA).[62]

As an independent women's order, unaffiliated with a men's group, the Unabhaengiger Orden Treuer Schwester (Independent Order of True Sisters) was unique. Although it began in 1846 as a ladies' auxiliary to congregation Emanu-El, by 1851, it could claim to be the first independent national Jewish women's organization, with six lodges, two in New York City. The True Sisters had all the trappings of a fraternal order, including not just material benefits but also a system of four degrees of membership, named after Jewish heroines: Miriam (sisterly love), Ruth (friendship and loyalty), Esther (fidelity), and Hannah (piety). Although many of its members discovered fraternal forms through their husbands' B'nai B'rith membership, and the two orders maintained friendly relations, the Independent Order of True Sisters promoted "the development of free, independent and well-considered action of its members. The women are to expand their activities, without neglecting their obligations as housekeepers, in such a manner, that if necessary they can participate in public meetings and discussions, *besides* [*sic*] the man, not inferior to him." Although the True Sisters remained a small organization—with twenty-one lodges and 5,991 members nationwide (ten lodges with 2,412 members in New York City)—it offered a rare place in communal life for autonomous women's activities. When the National Council of Jewish Women was founded in 1893, many True Sisters played active roles in the new organization.[63]

B'nai B'rith evolved gradually to meet its members' needs. Initially they were German immigrants of modest means, but by the end of the century they were both German and English speaking and solidly middle class. Over time, B'nai B'rith simplified its rituals and deemphasized its benefits. Those who were in need still received support, and the New York District opened an old-age home in Yonkers in 1882; but as members moved up socially, they directed more of their attention to philanthropic efforts. For a time, B'nai B'rith took the lead in mobilizing for Jewish rights at home and abroad and in aiding and Americanizing new waves of Jewish immigrants. By 1917, although it retained its headquarters on upper Broadway, its center of gravity shifted outside the city: of 313 lodges and 35,422 members across the country, only 19 and 2,100, respectively, were in New York.

■ The Sabbath and the Jewish Street

One manifestation of the large German influence on Jewish organizational practices in the nineteenth century was their secularization practices. This carried over to Sabbath observance as well. In an editorial in the *Jewish Messenger*, an exasperated Rabbi Samuel Myers Isaacs noted that the average Jewish New Yorker desired to keep the Sabbath but felt that America's "climate" created "something in the air that opposes his intention."[64] This pattern held steady. Fifty years later, Rabbi Bernard Drachman, a staunch crusader for Sabbath observance, claimed that Sabbath laxity became significant in the mid-nineteenth century. Immigrants seeking freedom and economic opportunities "seemed to think there was something in the American atmosphere which made the religious loyalty of their native lands, and especially the olden observance of the Sabbath, impossible."[65]

What, exactly, transpired in New York's "climate" to make regular Sabbath observance difficult? Doubtless economic pressures weighed more heavily on Jews than on the Irish and Germans, since the Jewish Sabbath was an accepted workday for the city. Nevertheless, Sabbath practices differentiated not only Jew from Christian but also Catholic from Protestant and German from Anglo. New Yorkers debated the meaning of the Sabbath, how it should be observed, and whether it should be observed at all. German Christian immigrants contributed to the debate over appropriate behavior on the American Sunday. Even Germans who attended church regularly included "secular activities" as part of their Sunday routine, and these elicited criticism from native-born Protestants and even prompted legislation. While Sabbatarians wished to reserve Sunday for rest and churchgoing, more fluid definitions of Sunday behavior included attendance at a library, a voluntary association, or a lecture hall. As more immigrants entered the city, many supported the notion of a "Continental Sabbath," which encompassed leisure and amusement. Theaters, dance halls, and saloons beckoned many city dwellers but irked those who favored a strictly observed and government-protected Sunday as a day of church attendance and quiet contemplation. German immigrants, in turn, organized to proclaim their right to spend their day off from work as they pleased, appealing to American separation of church and state and individual liberties to fight against Sabbatarians and blue laws.[66]

Jews, of course, traditionally observed the Sabbath on Saturday. But they too joined in the debates. On a practical level, New York Jews grappled with whether to work on Saturday, at once the Jewish day of rest and an important commercial day. The Jewish network of peddling and business failed to insulate Jewish workers and businessmen from the tug of the city's commercial demands and the lure of its opportunities. As early as the 1840s, sermons and publications noted that Jews shirked their religious responsibilities. Jewish communal leaders denounced Sabbath desecration; but notably, an 1854 Sabbath debate among Jews actually addressed Christian worship patterns. This debate focused more on a Jew's place in Christian New York society than on Jewish Sabbath observance.

Indeed, just as German immigrants discussed the merits of the Continental Sabbath in their newspapers and in saloons, immigrant Jews considered the role of the Sabbath in secular spaces such as libraries and the Jewish weekly the *Asmonean*. In 1854, Professor Emanuel Brandeis delivered a lecture at the B'nai B'rith's Maimonides Library Association, at 56 Orchard Street, in which he focused on Chatham Street, a mere ten-minute walk away. But this lecture addressed work, not leisure, and must have hit home as many in attendance either lived and worked or had lived or worked on Chatham Street. What was wrong with Chatham Street? Given the tenor of other lectures and articles on Jews' neglect of their Sabbath, one might expect that Brandeis would have focused on Jews who opened their stores on Saturday, thereby disregarding the Jewish Sabbath. To the contrary, here, Brandeis lambasted those who opened on Sunday: "It is revolting to see people so regardless of public feeling as to desecrate a day of general worship, and to trade and deal openly, while the majority of inhabitants are going in pious devotion, to throw themselves at the feet of the divinity." Brandeis excused Sabbath observers from his critique, targeting only Jews who kept their businesses open seven days a week and thereby made Chatham Street "a crying abuse, a foul spot upon the New York Israelites." Brandeis chastised the seven-day-a-week storekeepers for disturbing the "pious devotion" of Christians on Sunday but ignored the distress that Saturday commerce must have caused Jewish Sabbath observers. Instead, Brandeis called on Jewish businessmen to close their shops on Sunday, to redress the fact that their commerce "lower[ed] [Jews] in the general esteem."[67]

Sunday work raised a larger theoretical question about Jews' place in New York and American principles. The *Asmonean* leveled a thorough critique of Brandeis's arguments. Its columnist claimed that the Jews' ability to open on Sunday was actually "an illustration of American freedom, a striking instance of independence and equality." Brandeis rejected this comparison, characterizing Chatham Street as a "crippled monument of American freedom and equality" and a manifestation of the "European ghetto." The *Asmonean* columnist took umbrage: "One of the most central, best located thoroughfares, tenanted on one side almost exclusively by Christians, a Ghetto! I could never have made that discovery." Here, the *Asmonean* columnist argued, Jews, along with Gentiles, composed a thriving, core artery of New York commerce. Jewish Sunday commerce demonstrated America's freedoms: "the real question at issue, namely the right, the inalienable right of every citizen to work or rest on the day he chooses!" Just as German immigrants invoked American freedom to justify their Sunday customs, so too did Jews turn to a language of rights. This debate suggests that the very presence of Jews, and of minorities, illustrated key principles of American identity even as they deviated from the social mainstream.[68]

The debate in the *Asmonean* demonstrates that even Jews who disregarded Jewish religious law had an identity as Jewish New Yorkers. Both non-Jews and other Jews considered them part of the Jewish community, and non-Jews could be offended by their disturbance of the Christian Sabbath, while Jews could worry about the possibility that non-Jews might take offense. In other words, deviating from religious precepts did not necessarily distance one from Jewish identity or community.[69]

■ The Growth of the Garment Industry

The Jewish arrivals of the mid-nineteenth century set many of the patterns followed by those who came later. Nowhere was this more visible than in the garment industry that became the basis of a large part of the New York Jewish economy. New York's assets continued to facilitate the growth of the garment trade, enabling clothing manufacturing to increase 600 percent between 1860 and 1880. The city already had numerous garment firms, which took advantage of the city's proximity to New England textile mills as well as European textiles and fashion ideas. New immigrants both provided cheap labor and fed a growing retail market in the city itself. And the simultaneous increase of catalogues, advertising, and department stores helped to expand markets across the nation. New York's role as the financial capital also provided funds for new and old firms eager to grow. While New York's lack of open space hindered other industries from taking root, the garment industry's adaptability and flexibility with regard to production meant that it could be decentralized in the city. Manufacturers purchased, designed, and cut fabric but then relied on contractors who managed the assembly and production of the finished clothes in tenement apartments throughout the city.[70]

The Civil War demanded the production of uniforms, and Jewish merchants stepped in to meet the demand. This effort helped propel Jews from the margins to the center of clothing manufacture. Both Jewish merchants who had already been involved in the clothing business and those who lacked any clothing experience whatsoever jumped at the contracts and set up shop accordingly. Without time to measure every single soldier, suppliers developed a system of standardized sizes for the first time. This helped in the rapid production of uniforms but also made possible mass production for a civilian market.[71]

German Jews used their experience in the garment industry and wholesale and retail trade to direct this expansion, with the help of an influx of cheap labor that came in the form of eastern European Jews in the 1870s, 1880s and 1890s. As eastern European Jews arrived in New York and settled in the same neighborhoods that had once nurtured the central European Jewish second-hand market, they soon learned of the importance of the garment industry and used neighborhood networks to find their way into it. By 1890, one-half of all employed eastern European Jews in New York worked in the garment industry, and by 1900 they composed the majority of both workers and employers.[72]

Mary Wasserzug's story illustrates the ways in which eastern European Jews followed the central Europeans into the garment industry. In 1876, a quarter century after Raphael and Julia Cowen settled in Five Points, twelve-year-old Mary Wasserzug arrived from Werbelow with her mother to find her elderly father living in a single narrow room on East Broadway. Having failed to launch a jewelry store, the father was barely getting by, and so Mary immediately sought employment. Neighbors secured her first position, as a domestic to established cousins on Grand Street, where she earned three dollars a week. As a newcomer, this position conferred certain advantages—despite demeaning treatment from the mother of the home, the older daughters, who also happened to be schoolteachers, helped Mary learn English. But almost from the beginning, Mary understood that the garment industry was the more respected occupational goal. With the knowledge that her older sister, Rivkah, a skilled seamstress, would be arriving, Mary saved money so that Rivkah could buy a sewing machine, bypass domestic work, and enter the garment industry. When tensions forced Mary to leave the domestic position, she too wanted to find work in the garment industry: she "tried hard to secure work in a shop, but alas, she could not sew."[73]

Mary turned once again to neighborhood networks to find work as a domestic in New Jersey, with people from Werbelow, her hometown. But when she learned that the mother of the home was pregnant, "it occurred to Mary that she had made a mistake to enter domestic service. There would be much company when the child was born, they would discover who Mary was, and the news would travel as far back as Werbelow—Mary the rabbi's grandchild had in America become a servant." Jews in neither Europe nor America held domestic work in high regard. Having a job in the garment industry, on the other hand, was perfectly respectable.

> Again, Mary sought a job. She came at last to a buttonhole factory, where an old fellow-townsman was "boss." He himself taught Mary how to hold a needle and sew with a thimble. In a week Mary had advanced to finishing machine-made buttonholes. After one week of the apprenticeship Mary got a dollar and a half. She joyfully ran home and gave her parents her precious earnings. Her industry was rewarded, for two weeks later she was earning three dollars a week. It was the busy season for buttonholes and she was offered $4.50 by another employer. Her countryman advised her to accept, since he himself was unable to pay that much.[74]

Though Mary advanced in this position, the slack season came, and she lost her job. And so Mary found a job with a landsman, working in a buttonhole factory at 4 Bayard Street. Within several years, she advanced to become a forelady at Schwartz's buttonhole factory. Her mobility in the garment industry translated into increased income for the family and a series of residential moves within the Lower East Side.

Eastern European Jews viewed the garment industry as a means to an end. As Jesse Pope explained,

> The statement has been repeated until it is trite that the Jew considers the industry as a stepping stone to something higher, and in no industry in this country has the upward movement been so pronounced as in this. Every year large numbers desert the clothing industry to go into such occupations as small shopkeepers, insurance agents, and clerks; the importance of this movement is seen by the study of the migration of the Jews into the better residence districts uptown. The Industrial Commission says: "Tailors who have been displaced by green immigrants of the same or other nationalities have found better positions as contractors, manufacturers or small tradesmen, or have created a new line of product of a better grade."[75]

Many eastern European Jews remained in the garment industry only as long as they had to; economists found that the longer an immigrant lived in the United States, the less likely he or she was to work in the garment industry.[76]

■ Rising in Retail

While some of the Chatham Street shopkeepers and their descendants transformed their old-clothes trade into the ready-made garment industry, others charted their advance through retail. In 1902, to take one extraordinary
example, Macy's opened its stunning new department store, a nine-story
castle of commerce on Thirty-Fourth Street. Two red marble pillars flanked
the Broadway entrance, and overhead an arch showcased a bronze clock and
statues of Greek maidens. Though bronze letters spelled out the name of the
store's founder, R. H. Macy, Isidor and Nathan Straus, the current owners, engineered the move and the $4.8 million construction.[77] Their father, Lazarus,
had come to the United States in 1852 and started a general store in Talbatton,
Georgia. After the Civil War, Isidor brought the family to New York City to
open a wholesale crockery business. In 1874, Lazarus Straus and his sons Isidor
and Nathan acquired the concession for Macy's china and glass department.
Though many central European Jews had opened dry-goods firms, department stores represented the next rung in commerce. By the time Lazarus arrived in the United States, A. T. Stewart had opened his marble palace of commerce on Broadway and Chambers and collected a number of departments
under one roof. In doing so, he transformed the shopping experience from
one that involved inelegant traipsing from one retail firm to another to a fashionable, convenient experience in which New Yorkers found all their needs
under one roof and could dine and socialize as well.

By the time the Strauses acquired Macy's in 1896, it had long surpassed A. T.
Stewart's and other New York department stores. The Strauses built on that
success, continuing to innovate as well as moving uptown and constructing
one of the largest department stores in the world. Macy's enticed New Yorkers
to pursue happiness through consumption, as they handled the finest linens,
tried on the most fashionable dresses, and purchased English teas. An army of
workers created splendid display windows and meticulously arranged departments. The frequent touting of best prices encouraged New Yorkers to shop
with ease, reassured that they enjoyed luxury goods at decent prices. The move
to Thirty-Fourth Street escalated the glamour of the shopping experience, as
the increased space meant more goods to peruse (additional departments)
and unsurpassed grandeur. Macy's close attention to holidays, including its
orchestration and extension of the holiday season, gave customers further rea-

sons to return, enjoy, and shop. Macy's continued success enabled the Straus brothers (a third brother, Oscar, did not join Isidor and Nathan in the business but went into law instead) to take a leading role in Jewish philanthropy and in public affairs.

In the 1840s, Chatham Street Jews took over the undesirable secondhand-clothing trade, a sector that others mocked and shunned. But secondhand clothes and dry goods offered hope for advancement, and many made the transition from peddler to owner of a small firm. The transformation of erstwhile peddlers into substantial merchants was symbolized by the loft buildings they began to build on Broadway. As early as 1850, the *Asmonean* carried an advertisement for cast-iron building construction. One can imagine the aspiring peddler eyeing the advertisement and imagining his own name on the pediment. By 1888, noted one observer, "Of the 400 buildings on Broadway, from Canal Street to Union Square, the occupants of almost all are Hebrews, over 1000 wholesale firms out of a total of 1200 being of that persuasion." Moreover, the observer, added, it was not Broadway alone that bore witness to Jewish commercial mobility; "Hebrew firms also predominate in the streets contiguous to Broadway within the territory named."[78] In the course of several decades, Jews had moved beyond Chatham Street to Broadway. But even as these impressive buildings had risen, with the names of Jewish merchants above their doors, tens of thousands of Jewish immigrants were pouring into miserable tenements to the east on Orchard, Eldridge, Rivington, and Hester Streets. When the owners of the Broadway warehouses had lived on those streets, they had been a part of Kleindeutschland; now their employees found themselves on the Jewish East Side.

This late nineteenth-century print shows immigrants filing into the offices of the United Hebrew Charities for assistance. Several leading Jewish charities merged in 1874 to form the UHC, through which the more established, uptown Jews helped first central European and later eastern European Jewish immigrants. Compare the clean-shaven, Americanized clerks behind the desk to the bedraggled immigrants in line. (Photograph courtesy of Butler Library, Columbia University in the City of New York)

CHAPTER 2

"Radical Reform": Union through Charity

In the late 1880s, Rebekah Bettelheim Kohut typically started her day at home on Beekman Place, a quaint two-block stretch of four-story brownstones between Forty-Ninth and Fifty-First Streets. Kohut described these houses as "a little world in themselves. High up above the East River, and seemingly cut off from the rest of the city, the residents were very neighborly. All of the houses were of the four-story brownstone type, with high stoops." Jewelers, writers, doctors, judges, marble dealers, and musicians gathered on the stoops and in the bay-windowed parlors to enjoy the cool evening East River breezes that made bearable the hot city summers.[1] But though she began her day in this serene residential outpost, midday often found Kohut walking briskly through the congested streets of downtown Manhattan, stopping at various tenement apartments to deliver aid and comfort to the city's Jewish immigrant poor. Kohut and members of her congregation's sisterhood climbed "flight after flight" of the East Side tenements' "creaking stairs" and experienced firsthand how "spaces were divided and subdivided into tiny cubicles called rooms, without air or daylight." In the tenements, they paid "friendly visits" intended to assess the state of immigrant families in need.[2] What motivated Kohut to leave her sunny, refined, comfortable brownstone for a district of ramshackle tenements? Middle-class New York Jews like Kohut felt an obligation to help immigrant Jews and labored actively to forge the formal charitable channels needed to connect Jews now living in separate neighborhoods and inhabiting very different New York worlds.

In 1890, a census study focusing on American Jewish families who had been in the country for at least five years found that they had achieved solid, middle-class standing. Throughout the nation, Jews had worked their way up from peddler to small businessman, wholesaler, and professional: of the 18,031 men surveyed, 5,977 were retail dealers; 3,041 were accountants, bookkeepers, and clerks; 2,147 were wholesale merchants and dealers; and 1,797 were commercial travelers. Nearly two-thirds of the families surveyed had at least one servant.[3]

Many New York Jews too had attained middle-class status, but the city likely had a heavier concentration of both the wealthy and the poor than did the American Jewish community as a whole. Just as the majority of the city's eighty thousand Jews had achieved middle-class status by 1880, hundreds of thousands of newcomers arrived to reinforce the city's Jewish working class. Central European and, increasingly, eastern European Jews streamed into the city with few material assets. At the same time, New York's vitality as the nation's economic center produced a wealthy elite. By the last quarter of the nineteenth century, the nation's wealthiest and most illustrious Jews made their home in New York City, including department-store magnates such as Nathan and Isidor Straus of Macy's and Lyman and Joseph Bloomingdale and such famed financiers as Joseph Seligman, Solomon Guggenheim, and Jacob Schiff.

Communal leaders not only enlarged the agendas of congregations and other associations to include increased charity for newcomers but also created entirely new forms of charitable and communal support. They devised the charitable communal channels to connect brownstone Jews with tenement Jews and to bring Fifth Avenue Jews to East Broadway. At base, charity work underlined a sense of social responsibility toward the newcomers on the part of the more established. But translating charitable impulses into formal networks and institutions took years and sparked heated debates. Fraternal orders and communal defense organizations offered alternative models of communal organization. Nevertheless, the creation of a New York Jewish community owes much to the fostering of charitable networks and institutions, and they served as its core and structure.

Established Jewish New Yorkers could look to broader New York charitable trends as well as their own tradition of giving. In nineteenth-century New York, as elsewhere in the country, philanthropic enterprises were organized along confessional lines. Even publicly funded services were often delivered by groups with religious affiliations, and, naturally, the majority of these agencies were Protestant. Missionary activity was never far from charitable work, and the Catholic and Jewish poor often received a dose of preaching along with whatever aid they sought. By the middle of the nineteenth century, as immigration swelled the potential clientele for aid, both the Catholic and Jewish communities began to expand and institutionalize their charitable efforts. The result was a "mammoth enterprise of social service" that sought to care for "the sick, the elderly, orphans, the unemployed, prison inmates, the hungry, and the destitute." Severe economic downturns such as the Panics of 1857 and 1873 further spurred the creation of private charities to tend to the poor.[4]

By the fourth quarter of the century, New York Jews followed Protestant charities such as the Association for Improving the Condition of the Poor and the Charity Organization Society in instituting a modernized "scientific" approach to charity. As they did so, Jewish women's role as actors and leaders in all these charitable endeavors assumed greater prominence. Women delivered goods to the tenement districts, staffed downtown offices, served as partners in the United Hebrew Charities, and held major leadership positions in the congregational sisterhoods that provided many of the direct services to the poor.

As New York Jews adapted *tsedakah*, or charity, to the city's economic and social circumstances, they not only cared for needy Jews but also began to reshape the entire Jewish community. In the early nineteenth century, synagogues and their associated societies directed the community's charitable impulses. But when, in the mid-1850s, congregations strained to cope with seasonal rushes, such as the annual demand for Passover matzo, they tentatively began to join forces for specific efforts. Beyond the synagogue, benevolent and philanthropic associations as well as individuals sponsored a Jewish hospital, orphanages, and other charitable institutions. By the 1870s, the need for strong, centralized action, and models set by both the Jewish community in London and Christian New York, prompted Jewish communal leaders to campaign for a United Hebrew Charities to supplant a myriad of smaller charitable organizations.

■ Jews' Hospital and the Hebrew Orphan Asylum

A Jewish hospital seemed a particularly pressing need, since "sick and dying Roman Catholics and Jews" were especially vulnerable to the entreaties of "evangelically inclined Protestant clergy." In an increasingly diverse religious and ethnic society, hospitals at midcentury had become "fields of religious combat."[5] Moreover, discriminatory hiring practices made it difficult for Jewish doctors and nurses to get training or to practice at the highest levels. In 1852, therefore, the Hebrew Benevolent Society called a meeting attended by delegates of the Young Men's Fuel Association, the Hebrew Assistance Society, the Bachelors' Loan Society, and the German Hebrew Benevolent Society to consider the creation of a Jewish hospital. The effort stalled, however, until seventy-two-year-old Sampson Simson stepped forward with an offer of land on which to build a new hospital on West Twenty-Eighth Street between Seventh and Eighth Avenues. An 1800 graduate of Columbia College, Simson had been the first Jewish attorney admitted to the New York State bar and a clerk to Aaron Burr. Now he took over leadership of the incipient institution, incorporated as Jews' Hospital in 1852.[6]

With widespread support in the community, Jews' Hospital opened in 1855. Its four-story building featured all the latest improvements, including gas lighting and water from the new Croton water system. The hospital's founders originally intended it for an exclusively Jewish clientele (except, of course, in emergency). But the Civil War and New York's Draft Riots of 1863 led to an increased demand for hospital beds and prompted the institution to accept patients of any religion. In 1866, Jews' Hospital became Mount Sinai Hospital.[7]

Orphans were another vulnerable group, similarly at risk for evangelization, so it is no wonder that many New York orphanages operated under sectarian auspices—either Protestant or Roman Catholic. The city's Jews lagged behind the times, even though plans for an orphanage had been mentioned at the time of the founding of Jews' Hospital and Sampson Simson had endorsed the effort to build one. Only after Rev. Samuel Myer Isaacs, the Dutch-born cantor and preacher of congregation Shaarey Tefilah and editor of the *Jewish Messenger*, took up the cause did the movement for an orphanage pick up steam. Isaacs won over Jewish public opinion by publishing stories of Jewish orphans who converted after being raised in Christian institutions. The kidnapping and baptism of Edgar Mortara in Italy in 1858 further heightened Jews' anxieties about the retention of their youth. In response, the Hebrew Benevolent Society undertook to open the Hebrew Orphan Asylum (HOA) in

1860. The institution's success helped make HBS for a time the most important Jewish philanthropic organization in the city.

Over the succeeding decades, HOA grew steadily. Its first home, a brick row house on Lamartine Place in Chelsea, housed thirty boys and girls, who were escorted to school through hostile Irish streets by HOA's superintendent (who, however, administered "black strap" discipline to them at home). Its next home, taking up an entire block on East Seventy-Seventh Street, housed about 150 orphans and boasted far superior facilities, including shoemaking and printing shops, where the boys learned these trades and prepared for future employment. In 1884, HOA moved into a forbidding Victorian home on the whole block at 137th Street and Amsterdam Avenue. With additions, it eventually housed a capacity of over twelve hundred, its pillared dining room serving hundreds of children at a time.[8]

■ Passover: New York, 1858

The movement for an orphanage had also been advanced by the Jewish response to the economic crisis of 1857–1858, a response that presaged efforts to unite an ever more complex Jewish community through its philanthropic institutions. On February 21, 1858, as Passover approached, Jewish communal leaders—merchants, synagogue leaders, and congregational presidents—convened at 107 MacDougal Street, the home of Rev. Dr. Morris Raphall, the leader of prominent congregation B'nai Jeshurun, to grapple with reverberations of the Panic of 1857. The businessmen among them—Harris Aaronson, Zion Bernstein, Michael Schwab, Phillip Levy—undoubtedly had already faced the effects of the Panic in their commercial dealings. That winter, a decline in international trade, the collapse of a building boom, and a slump in the textile industry had left reeling thousands of shipbuilders, construction laborers, garment workers, peddlers, and shopkeepers. The weakened economy not only contracted men's occupations by 20 percent, but it also reduced by half the number of jobs available to women wage earners. Families pawned household goods to make ends meet. As communal leaders, Bernstein, Aaronson, and Schwab now contended with the downturn's impact on the Jewish working class. In February, it was difficult to imagine how the Jewish poor would be able to afford the new dishes, thorough cleaning, and matzo and other foods essential to the proper observance of the holiday.[9] Not only did

Passover exact additional expense, but it also required taking time off from work. Those who were employed might have wondered if their liberation from work on four out of the eight days of the holiday might find them unwillingly liberated from a job completely by its end.[10] The men gathered at the Raphall residence realized that the tradition of individual synagogues attempting to supply the needy with Passover provisions would not suffice. Current conditions demanded a more organized system, and more far-reaching resources. Accordingly, they formed the Association for the Free Distribution of Matsot to the Poor.[11]

The formation of this association was a radical step, as it united more than a dozen congregations that fiercely valued their independence and had contributed to communal fragmentation. But the men at the helm of many of these congregations possessed and often acted on strong communal impulses. Indeed, Zion Bernstein valued Jewish communal life so much that in 1838 he left New York City to establish Sholem, a Jewish agricultural community in Ulster County, in upstate New York. When Sholem disbanded in 1841, Bernstein returned to the city and turned his talents to the city's Jewish organizations. He pursued an energetic career as a Bowery pawnbroker and devoted his profits and time to his role as congregational officer at Anshe Chesed.[12] Michael Schwab, who owned a dry-goods business on Grand Street, spearheaded the formation of B'nai B'rith and served as an officer of Anshe Chesed. Harris Aaronson helped establish the Jews' Hospital and held leadership roles in the Hebrew Benevolent Society and B'nai Jeshurun. Samuel Myers Isaacs led Shaarey Tefilah, and Jacques Judah Lyons led Shearith Israel. Together, these men represented the leading congregations and fraternal associations, and their Passover efforts bridged gaps between Bohemian Jews and English Jews, between long-established congregations such as Shearith Israel and relatively newly formed congregations such as Ahawath Chesed.

Regardless of where these men had come from, they had made their mark in the city and represented an established class of Jewish merchants. Aaronson lived in the vicinity of stockbrokers and men whom the census identified solely as "gentlemen," either American-born or successful Irish immigrants. Indeed, a survey of census material for men listed as the organizers of the Passover distribution revealed a fairly common pattern: they tended to live in their own homes and sire families of American-born and well-schooled children. Their neighbors were either American born or immigrants who had resided in America for fifteen years or more. In short, their residential and family lives unfolded in radically different ways than did those of their downtown coreligionists.[13]

People in need of Passover matzo that year were peddlers, glaziers, washerwomen, shoemakers, cap makers, tailors, cigar makers, and struggling shopkeepers who lived in buildings with Irish families, non-Jewish Germans, and usually at least one other Jewish family, often two or three. They tended to be more recent arrivals, many with older children born in Germany and younger children born in America. Widows headed approximately 22 percent of the households whose heads' marital status was noted. Though their arrival was often too recent and their financial circumstances too unsteady to enable them to be leaders in the type of communal efforts led by such men as Schwab or Aaronson, these immigrant Jews formed informal communities.[14] Jews who received matzo were bound by common neighborhoods, blocks, and, in many cases, even buildings. An analysis of the association's 1858 matzo distribution list shows that certain blocks of Willett, Ridge, Pitt, Houston, Mulberry, Baxter, and Stanton Streets accounted for the lion's share of matzo parcels. Analysis of census material and city directories indicates that immigrant Jews shared occupations with their neighbors and, in good times, perhaps helped them secure positions as peddlers, tailors, glaziers, cobblers, smiths, washerwomen, and tailors.

But the Panic of 1857 had diminished the power of neighborhood networks; in those winter months, forty-one thousand New Yorkers requested shelter in police stations, and the Association for Improving the Condition of the Poor depleted its treasury.[15] Furthermore, men such as Bernstein, Isaacs, and Schwab understood that a Protestant organization would not supply Passover matzos. Despite radically different occupational and residential situations, Aaronson, Bernstein, Isaacs, Schwab, and other leaders persuaded their congregations to unite to help the poor. Their Association for Free Distribution of Matsot to the Poor had to raise funds for a projected sixteen thousand pounds of matzo. Beyond this, it needed to streamline its distribution. Previously, individual congregations had tended to the needs of the poor, but that often created a situation in which individual applicants uncertain of receiving funds from any one congregation would be needlessly "compelled to apply to one congregation, and then to another, perhaps to be refused, from the many calls made upon them."[16]

The fact that thirteen congregations—including the city's oldest and youngest, Sephardic and Ashkenazic, German and Bohemian—united for this effort was impressive. But, unable to raise all the needed funds, the congregations appealed to the Jewish press, the *Asmonean* and the *Jewish Messenger*. Rev. Samuel Myer Isaacs of Shaarey Tefilah, editor of the *Jewish Messenger*, thus proved a more effective committee member than Rev. Jacques Judah Lyons of the more prestigious Shearith Israel, who chaired the committee. The press effectively extended the committee's reach beyond the congregational audiences. On March 21, the *Messenger* printed an open letter to the "Hebrews of New York":

> The number of poor unconnected with a Congregation is . . . so great, while misery and destitution are so much more widely and lamentably spread this year than ever before has been the case, that public charity—though carried by most of the united Congregations to an extent far exceeding that of any former year—is not sufficient to meet all applications, even in a limited degree. The present appeal is, therefore, addressed to private beneficence, as it is only by its aid that the funds placed at the disposal of the Committee can be raised to an amount at all adequate to the exigencies of the coming Passover.[17]

The need for Passover provisions thus proved to be a broader community problem—one for which the united congregations eagerly assumed responsibility but that they were unable to solve completely. In the absence of any larger organizational or communal framework, a union of congregations could steer the effort but still demand broader communal and financial support.

The fact that the committee turned to the newspaper to rally the broader Jewish community signified demographic changes within the New York Jewish community, as well as new leadership opportunities. No longer composed of overlapping immigrant networks in Five Points and Kleindeutschland, the Jewish community had spread out geographically. The expansion of street railways hastened this development, and by 1864, more than half of all New Yorkers resided north of Fourteenth Street. With horsecars running up and down Third, Sixth, Eighth, and Ninth Avenues and across Eighth, Fourteenth and Twenty-Third Streets, middle-class New Yorkers could now afford to live farther from work and the working class.[18] New residential neighborhoods beckoned more established New Yorkers of all backgrounds, separating them from newcomers—laborers, artisans, small shopkeepers—who could afford only the downtown districts and relied on their mix of commercial and residential space. As the *Asmonean* noted, "The wealthy do not come sufficiently into direct contact with the poor, and cannot realize the extent and intensity of misery that prevails." Because the more established and the newcomers had fewer opportunities to meet at the local synagogue or kosher butcher store, the newspaper became the venue in which encounters might take place. By printing descriptions of the poverty of members of the Jewish community, the *Asmonean* amplified its reminder that "not less than eight hundred families of Yehoodim [Jews], equal to four thousand human beings, are utterly destitute."[19]

The committee appealed through the newspapers to Jewish New Yorkers to generate communal and financial support. As important, it explained why they were all members of the same community—whether residents of Kleindeutschland or Gramercy, shirt manufacturers or laborers, employed or unemployed. The economic severity of the winter of 1857–1858 had created a caste of penurious people unaccustomed to asking for help: "The class of poor . . . is totally different from that of any former period. It is not the mendicant, the widow, or the orphan, but it is the sturdy mechanic, who is willing to work, but whose hands have found no employ from the scarcity of work."[20] Just as these people did not expect to find themselves in need of help, the article admonished its readers, you, too, might find yourself in need one day. Upward mobility or even economic stability in New York could not be assured, and the downturn that had hit as much as 10 percent of the Jewish community might spread. Jewish communal networks, therefore, proved necessary to help all members of the city's Jewish community.

Beyond providing practical reasons why individuals should help provide communal support to the needy, these articles and editorials also constructed a communal identity based on traditional Jewish understandings of charity. The Jewish press assured its readers that charity was not just for the recipient but also for the donor. In brief, proclaimed the *Asmonean*, only through charity could one fulfill a deeper, if not the deepest, religious and spiritual obligation to "love thy neighbor like thyself" (Leviticus 19:18): "To 'love' is the command, and the practical manifestation of that love, the active obedience of that command is summed up in the one word CHARITY." The editorialist invoked the Talmudic sage Rabbi Akiva in claiming that charity is the "most comprehensive principle in the Torah" and urged readers to regard it as "the one most essential to the maintenance of society in general and to the Jewish community in particular." Next, the article listed examples of European Passover charity efforts and lamented the situation in New York, where "each nationality" forms its own congregations, "with a love of independence and a distrust of dictation, that rendered united action extremely difficult." The author conceded that the relative newness of New York's Jewish communities partially accounted for this situation but prodded them to emulate the examples set forth by the Bible, the Talmud, and European Jewish communities. To do this, the New York Jewish community needed to limit the independence of individual congregations: "'Union is force,' says the old proverb; and if that be true, division must be weakness." In this editorial's depiction of general Passover obligations and the specific needs of the local poor, it aimed to convince New York Jews of their communal obligations and to show how charitable giving might offer opportunities for individual and collective betterment.[21]

By April, the committee had registered people in need, including, discreetly, those too embarrassed to sign up on their own; contracted with Canal Street matzo bakers Mark Isaacs and Robert Anderson; and arranged the distribution of matzo parcels for three dates at Congregation Shaarey Shamayim, at 122 Attorney Street. Through this effort, the committee distributed 14,330 pounds of matzo to an estimated 2,866 individuals, members of 640 families, or approximately 8 percent of New York's Jewish population. Beyond the direct action of the Passover provisions, New York Jews accomplished a remarkable feat of union, with those of means attending to those in need.[22]

For some of these people, simply the donation of funds fulfilled their obligation to Jewish peoplehood awakened by the holiday; but for others, their involvement with charity encouraged a closer interaction with the poor. On the days of the matzo distribution, one could imagine Harris Aaronson, forty-five years old, a prosperous shirt manufacturer and officer of B'nai Jeshurun, leaving his home at 170 West Fourteenth Street and heading downtown to the vestry rooms of Shaarey Hashamayim in the heart of Kleindeutschland to distribute Passover provisions. Aaronson had come to America from Posen but had lived in New York for at least twenty years. At five foot nine—relatively tall for that time—with a high forehead and roman nose, how dignified he must have appeared to twenty-six-year-old Sarah Meyer, a tailor residing a few blocks from Shaarey Hashamayim at 84 Ridge Street, the sole support of five-year-old William. Similarly, Bavarian-born Michael Schwab, the Grand Street milliner and dry-goods merchant, had been in New York for close to twenty years and might have passed provisions to a relatively newly arrived Bavarian, Joseph Mannheimer, a thirty-three-year-old who lived with his wife, Sophia; son, Marx, two; and daughter, Mina, a few blocks from the synagogue, at 228 Houston.[23]

Some recipients of aid had been in New York for as long as the donors but had apparently gained a tenuous hold on middle-class status, at best. Samuel Myer Isaacs had repeatedly reminded his readers that people in need of Passover charity that year included those who had already made it in America, only to find themselves in reduced circumstances or even back in the tenements. Isaacs, then, would not have been surprised to encounter Henry Berliner, who came to pick up thirty pounds of matzo for his wife, Sara, and their four children. The Berliners resided at 266 Third Street, and Henry worked out of their home as a tailor. Both he and Sara had been born in Bavaria and had lived in New York for at least twelve years, as their eldest son, Samuel, had been born in the city. Despite their class differences, then, donors and recipients shared backgrounds and experiences. Did their interactions remind some of the committee members of their own early days in New York, or did they seem remote? Did Michael Schwab treat Mannheimer as a fellow Bavarian, or was he more attuned to their now unequal stations in life? While we do not have the answer to these questions, we do know that Schwab and others spent hours canvassing the city, tracking the thousands in need, exerting their energies and funds to ensure that all of New York's Jews had Passover matzo and provisions.

The year 1858 was a milestone in New York Jewry's gradual realization that charity was one of the means to transcend the limited bounds set by local mutual aid associations or neighborhood synagogues. No longer knit together through downtown Chatham or Kleindeutschland neighborhood networks, the growing and ever more complex community forged citywide charitable endeavors through unions of congregations and newspapers to help Jewish New Yorkers in need. But though the 1858 effort ended with a vow to reconvene the following year, attempts to revive it floundered, and the only vestige of the formerly successful union was a lament from a subscriber to the *Jewish*

Messenger: "It is deeply to be regretted that the Union . . . will be discontinued." The editor replied that it was his understanding that the individual congregations had taken up the matter.[24] The 1858 matzo effort, a response to the Panic of 1857, was a remarkable success that Passover, even if it unraveled by the next season. It took another economic downturn—the Panic of 1873—to bring about a more permanent union.[25]

■ Purim Balls

Philanthropic enterprises served especially well to cement a sense of community among people affluent enough to provide for their support. Sponsorship of a philanthropic agency brought prestige, and as new leaders emerged from among the immigrant waves and the native-born, they sought to solidify their position by creating new organizations. In Europe, the community often possessed authority to tax its members, but in America, participation in communal functions was voluntary; so agencies had to work constantly to raise funds. In the middle of the nineteenth century, they encouraged widespread participation partly by tying fund-raising to the kind of extravagant leisure activities and entertainment that growing numbers of middle- and upper-class Jews enjoyed. Dinners, concerts, dances, theater and opera benefits, cornerstone layings, synagogue dedications, installations of rabbis, graduations, and even funerals became occasions for appeals for donations, often marked by great pomp and circumstance. Honors were distributed and social alliances made.[26]

One "American innovation" was the charity ball, often held to coincide with Purim.[27] In 1862, an entire organization was founded dedicated to giving "social entertainments for charitable purposes." The main social function of the Purim Association of the City of New York was its annual "fancy dress or civic ball." The association's first ball took place on Shushan Purim 1862 in the extravagantly festooned Irving Hall. The Seventh Regiment Band played a wide variety of dances, including polkas, waltzes, quadrilles, and reels. The revelers came in costume, dressed as Little Red Riding Hood, Hamlet, and Romeo, among others, though, interestingly, nobody dressed as characters from the Purim story. The ball lasted until four a.m. After the ball, the *Jewish Messenger* reported that it was "beyond a doubt the finest, most brilliant, and most successful affair of the season." The profits were divided between Jews' Hospital and the Hebrew Benevolent Society, with each organization receiving fifty dollars. In subsequent years, the balls grew larger and more lavish but also more closely tied to Purim themes. In 1866, for example, over three thousand people came to see the Academy of Music turned into a Persian temple, committee members dress as members of the Persian court, and the story of Purim acted out. The Purim Association of the City of New York created the model for Purim balls that became popular in other cities.[28]

■ United Hebrew Charities, 1874

The patterns and lessons of the 1858 Passover experiment and the charity balls of the 1860s charted a path even more promising and far-reaching than a union of synagogues, but it was an arduous process. As Samuel Myers Isaacs tried to revive the Passover union, he realized that the problem was more fundamental than the poor in need of matzo. Indeed, the Passover season exposed the fact that the poor needed an organized community "all year round": "When will our communal authorities arouse to a proper sense of the benefits to be derived from united action?" he asked. "When will a central Board of Relief be organized, to take exclusive cognizance of the wants of the poor at all seasons of the year, and to seek out and relieve cases of genuine hardship and distress?" he demanded. "We begin to grow weary of perpetually admonishing our congregational authorities of the imprudence of persisting in the dubious method of extending relief. Shall we not soon have the satisfaction of finding our words producing an effect on their minds?"[29] Failure to unite not only hampered the Passover season but also reflected a broader communal weakness.

By 1865, Isaacs took matters into his own hands by circumventing the congregations and appealing to his readers for support:

> They [the congregations] should unite, but, as from various motives, they have not done so, let not the poor, nor ourselves, be the sufferers. We cannot send the poor away empty handed, and we certainly cannot from our limited means relieve all applicants. For this and other reasons we seek assistance from those who are desirous of alleviating the distress of the poor Israelite, so that he, too, may have a glimmering of joy at the period of national thanksgiving, the anniversary of our emancipation from Egyptian thralldom.

The *Messenger* thus informed interested readers that the paper "shall be happy to take charge of any donations that they may please forward to [its] office."[30] The *Jewish Messenger* repeated this service the following year, assuring its readers—the potential benefactors—that their action would not only "stanch bleeding wounds" but would be rewarded "by the blessing they will receive from those they have benefited, and by the approval of heaven."[31]

Whereas in 1858, the committee had used the *Jewish Messenger* as an instrument to generate increased financial support, in the 1860s, Isaacs and the *Messenger* coordinated charitable efforts directly. In the absence of a united congregational front, or even a federation of benevolent or mutual aid societies, the newspaper knit the community together. The newspaper recognized the plight of the "unsynagogued" and spearheaded efforts to help them. With the rise of American newspaper culture, and in the absence of a strong rabbinate, editors assumed a significant leadership role. While a preacher might fear that his pulpit sermons might offend well-heeled congregants, an editor could be more critical of the community. Isaacs thus led the way with regard to Passover charity. By the early 1870s, his son, Myer Samuel Isaacs, helped him.

As the Panic of 1857 fueled the formation of the Association for Free Distribution of Matsot to the Poor in 1858, the Panic of 1873 provided the immediate impetus for the foundation of the United Hebrew Charities the following year. The Panic of 1873 severely disrupted the lives of many New York laborers, Jews among them. Approximately 25 percent of New Yorkers lost their jobs, and those who held on to employment found their wages decreased by one-third. Among those affected by the crisis were the members of the Gumpertz family of 97 Orchard Street. Natalie Rheinsburg Gumpertz had arrived in the United States in 1857, in her twenties, from Ortelsburg, East Prussia. She met and married Julius Gumpertz, an immigrant from Silesia. By 1873, the couple had four children. Julius worked as a heel cutter, or shoemaker, and his profession had encountered setbacks even before the panic. Thus, while overall trends augured well for Kleindeutschland immigrants, and many advanced from peddler to dry-goods-store proprietor or grocer to the coveted saloon keeper, technological advances and boom and bust cycles jeopardized immigrants' upward mobility.[32] In fact, in 1871 and 1872, Gumpertz had tried his hand as a clerk but then went back to heel cutting.

One day in October 1874, Julius Gumpertz left 97 Orchard at seven a.m. to cut heels at Levy's shop on Dey Street and never returned. Natalie enlisted the help of John Schneider, the proprietor of the saloon downstairs, as well as the landlord, Lucas Glockner. They failed to find him. Not knowing the cause of

Julius's disappearance, Natalie was left to care for her three daughters, Rosa, Nanne, and Olga, and infant son, Isaac. New York City's resources were severely taxed; in fact, due to the recent rush on the outdoor relief system, which provided food and coal, the city had circumscribed eligibility to include only the blind and "truly needy," which excluded Natalie, considered able-bodied.[33]

We cannot know whether Natalie Gumpertz ever applied for help, but the plight of people like her prompted the Jewish community to act. Yet while it took the economic crisis to propel the Jewish community to reform its charitable societies, the plan and method had been patiently devised and vigorously publicized for years. The *Jewish Messenger* had been promoting a "radical reform" of the existing charitable societies. Typically, the Jewish press had used the term "radical reform" to refer to heated debates over ritual, belief, and practice between emerging Orthodox and Reform movements in Judaism. The *Jewish Messenger*, on the other hand, shifted the focus away from arguments over religious practice to the broader challenge and opportunity posed to the community by charity. While the newspaper praised the Jewish community's generosity in supporting such organizations as the Hebrew Benevolent and Orphan Asylum Society, it questioned the lack of oversight of its funds. In its call for professionalization of charities, the *Jewish Messenger* criticized members of the merchant class who carelessly gave money to professional beggars who called with "some imaginary cause of distress."[34] Despite good intentions, the failure to pay attention to the ways in which the money was used allowed professional Jewish beggars to prosper, while deserving Jewish families suffered. Systematized charity would find employment for a head of household rather than simply doling out funds. The *Jewish Messenger* claimed, "It has always been our boast that, while the Israelites support the public charities, they take care of their own poor. What we lack is not the will of the spirit to give, but the knowledge how to give wisely."[35]

Myer Samuel Isaacs contended that personal charitable impulses, no matter how praiseworthy, needed to be adapted to modern times. What might have worked in the old neighborhoods—giving money to a peddler to start out, for example—could not meet broader communal needs. Models among American Christian charities and Jewish charities in other cities, specifically London, deserved emulation for their systematized and scientific philanthropy. Addressing the desire of congregations and small charities to keep their independence, the *Jewish Messenger* showed that even under American conditions of voluntarism, other religious and ethnic groups had devised united charities: "The Hebrew denomination should study the progress of other sects in this country. It will be found that the secret of success has been union."[36]

In praising the London system, the *Jewish Messenger* reiterated many of the same arguments it had raised over the course of the 1860s, as it had criticized the lack of a unified communal front in New York. First, it recognized the elemental social and economic conditions that sparked the need: "In a great city like London or New York . . . the ranks of the lower straits are recruited by the constant influx of foreign elements."[37] In other words, as long as there was immigration, there would always be a poor, working-class segment of the population. Moreover, though the city offered opportunity and mobility, its economic ups and downs created instability. The responsibility, then, of the more established Jewish community was to care for the poor in the most up-to-date manner, and here the *Messenger* held up the example of the London Jewish charity, which hired professionals to take charge of requests for aid and to determine in a scientific manner which should be approved and for how much.

As part of the effort to systematize service delivery, the *Jewish Messenger* divided the city into districts and sent uptown women to take charge of the Jewish communities within an assigned district. Inspiration from Christian missionaries in New York, such as the New York Association for Improving the Condition of the Poor, whose leader, Robert Hartley, had divided the city into districts for oversight, may have inspired Isaacs. And, indeed, by the Civil War, many New York charities had adopted this model.[38] Because many of the needy, especially those deemed "deserving" by their benefactors, were ashamed to ask for assistance, aid groups would send representatives to scout actively the various districts in search of the deserving poor. The emphasis on districts, too, pointed to the need to replace with a formal structure those social connections once fostered informally by neighborhood networks.

As charity became more systematized, women assumed leadership roles. Here, too, Protestant groups provided models: the New York Ladies' Home Missionary Society, for example, had been sending uptown women to Five Points since 1848.[39] In 1864, Isaacs appointed the Ladies Benevolent Society, connected to his own synagogue, Shaarey Tefilah, to distribute matzos and groceries to over one hundred Jewish families.[40] And in 1868, the *Jewish*

Messenger described how members of Ladies Benevolent Societies visited the city's "plague spots," the neighborhoods of the Jewish poor, to deliver fuel and food and to help Jews find employment. At Passover time, these "women of Israel . . . neglected their domestic duties, devoting the whole of their time to rob sorrow of its smarting pain, and to infuse joy into the tortured breast."[41] While Isaacs issued the call for funds, and many male readers donated, women actually distributed the Passover aid. Now, Isaacs wanted to formalize their participation in the districts he proposed.

As the momentum for a united Jewish charity built, leaders of congregations and independent benevolent associations chafed at the challenge to their direction. In response, the *Jewish Messenger* intensified its calls for action in the months preceding Passover 1873 and in advance of the annual meeting of the city's largest charitable organization, the Hebrew Benevolent and Orphan Asylum Society. The *Messenger* realized the importance of the support of the leading Jewish philanthropy of the day and therefore crafted a message that at once praised the institution for the work it had accomplished and stressed the necessity of "radical reform."[42]

At the annual meeting, Myer Stern, the president of the Hebrew Benevolent Society, acknowledged the pleading of the *Jewish Messenger* and introduced Myer Isaacs as the first speaker. Isaacs then recommended that a Committee of Fifteen be appointed to investigate the current method of "distribution of relief" and the potential for cooperation among the city's charities. While many members supported this motion, P. W. Frank, chairman of the Hebrew Benevolent Society's Charity Committee, expressed his frustration: "It is useless to disguise the matter any further. A Jewish paper has been endeavoring to mislead the public, and claiming that our funds are not properly distributed. What does the editor know about it? We assist only the deserving, whereas it is the beggars and the bummers who go to Isaacs' office, and there complain." Though the meeting's chairman called Frank to order, "he continued his tirade, exhibiting an extract from the *Messenger* which he had carried in his vest pocket, and he repeated that if any man said that the $19,000 have been expended for beggars, he says what is false from 'bottom to top.'" Isaacs, in turn, defended himself, explaining that he was praising the work of the Relief Committee but encouraging it to investigate ways to be more efficient by establishing a "new and proper system." Isaacs professed, "I simply want our poor Jews living in the byways of the city, in horrible poverty, to be raised from their condition and be made decent citizens, and that is the whole of the subject." The meeting ended with an appointment of a committee to do just as Isaacs and the *Jewish Messenger* had encouraged for months, yet the resistance expressed by Frank and others shows just how formidable and radical the plan for union proved.[43]

The resulting study justified the formation of a United Hebrew Charities, but it was the Panic of 1873 that lent urgency to its formation. Isaacs described the severity of New York conditions that winter and turned to Jewish tradition as he invoked the Shema, the core Jewish prayer that proclaims the oneness of God: "As we have one God, one law, and are one people, so should we have one institution, where every case of distress might appeal with the certainty of immediate relief."[44] Finally, in October 1874, five core institutions—the Hebrew Benevolent and Orphan Asylum Society, the Hebrew Benevolent Fuel Association, the Hebrew Relief Society, the Ladies Benevolent Society (Gates of Prayer), and the Yorkville Ladies Benevolent Society—formed the United Hebrew Charities.

In subsequent years, the United Hebrew Charities helped thousands of families facing plights similar to that of Natalie Gumpertz. The organization's first annual report stated, "The character of the aid given has been largely in money to pay rent, to support neglected little children, and to relieve temporary wants." Those "poor families" who received this aid lived "crowded in tenements, deprived of sufficient air, exposed to disease and crushed in spirit." Further, the first set of problems to engage the UHC in its formative years included "ways to reduce desertion among Jewish husbands." Thus, Gumpertz was not alone in her plight: economic vicissitudes, increasingly congested neighborhoods and tenement dwellings, and desertion plagued many Jewish New Yorkers.[45] The UHC aimed to restore families to "self-support" and to that end purchased sets of tools, pushcarts, and, in some cases, stock for small stores. While an initial payment might have helped women such as Natalie Gumpertz pay rent and purchase food, it was not a long-term answer. She may have turned to the UHC for assistance in earning a living. Since Natalie had four children to tend to, becoming a tailor seemed the most sensible solution, as it would allow her to work at home, near her children. By 1875, thirty-five thousand women in New York worked as dressmakers or milliners.

The UHC encouraged this trend: "Sewing machines were supplied to tailors and to tailoresses, who had been recommended by the respective district committees."[46] In 1878, Trow's New York City directory listed Natalie Gumpertz as a dressmaker.

Initially the United Hebrew Charities responded chiefly to the "effects of the panic of 1873," with strong support from the Jewish community: subscriptions of $37,007 more than covered expenditures of $29,312. As the UHC report noted, while the five core institutions provided $18,238.89, additional individual and congregational support yielded $18,227.90: "It is therefore apparent that public opinion sustains the plan and action of the United Hebrew Charities."[47] Not until the 1880s, when hit by the sheer numbers of eastern European Jews, did the organization run into financial difficulties.[48] Yet even then the UHC served one out of ten Jewish immigrants.

By the first decade of the twentieth century, even as the UHC was overshadowed by newer, more innovative social welfare agencies, its building at 356 Second Avenue "gave the Jews a headquarters," as one observer put it. This three-story structure, with its large arched windows and ornamental cornice that "suggested a Florentine Renaissance palace," was situated at the corner of Twenty-First Street, in neutral territory, several blocks north of the teeming Lower East Side, where many of its clients lived, and well south of the fashionable upper Fifth Avenue neighborhood to which its patrons were then moving. A number of important Jewish social welfare agencies lined its corridors. It hosted important events, including the founding meetings of the American Jewish Committee in 1906 and the Kehillah in 1909, and projected an image of professionalism and solidity to Jews and non-Jews alike.[49]

■ From Beekman Place to the Bowery

At the age of twenty-five, Rebekah Bettelheim Kohut ventured beyond her duties as rabbi's wife and stepmother to eight children to forge a public career in social action. This was not necessarily a natural or easy transition. Not only did she have to tend to the children and manage her household, but when a speech she gave on behalf of a neighborhood association made the newspapers, tensions arose at home. "My husband," she later recalled, "while rather proud that what I had said seemed worthy of quotation, was dubious of the wisdom of a public career for me. He felt that I had much to do at home, and

Rebekah Kohut, when she was president of the New York section of the Council of Jewish Women. Kohut's impressive career as a Jewish communal leader began when she organized a sisterhood at Ahawath Chesed (later renamed Central Synagogue). The sisterhood earmarked a district of responsibility in the downtown tenement districts. There, the uptown women provided classes and material assistance to immigrant families. (Photo by Underwood and Underwood, courtesy of Central Synagogue Archives)

was more or less jealous of any time I gave to others." Yet precisely by virtue of Alexander Kohut's position as rabbi at congregation Ahawath Chesed was Rebekah able ultimately to carve out and legitimate a markedly public role. At several meetings at nearby Temple Emanu-El, she had listened to Rabbi Gustav Gottheil address his congregation's newly formed sisterhood. Inspired, she described her next step: "Realizing that an organization of this kind gave women opportunities for worthy service among the poor, I urged upon my husband that a similar institution be formed among the women of his congregation. It seemed to be the work that I could do for him, and he consented."[50] Like other clubwomen, who justified their expanded sphere by rooting it in domestic values, Kohut carefully framed her public work as a continuation of wifely and motherly virtues rather than a radical rupture; even in her autobiography forty years later, she emphasized her husband's approval.

However justified, the work took Kohut far from her parlor in the East Fifties all the way to the Bowery-district tenements. One of the genteel neighbors Kohut and her husband socialized with on summer evenings was Henry Harland, who, in a roundabout way, could take credit for the Kohuts' residence on Beekman Place. Harland, a Protestant, assumed the more Jewish-sounding pen name Sidney Luska to detail the social and romantic lives of New York's Jewish community in his popular novels. According to Rebekah, Alexander

Kohut attached special meaning to Luska's 1887 *Yoke of the Thorah*, as it was the first English-language novel he read upon moving to the city. Inspired by the heroine, who resided on Beekman Place, and taken by the coincidence of a "for sale" sign on the lot a month before his wedding to Rebekah, he purchased the corner home for the family in 1887.

As Tillie, Harland's heroine, described Beekman Place, "It's fearfully out of the way, but it's grand when you get there."[51] Scenes from the novel, as well as architectural descriptions of Beekman Place, indeed give one the sense that Rebekah Kohut's domestic life, no matter how busy, was sheltered from the roughness of city life. In the novel, guests first gather in the back parlor and enjoy the "view from the bay-window—up, down, and across the river" and then reconvene in the backyard for an outdoor dinner:

> Elias thought it exceedingly pleasant thus to feast in the open air, while the sky and river glowed with the reflected splendor of the sunset; and said so to Miss Tillie. She replied that it was simply ideal, that they always did it in good weather, and that it was quite the rage among the residents of Beekman Place. Beekman Place, she went on, was the grandest street in the city, and she was awfully attached to it. She'd lived there most all her life, and all the memories of her childhood were associated with it. She remembered when she used to go fishing, with a thread and a bent pin, off the docks below there.[52]

Kohut's routine was undoubtedly more encumbered than that of Luska's Tillie —she battled constant financial strain and described a social life that revolved around her husband, not her. Still, the ability to gather people for a comfortable, airy summer evening or to gaze out of an oriel window onto the East River offered a middle-class lifestyle unimaginable to the Lower East Side tenement residents to whom she tended.

Beekman Place also gave Kohut her first taste of public social work: in New York, increased opportunities for middle-class women were in the air, as evidenced by the fact that Rebekah had only to walk outside her home to be recruited to her first public project. Her neighbor invited her to work for the Women's Health Protective Association, a secular organization that fought for more street cleaning and sanitation. But only when Rebecca linked her public work to religious duties did she win Alexander Kohut's hearty encouragement.

Though some of the women of Kohut's sisterhood, such as Julia Richman's family, had resided on the blocks surrounding Ahawath Chesed's previous synagogue at Avenue C, the neighborhood that became the base of their sisterhood's activities had changed considerably by 1889; so, too, did the nature of their religious activity. The downtown neighborhood had increased in population density, while the influx of eastern European immigrants steadily accelerated the German-speaking migration uptown and to Brooklyn. The formation of the sisterhood linked these women to the very neighborhood that they—or at least their congregational forebears—had left behind: the area bounded by the Bowery and the East River, from Houston Street to East Fourth Street, which had been part of Kleindeutschland but now was becoming the Lower East Side. Yet even if this journey to the neighborhood was not entirely new for them, since some had perhaps traveled to Avenue C for services, the nature of their engagement departed radically from their previous visits. Now their religious work and identity consisted not only of worship but also of direct interactions with the city's working class and Jewish poor.

The sisterhoods' social work rested on the opportunities for service that arose from the dislocations brought about by the rapid development and growth of New York City. Between 1870 and 1915, the city's population expanded dramatically from one and a half million (including the areas incorporated into New York in 1898) to five million. The inability of municipal government to keep up with the needs of a growing population opened opportunities for citizens of all backgrounds to forge distinctive charitable and social work roles and offered women the possibility of involvement in public affairs. Meanwhile, the city's poor mushroomed in number, largely due to immigration from southern and eastern Europe. Jewish immigration tested the Jewish charities, and they sought ways to rise to the challenge.[53] Jewish communal leaders redirected and reinvigorated preexisting organizations, shifted congregational charitable focus to the newly arrived, and established new settlement houses, hospitals, and schools. The UHC assumed the major responsibility of helping newly arrived immigrants by providing lodging, meals, medical assistance, and burial services and administering employment bureaus.[54]

As both a middle-class New Yorker and Jewish woman, Rebekah Kohut—and the other women in the sisterhoods—participated in broader urban trends charting new paths in the incipient professionalization of social work.

In the past, women's charitable work at Ahawath Chesed had consisted of sewing circles and raising money; but these efforts kept almost all members in their own neighborhood parlors. The growing women's club movement propelled Jewish women outside their homes to work directly with the poor. They set priorities, managed budgets, and cast their net far beyond the confines of home, synagogue, or neighborhood. Though the sisterhoods drew inspiration from Christian women's organizations, they distinguished themselves by emphasizing their Jewish identity. Their work benefited coreligionists; moreover, they viewed the nature of the work as religious.

Rebekah Kohut thus exchanged her oriel window's view of the East River boats and her placid Beekman Place for the hustle and bustle of pushcart-packed streets. More than simply an exchange of scenery, though, the distance of two miles brought her from a world in which Judaism towered above the streetscapes in the form of bronze minarets, and middle-class Jews casually gathered with Christian neighbors on brownstone stoops, into a world where people worked for fourteen hours at a time over sewing machines in tenement apartments, worshiped in spaces carved out of tenement halls, and socialized on tenement stoops. Indeed, this setting differed so remarkably from the sisterhood women's accustomed territory that it transported them: "There was a fascination in walking along Hester, Canal, Grand, Allen, Varick and Essex Streets and East Broadway, and losing one's self in the throngs of newcomers to America."[55] What distinguished the sisterhood women from other uptown visitors was how deeply they penetrated the downtown district. Not content, as others, merely to sample the "Oriental bazaar" of the market, Kohut and the sisterhood delved further into the heart of the downtown district. They established an office at 71 East Third Street and, from there, monitored their district, which covered the entire Lower East Side.

This charity work differed qualitatively from past types of Jewish women's charity with regard to both mission and organizational networks. "We do not wait until the poor come to our house but by means of our society we go out to meet the poor," relayed the sisterhood's annual report.[56] In forming and leading the second sisterhood in the United States in 1889, Rebekah Kohut and her congregation used a shared religion, a heightened sense of women's role in the world, and social work to build a more direct bridge to downtown's Jews. By 1895, Kohut's sisterhood had a membership of 350. They ran a kindergarten, a sewing circle for girls, and a religious school at their headquarters, and they dispersed throughout the neighborhood to "alleviate the misery and relieve the wants of 200 destitute families."[57] Ahawath Chesed's sisterhood drew inspiration from Temple Emanu-El's rabbi, Gustav Gottheil, and that congregation's sisterhood, led by Hannah B. Einstein. In 1890, the sisterhoods joined forces with the UHC, and, in 1896, ten sisterhoods formally organized an umbrella organization, the Federation of Sisterhoods of Personal Service, with Einstein as president. As a measure of the respect earned by the sisterhoods, the UHC accorded to each its formal district of responsibility.

From an early stage, sisterhood women discussed not only the work itself but also its larger significance with regard to class and religion. They emphasized that they performed the work in part to bridge class differences. As Hannah Einstein explained, the uptown sisterhoods aimed to forge genuine connections to the new immigrants not only in order to improve the charitable work but also "to overcome the estrangement of one class of the Jewish population from another and to bring together the well-to-do and the poor, in the relation, not of patron and dependent, but of friend and friend."[58] Ahawath Chesed echoed this notion that as coreligionists, the eastern European Jews merited real relationships: "These poor are in very truth our brothers and sisters; let us deal with them in brotherly and sisterly fashion."[59] In an 1899 report to the UHC, Einstein claimed that the moral, educational, and religious nature of the sisterhoods' work proved more valuable than more easily measurable material goals and outcomes.[60] In turn, communal leaders such as Shearith Israel's Rabbi David de Sola Pool used language with a religious tone to describe these women, recounting the activities of his congregation's sisterhood as focused on the "loyal conservation and transmission of Jewish religious values."[61] "Such personal service," wrote UHC director Dr. Lee K. Frankel, "is a phase of the old Jewish idea of 'gemilut hesed,' and the modern development of the thought that the best aid that can be given to the poor is to help them help themselves."[62]

The sisterhoods readily viewed their activities as religious in nature, and Ahawath Chesed's president, Hannah Leerburger, concluded her reports with the following words of thanks: "Grateful to the Almighty for whatever good we have done."[63] But they also translated their spiritual goals into quantitative terms. Over time, sisterhoods raised and spent millions of dollars and aided tens of thousands of immigrant families. In 1896, Ahawath Chesed's sisterhood distributed 109 pairs of shoes and 575 pounds of Passover matzo. In a given year, it might assist as many as 181 families and dole out close to $15,000 worth of clothing, food, and cash. While organizations such as the King's Daughters or other Christian social service agencies could have likewise provided shoes to the eastern European Jews, they certainly would not have provided matzo. This work promoted the religious lives of eastern European immigrants. The Reform Temple Emanu-El created a religious school, and though the Reform movement aimed to instill the idea that the spirit of the law trumped the letter of the law, it accommodated requests of Orthodox immigrants even when they countered its own Reform practices. Though Reform at the time privileged English over Hebrew and preferred that confirmation ceremonies supplant bar mitzvah classes, the sisterhood's religious schools leaned toward traditional forms.[64] Thus, sisterhood members avoided the heavy-handed imposition of their own cultural assumptions on their immigrant clients.

But sisterhoods proved powerless to resolve the fundamental fissure between Orthodox religious needs and the American workweek. As the daughter and wife of a rabbi, Rebekah Kohut developed an acute sensitivity to the fate of religious immigrants and expressed concern for the plight of Talmud scholars who could find no support for their study in their new country. She also noted that the American workweek collided with the Jewish Sabbath and discussed what the Sabbath, especially for the younger generation, often yielded: "Aside from the actual material suffering, the situation produced many a family tragedy. The younger generation was readier to adapt itself to American conditions, and while the old folk bitterly opposed their working on the Sabbath and in general assuming the ways of Gentiles, yet they found themselves dependent upon their children for support. It was a sad state of affairs."[65] In both cases, though, Kohut could not move beyond sensitivity; she had no solution and therefore could only focus on the practical side: the need for immigrants to make a living: "and I am willing to confess that I induced many an erudite scholar to join the army of sweatshop laborers in preference to being reduced to destitution."[66] Similarly, she lamented that though the sisterhoods devoted time to establish religious schools for immigrant children, they failed to provide much-needed spiritual guidance for adolescents and their parents.

Maintaining religious values while helping immigrants fit into the American economic system posed the sisterhoods with a dilemma that they were unable to resolve. Uptown Jews and downtown Jews alike knew that immigrants needed to adapt to New York's economy, which caused individuals to curtail or even to jettison religious practices and attitudes. While many of the uptown congregations had created a Reform Judaism that helped them fit into American society and maintain an identity as Jews, they knew their solution would not appeal to many eastern European Jews.

These uptown women devised new models of Jewish womanhood. In their adoption of "scientific" methods of social work and expanded notions of women's proper sphere, sisterhoods drew much from their Protestant neighbors, even as they retained, privileged, and created their own distinctive Jewish female identity. Whether uptown or downtown, New York City demanded a new form of Judaism—and this Judaism encouraged neither scholarly work nor Sabbath observance. New York's economic cycle required constant energy and attention from immigrant businessmen, leaving little time to attend services, much less lead them. Downtown, ambitious immigrant men quickly learned to forgo the Saturday Sabbath in favor of an extra day of sales or payday in the shop or store. Yet in both cases, New York life allowed Jewish women, as guardians of the home, whether a brownstone or a tenement, the chance to continue and to embellish their religious duties and obligations.

The second half of the nineteenth century was a period of great growth for New York City and even greater growth for its Jewish community. As the Jewish population expanded, it also became increasingly complex—internally differentiated by class, country of origin, religious inclination, and language. The face-to-face informal neighborhood networks that had characterized Jewish life at the beginning of the period continued to exist but proved inadequate to meet the community's needs. So New York's Jews began to elaborate a system of formal institutions to take care of the poor, the sick, the orphaned, and the widowed among them. In doing so, they reached beyond the boundaries of individual congregations and mutual aid societies, creating a broader communal structure that transcended internal differences and gave women a central role in the emerging core institutions of the community. They followed patterns common in the city as a whole, where social welfare agencies formed mostly along denominational lines. Continued immigration meant that the community's needs remained great, but part of New York's promise, largely fulfilled, was that Jews acquired the means to fill those needs. Philanthropy became one of the community's defining characteristics, competing with, and ultimately winning out over, alternative models such as those set by fraternal orders and defense organizations.

Ahawath Chesed's Moorish structure towered over its brownstone neighbors when it opened in 1872. Later renamed Central Synagogue, the building's towers, keyhole windows, and arches distinguished it from contemporary religious and commercial buildings in New York City. (Photo by C. K. Bill, 1872; Central Synagogue Archives)

CHAPTER 3

Moorish Manhattan

■ Moorish on Lexington

On December 14, 1870, close to five hundred New Yorkers—Christians and Jews alike—mounted a makeshift platform on Lexington Avenue and Fifty-Fifth Street. "Adorned with flags," the platform covered a construction site for what was to become congregation Ahawath Chesed's new synagogue. The December sun shone brightly as ticket holders filed in to take their seats for a cornerstone-laying ceremony.[1] Though there was very little for the eye to behold—yet. The day's speeches evoked pride in the heights achieved by an erstwhile tiny immigrant Kleindeutschland congregation and roused the attendees to look forward to the future structure that would soon tower over its brownstone neighbors. The nearby presence of the imposing Moorish-style Temple Emanu-El on Fifth Avenue and Forty-Third Street perhaps gave the group that was assembled an inkling as to the look and feel of the proposed building; newspaper articles promised that "when finished, [it] will be an ornament to this section of the City."[2] But precisely because there was little to see, words and symbolism carried the day. Many of those words resonated beyond that sunny Wednesday, finding their way into the city's secular and Jewish newspapers.

Isaac Mayer Wise, the country's leading Reform rabbi, whose B'nai Yeshurun synagogue in Cincinnati was also built in the Moorish style, delivered the keynote speech. Wise directly addressed Christian as well as Jewish members of the "worshipping multitude":

> You lay the cornerstone to a new temple in this Metropolis of our country, to rear upon it another proud structure beside all the gorgeous temples in this City and

country to add another link to the blessed chain of sanctuaries which encircle all climes and zones, all authentic history, from the first altar erected by the Patriarch Abraham in yonder Palestine to the tabernacles of the modern Israel of the globe; to invite all the sons and daughters of your congregation, of all the families of man, to come worship the sole sovereign of the universe.[3]

Ahawath Chesed's leaders used the onset of construction of their new building as an opportunity to invite the leading American figure of Reform Judaism, Christian neighbors, city politicians, and local religious and communal leaders to celebrate a tolerant, cosmopolitan city and nation. Together they affirmed that they shared an American identity elastic enough to contain individual and group differences. Those who were gathered did so ostensibly to witness the laying of a physical cornerstone for what was to be a grand Moorish synagogue. Yet the true cornerstone laid that day was Jews' intangible but very real sense of security and confidence in their city and country. In this way, Wise's use of the word "temple" could refer both to a chain of Jewish synagogues across time and place and also specifically to those forward-thinking and tolerant houses of worship in New York and America for "all the families of man," Christian or Jewish.

By the time Ahawath Chesed laid its cornerstone, New York hosted more Moorish-style synagogues than any other city in the world. On one level, "Moorish Manhattan" refers to the physical Moorish style as displayed by Ahawath Chesed. On another level, it refers to the openness, tolerance, and cosmopolitanism that enabled New York Jewish congregations to alter their rituals and customs to conform to American cultural standards, even as they maintained their distinctiveness. While many scholars have linked the Moorish style with the Reform movement, Henry Fernbach designed New York's second Moorish synagogue, Shaarey Tefilah on Forty-Fourth Street, for an Orthodox congregation, whose rabbi, Samuel Myers Isaacs, ardently defended tradition and routinely criticized Reform. The use of the Moorish style marks a wider Jewish engagement with modernity and with the surrounding religious and secular culture.[4] In the deliberate engagement with modernity, the Reform movement took the lead; but even many Orthodox synagogues, though hewing to Jewish law and tradition, similarly wished to adapt their Judaism to America. The flourishing of the Moorish style in New York speaks less to Reform or Orthodox denominational affiliation and more to the freedom and comfort experienced by Jews in the city. Congregations reflected a wide spectrum of religious identification, from Reform to Orthodox, but, with the exception of some eastern European rejectionists, they all sought to forge a workable New York Judaism.

Within sixteen months of the laying of the cornerstone for Ahawath Chesed, architect Henry Fernbach's design, the building committee's fundraising, the congregants' donations, and the labor of builder Samuel Cochran's work crews left little to the imaginations of the three thousand congregants and guests celebrating the completed structure's dedication on April 19, 1872. Set against those same rows of Midtown brownstones, a handsome structure of Belleville brownstone and yellow Ohio sandstone trim animated the skyline. People nearing the temple would catch sight of what looked to be five-pointed stars but were in actuality seven-pointed stars designed to give the appearance of having five points when viewed from any direction. These stars perched atop shiny, bulbous "ribbed globes of bronze." Two sturdy octagonal towers and lively ivory crenellation along the cornice provided a frame for a "beautiful rose-window" composed of white pine tracery and forming circles of five-pointed stars. Keyhole windows and geometric patterns punctuated and enlivened the muted tones of the façade. While the domes and stars dominated the view from afar, up close, arches, formed by alternating light and dark stones, articulated five sets of wooden double doors, themselves carved with six-pointed Stars of David. At night, specially designed streetlights highlighted the façade's patterns. Within the grand sanctuary, "rich glass" filled the shapely windows, and "profuse gilding" accentuated geometric patterns borrowed from Spain's Alhambra mosque and stenciled on the walls in shades of ochre, azure, and red.[5] Delicate-looking cast-iron pillars supported an arch, which in turn framed the bimah, or reader's platform, situated at the front of the sanctuary. A cupola crowned the room's focal point, the holy ark in which the Torah scrolls were kept. Overall the sixty-two-foot ceiling created a spacious feel for the sanctuary, with room for naves, an organ, and fifteen hundred men and women to sit together for decorous and inspiring spiritual services and sermons.

Wise did not return for these dedication ceremonies, but we can imagine that he would have been heartened to read an account in the *New York World* that responded to the cornerstone messages of optimism and progress. The *World* reporter reflected on the synagogue's meaning for Jews and for Judaism and also for America. In an article titled "Modern Judaism" that detailed the dedication ceremonies, he, like Wise, noted that this building represented progress for the Jewish people. The reporter viewed the structure as a source of pride to which Christian neighbors could likewise lay claim: "Such temples as Emanu-El and Ahawath Chesed are monuments of Christianity as well as of Judaism. They testify not only of constant Jewish zeal and munificence, but also of increased Christian humanity and tolerance."[6] The Moorish buildings that began to dot New York's cityscape served as a reminder and source of pride for a tolerant, cosmopolitan American spirit, one that reveled in the march of both Gothic churches and Moorish synagogues down its prominent avenues.

Before the Civil War, most Jewish congregations lacked the resources to build their own structures, instead buying downtown houses of worship from upwardly mobile Protestant congregations in search of more attractive uptown locations. Both Emanu-El (1847, Chrystie Street; 1854, Twelfth Street) and Ahawath Chesed (1864, Avenue C) remodeled downtown Protestant churches into synagogues. Many immigrant Catholic churches did the same; before the Civil War, 25 percent of Catholic congregations worshiped in former Protestant churches. But heightened economic activity in the wake of the Civil War positioned leading Jewish, Catholic, and Protestant congregants to funnel their success into the design and construction of magnificent houses of worship.[7] Between 1860 and 1870, synagogue construction, chiefly in New York City, increased New York State's synagogue property value by over 200 percent to $1,831,950 and doubled its seating capacity from 10,440 to 21,400.[8] New York City had the most well-appointed synagogues in the country, and they attracted attention. In 1868, Temple Emanu-El, the city's wealthiest congregation, constructed a striking Moorish temple on a prominent corner city lot on Fifth Avenue and Forty-Third Street. This was "the first building in New York that was clearly identifiable as a Jewish house of worship."[9] The *Manufacturer and Builder* hailed it as the "most important" of New York buildings erected that year, and praised it as "a fine example of the Moorish style of Spain and a very close copy of the Alhambra." The *New York Times* described it as "magnificent" and "splendid."[10] Within four years, Emanu-El (1868), Shaarey Tefilah on Forty-Fourth Street (1869), and Ahawath Chesed (1872) created the first aggregation of Moorish synagogues in one city, located within blocks from one another.

Moorish synagogues shared Gothic and Romanesque structural engineering with other religious institutions, but the decorations and details—minarets, finials, crenellations, domes, slender pillars, cusped arches, horseshoe windows—created an "all-over effect" of the "exotic." Jewish congregations' use of the Moorish style clearly distinguished their synagogues from the era's Gothic and Romanesque churches.[11] The Moorish style had rarely appeared in America until that time, including notable exceptions P. T. Barnum's home in Bridgeport, Connecticut (1848), and the Crystal Palace built for the 1853 New York World's Fair.

The architects for New York's Moorish synagogues thus drew inspiration mainly from several decades of synagogue designs in central Europe, as well as from brand-new synagogues in Cincinnati (B'nai Yeshurun, 1866) and San Francisco (Temple Emanu-El, 1866). Indeed, New York's promise of freedom can be understood in part by comparing it to the European experience with regard to both Moorish architecture and religious expression. In central Europe, Enlightenment ideas of freedom and liberty gained momentum in the nineteenth century, but old prejudices barred complete social and political acceptance for Jews. This limited acceptance influenced the ways in which new synagogues were built. Beginning in the 1830s and 1840s, more affluent congregations had the opportunity, means, and tacit permission by a relatively more tolerant and enlightened society to build notable houses of worship. In what style, however, should these synagogues be built? Many leading Christian architects argued that Jews could not claim as their own the Gothic and Romanesque styles commonly used for churches. Though no record of the appearance of the ancient Temple or synagogues existed, architects speculated that the Temple would have resembled the religious structures of the Jews' neighbors in "the larger Oriental world" of the ancient Near East. In the 1830s and 1840s, architects began to experiment with a Moorish, or Islamic, style; notable examples built during ensuing decades include synagogues in Dresden (1838), Vienna-Leopoldstadt (1858), Mainz (1853), Leipzig (1854), Budapest (1859), and Berlin (1866). Many leading Jewish congregations responded warmly to the appeal of the Orient—understood in Europe at that time to refer to the Middle or Near East—that the Moorish style evoked. The romanticism of Oriental roots offered an exotic identity that might find favor in the eyes of central European Jews' Christian counterparts. In adopting the Moorish style, synagogues in central Europe "hoped that they could convince the public of the nobility of their Orient blood." While many congregations found this concept intriguing and derived pride in the uniqueness of a heritage whose form was so beautiful and exotic, some German congregations rejected this style. If, it was argued, Islamic culture, however interesting and important in its time, had been superseded by European Christian culture, then to build in that style only gave concrete form to the idea that Jews, and Judaism, were less civilized and less worthy of the modern world. What was interesting and important about Judaism, they feared, would appear vestigial as opposed to operative, a curiosity rather than a vital element of modern European society.[12]

For the synagogues' design and appearance, architects of the Moorish style in New York drew inspiration from Moorish synagogues in central Europe. But the context and, therefore, the style's cultural meaning differed dramatically. In Europe, Christian architects had objected to the idea of Jews building synagogues in the Gothic or Romanesque style, but in New York City, Jewish congregations faced no such opposition, often meeting in former churches built in those styles. Further, when a few congregations in pre–Civil War New York had the funds to build a synagogue, they often chose the Gothic style (most notably Anshe Chesed's Norfolk Street Synagogue, 1850) or the Romanesque style (Shaarey Tefilah's Wooster Street Synagogue, 1837), resulting in structures that could be mistaken for churches. By the time congregations began moving uptown, and had the budgets for more substantial construction, they naturally looked to Europe for grand synagogue styles. Whereas in Europe centuries of discrimination and a separate status marked Jews as alien even as they became part of the emerging bourgeoisie, and even as political notables attended synagogue dedication ceremonies, in the United States tolerance rested on a firmer political foundation of equality and freedom of religion. In this way, Judaism could be understood as a crucial component in the creation of a cosmopolitan city. If Jews used the Moorish style to proclaim a sense of otherness, it was an otherness that did not threaten their social position.

By the 1880s, Moorish synagogues helped to shape the New York urban landscape. An 1882 story in *Atlantic Monthly* depicts a young lawyer and an acquaintance strolling through New York:

> They went down, past the unfinished Cathedral, the Moorish Synagogue, and the Egyptian reservoir, with the castellated dwellings opposite, on the battlements of which an Ivanhoe or Sister Anne, or the yellow dwarf might have appeared; past the

quaint tower of the Church of Heavenly Rest, with its angels trumpeting to the four corners of the heavens; past the incredibly tall hotels and apartment houses, past the scattered shop-fronts of the tailors, confectioners, and jewelers.[13]

"The Moorish Synagogue," undoubtedly Temple Emanu-El, thus appears without remark in the same sentence as other New York landmarks, including several churches. The lack of judgment or comment that Moorish synagogues elicited demonstrates the extent to which they had become an accepted part of the cosmopolitan city. Charles W. Hobbs's 1889 *Illustrated New York City and Surroundings* lauds the "beautiful and important" Temple Emanu-El and notes its Moorish architecture; it more quietly mentions the "Jewish Synagogue" on Lexington Avenue (Ahawath Chesed).[14]

Beyond simply hosting the most Moorish synagogues in the world, New York City's tolerant and cosmopolitan atmosphere lent entirely novel meanings to the Moorish style and encouraged the development of new expressions of religiosity for the American Jews who congregated within them or even just walked by them. The very tolerance, freedom, and cosmopolitanism that made multiple New York Moorish styles distinct from those in Dresden, Budapest, or Berlin allowed for a broad range of American Jewish expressions. Ahawath Chesed's Moorish synagogue on Lexington differed from Temple Emanu-El's Moorish synagogue on Fifth Avenue or Shaarey Tefilah's Moorish synagogue on Forty-Fourth and, in time, from Kahal Adath Jeshurun's Moorish synagogue on Eldridge Street. They expressed a panoply of ways to be Jewish in New York, sometimes within blocks of each other. Freedom from state-sponsored religious authority allowed each congregation to develop independently, creating a competitive terrain in which each congregation defined itself not only though its endorsement of reform or defense of tradition but also in comparison with its neighbors. The pulpits of these congregations became stages for vigorous debate about the direction that American Judaism should take. While sometimes divisive, such arguments lent new meaning to Jewish life, regardless of congregational identification. New York congregations paid attention to each other's choices, and the national Jewish papers and religious leaders did too.

Like the Moorish style of synagogue architecture, Reform Judaism had roots in central Europe, but it, too, found new form and meaning once transplanted to the United States, where freedom encouraged dramatic changes. In

This drawing of the Eldridge Street Synagogue predated the building and was used as an advertisement in the Yiddish press to attract members. Its Moorish architecture showed an awareness of uptown synagogue trends, but its retention of traditional rites spoke to its members' desire to adapt Orthodoxy to American life. *Yidishe gazeten*, 1887. (Collection of the Museum at Eldridge)

Europe, Reform Judaism developed with the spread of Enlightenment ideas and in response to a protracted emancipation process in which Jews sought to effect reforms in part to gain approval from a non-Jewish society that withheld full citizenship. Reformers sought to adjust Judaism to modern behavioral norms and philosophy. Middle- and upper-class Jews in Hamburg and Berlin spearheaded initiatives to orchestrate what they considered to be more uplifting services, adopting stricter rules of decorum and introducing instrumental music. In the 1840s, a series of rabbinical conferences in Brunswick, Frankfort, and Breslau led to innovations such as reading the Torah on a three-year cycle as opposed to a one-year cycle and the abolition of the second day of festivals. Even as Reform leaders and their congregations embraced new opportunities posed by an increasingly emancipated and enlightened society, and incorporated such practices as German-language sermons, mixed choirs, and organ music into their religious services, they encountered resistance from established Jewish communities and rabbis as well as intervention by governments sometimes hostile to reform. Whether opposition came from Jewish or governmental authority, it hampered the "free development" of Reform.[15]

Though central European Jews cultivated many Reform practices and developed justifications for change, Reform found its fullest expression in the United States. Taking advantage of economic and social opportunities, American Jews had a harder time meeting the obligations of traditional Jewish practice. Though they established congregations that observed traditional rites, observers in the early years of the nineteenth century noted laxity in practice outside the synagogue, where individual proclivities determined levels and styles of observance. Many immigrants, intent on getting a business off the ground or enjoying newfound social opportunities, neglected synagogue attendance. Jewish communal leaders complained that perhaps America offered too much freedom altogether for the formation of Jewish communities; statistics suggest that half of all American Jews chose not to affiliate with any congregation by 1850. As congregations attempted to alter tradition to match practice by modernizing the services, no centralized authority guided them; few ordained rabbis had settled in America. Isaac Leeser, leader of congregation Mikveh Israel in Philadelphia, observed, "Each congregation makes its own rules for its government and elects its own ministry, who is appointed without any ordination." This freedom resulted in variation, as each congregation found its own way to reconcile Judaism with American culture.[16]

As in Europe, young, upwardly mobile Jews led the charge for reform in New York City. In 1843, the same year B'nai B'rith was founded several blocks away, German immigrants, including Leo Merzbacher, who had served as rabbi at the leading German synagogues, formed a Cultus Society in Kleindeutschland to discuss change in synagogue practice. In 1845, they took the next step in establishing Temple Emanu-El. Emanu-El's founders voiced concern that the existing synagogues repelled the youth. They also sought to keep Jews together as a community. But unlike B'nai B'rith, which adopted prayers, signs, and symbols from Jewish tradition to affirm a secular Jewish identity, the Cultus Society explicitly desired a new religious community. In choosing the name Emanu-El—"God is with us"—they expressed their fervent desire to stay within the bounds of Judaism. While they hoped that reform would enable them "to occupy a position of greater respect among [their] fellow-citizens," they also desired to "worship better, with more devotion." Even as they made changes to gain the respect of Americans, they wanted to keep

Judaism relevant to other Americanizing Jews. Indeed, New York religious leaders such as Merzbacher and Max Lilienthal embraced reform in order to "save Judaism" from what they believed to be the straightjacket of outdated forms imposed by fanatical traditionalists.[17]

Like many other fledgling congregations, the founders of Temple Emanu-El rented rooms in a meeting hall, at the corner of Clinton and Grand Streets. As they undertook the formation of the first avowedly nontraditional, or Reform, congregation in New York, they could look to Charleston, South Carolina's Beth Elohim, the first Reform temple in the United States, or Baltimore's Har Sinai, the country's second Reform temple. But for the most part, Emanu-El charted its own course. The congregation changed the service to make it more decorous, aesthetically agreeable, and accessible to New Yorkers. While it kept the traditional prayer book, it eliminated several prayers and added vocal music, German-language hymns, and a German-language sermon. Even as it made these minimal changes, the congregation upheld many critical elements of traditional Jewish life: Jewish dietary laws (*kashrut*), separation of men and women during prayer, and the prayer shawl and head covering for men. Overall, Emanu-El's approach attracted new members, enabling the congregation to purchase a church on nearby Chrystie Street in 1847. Moving into the new building afforded an opportunity to introduce additional reforms; over the course of several years, Emanu-El adopted a German hymnal, decided to read the Torah on a three-year cycle, introduced an organ, and minimized the requirements for boys studying to become bar mitzvah. In doing so, the temple's leaders intended to strengthen New York Jews' Jewish identity. To this end, they hired the architect Leopold Eidlitz to renovate the interior of the church into a synagogue and to remove Christian markings from the façade of the building. Thus, they strove to modernize in order to strengthen, not diminish, Judaism.[18]

Though each of these changes alienated some congregants and drew ire from traditionalists in the press, Emanu-El flourished, attracting ever more worshipers and growing bolder in its reform initiatives. The growth of the city's population and the economic and social advancement of its Jewish residents gave Reform congregations the means to increase the visibility of their ideals. In 1854, Emanu-El purchased a Gothic Revival church on Twelfth Street and introduced a new prayer book, *Seder Tefilah*, authored by Merzbacher, which banished the observance of the second day of festivals. Most boldly, the congregation introduced family seating. Emanu-El was the first Jewish congregation in New York, and only the second in the United States, to allow men and women to sit together during services, as worshipers did in mainstream Christian denominations. Indeed, Emanu-El's purchase of a church with family pews made this transition seem almost natural. In many ways, for Emanu-El to introduce family seating seemed the next step in its efforts to meet the standards of American society. Congregations like Emanu-El enacted these changes chiefly to display their absorption of mainstream middle-class religious values and norms and to demonstrate that Judaism was modern and respectable.[19]

Yet these American norms directly conflicted with the Jewish tradition of seating women in balconies or behind curtains. To seat men and women together marked a radical and visible departure from tradition and even from Reform practice in Germany. Other New York congregations that had adopted some of Emanu-El's reforms initially shied away from family seating. In 1850, Anshe Chesed moved into its newly built Gothic synagogue on Norfolk Street; here the congregation introduced a choir with men's and women's voices and had its prayer leader face the congregation instead of the eastern wall; yet it kept its traditional prayer book and maintained separate seating of men and women.[20]

Yet by the end of the Civil War, many of the reforms that Emanu-El had spearheaded had been at least debated, if not implemented, by many New York congregations. The city's oldest congregation, Shearith Israel, remained Orthodox, with separate seating. But New York's second-oldest synagogue, B'nai Jeshurun, adopted family seating in 1875 after a fight that led to a civil court case and attracted the attention of the Jewish world. Those in B'nai Jeshurun who desired change wanted to bring the congregation in line with "the requirements of modern taste and culture," thereby making Judaism attractive to an American generation. The minority who opposed mixed seating expressed their view that bringing Judaism in line with American standards would erode its core values by making light of Jewish law and tradition. The judge refused to rule on matters of Jewish law but did uphold the majority's right to change the congregation's bylaws. By the 1870s, most New York synagogues, with the exception of a few Orthodox holdouts, such as Shearith Israel and the new eastern European congregations forming downtown, had adopted family seating.[21]

While the absence of a centralized Jewish authority allowed congregations to go their own ways, they often paid attention to what their counterparts were doing. As the B'nai Jeshurun case showed, debates offered individuals the opportunity to air their beliefs. When the case went to court, traditionalists collected affidavits from Rabbi Abraham Ash of Beth Hamedrash Hagadol and Samuel Myers Isaacs of Shaarey Tefilah; likewise, those who favored family seating called on Rabbi Gustav Gottheil of Temple Emanu-El, Rabbi David Einhorn of Temple Beth El, and Rabbi Isaac Mayer Wise of Cincinnati. As congregations enacted reforms in a piecemeal fashion, often led by the laity, strident voices for Reform and Orthodoxy battled each other in the Jewish press. The debates reached beyond the city's limits. By 1855, Emanu-El was the leading German congregation in New York, its influence extending throughout the country. Congregations in Albany and St. Louis used its prayer book, and Chicago congregations turned to it for advice. By that time, New York Jewry in general considered itself the leader of American Jewry; it was natural, then, that its premier Reform congregation exercised similar clout over Reform congregations.[22] What happened in New York attracted the attention of a national audience.

By 1880, the vast majority of congregations in the United States considered themselves to be Reform. In the 1850s and 1860s, trained Reform rabbis arrived from Germany, assumed leadership positions in American synagogues, and worked with a lay leadership to steer congregations eager for change. The reforms that had seemed so radical were now commonplace: shortened and decorous services (typically two hours), choirs of men and women, and family seating. To signal this new direction, many congregations called themselves "temples" as a dignified term that also signaled rejection of the hope for the restoration of *the* Temple in Jerusalem. Yet though they had a name, and they shared common practices, they had yet to agree on an ideological rationale.[23]

Even as New York Jews brought their Judaism in line with modern sensibilities, one problem plagued all congregations, Reform and Orthodox. Maintaining the traditional Jewish Sabbath proved a difficult issue for all because it conflicted with the standard American workweek that included Saturday. Only so much accommodation could take place with American norms that so directly obstructed Jewish observance.[24] Both Reform and Orthodox wrestled with the problems of Sabbath observance and synagogue attendance. Samuel Myers Isaacs chided Americans for their neglect of the Sabbath, reserving special ire for the comfortable classes who rode in carriages and sent their children to dancing lessons. Some Reform congregations experimented by offering Sunday sermons in addition to Saturday services. But even Emanu-El's second rabbi, Samuel Adler, who succeeded Merzbacher in 1857, firmly opposed a proposal to shift the sermon from Saturday to Sunday.[25] Even if congregants did not attend Saturday services, they often wanted their temples to hold them, loyalty to tradition outweighing accommodation.

In 1876, Adler's son, Felix, split from Reform Judaism to form the Society for Ethical Culture. This departure shocked the Jewish world, as Felix had been sent to Germany for rabbinical training and was slotted to take a leadership role at his father's Temple Emanu-El. When Felix returned from Germany, he tried on this role but found it not to his liking. Enamored of the optimistic universalism of Reform thinkers, Adler lost faith in the particularity of Judaism. "The intellectual and ethical challenges of the day" demanded a strong, humanitarian, and truly universal effort. "Judaism is dying," he pronounced as he gathered like-minded individuals, many of them young and Jewish, to form the Society for Ethical Culture. The Ethical Culturists met on Sundays to absorb the ideas of all world religions and to consider progressive ideas and deeds in their own city. In particular, they sought to model new forms of education for working people's children, establishing a school that would teach the tenets of Ethical Culture. The society attracted only a small percentage of New York Jews (many of whom also retained their membership in Reform congregations). But Adler's defection, as well as his religious challenge, disturbed Reform rabbis such as Kaufman Kohler, of Temple Beth El, who later provided an ideological response.[26]

Within this broadening spectrum of religious identification, debates over specific reforms shaped the trajectories of individual congregations. Ahawath Chesed, for example, embraced standard reforms such as mixed seating and a mixed choir, but it was never a leader in radical reform, as was Temple Emanu-El. When Rabbi Adolph Huebsch and his congregation moved into the Eleventh Presbyterian Church on Avenue C in 1864, Isaac Mayer Wise praised Ahawath Chesed's installation of an organ, trained choir, and family pews. But in his dispatch to the *Israelite*, he scolded the congregation for not taking further steps toward Reform and urged it to rid itself of synagogue practices imported from Prague.[27] The members of Ahawath Chesed did not heed his advice. Huebsch wrote a modernized version of the liturgy yet championed stricter Sabbath observance. After his death in 1884, the congregation turned its attention back to Prague, where it contracted with Alexander Kohut. The graduate of the Breslau Theological Seminary had already completed several volumes of a Talmudic dictionary, the *Aruch Completum*, and his selection signaled a more conservative direction.

Ahawath Chesed's choice of Kohut demonstrated a tentative stance toward Reform and a continued respect for tradition; it also showed how even one congregation might exhibit a range of behaviors and change course over time. Kohut's first sermon at Ahawath Chesed acknowledged these ambiguities. He criticized those who did not uphold the importance of Jewish law but carefully clarified that he directed his attack only against those who deny Jewish law "on principle" and not those who transgress due to the "exigencies of life." This distinction seemed designed to keep him in good favor with his congregation, many of whom did not follow Jewish law because of the demands of work and business. By isolating members' good intentions and their admiration for Jewish law, he aimed to steer them toward fuller observance. It appears that he made some headway. Indeed, Kohut reintroduced the observation of certain holidays such as Purim, Chanukah, and Sukkot and returned to reading the Torah in the traditional annual cycle. The congregation accepted these changes, indicating its openness toward greater conservatism.

Within weeks of Kohut's New York arrival in May 1885, he commenced a series of lectures on the rabbinical text *Ethics of the Fathers* and used it to challenge Reform ideology and practice. Without Jewish law, he argued, Judaism was a "deformity—a skeleton without flesh and sinew, without spirit and heart. It is suicide, and suicide is not reform." Kohut hoped to advance "the old and the new in happy and blended union," along more "conservative lines" that recognized the importance of Jewish law.[28] Rabbi Kaufman Kohler (1842–1926), leader of Temple Beth El (1874), just eight blocks north on Lexington Avenue, responded in kind, delivering five discourses, "Backwards or Forwards," in which he defended Reform.[29] These exchanges came to be known as the "Kohut-Kohler affair" and attracted press attention. Max Cohn, the editor of the *American Hebrew*, rushed to translate Kohut's sermons from German for his weekly paper. The exchanges were commented on and debated in the papers and within synagogue halls. The *New York Times* covered the controversy as well, printing Kohler's account: "In these discourses I defended my view, and Dr. Kohut responded each time from the pulpit at his temple; each with mutual recognition of the views and personal qualities of his opponent."[30]

Not only does this affair show the fluidity within a congregation, but it also reveals the dynamism of the debate and the excitement New York offered to Reform and traditionalist leaders alike. Rebekah Bettelheim, a daughter of a San Franciscan rabbi and soon-to-be fiancée of Alexander Kohut, recorded in her memoirs the apprehension she felt upon attending an open meeting at Temple Emanu-El in which prominent rabbis, including Kohut and Kohler, had gathered to discuss "The Conflict between Science and Religion." Bettelheim had been following the debates among rabbis in the press and feared experiencing the acrimony in action; however, she was pleasantly surprised by the proceedings:

> It was interesting to see all those rabbis of conflicting beliefs gathered in one assemblage, listening to their respective opponents. Face to face, people cannot hate each other as much as if either side recedes into a vague symbol of menace. Here were these men, leaders all, who had to state their viewpoint for their opponents. No flights of rhetoric, no appeals to lay prejudices and passions, no beclouding the issues were possible if these men were really sincere in their desire to arrive at amity.

In Bettelheim-Kohut's account, Kohut's address garnered the admiration if not the agreement of opponents such as Kohler and Gustav Gottheil. "I remember with what gratification I saw Dr. Kohler rush forward and congratulate his antagonist."[31] This action then caused Bettelheim-Kohut to reflect on the broader meaning of this open meeting and the stimulation the contestation of ideas provided. Despite antagonisms displayed in print, there seemed to be recognition at these cross-congregational meetings of the opportunity for collaboration, providing these men a chance to test and sharpen their viewpoints. New York's geography—with diverse temples within blocks of each other—surely heightened this dynamic, and "each man's synagogue was crowded to overflowing."[32] The impact of the debates spread beyond the synagogue halls, awakening public interest in the issues facing Judaism. The sheer concentration of leading congregations and rabbis made New York different from other Jewish centers.

The Kohut-Kohler debates crystallized two important viewpoints, both of which asserted New York's centrality in the direction of American Judaism. First, Kohler summoned like-minded Reform rabbis, including Isaac Mayer

Wise, to Pittsburgh for a convention. While Reform leaders, including Wise, had previously attempted to unite rabbis around an ideological justification for Reform, they had never succeeded. This time they did. The resulting Pittsburgh Platform, an eight-point articulation of American Reform Judaism, wielded tremendous power through the 1930s. The platform rejected the Talmud's hold on modern Jews, eliminating laws such as the regulations on diet and dress that did not meet the standards of "modern civilization." The platform championed an enlightened and universalistic spirit that encouraged Jews to espouse Judaism's moral and ethical teachings. Judaism, in the Pittsburgh Platform's light, became a "progressive religion ever striving to be in accord with the postulates of reason."[33] Thus, the debates with Kohut prompted Kohler and his colleagues to hammer out the most decisive ideological statement of Reform and American Judaism up to that point, a milestone in the American Reform movement.

In turn, the Pittsburgh Platform's rejection of the Talmud and the binding force of Jewish law pushed Kohut to join with other rabbis—Sabato Morais and Marcus Jastrow of Philadelphia, Henry Pereira Mendes of Shearith Israel, Henry Schneeberger of Baltimore, Aaron Bettelheim of San Francisco—to establish a rabbinical seminary in New York City. At the Jewish Theological Seminary (JTS), students would learn to deliver English sermons and immerse themselves in Western thought but would continue to study Talmud and traditional texts. According to an *American Hebrew* editorial, JTS aimed to train American rabbis in "English culture" and to effectively blend the "American spirit" with "the strong historical armor of historical Judaism."[34] Kohut had preached this balance to Ahawath Chesed, and these rabbis hoped such a synthesis could ensure proper leadership for American Jewry. Initially, lack of funds limited JTS's influence. But by the turn of the twentieth century, the eastern European immigration spurred demand for new leadership and prompted uptown leaders Jacob Schiff and Louis Marshall to support a renewal of the institution. Under Solomon Schechter's leadership, JTS expanded its reach, training not just rabbis but also teachers through its Teachers Institute. By the second decade of the twentieth century, JTS had moved away from Orthodoxy to create Conservative Judaism, a third branch of American Judaism. As Rebekah Kohut recalled, "Thus one of the great seats of learning, the training-place of many of the most distinguished leaders of today, the home of the greatest Jewish library in the world, owes its existence to the fevered controversy of the 1880s."[35] What began as congregational sermons escalated into a nationwide dialogue and debate over the course of American Judaism.

Wherever uptown synagogue members positioned themselves along the spectrum of religious practice, by the 1880s they surely reveled in their buildings' beauty. The uptown addresses and the distinctiveness of the Moorish style in contrast to other churches and residences in the city announced that their Jewish congregants, many of them immigrants or the children of immigrants from central Europe, had integrated into the American economy and lived in and worked at the vernacular offices and homes in the neighborhood. These merchants and manufacturers desired to preserve their Jewish identity and to pass this identity to their children. Having a space to do this, particularly such fine spaces as these, demarcated a place to be apart in a city of such power and force. It reminded congregants of the importance of their Jewish identity. This New York Jewish identity, however, was never static; rather, it took new shape as congregants attended and discussed sermons regarding the direction of American Judaism, responded to the needs of the next generation, and managed shifting economic conditions.

The next great challenge and opportunity came in the form of eastern European Jewish immigrants. These immigrants were arriving in multitudes and settling in the very same streets that had made up the former Kleindeutschland, now called the East Side, or the Jewish Ghetto. Five-story tenements housed Yiddish-speaking immigrants, and some of the garment shops owned by Ahawath Chesed's members employed eastern European Jewish laborers. Just as Ahawath Chesed's German-speaking immigrants had once gathered in a Ludlow Street hall to lead Orthodox services, these newcomers too adapted storefronts and tenements into houses of prayer. A church on Chrystie that had once been the home of Temple Emanu-El now housed the eastern European Orthodox congregation Mishkan Israel Suvalk.[36] But in 1886, Beth Hamedrash, located at 78 Allen Street, just a few blocks from Ahawath Chesed's founding home, bucked the trend, as it prepared to build its own new synagogue—and change its name to Kahal Adath Jeshurun—a few blocks to the south on Eldridge Street.

■ Moorish on Eldridge

By January 1887, the trustees of Kahal Adath Jeshurun must have been somewhat anxious. Construction of their new synagogue was proceeding apace; a cornerstone had been laid in November. But bills were mounting, and syna-gogue officers pinned all their hopes on opening in time for the September High Holiday season. The disparity between the congregation's 150 members and the new sanctuary's capacity of 735 must have been daunting. Just as the lay leaders of uptown temples such as Ahawath Chesed had to calculate how they would finance and maintain their new structures, and used the sale of seats as their primary means to do so, so too did the leaders of Kahal Adath Jeshurun. Thus, in January 1887, the congregation crafted and circulated seat contracts. These stipulated terms and prices for the purchase of pews. By this time, the trustees of the synagogue had copies of the Herter Brothers' water-color plans for the synagogue structure; a black-and-white etching had also appeared in the *Yidishe gazeten*. One imagines they would have used these images when trying to sell the seats.

After all, in a competitive market of 130 downtown congregations, one in which immigrants selected congregations based on hometown ties, the leaders of Kahal Adath Jeshurun needed to sell or market their congregation in novel ways. Eastern European Jews who settled in New York City tended to form small congregations and, lacking funds, rented halls for their worship services. They took turns leading services or, if more established, hired cantors and preachers to chant the prayers and deliver Yiddish sermons. Beth Hamedrash Hagadol, perhaps the largest eastern European congregation (which, along with Kahal Adath Jeshurun, could trace its roots to Beth Hamedrash, the Rus-sian congregation that formed in 1852 in Five Points), took the eastern Euro-pean synagogue to a new level when it purchased a church on Norfolk Street and renovated it into a handsome synagogue. But in general, most downtown congregations were hidden from view, distinguished only by a sign. So well did they blend into the Lower East Side streetscape that a *New York Daily Trib-une* reporter assigned to report on the "Hebrew quarter's" synagogues in 1896 characterized his quest as a veritable investigative endeavor:

> Scores, and even hundreds, of tiny synagogues [are] hidden away in this region of old buildings—synagogues consisting of a single floor, or at the most two, and giving no sign of their existence until they are stumbled upon. Some of the older tenements, dark of stairway and almost crumbling with age, have two, three and even four of these little worshipping places within their walls, where prayers are said thrice daily.[37]

Another early twentieth-century observer noted that most of the more than one hundred synagogues he surveyed were not "anything more than halls or large rooms in tenement-houses, sometimes above or below a drinking-place, and in a few instances in a ball-room, which on Saturdays puts off its unholy garb."[38]

In some ways, these randomly located and chaotic venues reflected the state of much of immigrant Orthodox Judaism into the twentieth century. A vacuum of religious authority existed, which even the more established congregations could not fill. By the 1880s, central European Jews had close to half a century's experience in creating congregations in America; the eastern European Jews were only beginning. But they had heard of the changes that uptown Jews had made, and to them Reform Judaism seemed utterly foreign, even heretical.

The Moorish structure arising on Eldridge Street might have called to mind images of temples uptown. Was there going to be a Reform synagogue in the heart of the Lower East Side? Anyone with the funds to build such a structure surely was an uptown, German Jew. For those who had such questions or impressions, the seat contract offered swift and unequivocal reassurance:

> As it is the intention of all persons connected with said congregation to preserve, maintain and adhere to the strict Orthodox faith, it is hereby agreed, that, if at any time an organ should be used in connection with the service, if males and females are allowed to sit together during divine services; or if a mixed choir (males and females) is allowed to sing during divine services, the said [seat owner] shall have the right to recover from the said congregation, twice the amount which he may have paid to said congregation from the dates of these presents, exclusive of interest and dues.[39]

In the late nineteenth century, the women's balcony guaranteed by this clause provided not just a physical separation of the sexes but a rigid conceptual dividing line between Reform and Orthodox Judaism. Ahawath Chesed's mixed choir and mixed seating—all the elements that marked it as Reform—would not be countenanced at the downtown Moorish synagogue.

By September 4, 1887, the hopes of opening in time for the High Holiday season were fulfilled. Throngs, including some uptown Jews curious to see what this new structure portended, assembled on Eldridge Street for a dedication ceremony. Regardless of their religious sensibilities, Jews gathered downtown in large numbers: in 1887, nothing in the neighborhood's architecture announced the Jewish presence as strikingly as the Eldridge Street Synagogue. Though it lacked the corner lot that such uptown congregations as Emanu-El and Ahawath Chesed had secured, Eldridge's three-lot perch in the center of the street was still impressive. Approaching from afar, one could detect the Stars of David atop finials, themselves lacier and more delicate than the solid masonry of Ahawath Chesed's sturdy octagonal towers. In place of crenellations, more sprightly iron crestwork danced along the cornice. The materials of Eldridge Street, without question, were less expensive and less impressive. How could brick compare with Belleville stone, or terra-cotta with sandstone trim? Yet the effect delighted the eye; the terra-cotta floral designs and Stars of David articulated the placement of keyhole windows and doorways as nicely as the stone arches did uptown. Uptown visitors praised the building—the *New York Herald* considered it among the finest synagogues in the city. While the brownstone of Lexington's synagogue matched its neighboring brownstone townhouses, here the brick of the Eldridge Street Synagogue aligned it with neighboring tenements; yet its use of cream-colored brick set it off in a distinguished manner. Once inside the sanctuary, an Ahawath Chesed member might have been reminded of his own synagogue's stained-glass windows and delicate pillars but would have been discomfited by the bimah, or reading platform, set in the midst of the sanctuary instead of in the front of the congregation and by the seating of women in the balcony rather than on the sanctuary floor.

Arriving on opening day, an uptown reporter from the *American Israelite*, a Reform publication with a national circulation, described the architecture as "elegant" and noted the "plentiful supply of air and light from the many and high windows."[40] But he complained that the serene setting failed to inspire decorum among the worshipers, and he sniffed at the women squabbling in the balcony, the babies crying, and the men grasping half-smoked cigars. In retaining Orthodoxy, and the habit of visiting the synagogue daily as opposed to a supposedly more reverential weekly or monthly basis, he suggested, the downtown Jews' Judaism was just as un-American behind an ornate Moorish façade as it was behind a vernacular brick tenement one. Their behavior made him question their very ability to Americanize. Reform, he suggested, remained the only true form of American Judaism.

In many ways, the Eldridge Street Synagogue and the wealth it represented stood as a rebuke to the ways in which uptown Jews like the *Israelite* reporter had reconciled their Jewish and American identities. While it was accepted that newly arrived eastern European Jews would form Orthodox prayer groups in tenements, Orthodox worship in an architecturally prominent building raised eyebrows. The ability to build such a synagogue implied that a significant segment of the congregation had Americanized sufficiently to raise funds and navigate courts. Should not these businesspeople and communal leaders have embraced Reform? Instead they used their American business sense to proclaim their Orthodoxy. The speeches that resounded throughout the handsome interior finishes of "cherry and ash" signaled the adamancy with which this congregation defined itself in contrast to Reform Judaism. Rabbi Henry Pereira Mendes, leader of the pioneer New York City synagogue Orthodox Shearith Israel, implored congregants in the Eldridge audience to instruct their children "in the teachings of religion and be made familiar with Jewish history, otherwise they [would], in growing up, leave the synagogue and join the temples up town." Rabbi Bernard Drachman, another Orthodox rabbi, pleaded with his audience to maintain their traditions, lest "they might stand before their mirrors some morning and not recognize themselves as orthodox anymore."[41] These orators viewed Reform as a more profound threat than apostasy.

In truth, lack of decorum at a synagogue dedication was not the exclusive province of the Orthodox; an account of Temple Emanu-El's dedication in 1868 described how the crowd's anxiety to find seats was so great that when "the doors were opened there was a crushing and a crowding in which ladies' crinoline and gentlemen's hats suffered severely." Only the presence of a "large police force" maintained order. Yet beyond these shared infractions of decorum, both congregations strove for order. Downtown's retention of the Orthodox liturgy did not stop it from hiring a renowned cantor to lead the prayer service. At Eldridge, the cantor helped avoid what some Jews considered a cacophony of worshipers reciting prayers at their own pace, the cantor's status and control being further enhanced by the hiring of a "double male quartette." In addition, the congregation apparently had created a system by which trustees stationed throughout the sanctuary could signal the *shames*, or sexton, if crowds became too noisy; upon receiving the signal, the *shames* would thump the reading table with his fist "and a sort of small thunder reverberated through the synagogue."[42]

Like many downtown congregations, the Eldridge Street Synagogue did not have its own rabbi. In 1887, the congregation joined forces with fourteen other downtown congregations, including Beth Hamedrash Hagadol, to form the Association of Orthodox Hebrew Congregations (Agudes ha-Kehillos). They aimed to address the state of chaos in the regulation of kosher meat and the adjudication of other aspects of Jewish law. While many leading Orthodox downtown Jews had established important ties with uptown Orthodox rabbis, such as Drachman and Mendes, they knew they needed an eastern European luminary to rally the support of the downtown immigrants. Certainly, to their minds, the uptown Reform rabbis could not provide guidance. Thus, they resolved to import an eastern European rabbi, Jacob Joseph, from Vilna. Though they could import the rabbi and offer him a handsome salary, they could not import eastern European Orthodox communal structures. Joseph failed to gain widespread support in the New York community despite a warm initial greeting. Matters took a turn for the worse when the association decided to tackle the issue of *kashrut*. To help pay for Joseph's salary, the association placed a tax on kosher meat. Unfortunately, the downtown consumers reacted with horror at the tax, which reminded them of the hated Tsarist meat tax known as the *karobka*. Rival rabbis elected themselves chief rabbis of their communities, and hopes for a citywide Orthodox Jewish authority disappeared.[43] As a leading member of the association, the Eldridge Street Synagogue was forbidden to hire its own rabbi, as Joseph served as the spiritual leader of the constituent members. But Joseph's expertise did not extend to the temporal affairs of running a congregation; he left this to the congregation's lay leaders.

Just as Ahawath Chesed had relied on the good judgment and devotion of its lay leaders, so too did Eldridge Street depend on men such as Sender Jarmulowsky, Nathan Hutkoff, David Cohen, and Isaac Gellis, and in later years Barnet Goldfein and Simon Lazerowitz. Lay leaders of the downtown synagogue were leading businessmen, and many had been in America for over a dozen years. In its first few decades, the Eldridge Street Synagogue constantly battled neighboring congregations for the allegiance of the Orthodox public, a competition that often hinged on who could import the most talented cantor. In later years, leaders struggled to update and maintain their beautiful building to keep its place as one of the city's most attractive synagogues. The most pressing challenges occurred within a decade of its opening, as the most successful members began to migrate out of the Lower East Side to Harlem and the Bronx. Rather than move the synagogue uptown, the lay leadership constantly sought new ways to attract members and, when needed, secured mergers that maintained its downtown presence.

Though Eldridge Street's top leaders had established careers as bankers and businessmen and possessed the wealth to buy seats for hundreds of dollars, the congregation's base was much more diverse. As *Century Magazine* reporter Richard Wheatley put it, "Lawyers, merchants, artisans, clerks, peddlers, and laborers compose the dense and changeful throng. All are one in respect to race and faith, but many in regard to birthplace and speech. *E pluribus Unum* receives a new meaning here."[44] A *New York Herald* reporter even claimed that a fair share of those who were present at the congregation's opening were American born. Just as Ahawath Chesed became a place where Bavarian, Bohemian, and Prussian immigrants formed an American Judaism, so too did the Eldridge Street Synagogue become a place where Jews from throughout eastern Europe, along with some who were American born, undertook a similar project. To be sure, this Americanization occurred in steps; Ahawath Chesed relied on the German language to bind the newcomers from points throughout central Europe. Indeed, English did not become its official language until 1899. The unification of diverse groups of eastern European Jews rested heavily on the use of Yiddish in both congregational meetings and sermons.

The congregation's devotion to Orthodoxy did not mean it was unresponsive to American currents. On opening day, those who were assembled waved the Stars and Stripes; and in 1889, the congregation was decorated for the centennial of George Washington's inauguration. In 1900, the congregation hosted a mass meeting on the topic of neighborhood crime; the guest speaker was Dr. Felix Adler, former Reform rabbi and founder of the Ethical Culture Society, which rejected Judaism for humanist universalism. While the congregation would never have permitted Adler to lead a religious service or to deliver a sermon, they allowed him, as a leader in the city's progressive movements, to ascend the pulpit to hold forth on a pressing local problem. During World War I, the congregation showcased a specially designed American flag with stars representing children of the congregation who were now soldiers in the American army.[45]

Yet economic exigencies challenged Orthodox life. Even in a city like New York, with its enormous Jewish population, the Monday through Saturday workweek dominated; moreover, city blue laws expressly forbade Sunday commerce. Just as central European immigrants to New York often neglected strict Sabbath observance in favor of economic integration, so too did eastern European Jews grapple with the city's blue laws and Saturday work.

Eastern European immigrants proved powerless to change the city's work tempo on a weekly basis; however, they did organize to demand recognition of their holiday observance. Consider the case of Morris Simons, a pawnbroker and longtime member of the Eldridge Street Synagogue. In 1897, Simons penned a letter to New York City Mayor William Strong, requesting that "Israelite" storekeepers be allowed to open their doors on Sunday, September 26. While city and state blue laws normally kept businesses closed on Sundays, the fact that Rosh Hashanah, the Jewish New Year, fell on Monday, September 27, that year threatened to create havoc. Sandwiched between a Saturday, the Jewish Sabbath, when Jewish storekeepers were obliged by their religion to stay closed, and the following Monday and Tuesday, when all the district's stores would be closed in honor of the holidays, the Sunday in question was the only day in a four-day period in which Judaism permitted business. If Jews obeyed the Sunday blue laws and remained closed, not only would storekeepers lose a significant amount of business but Jewish households would be unable to prepare for the New Year. At this point, only the mayor's secular power could provide the relief Jewish immigrants needed to prepare for their holiday. In perfect English, Simons assured the mayor both that "the population of that district are all Israelites and we have no other customers" and that he and his son had kept closed on Sundays as long as they had been in business.[46]

Simons, and Lower East Side Jews in general, must have been pleased with the official decision to grant all Jewish businesses permission to open their doors that Sunday. The *New York Times* reported, "Orders were issued from Police Headquarters to permit Jewish dealers to transact business yesterday, and the marts of Hester, Orchard, and Ludlow Streets presented their usual Friday afternoon appearance. Brisk trading was the order of the day and the tardy buyers took advantage of the leniency of the police. Even the stores on the Bowery were open all day and did quite a good business."[47]

The exchange between the pawnbroker and the mayor highlights once again the central difficulty in reconciling Orthodox Judaism and American ways of doing business. That Sunday's suspension of the blue laws was an exception, granted in honor of a once-a-year event, and failed to address the weekly dilemma prompted by the Jewish Sabbath's collision with laws mandating a

Sunday Sabbath. The clash of calendars forced Jewish immigrants who wanted to preserve their Orthodoxy to hunt for jobs that allowed them to rest on the Sabbath. If one did have to work on the Sabbath, how could one remain an observant Jew? Uptown, Ahawath Chesed and Emanu-El had responded in part by emphasizing Friday-night services and promoting a Reform agenda that minimized the centrality of Jewish law. Downtown, aside from proclaiming that members could not "publicly desecrate" the Sabbath, the Eldridge Street Synagogue had no official answer for Jews who worked on the Sabbath.[48]

In truth, only a minority of New York Jews observed the Sabbath or affiliated with a synagogue; observers estimated that perhaps 20 or 30 percent prayed weekly and that only 5 to 40 percent belonged to a synagogue. But they also agreed that many more, perhaps three-quarters, visited the synagogue annually on the High Holidays.[49] The Eldridge Street Synagogue provided a venue for eastern European Jews who did not attend daily or even weekly to participate in services according to the holiday or life-cycle schedule. For example, in 1909, 72 percent of the Eldridge Street Synagogue's income came from the sale of High Holiday tickets, many of them to nonmembers, Sabbath desecrators, who nevertheless desired to worship in an established synagogue during the High Holiday season. Likewise, a bar mitzvah brought fathers and sons in closer contact with the community. The 1913 constitution made special accommodations for nonmembers who needed a place for their sons' bar mitzvah ceremonies and explained, "A Bar Mitzva whose father is not a member of this Congregation can be confirmed at the Synagogue on payment of such fees as the Board of Trustees may determine." The constitution also suggested the ritual's popularity, as it made provisions and rules for the order of honors and privileges on days with multiple bar mitzvah ceremonies.[50]

On Eldridge Street, Moorish finials and stenciled gilded stars shielded a congregation of Jews who strove to create an American form of Orthodoxy. Congregational leaders understood the broader challenges confronting Jews beyond the stained-glass windows. Though the congregation's involvement in the chief rabbi experiment yielded no returns, it tried again to organize Orthodox Jewry by leading the initiative for the Orthodox Union in 1898. Several of the congregation's leaders held office in the Orthodox Union, and the synagogue hosted the convention.[51] The Orthodox Union brought together uptown Orthodox rabbis such as Henry Pereira Mendes and Bernard Drachman with downtown leaders such as Judah David Eisenstein from Beth Hamedrash

Hagadol. The Orthodox Union defined itself in contrast to "the declarations of Reform rabbis not in accord with the teachings of the Torah." It also worked as a lobby to defend the interests of Orthodox Jews to avoid as much as possible the kinds of conflicts that took place over Sabbath observance. But like the early leaders of Temple Emanu-El, the Orthodox Union leaders desired to guide immigrants in balancing "their allegiance to Judaism with the drive to Americanize."[52]

Not all downtown Orthodox Jews shared the interest of Eldridge Street or the Orthodox Union in merging Americanism with traditional Judaism. The resisters, organized in the Agudath Ha-Rabbannim (Union of Orthodox Rabbis of the United States and Canada), viewed any compromise with American culture as a threat to traditional Judaism as practiced mainly in eastern Europe. They therefore lamented the introduction of English-language sermons in some congregations and fought a rearguard action against the modernization of the curriculum in Yeshiva Etz Chaim, an Orthodox day school established in 1886, and the Rabbi Isaac Elchannan Theological Seminary (RIETS), founded in 1897 and emerging as the primary training school for Orthodox rabbis. The rabbis of the Agudath Ha-Rabbannim considered their RIETS- and JTS-trained colleagues to be deficient in Talmudic learning, with the Americans' ability to speak idiomatic English, if anything, a strike against them. Rabbi Jacob Willowski summed up the resisters' attitude: "America is a treif land where even the stones are impure."[53] But the resisters were losing their hold on even the Orthodox segment of the community.

The funeral of Rabbi Jacob Joseph demonstrated the extent to which Orthodoxy had gained recognition from the broader community. Largely ignored in life, in death Rabbi Joseph came to be viewed as a symbol of Orthodox Judaism in America. On July 30, 1902, tens of thousands of mourners turned out for the rabbi's funeral, which wound its way, from his house on Henry Street, along Grand Street, toward the ferry to Brooklyn. The funeral has been remembered mainly for the melee that broke out between some of the mourners, the workers at the R. H. Hoe factory, and the police. But at the time, Rabbi Joseph's funeral was also touted as a demonstration of the power and maturity of Orthodox Jewry in New York. Observers as diverse as the Orthodox Yiddish daily *Tageblat* and the *New York Times* stressed the simplicity and dignity of the funeral and procession, which was, according to the *Tageblat*, "without order and yet without confusion." Moreover, a mayoral commission exonerated the mourners of any blame in the disturbance and disciplined a police captain.[54]

As represented by the leaders of the Eldridge Street Synagogue, the Americanizing Orthodox understood the importance not only of adapting the synagogue but also of supporting a wide range of Orthodox communal institutions. Just as central European leaders had turned to charity, so too did the leaders of downtown New York Jewry. The reach of the Eldridge Street Synagogue leadership throughout the community indicates the engagement of Americanizing Orthodoxy. Eldridge Street leaders also served on the boards of Jewish charities, from the Hebrew Sheltering House Association to the Beth Israel Hospital to an array of yeshivas and Talmud Torahs. In fact, a six-slotted *tsedakah*, or charity, box designated Yeshiva Etz Chaim as a beneficiary of the congregation's largesse. One of the congregation's first presidents, Isaac Gellis, served on the board of Beth Israel, Mount Sinai, and Lebanon Hospitals; the Montefiore Home; the Home of the Daughters of Jacob; and the Hebrew Sheltering and Immigrant Aid Association. Isaac's wife, Sarah Gellis, who was "very religious," left no record of formal organizational leadership but crafted her own charitable arrangements. On Friday afternoons, she not only prepared Sabbath meals for her family of seven children but also engaged two cooks to prepare foods for an "open house" throughout the Sabbath; her grandson recalled the "continuous run of people coming to sit and eat." During Passover, Isaac regularly donated one thousand pounds of kosher meat to Eldridge Street for its part in the traditional *maos khitim* communal outreach at Passover. Sarah went from business to business, gathering donations of clothes, shoes, and hats for 350 children.[55]

■ Religious Education

If Saturday work posed a problem for adult Jewish Sabbath observance, the popular American public school curtailed traditional religious study for children. Among the most important religious institutions elaborated by New York Jewry were thus those devoted to the religious education of its boys and girls. Running the gamut from Reform to Orthodox, religious institutions enthusiastically assumed the task of socializing the next generation in a synthesis of Americanism and Judaism. Others resisted accommodation with the local culture. Most took the form of supplemental schools that the children attended after the regular public school day: Sabbath and Sunday schools met once a week and were often tied to Reform congregations. Their curriculums included Jewish history, Hebrew language, and ethics, with the stress on history. Other congregational or communal "Hebrew schools" and "Talmud Torahs" met on weekday afternoons, after the regular public school day. An eclectic collection of institutions, they taught Hebrew language, the Bible, Jewish history, and "prayers, customs, and laws" in varying combinations. Some included music as well. Independent *hadorim* attempted to replicate the traditional eastern European style of elementary education and met in a variety of venues, including private homes and storefronts. Finally, secular Yiddish schools founded in the second decade of the twentieth century by immigrant radicals probably represented the greatest departure from educational tradition. These supplementary schools stressed Yiddish language (the Labor Zionist schools also taught Hebrew), modern Jewish literature, history, and folk customs, mixed with a healthy dose of socialism. Parents often sent their daughters to the secular schools to learn to read and write Yiddish. Boys went to religious schools for their bar mitzvahs.[56]

In 1917, not quite one thousand boys attended one of four all-day Jewish parochial schools, or yeshivas. In these schools, students studied traditional Jewish subjects including *Humash* with the commentaries of Rashi and Talmud, from nine in the morning until three in the afternoon. From three until seven, they studied secular subjects. The language of instruction for the Jewish studies was generally Yiddish. The oldest of the yeshivas was Yeshiva Etz Chaim, founded by eastern European immigrants in 1886, but the largest was the Rabbi Jacob Joseph School, with over five hundred students. In 1915, Etz Chaim merged with the Rabbi Isaac Elchannan Theological Seminary (RIETS) to form Yeshiva College. A year later, Yeshiva's high school division reemerged as the Talmudical Academy, which, like Jacob Joseph before it, promised a first-rate secular, as well as religious, education. Ultimately, Yeshiva University, with its high school, undergraduate college, rabbinical seminary, and graduate schools, became the flagship educational institution of modern American Orthodoxy, striving to balance *Torah u-mada*, traditional Jewish learning with secular scholarship.[57]

With New York Jews' diverse responses to the opportunities and pressures of American culture, religion ceased to unite them. Yet, beneath the surface, whether Reform or Orthodox, most New York Jews strove to fashion a new form of Judaism that suited their city and its lifestyle. In this respect, the Orthodox synagogue was as much an experiment as the Reform temple was. And for both, these experiments demanded certain essential ingredients, including congregational leaders who possessed legal and business acumen derived from experience in New York commercial life. This greatest asset paradoxically posed a challenge, as immersion in New York's business and commercial life threatened to overwhelm traditional observances and lifestyles. The synagogue could not contain all of religious life. Home life, directed by immigrant women, became another site for religious expression and adaptation.

When longtime Lower East Side banker Sender Jarmulowsky opened his new building in the spring of 1912, he highlighted capitalism's opportunities to the immigrant community. After the Jarmulowsky family was forced to sell the building in 1920, a succession of leading mainstream banks took over the first-floor banking hall. Factories filled the upstairs lofts, producing lace curtains, overalls, and nightgowns. By 1945, a piano manufacturer built and sold pianos—a hallmark of middle-class respectability—in the building.

CHAPTER 4

Immigrant Citadels: Tenements, Shops, Stores, and Streets

Though no one could trace the rumor's origins, by the afternoon of Wednesday, December 11, 1901, the devastating news had been repeated by thousands of lips. It gathered a force of its own, wending its way through the Hester Street pushcart market, across tenement airshafts, from one stoop to the next, and up into the garment lofts. Sender Jarmulowsky's bank had run dry! Shoppers stopped haggling, storekeepers shuttered their shops, and tenement housewives threw down their market baskets and formed "an excited mob, in which there were mingled shouts and cries of anger, pleading, grief, and despair." The crowd converged at the bank's entrance, on the corner of Orchard and Canal Streets. Though it soon appeared that the venerable Jarmulowsky had ample funds to satisfy all requests—he and his clerks disbursed $35,000 on Wednesday and kept their doors open past the standard closing hours—the lines showed no signs of abating. Rather, they continued to extend for blocks in several directions as "many terror-stricken depositors kept their places in line in front of the doors all night, and were desperate when the institution resumed payments at 10 o'clock [Thursday] morning, and other depositors by the hundreds arrived."[1]

A *New York Times* journalist surveyed the scene that morning, noting the diversity of the crowd. Some passbooks showed accounts as large as $1,000, others as small as $5 or $6. But the depositors' anxiety united them. The reporter sensed not just the sums of money involved but the many hours of rugged toil that those sums had exacted from the passbooks' owners and the broader hopes and ambitions they promised. Mary Geltman, of 4 Orchard Street, arrived at six a.m. Thursday to relieve her brother and redeem her $68 savings: "She blushingly confessed that she was going to be married soon, and wanted to take no chances on getting her bridal outfit."[2] Had the journalist elicited more "confessions," he might have reported a young husband saving money for ship tickets for his wife and children in Europe, a presser laboring in a garment shop with hopes of buying a sewing machine and starting his own enterprise, a mother in need of cash for the next installment on the family's prized piano, or perhaps a merchant who hoped to move his family beyond the teeming Lower East Side. These anxious East Siders, holding onto their passbooks like life preservers amid a swirling sea, were a microcosm not only of the neighborhood's Jews that day but also of the collective strivings of the hundreds of thousands of Jews who made the Lower East Side their first home in America in the decades surrounding the turn of the twentieth century. For close to fifty years, the East Side was known as the city's premier Jewish neighborhood, welcoming newcomers and sending the more Americanized on their way. Even as one family bade farewell to an East Side tenement apartment for the enticements of Harlem, Brooklyn, or the Bronx, a new family arrived to claim their apartment, perhaps applying a new layer of wallpaper but encountering similar challenges and nursing the same hopes for mobility as their predecessors.

These immigrants sewed, hawked, and haggled to build better lives. Pious synagogue-goers, Yiddish-theater devotees, and Socialist firebrands alike dutifully visited the bank weekly to deposit portions of their own paychecks or the collective earnings of their family's labor. On normal days, as they waited in line to deposit or withdraw, they perhaps entertained hopes for their future lives in New York. The potential for success was there, firmly rooted in the ethnic enclave. The story of Sender Jarmulowsky, reputed to be a "millionaire," showed how a Talmud scholar with ambition could start a bank and forge a career as a philanthropist and benefactor of schools, hospitals, and synagogues. The people in line could surely see the rooftop finials of the Eldridge Street Synagogue, an early product of Jarmulowsky's largesse. Businessmen also mingled with the crowd: "Several . . . Hebrews of the more intelligent class . . . told everybody that there was no need of uneasiness and cautioned all not to discount their claims." Another real estate merchant cum philanthropist, Jonas Weil, had an "enormous roll of bills in his pocket," and "whenever he saw a particularly tired and careworn woman with a baby in her arms or an old man in the surging line he took their pass books and gave them the amount of money called for out of his own pocket."[3] On the other hand, lacking the wealth of Jarmulowsky or Weil, but clearly desiring it, some East Side store owners took advantage of their neighbors' frenzy and with much cooler heads offered ninety and ninety-five cents on the dollar to those who were too anxious to wait. In this way, the shopkeepers earned not only 5–10 percent of the passbooks but also the interest for the second half of the year. One claimed to have made $1,000.[4]

To those who waited, Jarmulowsky and his clerks paid one hundred cents on the dollar and finally dispelled the rumor of collapse, and the crowds dispersed, returning to their sewing machines, kitchens, stores, and pushcarts. By Monday, December 16, so thoroughly had Jarmulowsky snuffed out the rumor that some of the very people who had rushed to withdraw returned to reopen their accounts.[5]

■ Immigrant Bankers: Capitalism and Community

A decade later, in May 1912, having withstood occasional runs on the bank and grown with the community, Jarmulowsky presented the neighborhood with its first high-class office skyscraper, proudly emblazoned with his name. Though he and other successful eastern European businesspeople and philanthropists no longer resided downtown, their banks and stores thrived on the burgeoning East Side, and they returned there each morning to serve, and profit from, their ethnic constituency. In many cases, they invested the money they had earned through business, whether dry goods, cigars, or the garment industry, in real estate, first on the Lower East Side and then uptown and in Harlem, Brownsville, and the Bronx. But Jarmulowsky was the first among them to introduce the relatively new "skyscraper" bank building to the Lower East Side.

Jarmulowsky's bank, just like his synagogue twenty years earlier, changed the physical landscape of the Lower East Side. No longer would Lower East Side banks operate from typical neighborhood three-story commercial structures or nondescript tenement storefronts. When enterprising bankers such as Max Kobre had festooned their buildings with terra-cotta beehives or wrought-iron initials, they had merely scratched the surface, dressing up ordinary structures but leaving the streetscape largely as it was. Jarmulowsky's architect son, Meyer, upped the ante in 1903 when he designed a seven-story Moorish-style building, "a miracle of white enamel, gold paint, of Oriental balconies of brass," for a branch he opened with his brother, Louis, on East Broadway.[6] But when their father's building opened nine years later, the *New York Times* described it as the East Side's "first strictly high-class tall bank and office building," akin to the "highest grade banking buildings" in Manhattan's tonier business areas. Indeed, the 1906 J. & W. Seligman & Co. headquarters on William Street, in the Wall Street financial district, appears to have served as one inspiration for the design. Both banks had rounded corners, announcing their structures' significance at street level, while circular towers at the roofline proclaimed their majesty far and wide. In modeling his bank after that of the "American Rothschilds," Jarmulowsky signaled his admiration for these successful German-Jewish bankers. Jarmulowsky's eye-catching rooftop, a domed circular pavilion wreathed by eagles, also elicited comparisons to McKim, Mead & White's Municipal Building, perhaps indicating Jarmulowsky's ambition to be viewed as the sovereign of the East Side.[7] The bank's popular neo-Renaissance-style skyscraper design thus linked the Lower East Side to the rest of the city.

By the time the "temple of finance" opened to the public, Mary Geltman, like many of the alumni of the 1901 run on the bank, might already have been living in Harlem or Brooklyn, unable to view the skyscraper. Yet, if she read any of the Yiddish newspapers available in those neighborhoods' candy stores, she could not have missed the full-page advertisements announcing the opening of the new bank building and proclaiming a "*yontef,*" or holiday, for the East Side. The advertisements in the *Jewish Daily Forward* promised special promotions throughout the month of May. When the fall busy season hit its stride, Jarmulowsky urged workers to "save what you can for the future. Each man and each woman who works can save some of his or her wages for a rainy day." As a convenience to workers, Jarmulowsky's bank kept its doors open until nine p.m., so no one need "stop his work and lose time during the day."[8] Leaving the noise and chaos of Canal Street, immigrants entering Jarmulowsky's bank gazed up to see the inscription "S. Jarmulowsky's Bank, Est. 1873," elegantly carved in stone, and a grand clock surrounded by rosettes and allegorical figures representing industry and commerce. The fact that the business had been around for nearly forty years must have been as reassuring as the solidity of the structure. But the two-story marble banking room, which rivaled those of established uptown banks, probably excited tenement dwellers even more.

If the Eldridge Street Synagogue two blocks to the west represented immigrant religion, and the *Forward* building two blocks to the east represented immigrant socialism, then Sender Jarmulowsky's bank symbolized both eastern European immigrant Jews' thrift and their entrée into New York capitalism. A late nineteenth-century mass-circulation guidebook advised newcomers, "Do not take a moment's rest. Run, do, work."[9] Regardless of background or occupation, immigrants worked day and night to maintain themselves and their families. In return for six days of running, doing, and working, they received a week's wages or netted a sales profit, and after paying rent, shopping for food, and purchasing stock for the cart or placing a deposit on the next contract, some of this money found its way into the bank. In this way, local banks served as an expression of immigrant ambitions and disappointments. Whether Socialist, Anarchist, Orthodox, or atheist, all immigrants worked, and many of them availed themselves of opportunities to save their money. If New York was the "Golden Door," then passbooks from Jarmulowsky's bank were the keys for many immigrant families. Immigrant banks like Jarmulowsky's point to the importance of neighborhood and ethnic economic niches that helped families of newcomers adapt to the city and that ultimately led them to become vital actors in its economy, especially in the garment trades, street commerce, and real estate. Yet as important as these neighborhood networks were, the bank also underscores the importance of the immigrant family, the basic economic unit that strategized to eke out a living in the tenement districts and negotiated the adaptation of traditions to New York.

In the 1870s, approximately 15,000 eastern European Jews arrived in New York, the majority settling in the same downtown neighborhoods—between Five Points and Kleindeutschland—where central Europeans had originally resided before moving uptown. In 1873, Sender Jarmulowsky, a Russian-born Talmudic scholar turned Hamburg banker, decided to try his luck in New York City at Canal and Mott Streets, the heart of the old Jewish section of Five Points. In 1878, Jarmulowsky moved eastward, renting an office on the southwest corner of Canal and Orchard. There he catered to many New York representatives of the 240,000 eastern European Jews who arrived in the 1880s, 391,000 who arrived in the 1890s, and 1,387,455 who arrived between 1901 and 1914. In the early years, bankers served primarily as ship ticket agents helping immigrants in America send funds, and eventually tickets, to relatives in Europe. It was extremely important that a banker inspire trust, so an early advertisement promised that Jarmulowsky's ship-ticket services were "Solid! Secure! Real!"[10] In New York, Jarmulowsky cultivated a reputation as an honest businessman, becoming well-known to families on both sides of the ocean. Within a few years, as his own sons and in-laws joined his business, Jarmulowsky assumed a paternal persona to the entire community. In 1902, an English-language account hailed him as a "patriarchal gentleman," an honorary relation to the "tailors and working girls" who constituted his clientele.[11]

Memoirs recall Jarmulowsky's role in the lives of immigrant families. Abraham Goldman's father arrived in New York from Lithuania, and his relative met him at Castle Garden and took him to the Lower East Side. The elder Goldman had earned a few dollars for some translation work he performed at Castle Garden and was anxious to send this home. Abraham remembered, "The next day Dad said he took a walk to see what New York looked like. . . . He saw a sign printed in Yiddish. It read 'Jarmulowsky Bank, Money sent to all parts of Europe.' Dad went in and sent the $15.00 he made to Mother in Neustadt."[12] This passage shows how quickly upon arrival immigrants encountered Jarmulowsky and how vital was the service he provided. Louis Lipsky recalled that Jarmulowsky helped his mother when she arrived and described the banker's cumulative impact on the "whole Jewish migration": "a simple, self-supporting, self-relieving operation with Jarmulowsky as the magician who made all the works go round."[13] By the time Jarmulowsky died in 1912, the *Tageblat* declared that "Sender Jarmulowsky was a name that was known to every Jew in the old and also in the new world. . . . His business brought him into contact with hundreds of thousands of immigrants to whom the name Jarmulowsky was the guarantee of honesty."[14] Even after his death, his name, now etched in English in Indiana limestone rather than printed on a Yiddish sign, continued for a time to preside over the first New York bank transactions of tens of thousands of immigrant tailors and working girls.

Arguably the most influential and famous of the East Side bankers, Jarmulowsky was by no means the only one. Adolf Mandel started his business in 1883. His Rivington Street bank attracted notoriety during a February 1912 run; but his neighbors vouched for his "excellent reputation," and he indeed fulfilled his assurance that their deposits were "as good as gold." Like Jarmulowsky, Mandel by then lived uptown, on East Eighty-Seventh Street. A "large owner of Bronx real estate," he continued to run his bank on the East Side, where he maintained "large financial interests."[15] A 1903 *New York Tribune*

In February 1912, immigrant depositors stormed Adolf Mandel's Rivington Street storefront, after hearing rumors that the bank had run dry. The Delancey Street Station promptly dispatched police officers to keep order while Mandel and his clerks patiently refunded depositors. (Prints and Photographs Division, Library of Congress, Washington, DC)

survey of East Side banks likewise counted the hundreds of East Side bankers, some who had deep roots in the neighborhood, others who were "bankers by the grace of having come over a steamer or two ahead of the other fellow."[16]

Bankers flourished in immigrant neighborhoods because they met critical needs of their communities. In New York, Hungarian bankers usually served Hungarian communities, Italian bankers Italian communities, and Jews Jewish communities, as the city's "more established financial institutions . . . tended to eschew immigrant neighborhoods."[17] In place of the mainstream banks, immigrants who had already succeeded as grocers, saloon keepers, and merchants started banking as a side business. They sold ship tickets to newcomers anxious to reunite with family members they had left behind in Europe, featured installment plans that made many purchases possible, watched over their patrons' savings, and offered business loans and credit to ambitious

M. & L. Jarmulowsky (dinner), ca. 1906. The extended Jarmulowsky family gathered to celebrate the opening of Meyer and Louis's branch on East Broadway. Sender is at far right. (Byron Co. Collection, Museum of the City of New York)

shopkeepers. In turn, the banks invested in real estate, spurring development of the Lower East Side and, increasingly, neighborhoods in Harlem and the Bronx. Some bankers would take funds entrusted to them to more established banking houses to collect interest, and some would "borrow" these funds for their own business needs. Overall, these immigrant banks became "reservoirs for local investment capital," enabling small entrepreneurs to access capital and also to directly invest funds in real estate.[18] Ultimately, the growth of immigrant businesses attracted the city's larger banking houses. In 1903, a *New York Tribune* article noted that the Jefferson and Corn Exchange banks, the Van Norden and Mutual Alliance trust companies, and the Federal Bank of New

York had recently opened branches on the East Side, having recognized that dealing with neighborhood resident merchants was a "profitable business."[19]

Still, the majority of immigrants patronized immigrant bankers, who fulfilled an overarching social function, uniting friends and family, dispensing news, and selling ship tickets. Consider the role that Max Kobre's Canal Street bank played in the lives of immigrants from the area surrounding Slutsk:

> When a letter arrived for one person, everyone read it. Letters were received at the address of Max Kobre's bank on Canal Street. Kobre was like an older brother to all the Slutsker *landslayt*. As with the man of wealth in a town back home, everyone deposited their money with him. We also paid Kobre weekly installments for the ship's tickets with which we ourselves had come and which we sent to relatives and family. Kobre's was the "clearing house" where we exchanged news from the entire region.[20]

In addition to exchanging news and setting newcomers on their feet, the men of Slutsk gathered at the bank to discuss work and find positions for themselves and their friends.

■ In the Tenements

Eastern European Jewish immigrants, uprooted by economic change in their home countries, came to New York seeking opportunities. Throughout eastern Europe—Russia, Austria-Hungary, Romania—industrialization had brought extreme dislocation as struggling merchants and artisans found their production of goods and services far outpaced by Western output. Overpopulation in Jewish communities compounded the economic stress, spurring migration to large cities throughout Europe and the United States. In Russia, outbreaks of pogroms in the aftermath of Tsar Alexander II's assassination in 1881 and ensuing restrictions on Jewish educational, residential, and occupational options further stimulated Jews, especially the young, to seek a better life in America. Between 1880 and 1924, two and a half million eastern European Jews came to the United States. Close to 85 percent of them came to New York City, and approximately 75 percent of those settled initially on the Lower East Side, which by 1890 "bristled with Jews." These huge waves of Jewish immigrants from Russia, Poland, the Austro-Hungarian Empire, and Romania far outnumbered the previous ones. They also came at a time of unprecedented immigration to the United States; between 1880 and 1920, America became the new home for twenty-three million immigrants. And eastern European Jews arrived intending to stay, unlike many of their immigrant contemporaries. Strikingly, between 1908 and 1924, 33.3 percent of all immigrants returned to their home countries, while only 5.2 percent of Jews returned to eastern Europe.[21] Jews also settled in New York City in larger numbers than did other immigrant groups arriving at the time.

Jewish immigrants came in family groups, increasing pressure to find jobs immediately upon arrival. Each Jewish wage earner supported 1.8 people, as compared to a non-Jewish immigrant, who supported 1.3 people. Between 1899 and 1914, women constituted 30 percent of all other immigrant groups to the United States, while among Jewish immigrants, women accounted for 44 percent. In the same time period, children under the age of fourteen made up 25 percent of Jewish immigrants, but only 11 percent of non-Jewish immigrants.[22] Often, Jewish families came as part of a chain migration, with husbands and fathers leaving first, securing a job and a place to live, and then sending funds home to bring over the rest of the family.

The Jewish East Side served as a gateway to America. In addition to Irish, German, and Italian immigrants, many Jewish immigrants met Jews from different regions or towns. While a contemporary observer might consider the Lower East Side to be one homogeneous neighborhood, simply a "Jewish ghetto," a Lower East Side resident from Hungary would have bristled at being lumped together with Russian or Polish immigrants. Indeed, a closer look at the Lower East Side, the stretch of territory bounded by Fourteenth Street, the Bowery, the East River, and Market Street, reveals multiple subethnic enclaves. Hungarian Jews clustered above Houston Street; Galician Jews in a section bounded by Houston to the north, Grand Street, to the south; Romanian and Levantine Jews between Grand and Houston, Allen and the Bowery; Russian Jews south of Grand Street. This enclave pattern recalled the one set by German-speaking immigrants—in the very same sections just a decade earlier, sons and daughters of Hesse-Darmstadt, Bavaria, and Wurtemburg found favorite blocks. These disparate backgrounds shaped their encounter with New York and the Lower East Side—they sought out former neighbors (*landslayt*) to share distinctive foodways and religious customs and to adapt old-world networks to their new geography. Of these various streams of Jews, Levantine Jews, those arriving from Greece and Syria, appeared most distinct, their difference reinforced by their language, Ladino, a Spanish-based Jewish language. Most of the eastern Europeans spoke Yiddish.[23]

But though a Sephardic Jew might seek a particular block on Allen Street, while a Galician settled on Ridge Street or a Russian on Madison Street, they all became denizens of the tenement. For the many immigrants who arrived as children, and for those children born to immigrant parents in America, the tenement community offered more of an identity marker than did an increasingly remote Romanian, Greek, or Russian town. The tenement provided the stage for immigrants' first encounter with American daily life, a remarkably consistent stage over the twenty-five blocks of Manhattan's Lower East Side, where three hundred thousand Jews lived by 1893.[24] By 1900, over 90 percent of Jews lived in tenement rooms. Tenements even blanketed many areas of secondary settlement, including Harlem and Brownsville, where 88 percent of the dwelling units were in tenements by 1904.[25]

Though tenements came to be synonymous with overcrowded and unsanitary conditions, the first tenement apartments were built in the 1860s and 1870s as a solution to the overcrowding of available housing stock. Irish and German immigrants had started then to subdivide one-family homes, stringing up sheets to serve as "walls." The tall tenements, with five or six floors of apartments, offered each family its own space and kitchen and had the overall effect of dispelling the crowdedness of subdivided two-story homes. Imagine: in the same lot that uncomfortably held three families now stood a commodious and well-partitioned space for twenty families and two stores! But the aggregate growth of these tenements over a block severely restricted light and air. Tenement buildings filled 90 percent of the lot, leaving no room for side windows, and each new tenement further strengthened the barrier between tenement dwellers and sun and sky. While front rooms of the front apartments looked onto the street, and front rooms of rear apartments overlooked a rear yard, all interior rooms lacked direct light and air.

Of course, the tenements did not grow on their own; landlords, many of them immigrants themselves who had accumulated some savings, bought narrow lots as investments and possible stepping-stones to prosperity. They hoped to reap as much profit as possible, and that meant creating as many rental units as feasible. Incoming immigrants provided the incentive to build, while the city did little to regulate this construction. Until 1879, very few standards applied to tenements. With each passing year, the housing stock deteriorated, as increasing numbers of immigrants created ever more crowding. In one tenement, apartments that held an average of three to four people in 1870 accommodated an average of six in 1900 and often as many as ten or twelve. This crowdedness, in tandem with a lack of regulation, created the most infamous housing stock in the nation's history. In 1878, the *Plumbing and Sanitary Engineer* journal's competition for a model housing type yielded Robert Ware's "dumbbell tenement," so named because the buildings' shape resembled a dumbbell, narrow in the middle and wider at each end. When two such tenements adjoined, their narrow waists formed a shaft designed to let in light and air to interior rooms. Though this model became a law in 1879, its standards did not apply to the majority of tenements already standing. Even when it governed new plans, the resulting air shafts were too small to address effectively the ventilation issues and, in fact, could be faulted as combustible garbage receptacles.[26]

Before the 1901 Tenement Housing Law, a typical tenement hallway was dark, because wooden doors at both back and front blocked out the sun and no facility for gas lighting existed. One immigrant who arrived in 1880 recalled that in the first tenement he entered, the staircase was so dark that he had "to feel his way up."[27] In fact, at 97 Orchard, windows were cut into the walls of apartments next to hallways so that the unlit hallways could leech light from the apartments. Most immigrants lived in 325-square-foot apartments. They lacked indoor plumbing. Water needed for laundry, cleaning, and cooking had to be fetched from a faucet in the rear yard, which also housed laundry lines and privies. Bare-boned tenement kitchens had room for a coal—and later gas—stove and a sink (but no running water). There was no refrigeration at this point and very little storage, which necessitated daily shopping. Privacy was virtually impossible. Despite the hallways' darkness, a tour through the tenement halls must have been an exercise in sensory overload: the aroma of a neighbor's cooking, the screeching of toddlers, odors of chamber pots, the brisk footsteps of a contractor bringing in the next bundle of clothes to be assembled, a Yiddish conversation among third-floor housewives, echoes of children's street games from street or roof, and the never-ending hum of sewing machines.

The 1901 Tenement Housing Law, launched by Lawrence Veiller and Robert de Forest, the first comprehensive and retroactive law, led to radical restructuring of preexisting tenements, as well as molding the shape of those to come. Landlords of preexisting tenements now had to improve lighting in public hallways and individual apartments and to provide one toilet per two families. This often required adding skylights, installing gas lighting fixtures, and stealing space from bedrooms to create room for toilets and air shafts. This law finally had teeth, as it established the Tenement House Department to ensure that landlords complied with these standards.[28] But many of these changes came too late to affect the first generations of immigrants, who had by the turn of the century moved to other neighborhoods. Those who remained now had running water, indoor toilets, and perhaps more light and air. But these features did not reduce overcrowding or poverty.

Upon first glance, immigrants often registered dissatisfaction with their tenement apartments. Bessie Mischaloff and her husband and young child arrived in New York in the late summer of 1914. They initially stayed with her parents on Rutgers Place: "The heat was terrible. The rooms were small, and there were ten of us altogether. So people slept on the floor and on the fire escape." The crowdedness on Rutgers Place propelled Bessie and her husband to hunt for a place the very next day. They found two rooms on Madison Street, borrowed money from a brother-in-law for the deposit, and rented a pushcart to bring over their belongings. When they arrived, the janitor took them first to the basement, where she sold them beds and a carriage that previous tenants had left behind. Once settled, Bessie surveyed the room: "My heart sank. The walls were painted dark green and spread gloom." Yet she roused herself from these thoughts: "But I did not have that much time to think. I immediately went to work on the children."[29] Indeed, tenement conditions left little time and space for reflection; whatever one's initial reaction, one was overwhelmed with figuring out how to manage a household and raise a family.

But with time, even crowded tenement apartments sometimes reflected immigrant aspirations for respectability and material comfort. The right kinds of furniture set in rooms differentiated by function marked a family as having middle-class standards, if not income. Reformers from outside the neighborhood preached a "gospel of simplicity," seeking to convince immigrant housewives of the aesthetic and practical virtues of mission-style furniture with "good, honest, straight lines," muslin curtains, uncluttered shelves, whitewashed walls, and plain wood floors. But immigrant householders had other ideas, preferring "colored wallpaper, brightly patterned linoleum, and yards of lace and fabric trimmings." Above all, they favored heavy, plushly upholstered furniture.[30] Memoirist Aaron Domnitz recalled a cloak maker's apartment on Cherry Street in which he lived as one of three boarders. Although the family slept in one room, two boarders in another, and the third boarder in the kitchen, "one room, the parlor was not used. Large pieces of furniture were set up in that room: a big round table with chairs and a cabinet with a mirror. In the cabinet stood a platter with a set of six large glasses with colored edges that they never used. On the table was a large lamp that they never turned on. One could barely push one's way through all the furniture set up in there. That was the fashion in those days in immigrant homes."[31]

Merchants in the immigrant neighborhood, such as Deutsch Brothers on Avenue A or Daniel Jones on Orchard Street, catered to these tastes, advertising their installment plans in the Yiddish press. As Jews moved to more commodious dwellings uptown or in the Bronx or Brooklyn, they brought their tastes in furniture with them: "Wherever there is an upholstered surface, it is tufted; wherever a wooden one, it is carved into sinuous outlines and adorned with gilded leather."[32]

Another important acquisition for a family with ambition was a piano. A "piano in the parlor" became the sign of a rise to "the height of social respectability," a rise made possible by the Steinway company's development of an affordable and less space-consuming upright model, and installment plans offered by such merchants as Joseph Spector, who opened the first piano store on the Lower East Side at Grand and Orchard Streets. The piano served a number of purposes, all of them related to enhancing social status. Yiddish theater composer and conductor Joseph Rumshinsky recalled giving piano lessons in his youth: "I got busy, busy, busy. . . . From ten in the morning until three in the afternoon I taught young women, recently married, who wanted to show their husbands they play the piano. From three until seven I taught schoolchildren. And from then until ten or eleven in the evening I taught shop girls and office girls who wanted to get married."[33] The piano also opened the Jewish home to the influence of popular culture through the purchase of sheet music, not only of Yiddish songs such as those published by the Hebrew Publishing Company but also of those emanating from Tin Pan Alley for general audiences.

But some basic adaptations took place in the tenement world even before the acquisition of a piano or tufted furniture. One of the first things an immigrant did after arriving in the neighborhood was to transform him- or herself from a greenhorn into an American via the acquisition of a new suit of clothes, often with the aid of already-settled friends or family. Having completed the transition, the new American then proceeded to a photographer's studio to have his or her picture taken to send to relatives still in Europe. American goods were presumed to be superior to those of Europe, quite apart from the higher social status they implied. Aaron Domnitz recalled that *landslayt*, natives of the same hometown, "devoted" themselves to the greenhorn. When an immigrant arrived, Domnitz wrote, "we clothed him: *Landslayt* would go with the greenhorn to Canal Street to purchase a suit, a hat, and shoes. Everything had to be American. Clothes from home were defective, even if they were of good quality and well sewn. Going to the stores with the greenhorn was a joyful procedure, like a Jew back home picking out an *esrog* [citron used for the holiday of Sukkot]." Jews were not the only immigrants to reinvent themselves through dress, and of course, not all immigrant Jews cared for American fashion. But whether or not Jews were "unusually attuned" to American fashion, some contemporary observers thought that fashionableness marked the Jewish neighborhoods: The "wide sidewalks" of Grand Street, wrote a reporter for the *New York Tribune* in the summer of 1900, "show more fashion to the square foot on a Sunday than any other part of the city."[34]

Just as new clothes promised to Americanize the immigrant, they also held open the promise of upward social mobility, symbolizing America's open and apparently egalitarian class structure. New York Jews, of course, had already played, and were continuing to play, an important role in the revolution in garment production that made possible the democratization of clothing. With the advent and refinement of mass production, middle- and even working-class people could lay claim to apparel that previously had been within reach only of the upper class. Some observers simply argued that with a keen eye, one could still distinguish clearly among the classes. In 1904, one wrote acidly,

> Purposeless imitation! . . . The Fourth Avenue shop says to the Fourth Avenue buyer: "Behold my clever imitation. For less than you could pay in a Fifth Avenue shop, I can give you a perfect imitation. You would not be behind the styles, I know. I can make you look like a real peacock." The Third Avenue shop scans the windows of the Fourth Avenue shop and returns the same to its customers. The First Avenue shop has a still cheaper imitation, and in Hester Street, on the pushcarts, ghosts of the real are "Going, going, going" for thirty-nine cents.

Actually, since the working-class women wearing the "imitations" were often the same workers who had made the originals, the likeness was apt to be more exact than this snobbish writer wanted to admit. Moreover, the immigrants measured the transformation wrought by the clothes against the norms of the society they had come from, where lower-class women wore shawls and only ladies wore hats. Here, it seemed, virtually any woman could don a hat and become a "lady," while her male counterpart became a "gentleman." Self-reinvention—whether by means of a new suit of clothes or a piano—was another promise held open by America and New York.[35]

■ Work

Neighborhood connections were also indispensable for finding jobs. While Jews arrived with more urban skills than other immigrant groups had, they still needed to adapt them to American industrial conditions. They could not simply be transferred. Charles Bernheimer's survey of 333 Lower East Side wage earners in 1909 found that two-thirds of arriving immigrants secured jobs in occupations different from those they had held in Europe.[36] Thus, social connections in New York were extremely important, and these could be rekindled in the immigrant neighborhoods and tenements.[37]

Landslayt helped newcomers find jobs. As Aaron Domnitz recalled, "We knew which landsman was looking for a new place and who could take someone in to work. To take someone into your shop was considered the greatest good deed, almost the only good deed, that the greenhorns performed in their new country. We mainly devoted ourselves to greenhorns." Domnitz himself was aided by his *landslayt* in securing a position. He initially tried to find work as a plumber and then in the metal trades. But when these options did not pan out, he resigned himself to the overwhelming pressure to enter the garment industry: "I got tired of constantly changing jobs and looking for work. I felt the need to have steady employment with a more or less secure income. My relatives and *landslayt* lectured me that it was now time to settle down and do what everyone else did—become a tailor. I became a tailor."[38]

Indeed, just as immigrants found their way to an immigrant bank, whether for a steamship ticket or to open an account, most immigrants secured their first employment in the needle trades. By the first decade of the twentieth century, observers noted that the garment industry employed 53 percent of Russian-Jewish men and 77 percent of Russian-Jewish women workers. Though many immigrants claimed to have been tailors or seamstresses in Europe, their former craft skills did not necessarily translate into job readiness for New York shops, due to garment industry mechanization and its breakdown of tasks. On the other hand, garment jobs in the United States could be learned fairly quickly, and many Jewish immigrants became "Columbus tailors," discovering the needle in America. So thoroughly did this industry employ the Jews that it caused one observer to declare, "The needle has saved the Russian Jew in New York."[39]

Weaving through the pushcarts, boys carried bundles of fabric already cut to pattern to tenement contractor shops throughout the neighborhood, where they were assembled into garments. The contracting system prevailed in the garment industry, relieving manufacturers of the responsibility of managing the workforce. Manufacturers hired skilled workers to design the garments and cut the cloth, which they then farmed out for assembly to an army of small contractors. The contractors hired the sewing-machine operators, pressers, basters, and finishers and organized the assembly of the garments, which were then returned to the manufacturer. This flexible system expanded during the busy season and contracted during slack season, leaving both workers and contractors bereft of work and pay but insulating manufacturers from any wasted expenditures for overhead and wages. Although the contracting system put relentless downward pressure on wages and conditions, it also allowed workers to become "bosses" by opening their own shops with little capital. All that was needed to do so were a sewing machine, a pressing table, and a stove for the irons. Sewing machines could be purchased on installment, and one could use a tenement apartment for space. Immigrants also needed a strong will to compete. At the turn of the century, a third of all contractors went out of business each year.[40]

These tenement sweatshops became infamous for their crowded and unsanitary conditions. Laborers worked up to fourteen hours a day during the busy seasons, and the stove, needed to heat the irons, operated even throughout torrid summers. Operators sat by the windows for the sunlight, but in winter this weakened by late afternoon, straining their eyesight. One tenement at 7 Ludlow Street held several small factories:

The first shop that we entered consisted of a small room with two small grimy windows, and another room that had once been a bedroom. It was without windows, having only grates that looked out into the dark hallway. Several sewing machines stood in this small room. It was so crowded there that we could barely reach the operators, who sat closely together. Under the mantelpiece was a fireplace, where a lit oven was covered with pressing irons. Several girls sat working on the floor.[41]

The term *sweatshop* applied not because of the heat but rather because of the manner in which manufacturers "sweated" profit from contractors, who in turn sweated profit from laborers. Given the close margins of this system, and the fact that contractors received from manufacturers a fixed price per garment that was often very low, contractors' only chance of yielding a profit came from "sweating" as much work out of their workers for as little wages as possible. Though the garment industry offered opportunity for mobility, it also produced setbacks: "Today's workers might become tomorrow's bosses and to-day's bosses could easily fall back into the ranks of the proletariat."[42]

After the turn of the century, the growing availability of electric sewing machines, coupled with increasing regulation of tenement factories, stimulated manufacturers to relocate to more spacious uptown lofts with electricity. Between 1901 and 1911, eight hundred new loft buildings rose in Manhattan, providing ample space for garment shops.[43] Compared to tenement sweatshops, these factories provided high ceilings and sun-washed spaces. They proved especially appealing to young women—often teenagers—who entered the garment industry and preferred these more modern spaces to cramped tenement sweatshops. But although physical conditions improved, exploitation continued to characterize the work.

Jewish immigrants' "restless ambition" propelled them to take advantage of the opportunities for advancement presented by the city. Some improved their status by remaining in the garment industry as contractors or even as manufacturers. But as one observer noted, "Every year large numbers [of Jews] desert the clothing industry to go into such occupations as small shopkeepers, insurance agents and clerks." By the turn of the twentieth century, more and more Jews were entering the professions, though as a percentage, this number remained small until the 1920s. Most immigrants exited the working class by opening their own small businesses.[44]

According to one survey of the Lower East Side, 23.5 percent of the Jewish immigrants worked as "merchants," half of whom, in turn, were pushcart peddlers and the other half proprietors of their own stores.[45] If a newly arrived immigrant did not enter the garment shop, he or she often began as a pushcart peddler; one needed only ten cents to rent a cart and often could borrow a few dollars for the initial inventory. A peddler did not need to know English. In 1900, the city counted twenty-five thousand pushcart peddlers, many of them Jewish immigrants.[46] While Italian and Greek peddlers were known for their fruits and vegetables, Jewish peddlers made their mark on the city by selling nonfood items as well. One could find Jewish peddlers selling apples and cabbages on Hester Street; one could also find them offering eyeglasses, shoes, fabrics, clothing, toys, books, and hardware at prices that attracted shoppers from beyond the East Side. A city survey of seven hundred vendors selling nonfood items found that 95 percent were Jews.[47] A 1906 survey reported that peddlers earned fifteen to eighteen dollars a week, saving enough to open their own stores within five or six years.[48]

Indeed, many peddlers harbored the ambition to become a shopkeeper. With savings and perhaps a loan, a peddler might open up a store. Minnie Goldstein's father, for example, left Warsaw for New York, where his attempts to make a living as a cobbler failed. He changed course: "He took a wooden box, bought some baby shoes, took up position on Hester Street, and sold shoes at a profit of five or ten cents a pair. . . . Before long the women of Hester Street found out that my father would sell them a pair of shoes for thirty cents, while they had to pay fifty cents in a store for the same pair of shoes. Well, he started to earn some money, so he rented a small store."[49]

Storekeepers curried respect; they were their own bosses. One immigrant, Avraham Gollup, encouraged his teenage daughter, Rahel, to marry a young man who helped his mother run a grocery store: "He is a nice quiet man and the main thing, he is not a wage earner. The smallest businessman is worth ten workingmen." Despite this relative prestige, shopkeepers often worked themselves—and their families—as hard as contractors drove their workers. The young suitor whom Abraham Gollup so admired for his independence actually lived in a few small, unfurnished rooms behind the grocery, and the arrival of a customer at any time dispelled any notions of privacy.[50] Likewise, when Minnie Goldstein's father sent for her and her mother, Minnie was immediately put to work: "I worked from very early to late at night with my mother at home and my father in the store. And there was no talk at all of sending me to school."[51] Indeed, family members played essential roles in the management of stores. When Rose Radin's father, Louis Minsky, opened a store on Orchard Street, he sent for his wife and two children. His daughter recalled, "My mother would go into the store and sell. . . . And she had a way with her, a sweet way, and she sold, and then my father would come back and take over and she would go inside to take care of her children. . . . And she . . . took care of the store, took care of the children and she was a great help to him."[52]

Whatever job a Jewish immigrant took, when reunited with his family, an immigrant became saddled with additional expenditures. Simply put, the dollar went further in Russia than it did in New York, and the need to support a wife and children in the tenements strained resources. As Samuel Joseph explained in 1914, "Jewish immigrants are burdened with a far greater number of dependents than any other immigrant people." Between 1899 and 1910, because of the high proportion of women and children, 45 percent of Jews arriving in the United States listed "no occupation."[53] Jewish immigrants negotiated this responsibility, in part, by taking in boarders and relying on the wages of their immigrant children.[54] The 1910 U.S. Immigration Commission found that more than any other immigrant group, Russian Jews depended on their children's income. Whereas foreign-born families in general derived 21.1 percent of their household income from children's work, Russian-Jewish children brought in 30.7 percent of the household income. While mothers worked in the home or within the family businesses, fathers and the eldest children earned wages, and younger children attended school. Family members depended on one another as they formed an economic unit.[55]

Sociologist and settlement-house worker Charles Bernheimer's investigation of 225 families on one block in 1907 found that families relied on teenage children for between 44 and 69 percent of their total income. So crucial was the presence of multiple wage earners that in the absence of the traditional family, economic imperatives forced immigrants to forge new sorts of family arrangements. In one apartment, Bernheimer found a woman working as a pants finisher, earning $150 a year. Since rent typically was $10 a month, and the woman had an eleven-year-old daughter to support, she took in a seventeen-year-old cousin, who earned $325 a year as a dressmaker.[56] Moreover, the necessity to contribute to the family economy affected children's long-term life prospects. Before World War I, Jewish immigrant children generally achieved only an eighth-grade education, if that. The age at which students left school correlated directly with the age minors could obtain working papers. Thus, in the 1890s, twelve-year-olds could obtain working papers, and so the sharpest decline in school enrollment in the Lower East Side school district happened at that age. By 1903, when the age for working papers rose to fourteen, the steepest decline in enrollments happened at that corresponding grade. A full 37 percent of working papers issued in New York City in 1914–15 went to Jewish teenagers.[57] As Samuel Chotzinoff recalled, "Of course, everyone over fourteen years of age was employed in gainful labor. Not before the age of fourteen could one obtain one's working papers."[58]

Keeping boarders also provided crucial income for many Jewish families. In 1910, 43 percent of Jewish homes had boarders.[59] This mutually beneficial situation enabled a boarder to pay several dollars a week for room and board and not be bothered with housecleaning or food preparation, while a family earned extra income. For example, when Ben Reisman came to New York in 1896, he stayed with landsmen Yitskhok and Khanetshe Hammer. Yitskhok ran a soda stand on Essex Street, which apparently was not very profitable: "So they kept boarders. Six of us slept in a room. We paid three dollars a month with laundry, and one dollar thirty a week for supper." Aaron Domnitz's boarding situation included a landlady who did laundry and made nightly meals: "The main meal in the evening always consisted of the same courses, namely a piece of herring or chopped liver, pea or barley soup, cooked meat, and cooked plums, always accompanied by a pickle and a glass of beer." Even more prosperous families kept boarders. Domnitz's cousin earned fifteen dollars a week and even had a front room with fine furniture. But still, the cousin, wife, and two children slept in one bedroom, while two boarders shared a bed in the second and yet a third slept in the kitchen.[60]

The labor of tenement wives and mothers generated the income from boarders. Women handled the cash transactions and work involved in maintaining a boarder. Abraham Kokofsky's recollections of boarder management identified his mother as the decision-maker. Their Clinton Street tenement accommodated Abraham, his brother, and his father in one room and his mother and sisters in another; a third room housed boarders: "I'm sure that the only reason my mother was willing to give up that bedroom [was] because without that money she couldn't feed the family and pay rent."[61] Keeping boarders was thus closely bound to women's role as chief manager of household funds. This work demanded physical strength and keen strategizing. According to Harry Golden, with regard to the household and the renting of apartments, "Mother made all the decisions."[62] Women shopped daily and lugged water for cleaning, cooking, and laundry up and downstairs. This work also involved constant social networking. Boarders, almost by definition, were transitory and would have to be replaced; rent, however, was not transitory.

■ Remembering the Sabbath and Keeping Kosher

Eastern European Jewish immigrants made their homes in Jewish neighbor-hoods and often rented their tenement rooms from Jewish landlords and pur-chased their meat from kosher butchers and their vegetables from Jewish ped-dlers. They often worked for a Jewish boss and deposited money with a Jewish banker. Their children attended public schools with other Jewish children. Yet American conditions challenged many time-bound traditions. Sabbath obser-vance, for one, continued to be a contentious issue for the eastern Europeans, as it had been for the central Europeans earlier.

The threat to the Sabbath came from several directions. After the turn of the century, finding jobs that allowed for Saturday rest became increasingly difficult due to the garment industry's shift to the factory away from the neigh-borhood shop. As one garment worker recalled,

> [The garment trade] had started to migrate to new buildings uptown from the small, neglected little shops on Cherry, Forsythe, and Lispenard Streets. The migration brought with it small social transformations. In the old shops, people worked on Sundays. In the new ones, where the building had to be closed on Sundays, people started to work on the Sabbath. This caused something of a stir among workers and bosses alike.[63]

Thus, a changing factory system and the move to uptown factories greatly de-creased chances of finding a job in a Sabbath-observant garment shop.[64]

Sabbath observance came with a cost. Wage-earning Sabbath observ-ers worked in businesses that sold religious goods, such as sacramental wine stores or matzo factories, as well as Orthodox newspapers such as the *Morgen zhurnal* and the *Yidishe tageblat*.[65] Sabbath observers in the building industry could find work with Harry Fischel, who not only offered his laborers Satur-days off but also paid them for a half day.[66] Many memoirs, however, attest to the meager pay the more marginal jobs offered. Harry Golden recalled,

> The ragpickers and the peddlers who lived "in the back" were self-employed because they believed that was the only way they could observe the Sabbath which began on Friday afternoon. If they entered the open society they were afraid their employers would not forgive the necessary hours from sundown Friday until sundown Saturday, to say nothing of at least a dozen other observances during the year.[67]

Samuel Chotzinoff recalled how his father, a Hebrew teacher, hardly earned any money. The family managed to buy food for the Sabbath only because Samuel's three sisters worked in cigar factories while his brother worked as an assistant presser.[68]

One solution was to open one's own business and therefore to be able to set one's own hours. Anne Goldman surmised that her father started his own grocery store "as soon as he could because he was a strict Sabbath observer and would not have gone to work in a shop where you had to work on Saturday at that time."[69] But storekeepers still contended with unpredictable enforcement of Sunday blue laws that prohibited, or at least severely circumscribed, Sunday business. Enforcement seemed to depend on the whim of individual mayors or police commissioners. In some years, city officials strenuously enforced the laws; in other years, they did not. When Mayor Seth Low assumed office on a reform platform in 1902, his officials stringently enforced Sunday laws, leading one Canal Street storekeeper to exclaim, "They have spoiled the best day of business for us!"[70]

To rationalize working on the Sabbath, some immigrant Jews applied the concept of *pikuakh nefesh*—the understanding that one could break the Sabbath to save a life—to Sabbath work for family support. One Orthodox rabbi, Jacob Bauman, even wrote a responsum that used *pikuakh nefesh* to excuse Sabbath desecration by immigrant Jews who worked to support their families.[71] While most rabbis rejected this interpretation, the immigrant community in America accepted it. When Livia Garfinkel asked her Orthodox father how he could work on Saturday, he responded, "We are not in Jerusalem, for survival we are permitted."[72] So strong was the necessity to work on the Sabbath to feed one's family that it could be justified and excused in this way.

Another kind of threat came from within the community. Although the Sabbath problem was a labor problem, few labor leaders, many of whom adhered to radical secularist ideologies, cared about the Sabbath. Some radical organizers actively railed against religion, going so far in the 1890s as to hold annual Yom Kippur balls, raucous celebrations heaping scorn on traditional piety. The Socialist-led fraternal organization the Workmen's Circle forbade religious officials from holding office and regularly scheduled lectures to counter religion's power. But by the turn of the twentieth century, even such Socialist organs as the Workmen's Circle and the *Jewish Daily Forward* softened their stance on religion, in part because they embraced tolerance as an American principle and in part out of a practical recognition that the vast majority of immigrants fell somewhere along the middle of a spectrum that stretched from free thought to traditional Judaism, exhibiting interest and practices in both secular ideas and religious customs.[73]

In response, uptown Orthodox rabbis Bernard Drachman and Henry Pereira Mendes joined forces in 1905 with a downtown Jewish communal leader, J. H. Luria, to reorganize the Sabbath Association, an organization that aimed to encourage Sabbath observance and to counter the economic currents that militated against it. The organization strove diligently and creatively to address economic and political factors that made Sabbath observance difficult, negotiating with manufacturers to let workers stay home Saturday, organizing a boycott of bakeries that baked bread on Saturdays, opening an employment bureau to match Sabbath observers with sympathetic employers, and lobbying Police Commissioner Theodore Bingham for laxer enforcement of Sunday blue laws. Drachman also organized trips to Albany to persuade lawmakers to amend the blue laws permanently. Yet these efforts made little impact.[74] In 1913, the Kehillah, the Jewish Community of New York, reported that 60 percent of Jewish Lower East Side stores remained open on Saturday.[75] Drachman's employment agency found that the demand for Sabbath-observant positions far outweighed jobs available.[76]

Despite all the difficulties, the Sabbath left a mark on Jewish neighborhoods and homes, in large part due to the labor of the neighborhood women. Beginning on Thursday nights and accelerating on Friday mornings, Jews poured onto the streets for heated rounds of shopping and bargaining. A *New York Times* reporter advised readers, "Step off a Third Avenue car at the corner of Hester Street and the Bowery some Friday morning and walk east along the former street. I say 'Friday morning' because the market, striking and characteristic of the ghetto and its life, is held on that day. This is done so that an ample store of eatables may be laid in for *Shabbes* (The Jewish Sabbath) on the morrow."[77] Even the tenements dressed for the Sabbath: "On Friday afternoons the facades of many of the tenements were almost obscured by pillows and blankets being freshened, in conjunction with other pre-Sabbath sprucing measures."[78] In 1902, a reporter from the *Outlook* wrote, "In the Ghetto, Friday, the day before the Sabbath, is a day of agitation, of scrubbing, cooking, baking."[79] One contemporary observer, a reporter of *Century Magazine*, in attempting to depict the woeful conditions of the tenement apartments, conceded that Sabbath preparations improved the "interior rooms that would be more filthy than they are but for the Sabbath."[80] Settlement-house and social workers reported how a flurry of street activity on Thursday and Friday transformed the homes. A University Settlement Society worker concerned about the haphazard serving of meals in a working family household acknowledged how Friday night was an important exception: "Great preparations are generally made for the Sabbath menu, which is in most cases the only day when meals are taken in degree of regularity."[81] During the week, Abraham Kokofsky's family never ate meals together; the fact that they all held different jobs and would come home at various times made it impossible to do so. Friday, however, the family ate dinner together.[82]

That families could create such a distinct and meaningful Sabbath atmosphere in spite of contemporary currents testifies to their agency and continued respect for the Sabbath. Anne Goldman, who grew up on East Eighth Street, recalled how Saturday restricted children's activities: "We were not permitted to do anything that was not traditional on Saturday, and our outlet was to go to the library and read."[83] Reading was a central part of the Sabbath for many immigrant children; Helen Rosenfield recalled, "I went to the library on Friday afternoon—all my sisters took out books. That's all we did—we read books on Saturday 'cause we never went to a movie on Saturday."[84] Many children of immigrants remembered how Friday night marked the end of gaslight and recalled how dependence on candlelight affected their Sabbath: "When it came to be before candlelighting, we put out the light and we sat by candlelight. And when the candles burned out, we had to go to sleep because you couldn't read and there wasn't anything you could do."[85]

Closely related to the question of Sabbath observance was the issue of adherence to the dietary laws, or *kashrut*. The arrival of millions of eastern European Jews created a large market for kosher goods, and many companies, whether owned by Jews or non-Jews, began to offer kosher products. As early as 1900, food manufacturers began to target Jewish consumers with advertisements explicitly touting their products as kosher. Some companies, such as Gellis, Horowitz-Margareten, Rokeach, and Hebrew National, were founded by immigrant Jews and catered mainly to a kosher market. They added rabbinic seals of approval to their packages, testifying to their ritual purity. Soon national brands such as Quaker Oats, Babbit's cleanser, Borden's Condensed

Milk, Uneeda Biscuits, and many products from General Foods and Heinz 57 Varieties carried rabbinic seals as well.[86]

Just as immigrant housewives worked to bring the Sabbath to the tenements, so too did they fight to keep the cost of kosher meat affordable. In May 1902, when the price of kosher meat rose from twelve to eighteen cents a pound, women proclaimed a boycott, battling with butchers, uncooperative consumers, and police for control of the Jewish streets, first on the Lower East Side and later in Harlem, Brooklyn, and the Bronx. On May 15, thousands of women "streamed through the streets of the Lower East Side, breaking into butcher shops, flinging meat into the streets and declaring a boycott." The rioters, termed "strikers" in the Yiddish press, attacked customers of those kosher butchers who remained open, seizing and destroying their purchased meat. "Women were pushed and hustled about [by the police], thrown to the pavement, . . . and trampled upon," reported the *New York Herald*. Some seventy women and fifteen men were brought to court, charged with disorderly conduct.[87]

Over the next several days, mass meetings were held, and the Ladies' Anti-Beef Trust Association formed. Women canvassed the Jewish neighborhoods and visited synagogues across the city to gather support for their cause. The Socialist sector backed the movement, but so did a coalition of synagogues, mutual aid societies, hometown associations, and unions, headed by David Blaustein of the Educational Alliance. Orthodox leaders voiced their approval, as did even retail butchers, who hoped to deflect attention to the wholesalers. Taking advantage of a rift in the leadership in the Ladies' Association, male supporters created the Allied Conference for Cheap Kosher Meat and seized control of the boycott, which finally came to an end on June 5 with a negotiated (but, as it turned out, temporary) reduction of the wholesale price of kosher meat. Although only temporarily successful, the boycott showed that immigrant women had adopted organizing methods from the labor movement to maintain their access to kosher meat, and it also demonstrated the power of dense Jewish neighborhood networks.

In later years, it became easier to keep kosher. But a second, contradictory, trend set in at the same time. Fewer and fewer Jews kept strictly kosher, though they might prefer Jewish-style dishes and adopt stricter standards at holiday times. Between 1914 and 1924, consumption of kosher meat in New York City fell by 25 to 30 percent. At the same time, many Jews transferred their previous concern for ritual purity to an interest in high sanitary standards in processed foods. Advertisers soon recognized the implicit equation, and as early as 1912 Borden's adopted the slogan "Pure Means Kosher—Kosher Means Pure." By the 1920s, many Jews had abandoned *kashrut* altogether, embracing instead a modern preference for recognizable brands of packaged goods with reliably predictable quality.[88]

▪ Mobility

In 1920, Jarmulowsky's bank was sold at a bankruptcy auction, a victim of a 1917 run on the bank and the mismanagement of his sons, who had taken over the business upon his death.[89] This time when the crowds arrived, the sons could not even come close to paying the one hundred cents on the dollar as their father had done so efficiently. By 1920, the majority of New York's Jews banked in the boroughs or in Harlem, a subway ride away from the once-bustling Lower East Side. Banks like Jarmulowsky's helped spark these neighborhoods' growth by fostering real estate development in Harlem, Brooklyn, and the Bronx. Throughout New York, immigrants invested in new neighborhoods by building tenements. On the Lower East side, Jewish names accounted for 9.2 percent of property owners in 1860; however, in 1900, they accounted for 62.8 percent.[90]

By the turn of the century, Jews had also begun to transform other parts of the city, as builders, landlords, and tenants. Jewish real estate speculators and builders filled in open spaces with tenements and tore down individual houses to erect apartment blocs. *Forward* editor Abraham Cahan recalled how in the 1890s Jewish real estate operators did business in cafes and restaurants:

> There was a fever of real estate speculation. Lots, completed buildings and half-completed buildings were bought and sold. Anyone who had even a couple hundred dollars took to real estate. In the Jewish quarters, the fever overtook quite a few of our immigrants. Sitting over a bowl of soup or a glass of tea in a restaurant, they would buy and sell lots or five-story buildings, or a written commitment to make such a deal. Brokers took commissions. Someone who put down a deposit and secured a contract might have sold the contract to someone else and made a couple thousand dollars profit before he ever finished the glass of tea.[91]

The tenement real estate market's hierarchy paralleled that of the garment industry—both had layers of investors and workers, and with so many investors and middlemen seeking returns, tenants suffered just as sweatshop workers did. While both investments offered opportunity for people with relatively small amounts of capital, both posed tremendous risks and challenges. In the working-class Jewish neighborhoods, landlords typically employed lessees to manage the property. While more established, uptown Jews bought large parcels of land along planned subway routes, they then divided them and sold them in lots to smaller investors, who in turn sold them to builders, often downtown Russian Jews with loans from immigrant bankers. The builders quickly erected tenements, which they often sold to purchasers, who in turn sought out lessees to collect rent and attend to maintenance. The lessees' only hope of making some kind of profit was to raise rent and spend very little on repairs.[92]

More broadly, tenement construction along subway routes helped to create new working-class neighborhoods accessible to Lower East Siders. Almost as soon as the neighborhood started to make a name for itself—indeed, the term *Jewish Lower East Side* first appeared around 1905—it began to diminish in importance, as satellite or secondary neighborhoods grew. In 1892, the Lower East Side hosted 75 percent of the city's Jews. But the expansion of the elevated railroads, the opening of the East River bridges (Brooklyn Bridge in 1883, Williamsburg Bridge in 1903, and Manhattan Bridge in 1909), and construction of the subway system in 1904 led to the growth of Jewish neighborhoods in Central Harlem, Brownsville, Williamsburg, and, later, additional neighborhoods in Brooklyn and the Bronx. By 1903, the Jewish Lower East Side was home to only 50 percent of the city's Jews, and by 1916 only 25 percent.[93]

In the 1920s, the Lower East Side's Jewish population declined by 160,000, leaving behind a population of 100,000.[94] Yet the neighborhood still proved to be an anchor. In the 1920s and 1930s, 39 percent of the Lower East Side's residents were Jewish, but 75 percent of the businesses were owned by Jews. In fact, the commercial vitality of the neighborhood actually increased with the widening of streets and better transportation connections to the rest of Manhattan and Brooklyn. Those who had moved away continued to return to the Lower East Side to shop and to dine. Much in the same way that Philip Cowen remembers how his father returned to Mulberry Street and the Chrystie Street synagogue for religious goods or in the same way that Harris Aaronson left

Union Square for Attorney Street to distribute matzos, communal affection and responsibility bound New York Jews to the Lower East Side. Communal organizations continued to flourish, as did the array of Yiddish newspapers.

Meanwhile, new neighborhoods began to take on a Jewish caste. This was apparent not only in the stores and restaurants along the new shopping streets but in the very shape of local buildings. Despite all the speculation and subcontracting, the new buildings proved attractive to those who were looking to leave the Lower East Side. Cahan recalled that in the new Jewish sections of East Harlem, apartments had all the "latest improvements," including bathrooms with porcelain tubs, electric lights and buzzer systems, hot and cold running water, dumbwaiters, and, especially, light and air. The new apartments were snapped up before they were even finished.[95] By 1910, there were one hundred thousand Jews in Harlem, the better-off among them west of Lexington Avenue, the poorer to the east.[96]

Another immigrant quarter took shape in Brownsville, Brooklyn, named for developer Charles Brown, who had bought up farmland and subdivided it in the 1860s. By the 1880s, Jewish immigrants were moving to the area, attracted by the open spaces and garment factories opened by Elias Kaplan and other contractors who moved from the Lower East Side. By 1900, there were twenty-five thousand people in the area, mostly Jews living in modest wood-frame, two-family houses. But even by that time, most of the new buildings being erected by the Jewish builders and real estate speculators who congregated at Mrs. Axelrod's restaurant on Thatford Avenue were multifamily tenements. The population continued to grow, spurred by the construction of the Williamsburg and Manhattan Bridges. By 1910, one observer noted the transformation of what had been swampy wasteland into "rows miles long of four and five story modern pressed brick tenement houses." By 1920, 80 percent of the 100,854 residents of Brownsville were Jewish, and the neighborhood resembled the Lower East Side in its density, poverty, and Jewishness.[97]

Not everyone greeted with equanimity Brownsville's transition from semirural fringe of Brooklyn to Jewish tenement neighborhood. The *Brooklyn Eagle* complained early on that the area had "very much deteriorated by the settling of a low class of Hebrews who have disfigured many of the dwellings by converting them into small business places." Clashes between Jews and non-Jews took place, especially along the shifting borders of the section. Jews complained of attacks by Gentile hooligans on Rosh Hashanah and Tisha b'Av.

But if the *Eagle* was to be believed, the violence went both ways: "Since their advent to this portion of the town not a day has passed without a fight of some kind. In fact, many an unfortunate Christian who has had occasion to pass through the streets of Brownsville at night has been roughly handled." Indeed, in later years, Brownsville gave rise to a number of "tough Jews," including members of the mixed Italian-Jewish Murder Incorporated gang.[98]

Evidence of Brownsville's Jewishness came in a number of forms. There were dozens of synagogues, most of them in storefronts or converted houses, as well as other religious institutions such as the Stone Avenue Talmud To-rah and the Rabbi Chaim Berlin Yeshiva. There was the Labor Lyceum, where radical organizations such as the Workmen's Circle met. But since Browns-ville Jewish organizations erected few grand buildings, the neighborhood's Jewish character was most marked in the informal interactions of residents on the streets and in their homes. The marketplace on Belmont Avenue, be-tween Thatford and Stone Avenues, came alive on Thursdays and Fridays, as housewives and their husbands shopped for the Sabbath in the stalls that lined the sidewalks selling fish, live fowl, vegetables, salt herring, rye bread, and dry goods. A step up from the outdoor market on Belmont, Pitkin Avenue became Brownsville's mile-long main shopping street, lined with food and clothing stores, as well as Jewish-owned banks, theaters where movies were shown and live Yiddish plays produced, kosher delis, and Chinese restaurants. Newsstands sold Yiddish as well as English newspapers, including the weekly *Bronzviler Post*.[99]

Meanwhile, settlement of the Bronx was just beginning, with the densest concentrations in two patches, one east of Crotona Park, between the park and the Bronx River, the other to the west, between Crotona and Claremont Parks. When Aaron Domnitz moved to the Bronx in 1907, he recalled it as "new terri-tory for Jews," who traveled to Harlem to get kosher meat. Little by little, how-ever, signs of Jewishness appeared. Early on, the pioneers discovered which restaurants were Jewish owned and served "herring, borsht . . . , and Jewish bread if you asked." Soon, however, "Jewishness was revealed in the windows of the butcher stores, on the shelves of the bakery stores." Yiddish newspapers appeared on the stands. Jews brought urban development as well: "As the gen-tiles left, the grass on the hills, the bushes, plants, and flowers gradually disap-peared. More stores and tenement houses grew up in their place."[100]

Much of a district's Jewish character came from the people walking the streets, and much of this traffic was prompted by the daily business of buying and selling. To some extent, it was the style of commerce that made a street appear Jewish—pushcart markets arose in neighborhoods such as Harlem (98th to 102nd Streets along Second and Third Avenues), Brownsville (Belmont Avenue), and Mott Haven (137th Street between Brook and St. Ann's Avenues), as they became more Jewish.[101] To some extent, it was the presence of goods aimed at a Jewish market. Yiddish newspapers, for instance, appeared on the newsstands. But more important, establishments aimed at Jewish culinary tastes provided the neighborhoods with their special quality. In 1899, the 631 food sellers in the Eighth Assembly District on the Lower East Side, according to one study, included "131 butcher shops which proclaimed their wares in Hebrew characters," in addition to numerous bakeries, "bread stands," delicatessens, fish stores, herring stands, "grape wine shops," and two matzo stores.[102]

Besides kosher meat, certain foods stood out especially as Jewish favorites. Soda water, for example, which when unflavored became seltzer, the "workers' champagne," gave rise to more than one hundred Jewish-owned soda-water companies, 90 percent of such firms in the city. More than one observer noted that Jews also ate more fish than did "any other race in the city." This proclivity for fish, along with the tradition of keeping milk and meat separate, led to the elaboration of the fish stores and herring stands noted in the 1899 survey into "appetizing stores," which sold prepared fish, salads, and dairy products. Sausages and other prepared meats—salami, pastrami, corned beef, tongue, and bologna—were sold in delicatessens, which the Jews inherited from the Germans but which became such an iconic New York Jewish institution that their presence marked a Jewish neighborhood more clearly than even that of a synagogue.[103]

Full-fledged "sit-down" restaurants sometimes evolved out of the delicatessens, "coffee and cake parlors," and Romanian wine cellars of the Jewish neighborhoods. A handful of large, elegant kosher restaurants even appeared in the Jewish sections and in Midtown Manhattan, where they served a clientele of businesspeople and upwardly mobile families. In addition to meat restaurants, "dairy restaurants" offered vegetarian dishes purported by their proprietors to be more healthful than meat. Even when they were not actually kosher, the division between meat and milk restaurants remained as a cultural trait. By 1920, though, another ethnic preference became apparent on the main streets of Jewish neighborhoods, where Chinese restaurants began to appear, especially popular among the more adventurous younger element. In time, the Jewish taste for Chinese food became a kind of in-joke among Jews, even if it was less well-known outside the community.[104]

Jews put public and semipublic spaces to different use than did other people. One common observation was that Jews avidly patronized local public libraries. The branch on East Broadway was reputed to be the busiest in the city. Similarly, when the Brownsville branch of the library opened on Glenmare and Watkins Streets in 1908, it was "immediately filled to capacity," with the largest annual circulation in Brooklyn. To relieve the overcrowding, a separate children's branch was opened, housed in its own imposing building. In the Bronx, too, the library became a livelier place as Jews entered the neighborhood, and tastes in reading matter changed as well, tending toward European literature and books on social problems.[105] Jews also flocked to the city's parks. Of course, parks in the Jewish neighborhoods—such as Seward Park opposite the Forward Building on East Broadway, Brownsville's Betsy Head Park, completed in 1914, or Crotona Park in the Bronx—could be identified as Jewish spaces by the language or accents of the visitors or by the topics they discussed.

To what extent did migration out of the Lower East Side signal a movement into the middle class? While Jews had started to enter the professions, most advanced due to business. The great immigrant Jewish working class proved to be a one-generation phenomenon. Their fathers had been petty merchants, and their sons became clerks, shopkeepers, and professionals. Building, social work, and law attracted Jews. By the 1920s, those still working in the garment industry benefited from the growth of unions. These advances also facilitated and generated movement out of the East Side. Seward Park Library's annual report noted the movement of Jews out of the Lower East Side and explained that the only ones who wished to remain were older immigrants attached to neighborhood institutions. But even they might move on for family reasons. When the librarian asked one elderly man, a library regular, why he was moving to the Bronx, he responded, "Vell, I haf a daughter to marry"[106] Some upwardly mobile Jews remained in the Lower Manhattan neighborhood, which included wealthier sections on the streets south of East Broadway, such as Henry Street and Madison Street. But many settled immigrants and their children moved out to newer sections of Brooklyn and the Bronx, where they sought recently constructed apartment buildings, complete with elevators.

In adapting to the Lower East Side, Jews from the Russian and Austro-Hungarian empires, Romania, and the Levant had often relied on old-world communal networks to adapt to the world of the tenement, sweatshop, and pushcart. But by World War I, Jewish immigrants and their children lived well beyond the Lower East Side and constituted close to 28 percent of the city's population. As they moved into neighborhoods of secondary settlement, they drew on East Side networks and underwent a new process of adaptation. Though they were entering white-collar as opposed to blue-collar work, and though their children now took full advantage of New York's educational opportunities, they continued to live and work together. Just as they had in the Lower East Side, Jews now shaped a variety of American Jewish identities to fit the circumstances in their new neighborhoods in Harlem, Brooklyn, and the Bronx. The Jewish home was an important space, where families freely determined how Jewish they wanted to be and in what ways: how they dressed, what they ate, how they furnished their apartments, and what they did with their leisure time all contributed to a sense of identity conditioned by class and distance from the immigration experience. These domestic decisions reverberated well beyond the home, shaping neighborhood businesses, political clubs, and cultural associations. Jewish households, hundreds of thousands of them by 1920, thus helped define New York as a Jewish city through their creation of vibrant and distinctive neighborhoods.

During and after World War I, the American Jewish community, represented here by a female allegorical figure bearing a tray of food, raised tens of millions of dollars for the Jews of war-torn Europe. Note the New York skyline with the Statue of Liberty in the background. (Prints and Photographs Division, Library of Congress, Washington, DC)

CHAPTER 5

Capital of the Jewish World

In 1918, the Kehillah (Jewish Community) of New York City published the *Jewish Communal Register*, a massive 1,597-page compendium of Jewish organizational life in the five boroughs. To compile the organizational directories at the heart of the *Register*, a cadre of male Jewish student census takers of "good appearance, personality and . . . knowledge of things Jewish" traversed one hundred specially demarcated districts. They combed every street of Manhattan, the Bronx, and Brooklyn, as well as selected areas of Queens and Staten Island, for signs of Jewish organizational life—literally, for one of their methods was to hunt for signs posted in Yiddish or Hebrew. They also approached proprietors of meeting halls, groceries, and kosher butcher shops for tips on local groups. They discovered an astonishing array of "religious, educational, recreational-cultural, economic, philanthropic, correctional, research and coordinating, central and national, and national and international agencies"—approximately four thousand in all, large and small, in all parts of the city.[1]

The dense and diverse network of organizations, institutions, and movements documented by the *Jewish Communal Register* contrasted starkly with the one synagogue and associated burial society that constituted the formal Jewish community a century earlier. In the meantime, of course, the city had absorbed a tremendous influx of central European and eastern European Jews. The tens and hundreds of thousands, and later millions, of Jews who made New York a Jewish city by the late nineteenth and early twentieth centuries took advantage of the American promise of freedom by developing a communal structure to fit their many needs on their own terms. Often this meant a declaration of independence from traditional Judaism as much as from outside interference. By the early twentieth century, Jews often elaborated on patterns of organization established during the mid-nineteenth century.

The same conditions that produced so much vitality also provoked a high degree of fractiousness within the community. Organizations reflected the religious, social, linguistic, economic, and political cleavages within the Jewish population. Conflict was common, as was duplication of effort. The ethos of voluntarism and pluralism that characterized New York's Jewish community meant that true unity proved elusive. Not everyone believed unity was desirable in any case. Attempts to form an overarching corporate Jewish community organization, such as had existed in Europe but on a more democratic footing, failed. Federations and alliances for practical ends more often succeeded. But the freedom to remain outside the formal community was another of New York's promises, and many individuals chose to do so.

As New York Jews shaped their own local Jewish polity, they also took steps to aid Jews throughout the world. New York became the unofficial capital of the Jewish world. Not only was it now home to more Jews than any other city in the history of the Jewish people and not only did many of the world's most prosperous Jews live there, but New York Jewry suffered none of the wars, famines, pogroms, and oppression that characterized the Jews' lot in parts of Europe and elsewhere. From their relatively safe haven, New Yorkers took the lead in organizing American Jewry's political and relief efforts for Jews abroad. Many of these same New York–based agencies mobilized to counter anti-Semitism in the United States as well.

■ New York Jewry and Early Efforts at Jewish Defense

Even before the Civil War, New York's Jewish community began to establish itself as the capital of the Jewish world by asserting itself on behalf of threatened Jewish communities abroad and in defense of Jewish rights and interests at home. In 1840, when thirteen Jews were accused of ritual murder in Damascus, Syria, New Yorkers called a mass meeting to protest the accusation and to pressure the American government to intervene. Although too late to have much effect, the community's efforts set a precedent for organizing across congregational lines to speak out in solidarity with persecuted Jews abroad. The aging Mordecai Manuel Noah provided the ideological justification for such actions:

It may be said that we are remote from the scene of these cruelties . . . , that the Almighty has cast our lot in a country of laws administered alike to Jew and Gentile, that . . . we are exempt from such outrages. . . . We thank God that it is so. . . . But, sir, in every country on earth in which the Almighty has fixed the destiny of the Jew, . . . scattered by a wise Providence among every nation, we are still one people, governed by the same sacred laws and bound together by the same destiny.

Noah reminded New Yorkers, "the cause of one is the cause of all, . . . and if the time has not arrived when the strong arm of Israel can once more be uplifted in defense of the nation and its rights, we can yet raise our voice against . . . aggression."[2] The Damascus affair marked the first collective action by American Jews on behalf of Jews abroad and their "first effort at creating a distinctive political agenda."[3] Ten years later, when New York Jews similarly protested an American-Swiss trade agreement that allowed Swiss cantons to discriminate against American Jews, they were defending their own position as citizens deserving of equal protection from their government.[4]

If the Damascus and Switzerland affairs set precedents for ad hoc action, the Mortara affair led to the first successful attempt to organize American Jewry on a national scale, with New York as its headquarters. The move came in 1858, in response to the forcible separation of Edgardo Mortara from his family in Bologna, Italy. Church officials there revealed that a Catholic domestic servant had had the Jewish seven-year-old baptized in secret five years earlier. Outraged, American Jews engaged in public protests and once again called, unsuccessfully, for the U.S. government to intervene. In New York, more than two thousand people, Jews and non-Jews, attended a rally at Mozart Hall demanding Edgardo's release. The affair pitted Jews against Catholics in a battle for public opinion and influence. During the uproar, Jewish spokespeople appealed for Protestant support by playing on prevalent anti-Catholic nativist themes. Rabbi Isaac Mayer Wise, for example, railed against "the most odious act that ever emanated from the Prince of Darkness, . . . recently perpetrated in the dominions of Pio Nono, the Pope of Rome." Warning Protestants that they might be the next victims, Rabbi Wise concluded, "The history of these incarnate fiends, written in the blood of millions of victims, fully justifies such a conclusion." In fact, Jews largely won the battle for Protestant public opinion against Catholic attempts to defend, or to deflect attention from, the abduction. But Catholics won the political war, as the Buchanan administration's refusal to intervene tacitly acknowledged rising Catholic influence in the Democratic Party.[5]

In the wake of the Mortara affair, New York began to assert its primacy as a Jewish center over such rivals as Philadelphia and Cincinnati. Rev. Samuel M. Isaacs of New York's congregation Shaarey Tefilah raised the possibility of a national convocation of Jewish congregations to discuss how they might protect the civil rights of Jews around the world. The meeting in New York in November 1859 resulted in the formation of the Board of Delegates of American Israelites as a unified body empowered to speak for American Jewry. Regular meetings of the executive committee would also take place in New York. The varied agenda that the Board of Delegates set for itself touched on Jewish interests both domestic and foreign. In the United States, the board successfully lobbied Congress during the Civil War to permit Jewish clergy to serve as army chaplains and protested a proposed North Carolina constitution that would have restricted Jews from holding office. At the same time, the board came to the aid of Jews in Morocco, Palestine, Persia, Tunis, Galicia, East Prussia, and elsewhere; and lobbied to secure equal rights for Jews in the Swiss cantons. In 1867, the board offered support to the short-lived Maimonides College in Philadelphia and in 1872 reestablished a Jewish Publication Society. Lastly, in 1873 and 1877, the board undertook surveys of American Jewish congregations and communities to gather statistics about Jews in the United States. The Board of Delegates merged with the Union of American Hebrew Congregations in 1876.[6]

■ New Challenges

Over the next several decades, New York Jewry faced three interrelated challenges: the rise of local anti-Semitism, the often violent persecution of Russian Jewry, and—linking them together—the question of mass eastern European Jewish immigration, which was spurred by economic dislocation and persecution and in turn helped fuel a new wave of nativism tinged with anti-Jewish sentiment. Both established Jews and new immigrants tried to deal with these issues, sometimes together and sometimes in conflict with each other. By 1910, the Russian issue in particular had demonstrated the increasing importance of American Jewry, led by New Yorkers, on the world stage.

Ironically, the rising economic fortunes of the central European Jews and their children, coupled with increasing conformity to Anglo-American cultural norms, exacerbated hostility against them on the part of native Protestant elites. The Anglo-Protestant upper class, anxious in the face of tremendous social and cultural change in the last decades of the nineteenth century, came to view Jews as parvenu upstarts, vulgar and ostentatious symbols of class instability. Social discrimination now barred American Jews from clubs, hotels, schools, and professional organizations, even ones that they had previously had access to. In the most infamous incident, the Grand Union Hotel in Saratoga refused accommodation to Jewish banker Joseph Seligman in 1877, claiming that "colonies of Jewish people" would drive away Christian guests who felt that the Jews were simply "obnoxious."[7]

The new wave of nativism featured an element of racialism previously muted by an obsession with the perceived religious dangers posed by immigrant Roman Catholics. Nativism in the 1850s had largely been directed against the Catholic Irish, and it had been possible occasionally, as in the Mortara affair, for Jews to make common cause with native Protestants against the Catholic threat. The new nativism, however, questioned the racial admissibility of Jews, along with Italians and other immigrants from eastern and southern Europe. Influenced by racist thinkers in Europe and the rise of social scientific thought, American nativists began to doubt whether Jews (and Italians and others) were genetically capable of *ever* assimilating into the American nation.[8]

The resurgence of nativism, not coincidentally, corresponded with an increased number of immigrants coming from the southern and eastern peripheries of Europe, including Russian Jews. In New York, unsympathetic observers noticed a new type appearing in the city's public places. "Numerous complaints have been made in regard to the Hebrew immigrants who lounge about Battery Park, obstructing the walks and sitting on the chains," reported the *New York Tribune* in 1882. "Their filthy condition has caused many of the people who are accustomed to go to the park to seek a little recreation and fresh air to give up this practice," it continued. "The immigrants also greatly annoy the persons who cross the park to take the boats to Coney Island, Staten Island, and Brooklyn. The police have had many battles with these newcomers, who seem determined to have their own way."[9]

The established Jewish community worried that their association with uncouth newcomers might undermine their already shaky social status. But Jewish leaders generally rejected calls for immigration restriction. On the contrary, in addition to lobbying to keep America's borders open to Jewish immigrants, Jewish communal leaders such as Simon Wolf, Oscar Straus, Jacob Schiff, Jesse Seligman, and Louis Marshall strove to awaken sympathy for Russian Jewry among the American public and government officials. In the early 1890s, they successfully urged the appointment of a presidential commission on the sources of the mass migration from Europe to America, engineered the replacement of the American envoy to Russia with one more sympathetic to the Jews, and paid for *New York Times* correspondent Harold Frederic to go to Russia and report back on the dire Jewish situation there.[10]

Meanwhile, old and new social welfare agencies started to deal with problems of poverty, adjustment, and image posed by recent immigrants. Influenced by rising theories of scientific social work, for example, the United Hebrew Charities (UHC) attacked the behaviors and dysfunctional family structures that it saw as causes of poverty. In practice, this meant that indolence would not be tolerated among clients, whose worthiness for aid would be thoroughly investigated. It also meant an emphasis on productivization and self-help. In addition to distributing relief, the UHC thus founded the Hebrew Technical Institute in 1884 to provide young people with skills that would help them move beyond the garment industry. It established employment bureaus, loan funds, and scholarships. Its "work room" employed women while training them for industrial work.

In the first decade of the twentieth century, the UHC saw the desertion by men of their families as a central problem, one that led to such additional social ills as prostitution and increased institutionalization of children. By 1911, desertion had become so serious that it warranted its own agency: the National Desertion Bureau. In its first six years, the bureau handled nearly ten thousand cases by hunting down husbands and either effecting reconciliations (some apparently forced), securing family support from the men, or remanding them to the authorities for prosecution under a 1905 law that criminalized nonsupport (17 percent of cases). The *Jewish Communal Register* recounted some typical cases:

> Man left family in Brooklyn without warning; had been away for almost a year and made no contribution toward their support. Through publication of the man's picture in our "Gallery of Missing Husbands" he was located in Selma, Ala. He had established a business in that city and was induced through our correspondence with a

rabbi there, to send for his family. The reconciliation was complete as our applicant later advised us.

Family deserted in New York. Man located in Chicago, where it was ascertained he had instituted divorce proceedings. An indictment was secured under the Child Abandonment Law, and he was extradited thereunder. Man pleaded guilty; sentence suspended, family reconciled. Man had labored under the impression that the law was as light as his profession (he was a comedian). He had the audacity to institute a suit, alleging that his wife deserted him for a period of two years, although it was apparent that he left home but a month before. He has now learned his lesson and we have had no trouble with him since.

Man deserted family in Russia in 1904. Family arrived here in 1911 and filed immediately a complaint with the Bureau. Applicant had not seen her husband since her arrival, but countrymen had advised him of her presence. Man located in Brooklyn, invited to call at the Bureau, where a complete reconciliation was effected.

Charles W., a baker by trade, deserted the family in 1911 in New York. Three months later located in St. Joseph, Mo. He expressed regret for his act. Wished to return to family but was stranded without means. St. Joseph Charities communicated with Bureau and man returned at our expense. 1913, man deserted again. This time he was located in St. Louis, where he was living under an alias. He was indicted and rendition to this state followed. Sentenced to serve a term in the Penitentiary, but the Bureau secured his parole about six months thereafter.

The Desertion Bureau thus effectively worked with governmental and non-Jewish private agencies, as well as with the Yiddish-language *Jewish Daily Forward*, in which the "Gallery of Missing Husbands" was a popular feature for years.[11]

By that time, however, more innovative social welfare institutions had eclipsed the UHC. One of the most remarkable was the "settlement house," a concept imported from Britain, where East London's Toynbee Hall had opened its doors in 1884. The settlement house differed from traditional charities in that its workers, usually idealistic young college graduates, the majority of them women, actually settled into houses in the midst of the teeming immigrant slums they hoped to improve. In 1886, Stanton Coit founded the first American settlement house, the Lower East Side's Neighborhood Guild, later renamed the University Settlement. Motivated by the "social gospel," which sought to apply Christian ideals to the social problems posed by urbanization, immigration, and industrialization, settlement workers brought English and citizenship classes and social services to the urban poor. But, influenced by moderate forms of socialism as well, they often worked in the political realm for social reform.

Lillian Wald, founder of Nurses' Settlement in 1895, became New York's most famous settlement worker. Born to German-Jewish immigrant parents in Ohio in 1867, Wald came of age in Rochester, New York. Her father was an optical-goods salesman, and her mother was active in charitable work. Wald grew up on the fringes of the acculturated German-Jewish milieu in Rochester; her highly cultured family raised her in a universalistic spirit that drew more from liberal Christianity than from Jewish tradition. With her dark eyes and hair and full lips, Wald was self-conscious about her "oriental" appearance, which caused her to shy away from Jewish identification even more strongly during her long career. An ardent universalist, Wald believed in the "fundamental oneness of humanity." She received what she called her "baptism by fire" in social work shortly after her graduation from nursing school in 1889. Wald recalled that she was asked to teach a class in home nursing for an East Side technical school and that a young girl entered the classroom and begged Wald to help her family:

> All the maladjustments of our social and economic relations seemed epitomized in this brief journey and what was found at the end of it. The family to which the child led me was neither criminal nor vicious. Although the husband was a cripple, one of those who stand on street corners exhibiting deformities to enlist compassion, and masking the begging of alms by a pretense at selling; although the family of seven shared their two rooms with boarders,—who were literally boarders, since a piece of timber was placed over the floor for them to sleep on,—and although the sick woman lay on a wretched, unclean bed, soiled with a hemorrhage two days old, they were not degraded human beings, judged by any measure of moral values.[12]

This experience convinced Wald to make a career of working with and for the poor and ultimately led her to the settlement movement.

Wald's Jewish social connections led her to the financier Jacob Schiff, who became her chief benefactor. After a stint at College Settlement, Wald opened Nurses' Settlement in a house that Schiff bought for her at 265 Henry Street. The Henry Street Settlement, as it soon became known, offered all the services common to settlements: classes in English, citizenship, arts and crafts, and home economics; and a venue for youth clubs, lectures, and amateur theater. New York's Visiting Nurse Service started as a program of the Henry Street Settlement before it became an independent agency. Wald also fought from her base at Henry Street to improve the neighborhood through parks and playgrounds, public health measures, and better housing and working conditions. She offered the Henry Street Settlement's parlor to help launch the National Association for the Advancement of Colored People. A pacifist, she actively opposed American entry into World War I and defended civil liberties.[13]

While the Henry Street Settlement was resolutely secular and nonsectarian, the Educational Alliance was founded earlier by Jewish philanthropists a few blocks away on East Broadway as an explicitly Jewish institution with Jewish concerns. In 1889, three prominent preexisting Jewish institutions —the Hebrew Free School Association, the Young Men's Hebrew Association, and the Clara Aguilar Free Library—merged to form the Hebrew Institute, which became the Educational Alliance in 1893.[14] Not technically a settlement house, since it lacked resident "settlers," the Educational Alliance imaginatively blended Jewish education with Americanization. It shared lecturers with the University Settlement and, like the settlements, Americanized its clients through civics and English courses, flag-waving lessons, and exuberant celebrations of national holidays. But it also offered Hebrew lessons, Sabbath services, and Jewish holiday celebrations. This blending sometimes became apparent in small but immediate ways. For example, when Hebrew-school teachers noted with annoyance that young boys wore their caps inside the classroom in violation of American standards of decorum, the teachers distributed yarmulkes. As a board member reported, "It gives the classroom the appearance of uniformity and is a marked improvement over the former boorishness and un-American custom of wearing hats in the class room."[15]

In 1891, the Educational Alliance moved into a magnificent new building that seemed to the *New York Times* to be "a magazine for the storage of air and sunshine." The expansive five-story, "yellow pressed brick" corner building became an island of order, light, and American culture in a congested, dim, and chaotic neighborhood.[16] There immigrants of all ages studied English, learned vocations, played ball, and discussed literature. In 1895, the *Times* surveyed the Educational Alliance from bottom to top. The lower level held a 710-seat auditorium, where immigrants and their children could enjoy concerts and lectures. The main floor housed offices, an industrial school, and kindergarten classrooms. On the second floor were additional classrooms, where students gathered after school for art and music classes, drama groups, and clubs of all kinds. The third floor included still more classrooms, a chess and conversation room, and the Aguilar Free Library and reading room, where visitors could choose from twelve thousand books. Those who climbed the stairway up to the fifth floor found a gymnasium "on the most approved plan" and "a series of baths, walled in with marble, and lockers with open wire panel construction." Seeking open air, especially in short supply before the opening of Seward Park in 1903, local residents gathered in the Educational Alliance's roof garden.[17]

While a tour through the building provides a sense of the range of activities, a glance at the weekly schedule of a single classroom shows the kaleidoscopic and wide-ranging nature of its educational offerings. Take, for example, classroom number 12. Monday through Friday, it housed a kindergarten class from 9:00 a.m. to 12:30 p.m. Then, from 1:00 p.m. to 6:00 p.m., public school children learned Hebrew. By 7:15 p.m., men and women arrived for two-hour English classes. On Saturday nights, an American history class met at 7:00 p.m., and on Sundays, more Hebrew-school children filed in between 9:00 a.m. to 2:30 p.m. On Sunday evenings, a singing class for men and women convened from 5:00 to 6:00 p.m., a biology class at 7:00 p.m., and, finally, a literary society gathered from 8:00 to 10:00 p.m.[18]

The Educational Alliance altered its program to meet the desires of its clientele. Initially, religious activities reflected the founders' uptown Reform sensibilities, but interaction with the immigrant population brought lessons and servics more in line with Orthodox Judaism. An early ban on Yiddish was soon lifted. Tsvi Hirsh Masliansky, half traditional preacher and half Zionist orator, regularly held forth in Yiddish at the Educational Alliance. Its programs thus bridged a generation gap between immigrant parents and children, a goal frequently enunciated by the settlement movement. Board members even proudly reported that the Socialist *Forward*, often suspicious of uptown interventions and generally indifferent to religion, had responded favorably to a Passover play and "commend[ed] . . . the work of the Educational Alliance."[19]

With mixed motives of social concern and social control, the Educational Alliance had its critics on the Socialist left and the Orthodox right. But the masses spoke with their feet, and those feet actually wore out the Alliance building's marble stairs within thirty years. In 1895, 26,600 people used the building each week.[20] And the numbers kept growing. That a sizable proportion of its visitors were children and young adults spoke to its influence on the future of American Jewry.

Across the river in Brooklyn, the Hebrew Educational Society (HES) played a similar role. Founded in 1899 on the initiative of the Baron de Hirsch Fund and Abraham Abraham, owner of Brooklyn's Abraham & Straus department store and an in-law of the Manhattan Strauses, HES reflected many of the same concerns as the Educational Alliance. Brooklyn's Jewish elite anxiously read editorials in the *Brooklyn Eagle* criticizing uncouth Brownsville immigrants. But its members also looked nervously over their shoulders at their richer Manhattan counterparts. At the founding of HES, Abraham thus called on the "well-to-do Brooklyn Hebrews" to show "that the Brooklyn Hebrew is not behind his New York brother." The HES building at Hopkinson and Sutter Avenues housed "children's and youth clubs, English and citizenship classes, religious instruction and worship, a gymnasium, a variety of manual training and vocational courses, a kindergarten, recreation rooms, a seasonal children's farm garden, a summer roof garden, a milk station and baby clinic, a library, a branch of the penny provident bank, a music school, a citizenship bureau, community theaters in English and Yiddish, a study room, dances, and holiday celebrations." As many as 360,000 people used the building each year.[21]

Like the UHC, the settlements, and the Educational Alliance, the National Council of Jewish Women (NCJW) saw family stability as a cornerstone of healthy communal life and undertook practical work with new immigrants on a national scope. NCJW arose from the Jewish Women's Congress, which met during the World Parliament of Religions at the 1893 World's Columbia Exposition in Chicago. Sadie American, a local activist with links to the Maxwell Street Settlement and Temple Sinai, delivered the final speech of the Congress. The thirty-one-year-old daughter of a successful German immigrant merchant ended her speech with an energetic call for a permanent Jewish women's organization. Headquartered in Chicago, NCJW successfully organized sections in various cities among well-off Americanized women, many of them oriented toward Reform Judaism. Three years later, NCJW boasted more than four thousand members in fifty sections; by 1905, it claimed a membership of ten thousand.[22]

The outspoken and widely respected Rebekah Bettelheim Kohut led a New

York Section filled with highly accomplished women. In addition to Kohut, the New York Section at various times included educator and writer Minnie Louis; prison reformer Alice Davis Menken; author and Barnard College founder Annie Nathan Meyer; future political figure Belle Lindner Israels Moskowitz; Consumers' League leader Maud Nathan; and Julia Richman, the first Jewish principal and woman district superintendent in the New York City public schools.[23]

Soon, NCJW moved away from its early emphasis on religious self-education to focus on social service. In particular, it took an interest in the growing numbers of eastern European immigrants, work that embodied a combination of Progressive-era concern for efficient and systematic social work, Reform Jewish commitment to "universal ethics," and a sense that women possessed a special talent for ameliorating social problems. As early as 1894, when the New York State legislature's Lexow Commission had revealed the extent of Jewish involvement in prostitution, NCJW members decided to protect immigrant women from the dangers of the "white slave trade."[24]

This emphasis on immigration moved NCJW's New York Section to the forefront of the organization's work. NCJW cofounder Sadie American relocated to New York in 1900, solidifying the section's leading position. Indeed, the two were closely connected since "immigrant aid work" was in fact American's "pet project." American often served as NCJW's public face. As corresponding secretary (1893–1905) and then as paid executive secretary (1905–1914), she presided over the organization's growth in its early years, often traveling from city to city to establish new sections. With experience as an activist with the Maxwell Street Settlement, the Illinois Consumers' League, and the Chicago Women's Club, American had established her interest in social welfare and social reform by the time she reached New York. Within a couple of years, she became the New York Section's president.[25]

American led NCJW's efforts to aid immigrant women. In 1903, NCJW established a Department of Immigrant Aid and, two years later, an aid station at Ellis Island, staffed by Yiddish-speaking social workers. They interviewed every Jewish female immigrant between the ages of twelve and thirty, counseling them on the process and prospects for settlement and warning them emphatically about dangers posed by pimps and traffickers. NCJW's station at Ellis Island became the "hub" of its programming, but it was only part of what American called "the complete chain of protection" that NCJW provided to vulnerable single immigrant women. NCJW workers helped women settle into their homes and continued to monitor their progress for as long as three years afterward.[26]

But American was also a lightning rod for controversy. Her "brusque manner and autocratic style" alienated some and, combined with resentment over the ascendancy of the New York Section and immigration work over religious education, led to calls for her ouster. That American was a "Sunday-Sabbath observer" did not help her image in some circles within NCJW. Nor did her reputation for extravagance on the organization's budget. Finally, in 1914, allegations of financial mismanagement forced her out of her national position. Many local activists found her abrasive as well and eventually ousted her from her New York Section presidency too. She left NCJW and never returned.[27]

Meanwhile, the separate Brooklyn Section continued on its relatively more serene way. Its activities followed the priorities of the national and New York organizations: immigration work, much of it carried out at the Hebrew Education Society in Brownsville; assistance to Jewish women incarcerated or on probation; education in housekeeping; and aid to the blind. It also maintained the Council Home for Jewish Girls in Jamaica, Queens, for girls at risk of delinquency. Rose Brenner, elected section president in 1912 at the age of twenty-eight, provided dynamic leadership, increasing membership fivefold during her tenure. A Brooklyn native, daughter of a local judge, and member of congregation Beth Elohim, Brenner went on to head NCJW in the 1920s.[28]

■ New Immigrants Organize

New immigrants from the Russian and Austro-Hungarian Empires also organized on their own behalf. Many joined older organizations established by earlier immigrants. Jewish fraternal orders, for example, attracted a new cohort of members. In the second decade of the twentieth century, these orders peaked with half a million members nationwide. Two-fifths of the entire Jewish fraternal membership belonged to Independent Order Brith Abraham, and of IOBA's total membership of over two hundred thousand, nearly half—or ninety thousand in 354 lodges—were in New York City. Officially, IOBA was bilingual, with German and English as its languages. In fact, as it recruited heavily among eastern European newcomers, it added Yiddish. One-third of IOBA's New York lodges carried names of eastern European towns from which their members hailed. For example, the First Jablonower Lodge 447, made up of immigrants from Jablonow, Galicia (then Austria, now Ukraine), met on first and third Saturdays at 352 East Third Street, presided over by President Selig Fleisher, a thirty-five-year-old tailor just seven years in the country. Other lodges bore the names of American heroes and politicians (William Gaynor, President Wilson, George Washington), famous rabbis (Akiba Eger), modern Jewish cultural figures and heroes (Moses Montefiore, Moses Mendelsohn, Solomon Schechter, Mendel Mocher Sphorim), German cultural figures (Schiller, Heine), or local communal leaders (Judge Leon Sanders, Isidor Straus). Some simply designated the area where the members lived (Crotona, Williamsburg City, Yorkville, Star of Brooklyn). A few lodges catered to women, and this too was indicated in the name (Sarah Weinstock Ladies', Lady Garfield, Lady Roosevelt).[29]

The number of independent mutual aid societies also exploded. The *Jewish Communal Register* located 1,016, certainly an undercount. Most were *landsmanshaftn*, made up of immigrants from a particular hometown in eastern Europe. *Landsmanshaftn* often reflected an array of political, social, religious, and gender divisions in the community, and as a result, one small European town could give birth to multiple societies in New York bearing its name. The town of Rakov, Belarus, for example, had three *landsmanshaftn* in New York: Chevrah Beth David Anshei Rakov (Congregation Beth David People of Rakov; religious), organized in 1890, whose fifty members met at 225 Clinton Street, presided over by seventy-year-old Samuel Berman, who had been in the country since 1877; Rakower Young Men's Benevolent Association, founded 1904 (younger generation), which met down the street at 151 Clinton; and Branch 428 of the Workmen's Circle, the labor fraternal order (Socialist). In 1931, women established their own Rakover Froyen Klub (Rakover Women's Club). This dynamic increased among immigrants from larger cities, such as Warsaw or Minsk, which could have dozens of societies in their name.[30]

Surprisingly, *landsmanshaftn* and other societies served as schools for Americanization, albeit on terms defined by the immigrants. Their meetings alone constituted civics lessons, at which members learned the meaning of citizenship in a free republic. No matter their ideological orientation, they all possessed the same basic structure, derived from American sources, which immigrants learned from experience in older organizations or from a variety of instructional manuals and books published in Yiddish. One member recalled the profound transformations that could take place within the society.

As a newcomer, he had been depressed about his lack of success in adjusting to America and had considered returning to Europe.

> But something else happened, something extraordinary, that affected me very strongly and completely knocked out of my head the idea of going back. This is what happened. During the months that I was hanging around like that, my *landslayt* brought me into a society. And there I was, sitting at a meeting when one of the members—a man with a very good appearance—was speaking about a question very intelligently, nicely, and logically in good . . . Yiddish. I asked who this man was. When I was told his name my mind was changed completely—my thoughts about going back disappeared.
>
> What had happened? Here I must tell a little of the past of the man, the speaker at the meeting, who had made such an impression on me. He was a childhood *landsman* of mine, from the same street and from the same synagogue. As children we kept far away from each other. He was very poor, of a bad, even ugly appearance—dirty and ragged. He did not study in either a *heder* or a modern school. It is likely that he could not even read the prayers, though he used to hold the prayer book open. I quickly left him behind and forgot about him until this encounter at the meeting.
>
> So my whole way of thinking took a turn. A poor boy there! A fine, intelligent householder here, with a nice family and fine children! Dirty there! How clean and neat he is here! Of ugly appearance there! How nice and respectable he is here! In my ears I can hear the words as he would have actually pronounced them: "Do not scorn me because I am swarthy," and of course David's verse: "The stone forsaken by the builder has become the cornerstone."
>
> How could all of this have happened—this change from there to here? And then and there I decided no longer to think of going back. Here in America, in the free land with all opportunities for everyone equally, here is my home. I shook off the last bit of dust from the old country.[31]

The writer was not alone. Hundreds of thousands of immigrants "shook off the last bit of dust from the old country," prepared to take advantage of New York's social and economic opportunities surrounded by friends and acquaintances from the same old-country town.

By the first decade of the twentieth century, the individual *landsmanshaftn* began to combine into federations based on country or region of origin. The Russian, Polish, Galician, and two competing Romanian federations amplified the voice of the societies in the larger Jewish community, emphasizing a synthesis of Americanism and Zionism. As constituents of federations, societies built practical institutions such as hospitals and contributed to efforts to forge larger Jewish communal structures such as the Kehillah. The federations pushed to the fore a new class of leaders to represent the immigrant masses. These leaders included physicians, lawyers, and politicians who had come to the United States at an early age. Fluent in English, they were comfortable interacting—and sometimes competing—with the established Jewish leadership, the wealthy "uptown" elite. One observer characterized *landsmanshaft* leaders as "a type of truly democratic servant of the people, a type which possesses American energy and Jewish loyalty."[32]

Eastern European Jews also created their own philanthropic institutions, sometimes in direct response to perceived deficiencies in established agencies. Mount Sinai Hospital, for example, failed to meet the needs of all New York Jews. Indeed, its attitudes toward its immigrant patients often seemed indistinguishable from those of the Protestant missionaries whom it was originally designed to displace. The Americanized Jewish staff and lay leadership had especial contempt for the practices of the Orthodox eastern Europeans who composed an increasing proportion of their clientele by the 1890s. A particular sticking point was the lack of kosher food. As the Orthodox Yiddish daily *Tageblat* complained, "It is an open secret that in most of the Jewish hospitals in New York the food is not kosher, and that pious Jews who do not want to eat it are ridiculed." Reports of hospital staff shaving the beards of pious patients further roiled Orthodox circles. Former Socialist firebrand turned Zionist Joseph Barondess referred to Jewish-sponsored hospitals such as Mount Sinai when in 1911 he decried the "plight of the Jewish patient who arrives at a hospital where they understand neither his language nor his psychology."[33]

The eastern European community responded as early as 1890, when a group of forty Orthodox Jewish men met in a tailor shop to consider the need for a hospital to serve the impoverished Jews crowding into the Lower East Side. Though they possessed limited resources, founders of the Beth Israel Association of New York moved swiftly, opening Beth Israel Hospital in leased quarters at 196 East Broadway, the heart of the Jewish quarter, on May 10, 1891. Not only did the new hospital make a point of serving kosher food, but its doctors and nurses also conversed with their patients in Yiddish. Demand quickly outpaced the space available in the twenty-bed hospital, and Beth Israel expanded rapidly.

By 1917, Beth Israel boasted not only of its hospital but also of its free dispensary, its work treating newly arrived immigrants threatened with deportation because of trachoma, and its training school for nurses. About to move into a new building just outside the Lower East Side at East Sixteenth Street, the hospital's leadership represented the new elite emerging from the "downtown" community. While a German-born investment banker presided over Mount Sinai, Joseph Cohen, a cloak and suit manufacturer who had arrived in New York from Poland in 1874 at the age of ten, took the helm of Beth Israel. By that time, a number of other hospitals served the burgeoning Jewish population not only in Manhattan but in the Bronx and Brooklyn as well. Brooklyn's own Jewish elite, headed by Abraham Abraham of the Abraham & Straus department store, opened the Jewish Hospital of Brooklyn to much fanfare in 1906. Lebanon and Montefiore Hospitals, the latter headed by Jacob Schiff, provided medical care in the Bronx. Several *landsmanshaft* federations also ran their own small hospitals.[34]

Likewise, dissatisfaction with established agencies, in particular the UHC, led to the establishment of the Hebrew Immigrant Sheltering and Aid Society, known as HIAS. HIAS had its origins in two separate organizations. One, the Hebrew Sheltering House Association—also called by its traditional Hebrew name, the Hakhnoses Orkhim—had been founded in 1889 under the leadership of Orthodox Yiddish newspaperman Kasriel Sarasohn and the following year opened a shelter for homeless immigrants. The other, the Hebrew Immigrant Aid Society (also called HIAS), came into being when a *landsmanshaft* committee sent to Ellis Island to investigate the pauper's burial of a landsman who had died at the station decided to form a permanent agency to assist newcomers in need. Concerned that the UHC representative at the immigration station was unable to speak Yiddish, HIAS struck a chord in the immigrant community and raised enough money to place its own worker there. In 1909, the two organizations merged.

Within a decade, HIAS headquarters occupied a four-story building on two tenement lots on East Broadway, with the word "Welcome" inscribed in English above the door. That year the agency maintained its Ellis Island bureau, as well as branches in other port cities; helped immigrants "to land"; provided information; guided newcomers to locate relatives, jobs, and lost luggage; assisted with the process of naturalization; offered free legal advice; looked after the transportation needs of immigrants proceeding beyond New York; sheltered thousands in its hostel; distributed clothes to the needy; and staffed a Social Service Bureau and an Agricultural Bureau. HIAS distinguished itself by its determination and energy to assert the immigrants' rights—in appealing deportation orders, investigating conditions on arriving ships, and lobbying for proimmigrant legislation. Over time, HIAS helped hundreds of thousands of newcomers, winning the trust of the immigrant community.[35]

■ Jewish Defense at Home and Abroad

By April 1903, when more than forty Jews were slaughtered in a vicious pogrom in the Bessarabian city of Kishinev, a large eastern European Jewish population in New York closely followed events in the "old home." The Yiddish press broke the dreadful story of the pogrom, "galvaniz[ing]" the community and prompting it to wage an "unprecedented and vigorous campaign in American Jewish communal life."[36] The Socialist *Forward* called for a "monster demonstration," collected funds for relief, and gathered signatures on a protest petition. Although some Jewish Socialists objected to what they saw as a wave of nationalist hysteria in Jewish responses to the pogrom, others, such as Abraham Cahan, defended their concern for their fellow Jews: "[Jews] are slaughtered and raped in Kishinev because they are exactly what I am. . . . Can a man who suffers nothing when people with his blood, with his looks, are hacked to pieces, really suffer with the problems of mankind?" Cahan struck some of the same themes as Noah had not quite a century before.[37]

The Jewish elite reacted more slowly but soon showed that they too had taken events at Kishinev to heart. Responding to a call from the Alliance Israelite Universelle, Schiff and others organized the so-called Bankers' Committee that soon raised over $1 million, dwarfing not only the *Forward*'s $8,000 but British Jewry's £4,000. The effort marked a milestone in establishing American Jewry's preeminence. As even the *Forward* had to admit, the fact that the Jewish elite had the ear of some of their Gentile counterparts enabled them to make Jewish voices heard in high circles. Mayor Seth Low, facing a tough reelection battle, chaired a large protest rally, held at Carnegie Hall. Speakers included former president Grover Cleveland and Catholic archbishop John Farley. Meanwhile, B'nai B'rith initiated diplomatic efforts, presenting a petition to a sympathetic but reluctant President Theodore Roosevelt to convey to the Russian government, which refused to accept it.[38]

If after Kishinev downtown and uptown had worked largely on parallel but separate tracks, they found a way to work together in response to waves of bloody pogroms that followed the failed Russian Revolution of 1905. At a meeting held at the elegant Temple Emanu-El, the flagship Reform synagogue, "There were the 'native born,' the German element, Nationalists, Zionists, Reformers, Orthodox, Social Revolutionaries—in short . . . a united Jewry." The resultant American Committee for the Relief of Russian Jews quickly raised $1 million, half of which came from New York City. At the same time, a group of "Socialist Revolutionaries" issued a call for a Jewish Defense Association (JDA) to fund the purchase of arms for Jewish self-defense units. Under the slogan "The Jewish people is arming itself. We must create the means," JDA came to include not only Socialists but also Zionists and others. Even Schiff gave a nominal hundred-dollar donation. Judah Magnes, a Reform rabbi and Zionist with radical inclinations and family ties to Louis Marshall, headed the effort. Magnes clearly hoped that JDA would evolve into a permanent organization that would bridge the gaps between uptown and downtown, Orthodox and Reform, nationalist and cosmopolitan, radical and conservative sectors of the community. JDA's efforts peaked in a massive two-hundred-thousand-person march from the Lower East Side to Union Square, largely organized and attended by eastern European Jews.[39]

After Kishinev, and again in 1905–1906, various elements called for the establishment of a national representative Jewish body that might respond to crises in a more systematic manner than had the recent ad hoc campaigns. With many American Jews judging the response to Russian events inadequate, and calls for "organization in the air," a small and exclusive monthly New York social and discussion group known as "The Wanderers" met to assess the situation. They concluded that a permanent national organization to defend Jewish rights was needed and that they should take the lead in establishing it to make sure that it be "free from all objectionable tendencies." A committee headed by attorney Louis Marshall invited a small group of "leading Jews" from across the country to a closed-door meeting at the UHC building on Second Avenue. Most of the attendees were successful businessmen, lawyers, and rabbis of central European or American birth. Most adhered to Reform Judaism and rejected the nationalist view that Jews constituted a people apart from religious belief and practice. Several of them—Jacob Schiff, Marshall, Oscar Straus—had for decades acted as Jewish intercessors with the government on an unofficial basis. Only a small number represented the growing eastern European community or Zionist or radical political perspectives.[40]

After much debate over the course of several meetings, the assembled leading Jews rejected proposals for a democratically elected representative body —a Jewish "congress"—and settled on a small, self-selecting group of sixty. Although the American Jewish Committee (AJC) was to include members from all regions of the country, and its first president was a Philadelphian, New Yorkers formed the inner circle on its executive committee. In its early years, this inner circle represented a rather insular group, united by similar background and family ties. The location of AJC's small office and staff in the UHC building bolstered their dominance, as did the New Yorkers' tremendous individual wealth and personal influence.

Jacob Schiff and Louis Marshall were the dominant personalities on the committee. Born in January 1847 into a prosperous family in Frankfurt-am-Main, Schiff immigrated to the United States just after the Civil War. After a brief sojourn back in Germany, he returned to the United States, where he joined the investment bank of Kuhn, Loeb & Company, married Loeb's daughter, and rose to head of the firm. "Medium in build and fastidiously groomed," he sported a goatee, a walking stick, and a quick temper. As a leading financier and one of the wealthiest men in America, Schiff gave generously of his fortune to Jewish and non-Jewish causes. In fact, it sometimes seemed that there was scarcely a Jewish cause that did not receive funding from Schiff. Although a Reform Jew himself, he contributed liberally and ecumenically to any undertaking that he felt furthered Jewish learning or defended Jewish rights. In reaction to Russian anti-Semitism he had gone so far as to help finance the Japanese war effort during the Russo-Japanese War. With his extensive connections with Jews and Jewish organizations abroad, Schiff filled the role of the "elder statesman."[41]

Louis Marshall, a close ally of Schiff, became AJC's second president in 1912. A talented corporate lawyer, Marshall was born in 1856 in Syracuse, New York, to recently arrived German immigrants. A "short, stocky man of stern appearance," Marshall was always "confident in his opinions" and impatient with those who disagreed. His dour public persona certainly did not recommend him for mass leadership, and he harbored a suspicion of too much democracy in Jewish life. But his tireless efforts on behalf of Jewish rights and interests, including an intervention to settle the 1910 cloak makers' strike, elicited respect beyond the narrow confines of his social milieu. At one point, he even learned Yiddish and enlisted Tsvi Hirsh Masliansky to publish a Yiddish newspaper to reach the immigrant community. By the 1920s, he was so influential that critics complained that American Jewry lived under "Marshall Law."[42]

The American Jewish Committee aimed to defend "the civil and religious rights of Jews in any part of the world," to "secure for the Jews equality of economic, social and educational opportunities," and to provide "relief from calamities." It preferred to work quietly and politely, behind the scenes, through intercession with the people in power and through the force of moral argument based on carefully gathered and presented evidence. Accordingly, AJC established a bureau of statistics and undertook, together with the Jewish Publication Society, to issue the *American Jewish Year Book*. In AJC's first decade, it opposed questions regarding race on the U.S. Census, limitation of naturalization rights to non-Asians, and local laws banning kosher slaughtering. It defended Russian-Jewish revolutionary exiles faced with extradition to Russia, the rights of Balkan Jews, and Mendel Beilis, accused of ritual murder in Russia. In 1913, it helped push through the New York State legislature a bill banning discrimination in "public resorts."[43]

AJC also addressed the issue of Russian discrimination against Jewish travelers bearing American passports. Russian policy subjected American Jews traveling within the country's boundaries to the same discrimination that Russian Jews faced, a policy that seemed to violate provisions of an 1832 commercial treaty between the United States and Russia. When the State Department announced that the United States would no longer issue passports to former Russian subjects or to Jews without Russian consent, AJC protests induced Secretary of State Elihu Root to reverse the policy. In a May 1908 memorandum to President Roosevelt, however, AJC went even further and called on the administration to abrogate the 1832 treaty. Though launched by the American Jewish Committee, the abrogation campaign gained the support of a wide swath of American Jewry, including B'nai B'rith and the Reform movement's Union of American Hebrew Congregations. In January 1913, the United States terminated the treaty.

From AJC's inception, it fought to keep the borders of the United States open to Jews and all other immigrants. It lobbied Congress and presidents, testified before committees, produced proimmigrant studies, and interceded with immigration officials in procedural and administrative matters. Cooperating with B'nai B'rith, the National Liberal Immigration League, and other organizations, AJC for years managed to prevent the enactment of a literacy test for entry into the country and to fend off an explicit exclusion of "Asiatics" from citizenship.[44]

The American Jewish Committee's position as representative of American Jewry did not go unchallenged. Although it claimed to speak for American Jewry as a whole, it was hardly a representative body. Wary of too much democracy, its members jealously guarded their status as the country's "leading Jews." Hostile to Jewish national aspirations, AJC expressed the opinions of those who regarded themselves Jews by religion, not nationality or ethnicity. The nascent Zionist movement, to the contrary, gave voice to those who hoped for a Jewish national revival. Although Zionism remained small in numbers until the time of World War I, it claimed a mass base among eastern Europeans and a small but intellectually impressive following among educated Americans. It was a force not only for a vibrant Jewish culture but also for the democratization of Jewish life.

As in Europe, the Zionist movement emerged in America in the 1880s and 1890s. Some Americanized Jews responded enthusiastically. After reading Leo Pinsker's proto-Zionist tract *Autoemancipation*, poet Emma Lazarus proclaimed herself "one of the most devoted adherents to the new dogma." But at the grass roots, Hibbat Zion (Love of Zion) clubs began to form mainly in immigrant neighborhoods of New York and Brooklyn. After the first World Zionist Congress in 1897, these groups coalesced into the Federation of American Zionists (FAZ). Although most of its leaders were eastern European intellectuals such as Kasriel Sarasohn, the publisher of the *Yidishe tageblat*, FAZ attracted a number of American born or educated Jews, including its first chairman, Columbia University Semitics professor Richard Gottheil and Reform rabbis Judah Magnes and Stephen Wise. At first, FAZ adhered closely to Theodore Herzl's political Zionism, but it soon embraced cultural concerns. It also developed a number of allied organizations, including a fraternal order, Sons of Zion, and a youth group, Young Judea.[45]

Other branches of the Zionist movement emerged outside the FAZ framework. The Mizrachi movement organized those who sought to combine modern Jewish nationalism with traditional Judaism. It expressed its synthesis through the slogan "The Land of Israel for the People of Israel according to the Torah of Israel." On the other side of the spectrum, Poale Zion (Workers of Zion) united Zionism with socialism. It aimed to effect the national and social liberation of the Jewish working class through a socialist Jewish state in Palestine. In the meantime, it participated in both the Jewish national and the labor movements. The tiny Poale Zion party expanded its reach through its respected journal, *Yidisher kemfer* (Jewish Militant) and its allied fraternal order, the Jewish National Workers' Alliance.[46]

In 1912, the middle-class English-speaking members of one Zionist women's study group, the Hadassah Study Circle, issued a call for women to "stop talking and start doing something" for the Zionist cause. Meeting at Temple Emanu-El, they founded the Hadassah Chapter of the Daughters of Zion, which evolved into Hadassah—the Women's Zionist Organization of America. Hadassah eventually became not only the country's most successful women's association but also its largest Jewish organization. Although, as one of its founders put it, the women of Hadassah "did not stop talking," they nevertheless accomplished much based on their dual ideology of "collective motherhood" and practical action. Despite occasional criticism from male Zionists that Hadassah was *too* practical and not ideological enough, Hadassah continued to educate its members and the public in Jewish history and culture and in Zionist philosophy.[47]

Henrietta Szold guided Hadassah in its early years. By the time she helped found Hadassah, the dynamic and determined Szold was an accomplished Jewish communal activist and probably the most influential female member of the Jewish establishment. Born in Baltimore in 1860, she had received an American high school education and a thorough Jewish education from her father, Rabbi Benjamin Szold, a "liberal-minded" traditionalist. For many years, she worked as executive secretary of the Jewish Publication Society and as a noted translator and author. It 1893, she joined the Hibbat Zion circle in Baltimore. As she recalled, "I became a convert to Zionism the very moment I realized that it supplied my bruised, torn, and bloody nation, my distracted nation, with an ideal—an ideal that is balm to the self-inflicted wounds and to the wounds inflicted by others—an ideal that can be embraced by all, no matter what their attitude may be to other Jewish questions." Szold enrolled in

FAZ and joined the Hadassah study circle in 1907. She held that Zionism was the only path to "the re-establishment of Jewish life for the Jews."[48]

The promise of Jewish spiritual regeneration may have attracted Szold to Zionism, but a 1909 trip to Palestine with her mother turned her in a more material direction. Disgusted with the disease and poverty that she saw there and inspired by the American settlement-house movement, Szold devised a plan to aid the Jews of Palestine along similar lines. Szold and Hadassah volunteers, "influenced by their time and place," thus sought to provide the best of American medical standards and practice to the Jewish communities of Palestine. With funding from the non-Zionist philanthropist Nathan Straus, Hadassah sent the first American nurses to Palestine in 1913, opening a clinic in Jerusalem. Hadassah continued over the coming years to send nurses, doctors, and medical supplies and to fund clinics and, eventually, a famous hospital; in short, it built a modern Jewish infrastructure in Palestine.[49]

In terms of formal membership, the Zionist movement remained small until the onset of World War I, when the war and ascension of prominent Boston attorney Louis D. Brandeis to head FAZ enrolled tens of thousands of new recruits. By 1917, hundreds of Zionist societies, branches, lodges, and even synagogues flourished in New York City. The largest numbers by far were located in the neighborhoods of the eastern European immigrants and their children—especially the Lower East Side and Brooklyn neighborhoods such as working-class Brownsville and middle-class Borough Park. Members gathered in "camps" of Order Sons of Zion, branches of Mizrachi, Poale Zion and the Jewish National Workers' Alliance, and independent societies such as the fifty-member Hebrew-speaking B'nai Am Chai or the fifteen-member Tiphereth Zion Club of the Bronx. College students at City College, Columbia, Hunter, the Jewish Theological Seminary, New York University, and the Rabbinical College of America rallied to the Inter-collegiate Zionist Association. Two Hadassah sections covered "New York" and Brooklyn. Of the 119 Young Judea clubs in the city, 28 existed in Brownsville, where Zionist youth could be seen collecting money along Pitkin Avenue for the Jewish National Fund.[50]

While Zionists called for Jewish national revival in the Land of Israel, and the American Jewish Committee called for the integration of a Jewish religious community into the American nation, the Jewish Socialist movement harbored a range of attitudes toward the twin questions of the nature of

Jewish identity and the shape of the Jewish future. Some Socialists, especially among the older comrades who had arrived in America in the 1880s and '90s, struck a resolutely cosmopolitan stance, insisting that they spoke to and for the "Yiddish-speaking," not the "Jewish," proletariat. They looked forward to a world without national divisions and shared the assimilationism of AJC. Unlike AJC, however, they hesitated to join efforts they felt raised national, ethnic, or religious solidarity above that of class.

But increasingly after the turn of the century, Socialists adopted a more positive stance toward Jewish national identity. The most important intellectual proponent of the synthesis of political radicalism and Jewish nationalism was Chaim Zhitlovsky, who visited New York in 1904–1905 and then settled permanently there in 1908. Born in 1865, Zhitlovsky grew up in a Hasidic family in Vitebsk. He had been radicalized in his youth and as a member of the Russian Socialist Revolutionary Party remained an adherent of a non-Marxist form of socialism. After experiencing a reawakening of his Jewish identity, he developed a theory of diasporic Jewish nationhood with the Yiddish language as its central expression. A "handsome man with sparkling blue eyes and thick blond hair and beard," Zhitlovsky possessed a "sonorous voice" with which he spoke elegantly in Yiddish, Russian, and German. With a Ph.D. from the University of Berne, Zhitlovsky captivated audiences as a brilliant speaker and formidable debater. On one memorable occasion, he decisively defeated Cahan in a debate on the question "Is Marxism scientific?," concluding witheringly, "Comrade Cahan, you do not understand what we are dealing with here." Although he could be rigid and dogmatic in his espousal of a modern, secular Jewish culture in Yiddish, Zhitlovsky exerted enormous influence on a range of radical Jewish movements, including the Jewish Labor Bund (which saw itself as "national" but not "nationalist"), the Socialist-Territorialists (who believed that the Jews needed a territory but not necessarily in Palestine), and the Labor Zionists. Partly under Zhitlovsky's influence, adherents of these movements saw no conflict between Jewish peoplehood and Socialist internationalism.[51]

The supporters of the national-radical synthesis grew in number in New York as many young Bundists and Territorialists joined the migrant stream following the failure of the 1905 Russian Revolution. Entering the immigrant labor movement, they made it more overtly Jewish. In the Socialist Party, for example, they helped form the Jewish Socialist Federation (JSF) in 1912, over the objections of the old guard that protested such a move as an expression of Jewish separatism. In the Workmen's Circle, they pushed for more cultural projects—publications, classes, lectures, a theater, and, eventually, a network of children's schools—that would further develop a modern Yiddish culture, "purely secular" and "thoroughly Jewish." Although they still sometimes hesitated to join cross-class alliances, these Jewish Socialists spoke out vociferously on "Jewish issues" at home and abroad. They looked forward to the continued existence of a distinct Jewish people within an American "nation of nations." In 1917, the non-Zionist labor movement, including JSF, the Workmen's Circle, and other auxiliary organizations, still outdrew the Zionist societies.[52]

■ The Kehillah

These trends toward general organization of the Jewish community, and efforts for its democratization, received an ironic boost when in September 1908 New York City police commissioner Theodore A. Bingham published an article in the *North American Review*, titled "Foreign Criminals in New York." Backing up his accusations with statistics, Bingham blamed immigrant Jews for much of the crime in the city. "It is not astonishing," he wrote,

> that with a million Hebrews, mostly Russian, in the city (one-quarter of the population) perhaps half of the criminals should be of that race when we consider that ignorance of language, more particularly among men not physically fit for hard labor, is conducive to crime. . . . They are burglars, firebugs, pickpockets, and highway robbers —when they have the courage; but though all crime is their province, pocket-picking is the one to which they take most naturally.[53]

The Jewish community reacted angrily, with the Yiddish press and many organizations and leaders demanding Bingham's resignation. But questions lingered, even after Louis Marshall quietly arranged for Bingham to retract his statements in return for an end to the Lower East Side campaign against the commissioner.

Many Jews suspected that Bingham told an unfortunate truth. Indeed, significant Jewish criminal activity among immigrants on New York's Lower East Side had been the subject of several official inquiries since the 1890s. Two state investigations, those of the Lexow Committee in 1894 and the Mazet

Committee in 1899, had revealed Jewish involvement in such criminal activities as political corruption, prostitution, and extortion. By the time Bingham made his accusations, Jews controlled much, though apparently not a majority, of the prostitution in the city. In response, the uptown Jewish elite began to build social welfare agencies specifically designed to "'mitigate the dire consequences' of Jewish criminality." The question of Jewish criminality acquired increasing political importance as nativists sought to make a connection between immigrants and crime.[54]

The Bingham affair thus added fuel to the movement within the Jewish community toward greater centralized organization. Rabbi Magnes called on New York Jews to form a "permanent and representative organization that may speak on their behalf, that may defend their rights and liberties and that may also cope with the problems of criminality."[55] And a month later, a committee of downtown notables, headed by Magnes, convened a conference at Clinton Hall to discuss the creation of just such an organization. That meeting led to the official founding convention of the Kehillah (Jewish Community) of New York City, an attempt to merge traditional corporate Jewish communal organization with an American ethos of democracy and Progressive-era faith in technical expertise. The founding convention at the United Hebrew Charities building demonstrated that the Kehillah movement had a mass base, though not necessarily a majority of the community. Present were three hundred delegates representing 213 synagogues, charitable associations, mutual-benefit societies, lodges, educational institutions, Zionist groups, *landsmanshaft* federations, and other organizations. The leading lights of AJC, including Schiff and Marshall, also attended.

Judah Magnes held together this fragile coalition of uptown and downtown, Zionist and anti-nationalist, Orthodox and Reform, radical and conservative. Born in San Francisco in 1877, he had spent his youth in Oakland, California, excelling in journalism, sports, and oratory. Ordained as a Reform rabbi by Hebrew Union College in 1900, he arrived in New York in 1904 and by 1908 was rabbi of Temple Emanu-El, the congregation catering to the city's Jewish upper class. His marriage to Marshall's sister-in-law and his membership in AJC cemented his personal and political ties to the elite. Yet Magnes hardly typified its social milieu. Indeed, he cultivated a varied range of connections with the immigrant community. Rabbi of the flagship Reform congregation, he nevertheless occasionally prayed at a small Orthodox congregation in a tenement basement. An outspoken Zionist, he had radical and pacifist inclinations and enjoyed the company of Yiddish intellectuals. During the crisis of 1905, he had led the largest demonstration against the Russian pogroms. A brilliant preacher, with connections to widely varying Jewish circles in the city, Magnes was uniquely positioned to lead the Kehillah experiment.[56]

Magnes compared the Kehillah to a municipal government. One arm represented the democratic polity. Affiliated organizations sent delegates to the annual convention, which, in turn, elected an executive committee of twenty-five. These bodies expressed Jewish public opinion and set policy for the community. The founding convention resolved, uneasily, two contentious issues: One was a clause in the constitution that barred noncitizens from serving as convention delegates, passed after Magnes argued that it was necessary if the Kehillah was to avoid the image of an *imperium in imperio*. The other involved the relationship of the Kehillah to the American Jewish Committee. AJC disliked the idea of a truly democratically run community but went along anyway. In the end, a compromise made the Kehillah's executive committee the local district of AJC, giving AJC veto power over the involvement of the Kehillah in matters beyond New York City's boundaries. As it happens, AJC need not have worried. Its members consistently fared well in elections to the executive committee, often much better than self-proclaimed tribunes of the Lower East Side.

Based at the UHC building, the Kehillah's professional bureaus constituted the second arm of Magnes's Jewish municipal government. The first bureau, that of education, opened in 1910, and over the next several years the Kehillah established bureaus of social morals, industry, and philanthropic research. In addition, the Kehillah established the School for Jewish Communal Work and organized the Board of Orthodox Rabbis. Run by salaried staff, the bureaus attempted to coordinate, modernize, and professionalize Jewish efforts in their various fields. The Education Bureau created model schools and issued curricula and teaching materials; the Social Morals Bureau worked with police and maintained a staff of agents to gather intelligence on prostitution, gambling, and other vice in Jewish neighborhoods; the Bureau of Industry sought to mediate labor disputes. The Board of Orthodox Rabbis tried to set standards for the certification of kosher meat.[57]

In 1917, Samson Benderly, an educational reformer who headed the Kehillah's Bureau of Jewish Education, estimated that only 23.5 percent of Jewish children who attended public school received any sort of Jewish instruction at all at any given time. Though this meant that over the course of their school careers 68 percent of boys and 21 percent of girls would have acquired at least some Jewish education, Benderly also argued that what they got was dismally below the standards in the public schools. He had particularly harsh words for the traditional *hadorim* (classrooms), which he likened to "miserable holes." At best, wrote Benderly's associate Alexander Dushkin, the *heder* teachers were "earnest, mediaeval men, zealously trying to impart unwished for knowledge to the unwilling youngsters of the new world." At worst, they were ignorant peddlers and shop workers who passed themselves off as teachers to equally ignorant parents. The problem, Benderly and Dushkin both believed, was lack of systematic coordination and professionalism. Through their bureau, they raised pedagogical standards in all forms of Jewish school, calling for more professional training and institutional coordination.[58]

But by the time the United States entered World War I in 1917, the Kehillah was in crisis. Many of its problems stemmed from its attempt to form an all-encompassing corporate Jewish body in an open and pluralistic society. The community's large labor and Socialist sector remained aloof, unwilling to commit to an exercise in class collaboration. Even at its height, the Kehillah never won over more than a tenth of the thousands of individual societies and congregations, who jealously guarded their independence. And even among those who did affiliate, it was hard to impose order. The Orthodox failed to understand why they should follow dictates of Reform rabbis, and AJC resisted democratically arrived at decisions of the conventions. The war further damaged the Kehillah, as issues arising from it increasingly absorbed the community's attention. Having taken an outspokenly antiwar position, Magnes could no longer supply the glue to keep the enterprise together. It gradually dissipated, dissolving officially in 1922.[59]

■ World War I

World War I devastated the dense Jewish communities of central and eastern Europe, where a majority of world Jewry lived. Armies fought their way back and forth through Jewish cities and towns; Jewish men fought against each other as combatants on both sides; Jewish civilian populations suffered from the general ravages of war and from attacks specifically directed against them as Jews. The war uprooted hundreds of thousands and transformed them into refugees in Russia and Austria. Material losses were estimated at $400 million. Moreover, the hostilities severed previous channels of aid, from Berlin, London, or Paris, to the poverty-stricken populations of eastern Europe and Palestine and disrupted communal structures, whether traditional or modern.

American Jews almost alone remained unscathed by the war. Safe and relatively prosperous, they realized they had a special responsibility to aid their fellows in the war-torn areas of Europe and the Middle East. The Yiddish daily *Tageblat* expressed an opinion heard often as newspapers detailed the misery caused by the war: "It is important for American Jews to keep in mind that we are the only large Jewish community which is not caught up in the horrible tumult. We are the only part of the Jewish people which is living in peace and tranquility, so we should help, when we are able, the Jews on the other side of the ocean."[60] While connections between German Jews and Germany had weakened over time, those between recent eastern European immigrants and their home towns endured (though not necessarily with the governing authorities), and the detailed reports of devastation coming from those towns hit close to home.

Landsmanshaftn responded quickly. In the months following the outbreak of the war, disparate societies overcame their ideological and other differences to form united relief committees for their towns. Radical Workmen's Circle branches, Orthodox congregations, and everyone in between put aside their differences to raise thousands of dollars through mass appeals, theater parties, and balls. They held meetings where members heard firsthand accounts from recently arrived townspeople. The *landsmanshaft* federations channeled money to the old country and information to the new. The problem was getting the money across the frontlines to the intended recipients, who in many cases had fled and dispersed. By the end of hostilities, *landsmanshaft* relief committees had accumulated considerable sums.

The war-relief crisis once again stimulated calls for more centralized organization. Three national relief committees raised funds from distinct constituencies: the Central Relief Committee for the Relief of Jews Suffering through the War (CRC), founded at a meeting at the offices of the *Tageblat,* approached the Orthodox segment of the community; the American Jewish Relief Committee (AJRC) worked mainly with those associated with AJC; and labor and Socialist activists formed the Jewish People's Relief Committee of America (PRC). In an effort to rationalize the delivery of aid, however, CRC, AJRC, and PRC joined in the American Jewish Joint Distribution Committee (JDC, or Joint) to give relief with the "greatest directness and least duplication."[61] JDC ultimately survived the immediate crisis and its founding committees to become one of the most important American Jewish organizations, symbolizing American Jewry's role in providing material assistance to less fortunate Jews around the world.

The war also led to renewed calls for a centralized national organization that would speak for American Jewry on political matters at home and, especially, abroad. Proponents of an American Jewish Congress favored a more democratic, activist, and militant approach than did the American Jewish Committee. The idea of a Congress garnered most support among those who were inclined toward Zionism or other national conceptions of Jewish peoplehood, thereby generating more enthusiasm from the eastern European community than from the well-established central Europeans. Nevertheless, such "uptown" Zionists as Rabbis Magnes and Stephen Wise, as well as the newly converted Zionist leader Louis D. Brandeis of Boston, outspokenly supported the Congress idea.

The Zionist movement expanded greatly due both to the prestigious leadership of Brandeis, who stressed the compatibility of Jewish nationalism and American patriotism, and to American Jews' reaction to the devastation the war visited on European Jewry. The membership of the Federation of American Zionists (from 1918, the Zionist Organization of America) soared from 7,000 in 1914 to 150,000 in 1918.[62] New York also became the temporary headquarters of the world Zionist movement when the Provisional Executive Committee for Zionist Affairs (PEC) relocated there at the start of the war. Leading Zionists, such as David Ben-Gurion and Yitshak Ben-Tzvi, arrived in New York, having been expelled from Palestine by the Ottomans as nationals of a hostile power, and added prestige to the movement in the city. First under Brandeis and then under Wise, PEC played a leading role in raising funds for the Jewish community in Palestine and for refugees who had been expelled, negotiating with the British for recognition of Palestine as a Jewish national home and agitating for an American Jewish Congress.

As Brandeis gradually withdrew from active leadership after his appointment to the Supreme Court, Rabbi Stephen Wise took the reins of the movement. Wise, who later emerged as the preeminent Jewish leader of his generation, had been born in Budapest to a rabbinic family and had come to the United States at the age of six. A graduate of City College, with a doctorate from Columbia University, he received private ordination and embarked on a career as a Reform rabbi. Wise rejected an offer of the pulpit at New York's prestigious Temple Emanu-El because the trustees would not guarantee him enough independence to preach as he pleased. Instead, in 1907, he founded the Free Synagogue, "based on freedom of pulpit, free pews to all without fixed dues, outspoken criticism of social ills, the application of religion to their solution, and an extensive program of social welfare."[63] With his aquiline nose, jutting chin, and flowing mane, Wise became known for his soaring oratory and dramatic flair. An ardent liberal in politics and a passionate Zionist, he was, like Magnes, an uptown Reform rabbi who attempted to build bridges to the immigrant community downtown.

For three years, the American Jewish Congress sparked wide-ranging debates within the Jewish community. A dizzying array of players held meetings, attended rallies, and attempted negotiations. Finally, they reached compromises: the congress would seek to protect Jewish civil rights. "Group rights" were out, but the "rights of peoples," including the "Jewish people," were in. Three-quarters of the delegates were to be elected in open balloting and the rest appointed by organizations. Elections occurred on June 9 and 10, 1917, at polling stations across the country. In New York City, close to fifty polling stations, located in public and Hebrew schools, synagogues, YMHAs and YWHAs, and club rooms, including Temple Emanu-El, the HIAS building, and the Hebrew Education Society building in Brownsville, involved upward of 130,000 Jews. Nationally, over 300,000 people took part. Women had equal suffrage, a right they had already gained in New York State but not yet in the country as a whole. "We underestimated our forces," argued Yiddish journalist Joel Entin.

> As soon as the Sabbath was over, large groups of Jews thronged around the voting place. . . . There were many old people, Jews with beards, women in wigs and shawls.

. . . There were socialists, young and old, union people, Arbeter Ring Jews. . . . There were American Jewish girls who—judging by their manners and behavior—think, one could imagine, of nothing but enjoying themselves and dancing.

But, in fact, fewer people voted than organizers had predicted, possibly because of a last-minute Socialist boycott of the elections. Labor Zionists were well represented among the elected delegates, but no mainstream Socialists. Nevertheless, the elections constituted an unprecedented demonstration of communal democracy.[64]

When the American Jewish Congress finally met in Philadelphia in December 1918, after the war had ended and after several postponements, it named a delegation to represent American Jewry at the Versailles peace talks. There, however, the experienced diplomats of the American Jewish Committee carried out the real effective behind-the-scenes work. American Jews, who had already been in contact with President Woodrow Wilson and with the heads of the Polish government in formation, worked to write minority rights into the agreements leading to the independence of Poland and the other new central and eastern European states that emerged from the ruins of the Russian and Austro-Hungarian Empires. Marshall himself averred, "I am perhaps more responsible for the Minority Treaties than any other man."[65] Unfortunately, these liberal provisions for minority rights were more often violated than honored over the next couple of decades, handing American Jewry plenty to do in defense of Jewish rights abroad.

■ Federation

If the Kehillah and American Jewish Congress represented a vision of a democratic Jewish polity based on mass suffrage, the Federation movement based membership in the official Jewish community on the ability to provide charitable support to others. By 1916, dozens of Jewish philanthropic institutions, many of them with professional staffs, served a population of one and a half million and often competed for attention and dollars. Big donors, headed by German-born Felix Warburg of Kuhn Loeb, initiated a new round of centralization, this time in the form of a Federation for the Support of Jewish Philanthropic Societies. The Federation was intended as a joint fund-raising arm of its constituent agencies, which were to retain their autonomy in delivering services. The idea aimed to reduce duplication in fund-raising and to improve efficiency in service delivery by reducing pressure on organizations to raise their own money. New York was in fact a latecomer to the Federation model, which had been pioneered elsewhere. Even Brooklyn had a jump on Manhattan, having organized its own Federation of Jewish Charities in 1909. But the Manhattan and Bronx Federation dwarfed them all, raising over $2 million for eighty-four agencies by January 1917. (The New York and Brooklyn federations merged in 1943.)

The Federation attempted to mobilize a broad cross-section of the community—the minimum contribution was ten dollars, and the initial campaign attracted ninety-five hundred subscribers, upped to seventy thousand in January 1918. The Federation thus began to establish itself as the basic means through which middle- and upper-class Jews "paid their dues" for membership in the Jewish community at large. But the Federation idea was not really democratic. Its leadership remained in the hands of the wealthiest Jews—mostly at first of central European origin. In fact, meetings often took place at President Warburg's Fifth Avenue mansion, until they were moved to the nearby Harmonie Club in 1921. The Federation thus encouraged a "deferential community based on wealth."[66]

When New York Jews first responded to the Damascus blood libel in 1840, they were a small and insignificant community, with a correspondingly small and undeveloped communal structure and no permanent mechanisms to aid their sisters and brothers abroad. What distinguished them even then was that they lived in a relatively stable society that offered security and equality. Over the next eight decades, as their numbers exploded, New York Jews took advantage of that stability, security, and equality to elaborate a nearly innumerable array of organizations, ranging from very large to very small, some concerned primarily with their members' well-being and others with the state of the Jewish world. New York Jews sometimes sought unity, as when they established the Kehillah to speak for them in one voice, but most often their organizations divided them into multiple Jewries—English, German, Yiddish, and Ladino speaking; secular and Reform and traditionally religious; left wing and right wing; Zionist, Yiddishist, and assimilationist; uptown and downtown; rich and poor; immigrant and native born. One of New York's promises was Jews' freedom to organize their communal life as they saw fit and to be Jews as they wanted to define Jewishness. New York Jews took full advantage of that promise even as they also took advantage of the promise of security to make New York a base from which to aid Jews living in less favorable conditions abroad. In this way, New York became the capital not only of American but also of world Jewry.

In 1914, the Lower East Side sent Socialist labor lawyer Meyer London to the House of Representatives. His oratorical skills and ability to connect with the ordinary person helped propel Jewish immigrant Socialism to Washington. (Prints and Photographs Division, Library of Congress, Washington, DC)

CHAPTER 6

Jews at the Polls: The Rise of the Jewish Style in New York Politics

Even before the polls closed on Election Day 1914, people began to stream from all corners of the Lower East Side toward the building of the Yiddish-language *Jewish Daily Forward* towering over East Broadway. By nightfall, crowds filled Rutgers Square and Seward Park and flowed into the surrounding side streets. Those in the throng jostled for a better view of the screen hanging on the façade of the ten-story Forward Building, on which election results were to be projected. They were hoping for a Socialist victory in the heavily Jewish Twelfth Congressional District, a seat long held by Democrat Henry M. Goldfogle. The Socialist candidate, a popular labor lawyer named Meyer London, had run twice before. This time, it seemed he might win. But for hours there was no news. Only partial returns trickled in, and rumors spread that the Democratic machine was up to its old tricks, falsifying returns to swing the election to Goldfogle. At eleven o'clock, the conservative Yiddish daily *Tageblat* came out with an "extra" announcing Goldfogle's victory. But still the crowd stayed, waiting for word from the Socialist *Forward*.

Finally, at two o'clock in the morning, the official results were projected on the screen. Goldfogle conceded. London had won. The crowd erupted. People danced, sang, embraced, and kissed. At four o'clock, London was brought to the square, borne aloft on supporters' shoulders. A spontaneous procession snaked through the Lower East Side, the marchers waving brooms to signify a political housecleaning. At dawn, veteran Socialist Michael Zametkin, speaking from a balcony of the Forward Building, exclaimed, "Look, the sun is rising in the sky! And the sun is also rising on the Jewish Quarter, on the East Side!"[1]

The Forward Building, in competition with Jarmulowsky's bank to be the tallest on the Lower East Side, assertively proclaimed the rise of the Socialist sun in the Jewish community. Indeed, etchings of suns ran in bands along the top of the building, as if to proclaim the *Forward's* illumination even on cloudy days. Looking out on the open spaces of Rutgers Square and Seward Park, the

The architecture of the *Jewish Daily Forward's* building (1912) resembled that of the *Evening Post's* building. But whereas the *Post's* façade featured statues representing the spoken word, early written word, printed word, and modern editors, the Forward Building proclaimed its identity through busts of Socialist leaders and the name of the newspaper flanked by the Socialist Party's raised torch emblem. (Forward Association)

building visibly advertised the newspaper and its cause. The *Forward*'s name was emblazoned in large Yiddish and English letters on the top of the façade, along with the Socialist Party's arm-and-torch emblem. Above the front doorway were four relief portraits of Socialist heroes: Marx, Engels, Lasalle, and perhaps (the identity of the fourth is disputed to this day) Liebknecht. As the builders had hoped, 175 East Broadway became the main address for the Jewish labor and Socialist movements upon its completion in 1912. In addition to editorial and business offices and the printing plant of the *Forward*, the building contained meeting rooms and a thousand-seat auditorium. The Jewish labor fraternal order the Workmen's Circle was headquartered there, as were the United Hebrew Trades (a federation of predominantly Jewish trade unions) and the Jewish Socialist Federation. Union locals and radical *landsmanshaftn* used the meeting rooms.[2]

Not quite two miles to the north, at 141 East Fourteenth Street, stood Tammany Hall, headquarters of the controversial dominant faction of the Democratic Party in Manhattan. The three-story red-brick and marble edifice was actually owned by the Society of Saint Tammany, or the Columbian Order, a fraternal group that formed the political machine's inner circle. The cornerstone of the order's second "wigwam" had been laid with a great display of patriotic pomp in 1867, and when completed the following year, Tammany Hall also housed meeting rooms and a large auditorium, the scene of the 1868 Democratic National Convention. A pediment on the roof contained a larger-than-life statue of an American Indian chief—St. Tammany, the order's legendary patron—and the inscription "Tammany Society, 1789–1867." While Tammany's chieftains were wheeling and dealing in their offices upstairs, the downstairs was leased out to Tony Pastor's New Fourteenth Street Theater, a variety house. Tammany Hall, too, embodied the political power of an important ethnic group, for although the order was named for a legendary Indian chief and used pseudo-Indian lore, Irish dominated its leadership and political base.[3]

At Tammany Hall, as well as in its associated local clubs on the Lower East Side, the mood must have been rather glum on the night of November 3, 1914. Not only had Republican anti-Tammany crusader Charles Whitman won the governorship, but London's victory exposed the Democratic machine's weakness on its own front stoop. The immigrant communities in Lower Manhattan had long been Tammany bastions, and the machine had worked hard to

Tammany Hall (1868) on East Fourteenth Street housed the most famous Democratic Party political machine in the country. Controlled primarily by Irish Americans by the turn of the century, Tammany nevertheless attracted some Jews as well. (Photographed by Irving Underhill in 1914; Library of Congress, LC-USZ62-101734)

build bridges to the newer ethnic groups pouring into the area, especially eastern European Jews. Nevertheless, the Socialists represented an ethnic as well as political challenge, injecting a whole new style into the New York political scene.

The Forward Building and Tammany Hall symbolized opposing pulls on Jewish political allegiances, and each succeeded in attracting many Jews. Of course, there were other options as well: Jewish Republicans and anti-Tammany Democrats, reformers of various stripes, and other sorts of radicals. New York promised Jews that they would be able to participate in the city's political life. And Jews did take part, as voters, activists, and candidates. But although individual Jews played important roles in New York politics throughout the nineteenth century, only with the creation of large and dense Jewish districts at the end of the century did a distinctive Jewish position in New York politics emerge.

By the second decade of the twentieth century, Jews were poised to redeem the promise in full as a leading element on the New York political scene. Active on all levels, Jews' real, though divided, vote influenced elections. But obstacles remained. Jews could become active in Tammany Hall but soon ran into an "emerald ceiling" that prevented non-Irish from gaining decisive power. They could join the Socialist Party, but Socialists could not break out of their Jewish electoral ghetto and so proved of limited use as a means for exerting influence. The Republican Party might have been more open to newcomers than Tammany was, but as a minority party in the city, it too was of limited value.

Nevertheless, this period laid the foundation for the Jewish assumption of a full share of political power in New York (always in coalition with others, of course) in the 1920s, '30s, and beyond. What was distinctive about Jewish politics became a hallmark of New York City's general political culture—its practical use of governmental power to counter the capitalist market in favor of social justice, whether on the municipal, state, or national level. In alliance with such progressive politicians as Governor Al Smith, President Franklin D. Roosevelt, and Mayor Fiorello La Guardia, New York's Jewish social reformers and even Socialists ultimately entered the mainstream to help build New York's unusual social democratic polity.

In the early republic, Jews had inclined toward the Jeffersonians, who had an anticlerical streak and were more open to immigrants than their opponents were. Jews were even among the early leaders of the Society of St. Tammany, or the Columbian Order, then a fraternal organization with Jeffersonian leanings. The Jeffersonians evolved into the Democratic Party, and many Jews retained their loyalty, reinforced by mercantile ties with the cotton South as the Democrats became the chief defender of the slave system.[4] New York's Representative Emanuel Hart, for example, became a leader of the conservative "hunker" faction that embraced the cause of the slave states and resisted the intrusion of antislavery sentiment into the Democratic Party.

The Republican Party attracted support among central European Jewish immigrants and their children. New York Jews likely voted Republican in presidential elections between 1860 and 1916. In the late nineteenth century, a number of Jews occupied leadership positions in the party. Among New York's prominent Jewish Republicans was Abram Dittenhoefer, a native of South Carolina. He joined the party against his merchant father's wishes after hearing Republican Congressman Benjamin Wade's rebuke of Democrat Judah Benjamin for his support of slavery as an "Israelite with Egyptian principles." Later, Edward Lauterbach served as chair of the GOP in New York County in the 1890s. In 1892, former congressman Edwin Einstein became the first Jew to head a major-party local ticket when Republicans nominated him for mayor. Significantly, when he had first run for Congress in 1878, he was generally portrayed as a German, but now he was seen as a Jew. His candidacy had little hope of success and was meant primarily to attract Jewish votes to the state ticket. Tammany responded in part by increasing its nominations of Jews, most notably Ferdinand Levy, a multilingual immigrant and former coroner, for city register. Two years later, Tammany offered the mayoral nomination to the wealthy philanthropist Nathan Straus, but Straus withdrew when convinced by the editors of the *American Hebrew* that he was simply being used to draw votes for Tammany's other candidates.[5]

■ Tammany and the Jews

The heart of the Tammany Hall political machine was a fraternal order founded in 1786 and named for a semilegendary Lenape Indian chief. The Society of Saint Tammany, or the Columbian Order, was soon drawn into partisan politics, allied with the Jeffersonians. By the mid-nineteenth century, the Tammany Society became the nucleus of a powerful political machine that dominated the Democratic Party in Manhattan and, often, the government of New York City. Tammany cultivated a base of support among the city's working-class and immigrant communities, providing them with services, jobs, and entertainment, in exchange for the votes that kept Tammany in power. Some of the services and jobs came from the organization's own resources or contacts in private businesses, but most came from the expanding bureaucracy and technical machinery of local government. With control of the growing resources of local government at stake, winning elections became vital to the politicians and their followers. When persuasion and patronage failed, Tammany resorted to violence, intimidation, and fraud. It thrived in a hypermasculine environment of saloons, volunteer fire companies, and blood sports. Constant association with corruption tainted Tammany, occasionally erupting in spectacular scandals, the biggest of which involved Boss William M. Tweed. Tammany's leader between 1863 and 1871, Tweed headed a band of scoundrels known as the Tweed Ring, who looted the public treasury with great abandon. Their signature project, a court house behind City Hall, finished 5,100 percent over budget, with most of the excess cost lining the Ring's pockets.

The Tweed Ring garnered help looting the city from Judge Albert Cardozo, father of future Jewish U.S. Supreme Court justice Benjamin Cardozo. Tall and thin, with long thick curly hair and bushy eyebrows, Albert Cardozo was said to have had a face with "a slight Hebrew cast." A less friendly observer claimed that he had the "eyes of a serpent looking from the face of a corpse," an indication of a fatal character flaw. Cardozo displayed the "dignity and reserve" befitting a justice of the New York State Supreme Court, but as the Tweed Ring collapsed, he resigned in 1872 to avoid impeachment. Returning to private practice, he later became a "sachem" (executive committee member) of Tammany Hall.[6]

Tammany possessed the capacity to reform itself, and it did so periodically. By the twentieth century, it had muted the violence. But Tammany retained its special style of politics: as neither public service nor a means to change the world but as a business, with its chief trade in jobs and favors. In exchange for votes, supporters got aid in times of need or help with petty problems involving the courts or licensing authorities. Active members of the machine received jobs ranging from menial positions to commissionerships. Although Tammany leaders sometimes held public office, real power resided not in formal governmental positions but in party positions. These were organized hierarchically, from lowest-ranked election district "captains" or "ward heelers" through assembly district "leaders" to the chair of the county executive committee—the "boss." International and national issues mattered little to Tammany; its politics was local, personal, and face-to-face.

By the middle of the nineteenth century, Tammany Hall had become closely associated with the Irish Catholic community. As Irish immigrants and their children became Tammany's primary base of support, they, in turn, saw the machine as a source of needed social services, jobs, power, and upward mobility. When Honest John Kelly took over as the first Irish Catholic boss in 1871, after the Tweed scandal, he cemented the relationship. By the turn of the twentieth century, Tammany was an Irish stronghold.[7]

Jewish Tammanyites accommodated themselves to the Hall's largely Irish

Catholic culture. Some Jews found Tammany's highly personal, face-to-face, nonideological business model of politics very congenial, not to mention materially advantageous. As one early twentieth-century writer observed,

> The Russian Jewish young man, generally a lawyer, who casts his fortunes with Tammany Hall, gradually assumes the habits of his Tammany confreres. He chews, smokes, drinks, gambles, visits the clubrooms religiously, attends the politico-social functions of the year, is prominent in the purchase of chowder tickets, and is rewarded, perhaps, by being permitted to play at the Tammany chowder game of poker with the elite of the district. . . . As a rule, these young Russian Jewish men who make their way into Tammany Hall belong to a lower order. In some cases the office holders are taken from the most colorless class, having nothing but regularity and party fealty as their redeeming features.[8]

Along with easy sociability and a personal touch, Tammany's Jews, like its Irish, valued loyalty and a certain kind of honesty. A good man delivered on promises of a job, emergency aid, or a kickback. Generosity was valued too, and knowing whether it should be given discreetly or ostentatiously became an important skill. Where the means for the generosity were attained was seldom questioned.

Martin Engel emerged in the 1890s as one of the few Jewish influential Tammanyites when he became leader of the heavily Jewish Eighth Assembly District in the heart of the Lower East Side. Born in the neighborhood, Engel inherited his father's butcher trade, becoming known as the "Kosher Chicken Czar." "Stolid" and "squat," Engel was "physically unattractive," his face having been "smashed beyond all recognition" in a barroom brawl and then surgically reconstructed. A reporter noted Engel's lawsuit against his surgeon on the grounds that his kosher meat market was losing business because his flattened nose had not come out "Hebraic" enough. What he lacked in native beauty, Engel made up for by ostentatiously flaunting his wealth. Social worker Mary Simkhovitch recalled that he "used to drive through in an open barouche, his fingers laden with diamonds, and more diamonds shone from his cravat." At least some of that wealth was ill gotten, and for a time Engel personified Tammany's close association with prostitution and other forms of vice. Engel was heavily involved in the illicit sex trade as owner and protector of brothels in his district and beyond. Among his other civic activities, he served as an officer of the Independent Benevolent Association, a mutual aid society for brothel owners and associated politicians, saloon keepers, and real estate agents. When Charles Murphy took over the reins as boss in 1902, he endeavored once more to clean up Tammany's image. One of the first things he did was to depose Engel and install Florrie Sullivan, a member of the powerful—and Irish—Sullivan clan, in his place.[9]

Engel's Jewish associate in the Eighth Assembly District was Alderman Charles "Silver Dollar" Smith, a burly former paperhanger turned saloon keeper whose original name was most likely Charles Solomon. Born in Germany, Smith had been brought to America by his family at the age of one. (Or perhaps he had been born in the Eighth Ward, as he once told a court.) He acquired his nickname when he opened his saloon opposite the Essex Market Court. Embedded in the floor of Smith's establishment were one thousand silver dollars, a fifty-dollar gold piece in the center. The back room featured a chandelier with five hundred silver dollars, and the bar was decorated with a star and crescent made up of silver coins of various denominations. Smith claimed to have made back his investment within three days of opening, from trade brought by people who "wanted to see how this fool had wasted his money." Elected to the New York State Assembly in 1888 initially as a Republican, Smith soon switched parties. Although prone to violence (he was arrested twice during his first campaign), Smith was not without his virtues. When he died in 1899, his obituary noted that he was "one of the few politicians in the district who understood the Hebrew residents and their language." Rev. Gabriel Hirsch's eulogy paid him the ultimate Tammany compliment. "He never broke a promise to a friend," Hirsch averred, "and he had a warm and generous heart."[10]

By the time of Silver Dollar Smith's demise, many more politicians understood the "Hebrew residents and their language," as Tammany recognized the growing importance of the Jewish population by naming more Jews to the ticket. In 1900, Tammany nominated Judge Henry M. Goldfogle for Congress. Though he was not the first Jew to represent New York in Congress, Goldfogle *was* the first Jew to go to Washington representing a recognizably Jewish district. Born in New York in 1856, Goldfogle had graduated from local public schools. He read for the law, entered private practice, and in 1887 was elected to the municipal court. He served in Congress until 1914, returning for one more term in 1919–1920. Goldfogle was the "typical son of typical Jewish immigrant parents," according to Rabbi Stephen Wise, who eulogized him at his funeral in 1929. Tammany represented him as "not *a* Jewish congressman, but *the* Jewish congressman." And Goldfogle indeed fought explicitly for Jewish interests, whether having to do with Russian anti-Semitism or open immigration.[11]

Despite more frequent nominations for public office, Jews remained subordinate within Tammany Hall. With few exceptions, Irishmen retained the district leaderships well into the twentieth century, even in areas with Jewish majorities. As one Tammany boss reputedly argued, "The Irish are natural leaders. The strain of Limerick keeps them at the top. They have the ability to handle men. Even the Jewish districts have Irish leaders. The Jews want to be ruled by them." Whether or not it was true that the Jews wanted to be ruled by the Irish, the Irish district leaders managed to find enough Jewish support to keep their hold on the party. Partly, they did so by co-opting individual Jews into the machine.[12] In the Third Assembly District, straddling the Bowery, for example, Big Tim Sullivan ruled until shortly before his death in 1913. According to his biographer, Big Tim "liked Jews generally, thought they were smart, and admired their energy." As his district filled up more and more with Jews (and Italians, a group that fared worse than the Jews within the organization), he cultivated an image as a friend of the Jewish people. His associates liked to tell the story of how Sullivan had intervened with a street gang that had been harassing Jewish peddlers. Sullivan not only ousted the gang from its clubhouse but also had the venue turned into a synagogue. This act of philosemitism, according to the story, won for Sullivan undying admiration and support of his Jewish constituents. To cement their loyalty, he brought some in as captains. But Sullivan governed mostly with the help of an inner circle consisting mainly of relatives and other Irishmen.[13]

In the neighboring Fourth Assembly District, followers of leader John Ahearn and, after his death in 1921, his son Eddy told similar stories of their beneficence toward Jews: how the Ahearn Association made sure that firefighters hosed down the synagogue before Rosh Hashanah, distributed matzo and kosher food before Passover, and protected Jewish merchants from Sunday closing laws and wine-distributing rabbis from prohibition agents. Jewish club members became translators on the evenings when constituents would come to the club headquarters at 290 East Broadway to ask for help. "Mr. Ahearn would give a comforting nod," remembered one longtime Jewish worker, "then turn to me and say, 'Louis, talk to this man in his own language. He didn't come here to see a show.'"[14]

But the Ahearns also did more to incorporate Jews into the core of their organization. In fact, by 1920, most of the district's office holders were Jewish, and the inner circle of the Ahearn Association included Judge Aaron Jefferson Levy, Assemblyman Harry Schimmel, and Leon Stand. Ahearn loyalist and ward heeler Louis Eisenstein became the Irish dynasty's chronicler and Jewish apologist when he later wrote his memoirs. Eisenstein had an unusually benign view of Jewish-Irish relations. There was "never any religious friction," in his view, between Jewish businessmen and the police, who "winked at Sunday closing laws." Senator Barney Dowling was "our 'Irish-Jewish senator,'" and Father Byrnes of St. Mary's was "our 'Catholic-Jewish priest.'" Indeed, Eisenstein epitomized the Tammany ethos of loyalty to one's constituents and leaders. When he wrote that Jewish "assimilation into the club was complete," he was describing his own adjustment to Tammany's traditional political culture.[15]

■ Republicans

Republicans in the immigrant neighborhoods often differed little from the Democrats, except that they had to content themselves with patronage leftovers. As one observer put it,

> The Republican Jewish politician is another remarkable product of the metropolis. Socially he is, perhaps, a grade higher than the [Democratic politician]; his parents, by dint of hard work, have amassed a comfortable fortune, and their offspring has possibly had the benefit of a better preliminary education and has come in contact with wealthier young men, who are Republicans in their political affiliations.[16]

The rise of Samuel Koenig to the leadership of the Republican Party illustrates the relative openness of the local GOP to Jewish leadership. Born in Austria-Hungary in 1872, Koenig came to the United States as a child. At the age of nineteen, he was already campaigning for the Republicans, and soon he had founded his own organization, the Federal Club in the Sixth Assembly District. By 1911, he was the leader of the Republican Party in Manhattan, a post he kept for twenty-two years. A "neat, trim man with rimless spectacles," "without a trace of ruthlessness," Koenig was well liked. He ran his organization, as his friend Tammany ward heeler Louis Eisenstein put it, "along the familiar lines cut by Tammany, with some of the coarser edges smoothed out." Indeed, at one political dinner, Koenig told Eisenstein, "We Republicans and Democrats speak the same language. We fight only one day a year—from 6 am to the hour the polls are closed." The rest of the time, Koenig contented himself running the minority party in the city and collecting what patronage he could from federal and state governments when Republicans were in power and from Tammany for taking an occasional dive in an election.[17]

■ Socialists

By the 1910s, Socialism seemed to offer a more robust alternative to Tammany Hall than did the Republicans. Socialist power resulted from a long process of movement building that began in the early 1880s with the arrival of large numbers of immigrants from eastern Europe. Indeed, the movement had gotten off to a slow start. The first radical Russian-Jewish intellectuals formed a series of short-lived organizations that preached a mélange of Socialist and Anarchist ideas mostly in Russian and German. Although they professed a desire to reach masses of Jewish workers, their resistance to using Yiddish, which they considered a debased jargon incapable of expressing serious ideas, put a barrier between them and their Yiddish-speaking intended audience.

These early Jewish Socialists learned especially from the small but vibrant German radical milieu that already flourished in New York. The linguistic affinity between German and Yiddish aided the relationship, as did the Germans' largely secular orientation. *Forward* editor Abraham Cahan recalled that the German newspapers, especially Johan Most's Anarchist *Die Freiheit* and Sergei Schewitsch's Socialist *Volkszeitung* "played a major role in [the] intellectual development" of New York's Yiddish-speaking radicals.[18] With the help of the Germans, most Jewish radicals found their way to Marxism and the predominantly German Socialist Labor Party.

The year 1886 was a landmark one for the Jewish radicals, on both industrial and political fronts. Caught up in the mood of labor unrest that swept the city and the nation, over nine thousand mainly Jewish cloak makers walked off the job demanding an end to the contracting system. Other Jewish workers struck as well. On May 1, the Jewish Workers' Association led some three thousand Jewish workers as they marched to Union Square together with tens of thousands of German, Irish, and native-born American workers to demand the eight-hour day. The Jewish Workers' Association also organized support among immigrants for strikes of non-Jewish streetcar workers, waiters, and musicians.

Outraged at the arrest of several strike leaders, the labor movement decided to organize its own political party to contest New York's mayoral race that fall. The United Labor Party recruited as its candidate the radical social philosopher Henry George, who had begun to attract a following for his theories on the origins of poverty and inequality. The "short and scrappy redhead" ran on a platform calling for higher pay; shorter hours; better working conditions; public ownership of railroads, telegraphs, and streetcars; an end to police harassment of labor assemblies; and an end to collusion between politicians and business against workers' interests.[19] Above all, George stressed his signature issue, a single confiscatory tax on real estate, which, he believed, would finance a range of public welfare measures and end the monopoly on land that led to overcrowded housing conditions for the poor. George soon attracted a broad coalition of the disaffected, including most of the labor movement, Irish nationalists, middle-class reformers, German Socialists, and dissident Roman Catholic priests. Their vigorous campaign, featuring street meetings, rallies, and parades, rattled the upper classes, Tammany Hall, and the Catholic hierarchy, all of whom saw in it a threat to their control over the city.

The Jewish Workers' Association threw itself into the struggle. It opened an office on Canal Street and sponsored its own nightly rallies featuring Yiddish speakers. The highlight of the Jewish campaign for George came five days before the election, when George himself visited a rally in a Stanton Street hall and compared his movement to the exodus of the Israelites from Egyptian bondage. Despite his followers' enthusiasm, George lost the election to Democrat Abram Hewitt, gaining just shy of a third of the vote and finishing ahead of Republican Theodore Roosevelt. George carried the solid German and Irish working-class neighborhoods and most likely won a plurality of the as-yet-small Jewish vote. In the immediate aftermath of the election, the radical press hailed the results as a tangible demonstration of working-class mobilization. But soon the delicate coalition that had backed the campaign fell apart, and the movement, including its Jewish section, dissipated.[20]

Gradually, the Socialists overcame their resistance to using the language of the masses and attracted a following with their speaking and writing. Over the years, the migration of Jews already radicalized in Russia also augmented their numbers. Some immigrant Jews found in Socialism an answer to questions that plagued them—their downward social mobility in both the old country and the new, the long hours they worked in the factories, the miserable conditions in the tenements, and their marginalization as an ethnic minority. An immigrant sheet-metal worker recalled his first encounter with Socialist ideas shortly after his arrival in New York in 1896:

> The first couple of days after my arrival, my brother-in-law Motl took me to street meetings to hear various speakers about the election campaign. Suddenly, I heard a Yiddish speaker speaking from another corner of Suffolk and Rivington Streets. A young man was standing on a box and speaking full of enthusiasm. I pushed through the crowd to be closer to the speaker. . . . I had never heard such words in my town: "Worker freedom. . . . You toil bitterly in the sweatshops and your children go naked and barefoot. . . . Social, political, and economic equality and security" . . .
>
> It was the first time in my life I had heard the word "socialist." Excited by the speaker, I went home to sleep. As I lay on my bed, my mind worked over the speech that I had just heard: Work should be based on justice and right. . . . Your children go around in the street barefoot and naked. . . . With these and similar thoughts, I fell asleep.[21]

He soon joined a local Socialist club and remained active in the movement the rest of his life. Others had similar experiences, whether in the United States or Europe.

Socialists also began to build an organizational infrastructure that amplified their voice in the community and allowed them to touch directly the lives of tens of thousands of immigrants. On an April Sunday in 1892, ten workers met in an Essex Street tenement apartment to establish a class-conscious mutual aid society called the Arbeter Ring, or Workmen's Circle. Like the thousands of other immigrant mutual aid societies, the Workmen's Circle aimed to take care of its members in times of need, to provide medical care and burial expenses. More than the others, however, it explicitly emphasized education and solidarity with the working class in its "struggle against oppression and exploitation." In 1900, the several existing branches of the society reorganized as a national fraternal order. By 1917, the Socialist-led Workmen's Circle had 240 branches in New York City alone, with some twenty-five thousand members.[22]

The *Jewish Daily Forward*, or *Forverts*, established in 1897, influenced the rise of the Socialist movement even more than did the Workmen's Circle. The

Forward strove to be a lively and engaging newspaper, with language accessible to the average working-class immigrant reader and interests broader than orthodox Socialist doctrine or internecine party squabbles. For most of its first five decades, the *Forward* was led by Abraham Cahan, a veteran Yiddish Socialist propagandist and journalist with a talent for reaching a wide audience. By 1910, the *Forward* had become the most widely read Yiddish newspaper in the world and the most important Socialist daily in the country.

Born in 1860, Abraham Cahan grew up in Vilna, the intellectual capital of Jewish Lithuania. He received a traditional education and then attended the Vilna Jewish Teachers' Seminary, a Russian-language school that trained its students to become Jewish communal functionaries officially recognized by the Tsarist regime. Although he never attended university, Cahan fell in with a crowd of Russian-speaking revolutionary intellectuals, was forced into hiding, and in 1882 fled Russia. That same year, he gave the first Yiddish Socialist speech in America. In the 1880s and '90s, he had a hand in several early Yiddish newspapers. He also quickly learned English well enough to teach it to newcomers and to become an accomplished English-language writer.

The *Forward*'s founding editor, Cahan left after several months to join the staff of Lincoln Steffens's *Commercial Advertiser*. In almost five years as an English-language reporter for one of the country's premier muckraking newspapers, Cahan absorbed the methods of American popular journalism. When he returned to the *Forward*, he purposefully applied those methods to the Yiddish field. Dour and autocratic, Cahan was disliked by many of his writers, but he had a keen sense of his readers' tastes and interests. His many detractors among the left-wing Yiddish intelligentsia grumbled that he neglected serious issues, pandering instead to his uneducated readers with sensational stories on tenement fires and celebrity love triangles.

But despite the *Forward*'s critics, it continued to preach Socialism. It covered all the major events of the day from a radical perspective, and its inside pages contained analysis by leading European and American Socialists. It reported on labor struggles, Jewish and non-Jewish, not simply as an observer but as a passionate partisan—often raising money to aid striking workers. In fact, the *Forward* contributed some of its profits as a successful business enterprise to strike funds and Socialist campaign coffers. In election season, the *Forward* became a campaign sheet, urging its readers to vote the Socialist ticket.[23]

The Socialist Party (SP) superseded the Socialist Labor Party (SLP) as the main Socialist political body after the turn of the century. In contrast to the doctrinaire SLP, the SP's big tent accommodated progressive reformers and ardent revolutionaries, Christian Socialists and Marxist freethinkers, Oklahoma farmers and urban industrial workers. Joining the Socialist Party linked immigrant New York Jews to midwestern labor leaders such as Eugene Victor Debs, the party's perennial presidential candidate, and political operatives such as Victor Berger, head of the successful Socialist political machine in Milwaukee. In New York, the party included members of all ethnic stripes, but as the German population dwindled, Jewish neighborhoods emerged as the main bastions of Socialist strength.

The Socialist-led unions, especially in the garment industry, provided the final pillar of Socialist strength after the turn of the century. Throughout the 1880s and 1890s, Jewish workers had gained a reputation for waging spectacular strikes, only to let their unions dissipate once moments of acute conflict had ended.[24] This started to change after the founding of the International Ladies' Garment Workers' Union (ILGWU) in 1900 and culminated in the "Great Revolt" that shook the garment industry and the Jewish immigrant community in general between 1909 and 1914. In those five years, the ILGWU and other unions waged a series of giant, mostly successful strikes, mobilizing tens of thousands of members. In 1909, the United Hebrew Trades enrolled just five thousand workers in 41 unions. Five years later, its 111 affiliates claimed a quarter million members.

The opening battle of the Great Revolt came in late 1909, with the "Uprising of the 20,000," a strike of shirtwaist makers, two-thirds of them young Jewish women and most of the rest Italian. That summer and fall, strikes had broken out at a number of shops. The ILGWU's Local 25 began to press for a general strike in the industry, but the parent union held back, afraid that it lacked the resources to wage such a broad struggle. Finally, at a mass meeting at Cooper Union on November 22, a twenty-three-year-old member of Local 25's executive committee interrupted the leaders' speeches to appeal for a strike. "Curly-haired, dark-eyed, flirtatious," Clara Lemlich had arrived from Ukraine six years earlier. By the time of the strike, she had already established a reputation as a passionate Socialist street speaker in Yiddish and English and a militant striker willing to brave physical danger. Lemlich's brief speech, recounted in many variations, became legendary in the Jewish labor movement: "I am a working girl, one of those striking against intolerable conditions. I am tired of listening to speakers who talk in generalities. What we are here for is to decide whether or not to strike. I offer a resolution that a general strike be declared —now."[25] The next day, the first fifteen thousand workers went out on strike.

The strike was a qualified success. The largest companies held out longer than the small firms, resorting to violence and brutal arrests to intimidate the strikers. But the violence only helped to win over public opinion for the young women, especially when a notable contingent of middle- and upper-class allies from the Women's Trade Union League, including Anne Morgan and Alva Belmont, joined the protests. The strike ended in February 1910, without an industry-wide contract or union recognition in the big shops, but the workers had made gains in pay and working conditions. Most important, the membership of Local 25, about five hundred before the strike, now stood at twenty thousand.[26]

Five months after the end of the waist makers' strike, seventy-five thousand cloak-maker members of the ILGWU, most of them Jewish men, walked off their jobs. The cloak makers were more successful in gaining union recognition. In fact, with the intervention of Jewish lawyers and business leaders such as Louis Brandeis, Louis Marshall, and Jacob Schiff, union lawyers led by Meyer London forged an agreement with the employers' association. The "Protocol of Peace" established the garment industry's first permanent mechanism for settling grievances and disputes. By 1912, 90 percent of New York's cloak makers had joined the union.[27]

The Socialists also boasted the most articulate and intelligent leaders of all the political factions within the community. The same observer who commented on Jewish Democratic and Republican politicians noted that the Socialists were "the most remarkable of all. . . . As a rule the Socialist leaders are students, whose collegiate course has been prematurely cut off by reasons of migrations caused by anti-Semitism, or economic distress." Here they return to their studies and become "powerful debater[s] or excellent journalist[s]."[28]

Morris Hillquit fit that mold. Born in Riga, Latvia, in 1869 to a poor, German-speaking family, Hillquit (né Hilkowitz) received a Russian-language gymnasium education. He arrived in the United States in 1886 and went to work sewing shirts. Soon, however, he left the shops to work full-time in the labor and Socialist movement. After mastering Yiddish and writing for the Yiddish radical press, Hillquit turned to English-language writing and speaking, becoming a well-known popularizer of Socialist ideas. In the meantime, he graduated from New York University Law School and began to practice law. Hillquit made a good living as a corporate lawyer, even as he also took pro bono civil liberties cases and served as counsel to various unions. As he immersed himself in the Socialist movement on a national scale, he distanced himself from its specifically New York Jewish sector. He periodically returned to assist the garment unions in their struggles and to run for office. But although liked and respected, Hillquit never attracted a mass following in the immigrant community. One problem was his retiring public personality. Another problem was his ambiguous stance on immigration restriction, the result of an effort to find common ground with the prorestriction mainstream labor movement, but unpopular among immigrant Jews.[29]

Meyer London's career resembled Hillquit's in some respects but differed in that he continued to feel at home in the Jewish immigrant community and remained intimately connected with its life and its institutions. Born in 1871 in Kalvaria, Suwalki Gubernia, London grew up there and in Zenkov, Ukraine. He received both a traditional Jewish and modern Russian education and was hoping to enter gymnasium when his father, who had already emigrated to the United States, sent for the rest of the family. London arrived in New York in 1891, going to work in his father's radical print shop. London learned English and soon entered New York University Law School, graduating in 1898.

Quickly Americanized, London often addressed even immigrant audiences in English. Impatient with the SLP's doctrinaire leadership, he was one of the first in New York to join up with the midwestern group headed by Debs. But, unlike Hillquit, he confounded expectations by continuing to live on the Lower East Side, where his saintly nature became legendary. As an attorney for tenants, workers, and unions, he often refused payment for his services, and over the years he worked for the ILGWU and the Workmen's Circle. As the union's counsel and chief negotiator during the 1910 cloak makers' strike, London helped shape the Protocol of Peace. With his generosity, empathy with the powerless and oppressed, and devotion to the labor movement, London exemplified, in Irving Howe's words, a great "Socialist man." He spoke to audiences "from the heart to the heart" about the world's injustice. He also saw himself as a member of the immigrant *Jewish* community, though he rejected Jewish nationalism. Unlike Hillquit, London consistently opposed immigration restriction. When World War I broke out, London headed the People's

Relief Committee, the labor movement's effort to raise funds for Jewish war victims. Upon his election to Congress in 1914, he told a celebratory audience, "I hope that my presence will represent an entirely different type of Jew from the kind that Congress is accustomed to see."[30] Conscious of his visibility as a Jewish Socialist, London accepted his pioneering role in formulating a new form of American Jewish politics simultaneously committed to social justice and sensitive to ethnic concerns.

■ Reform

A variety of reform movements—whether of the good-government or social-reform type—enlisted the energies of middle- and upper-class Jewish activists. Like the Socialists, these reformers put principle above personal gain, but they thought in terms of a generalized "public good" rather than working-class interests. Middle-class reform movements were especially important as vehicles for women's activism before 1917, when women gained the right to vote in New York State. Jews among the reformers, wrote one observer, represented "the noblest type" of Jewish political activists, operating on the "highest planes of civic patriotism without regard to political preferment."[31]

Jewish "good-government" reformers such as Simon Sterne helped to overthrow the Tweed Ring in 1871 and pushed for honest, cheap, and efficient local government. Sterne, a native of Philadelphia and graduate of the University of Pennsylvania Law School, was one of several prominent Jews who served on the Committee of Seventy, the organization of respected citizens that led the indignant charge against Tweed. As the committee's secretary, he drafted a new charter for New York City that passed the state legislature but was vetoed by the Tammany-allied governor. Like many good-government advocates, Sterne believed in government by the "best men," by which he meant successful businessmen and professionals like himself. A social conservative, he enunciated a doctrine that local government was designed to serve and protect property owners. A surfeit of democracy, he believed, would only benefit the interests of the "tax eaters."[32]

But reform also elicited support among the broad Jewish electorate, including the new immigrants, especially if the candidates' platforms added a measure of social reform to the good-government mix. Despite Tammany mythology of a contented multiethnic working-class machine bloc, Jews did not always see the political machine as a benevolent protector against Sunday blue laws and police harassment. Rather, they were as likely to perceive a protection racket in which the district leader and his cronies benefited from both the fines gained from police crackdowns *and* fees and bribes paid to annul those fines. Tickets for the annual club "chowder" represented another unwanted and illegitimate cost of doing business in Tammany-dominated districts. The cultural strangeness of Tammany's ethos of politics as a slightly shady business enterprise, combined with its relative stinginess in doling out the proceeds of that enterprise to new immigrants, meant that working-class Jews often willingly followed their well-heeled brethren in voting for reform candidates.

Indeed, the outcome of the 1886 George campaign brought home to reformers and Tammany alike that Jews could not be counted on to accept blindly the dictates of party loyalty. They were inveterate ticket splitters, open to dissident appeals. Jewish districts gave crucial support to the reform victories of mayors William Strong in 1894 and (after the consolidation of the greater city) Seth Low in 1901. In both cases, reformers targeted immigrant neighborhoods for special appeals and put together successful coalitions of non-Irish ethnic groups, middle- and upper-class advocates of good government, social reformers, and Republicans. The Low campaign opened an office on Delancey Street and even spawned a Yiddish-language campaign newspaper. In both cases, however, the coalitions crumbled under the pressures of governance, as both mayors proved friendlier toward business interests than those of their working-class constituents—and added a dose of Protestant moralism by rigorously enforcing Sunday closing laws. The Strong and Low mayoralties set a pattern of reform administrations unable to survive beyond one term, partly because they lost the Jewish vote. In 1905, working-class Jewish districts once again voted for reform, but this time in the form of the radical populism of publisher William Randolph Hearst, running for mayor on a platform of municipal ownership of public utilities. Like Henry George, he helped demonstrate the new Jewish voters' unnerving propensity for radicalism.[33]

Reform politics also opened up space for women to participate in the public sphere, from which conventional morality barred them, by developing a sense of itself as essentially nonpolitical. Politics by definition was dirty, partisan, concerned with self-interest, and bound up with the masculine culture of vice. But reform was clean, nonpartisan, concerned with the public interest, and could be seen as an extension of women's duty to safeguard the morality of the home. Especially after investigations in the 1890s revealed Tammany's close connection with the commercial sex industry, groups such as the Women's Municipal League took an active role in reform campaigns, even when women could not vote. Jewish women such as Lillian Wald and Maud Nathan worked with the league to bring reform's message to immigrant Jewish neighborhoods, where, as Nathan recalled, residents had "confidence in [them] as . . . co-religionist[s]."[34]

Maud Nathan embodied the link often made by women between good-government reform and social reform. Unlike some of her colleagues, she also attempted to draw an explicit connection between Jewish values and social justice. Born in 1862 to a prominent old Sephardic family, Nathan early imbibed the "spirit of New York's social directory," but her privileged upbringing was interrupted when her father's business reverses forced the family to relocate to Green Bay, Wisconsin. After returning to New York as an adult, Nathan sought to leave the "narrow [Jewish] communal circle," even while remaining religiously observant. She saw "righteousness and justice" as the "heart of Judaism" and applied these values universally in her public activity. A vice president of the Women's Municipal League and an ardent suffragist, she left her deepest mark as cofounder in 1890 of the New York section of the National Consumers' League.[35]

Under Nathan's leadership, the Consumers' League desired to improve the conditions under which women worked, especially in department stores and garment sweatshops. The league's exhibits and publications educated the public concerning the problems faced by working women, appealing both to the conscience and self-interest of its middle-class audience. The league presented a twofold argument. First, it argued, "To live means to buy, to buy means to have power, to have power means to have duties." And consumers' duty involved making sure that their purchases did not support pernicious work environments or low wages. Second, the league reacted to prevalent fears of contagious disease by arguing that unhealthful conditions in tenement shops posed a threat to those who bought the clothing made in them. The league supported legislation, but its most innovative program was its label, issued between 1898 an 1918, to be sewn into garments produced under conditions it judged humane and healthful.[36]

Like Nathan, Belle Lindner Israels Moskowitz made connections between the causes of good government and social reform. But, unlike Nathan, Moskowitz came from modest immigrant stock, born in 1877 into the family of a watchmaker from East Prussia. Educated at the Horace Mann School and Teachers' College, she dabbled in Ethical Culture but remained affiliated with the Jewish community, especially while married to her first husband, architect Charles Israels. She began her career as a social worker at the Educational Alliance and the United Hebrew Charities and first achieved prominence with the National Council of Jewish Women as a crusader against the menace posed to young women by unregulated dance halls. From dance halls, she moved on to fight prostitution, which put her in frequent conflict with Tammany Hall.

Moved by the industrial struggles of 1909–1910 and the Triangle Fire of 1911, Moskowitz (then Israels; she married fellow reformer Henry Moskowitz in 1914) became involved in the "industrial field" and electoral politics. For several years during the period of the Protocol of Peace in the garment industry, she served as grievance clerk and chief clerk for the Dress and Waist Manufacturers' Association, a job that propelled her into the center of bitterly contested industrial and labor questions. She also joined the Progressive Party crusade in 1912, campaigning for Theodore Roosevelt and Oscar Straus, whose nomination for governor she seconded at the Progressive state convention.[37]

■ The Triangle Fire

The tragedy that brought Belle Moskowitz into the heart of New York industrial politics unfolded in the course of minutes late in the afternoon of March 25, 1911. A fire that day at the Triangle Shirtwaist Company influenced the direction of politics in New York for the next several decades and demonstrated the central role that Jews had come to play in the city's economic, social, and political life. Within about half an hour, 146 workers, most of them young Jewish and Italian immigrant women, died, either in the flames and smoke or by jumping to their deaths. Devastating to the communities that suffered most of the losses, the fire shook the entire city and set it on a course of social reform under the unlikely leadership of a coalition of Tammany Hall stalwarts and earnest reformers. The fire also contributed to an upsurge of the Socialist Party in the Jewish community.

Contrary to popular belief, the Triangle company did not run a sweatshop. Rather, Triangle employed hundreds of workers in a large (twenty-seven thousand square feet) factory on three floors of a modern (1900) loft building. The Asch building, a block east of Washington Square, was spacious, light, and airy. It had twelve-foot ceilings and elevators. It was considered fireproof. Unfortunately, the factory's contents were not fireproof. A carelessly discarded cigarette close to quitting time ignited tons of cotton scraps and cloth bundles scattered around Triangle's three floors. Panic ensued as workers tried to escape through locked doors or doors that opened inward, down inadequate fire escapes that buckled under the weight and heat, or down packed elevators that stopped running when the heat became too intense for their operators. Many victims fell eight, nine, or ten stories to their deaths, shredding fire department nets. Onlookers, including Consumers' League activist Frances Perkins, who lived just blocks away, and policemen who just thirteen months earlier had battled some of these same workers during their great strike, watched with horror from the streets below. The irony was not lost that the Triangle company had been one of the large firms that had successfully resisted the union.[38]

The neighborhoods from which the dead workers had come were momentarily stunned. The *Forward*, under the banner headline "The Morgue Is Full with Our Sacrifices," wrote on its front page, "Yesterday was one of the most horrific days in the history of the Jewish quarter. Our entire immigrant population moves about in a daze of horror and pain."[39] Then came a flurry of activity—protest meetings, memorial gatherings, relief drives—culminating in a symbolic funeral for the last unidentified victims and a mass meeting at the Metropolitan Opera House. Class tensions began to emerge. Jewish philanthropic groups, along with Mayor William Gaynor, feared that the mass funeral would get out of hand and tried to stop it. But a committee of Local 25, the Women's Trade Union League, the Socialist Party, the United Hebrew Trades, and other unions, chaired by shirtwaist maker and author Teresa Malkiel, proceeded with plans for a procession to the Workmen's Circle cemetery. When the day came, dreary and wet, thirty thousand people solemnly accompanied the carriages to the pier carrying their union banners.

At the Metropolitan Opera House meeting, workers filled the galleries while the wealthy philanthropists and reformers sat in the orchestra. Rabbi Stephen Wise of the Free Synagogue pointedly reminded the crowd that the tragedy had not been an act of God but the result of "the greed of man." But Rose Schneiderman captured best the defiant mood of the labor movement. At four foot nine, the redheaded Schneiderman, a former cap maker, a union activist, and Socialist, served as vice president and chief organizer of the New

York chapter of the Women's Trade Union League. Schneiderman made a career of forging cross-class alliances with middle-class friends of the labor movement. But that day she spoke bitterly to the assembled notables:

> The old inquisition had its rack and its thumbscrews and its instruments of torture with iron teeth. We know what these things are today: The iron teeth are our necessities, the thumbscrews are the high-powered and swift machinery close to which we must work, and the rack is here in the firetrap structures that will destroy us the minute they catch fire. . . .
>
> This is not the first time girls have been burned alive in this city. Every week I must learn of the untimely death of one of my sister workers. Every year thousands of us are maimed. The life of men and women is so cheap and property is so sacred!

Looking at her well-dressed audience, she bluntly told them, "I can't talk fellowship to you who are gathered here. Too much blood has been spilled. . . . It is up to the working people to save themselves."[40]

Schneiderman was not the only one to draw radical class-conscious conclusions from the fire. At a number of meetings, speakers made the connection even more explicitly than she did. At a cloak makers' rally, a worker in the crowd shouted, "Why shouldn't the working class elect its own candidates?" when a conservative labor leader called for the election of "honest men." At another meeting, Socialist editor A. M. Simons similarly declared, "We have the votes," and asked, "Why should we not have the power?" The SP staged a debate on the subject of how the Socialist victory in Milwaukee that year could be replicated in New York.[41]

Meanwhile, others closer to the political mainstream were also moved to action. Tammany Assemblyman Al Smith, who represented part of the Lower East Side in Albany, went to the morgue to talk with his constituents who had been affected by the fire. When a group of reformers approached him about setting up an investigative committee, he suggested it be made a committee of the legislature so that it would have political teeth. And when the Factory Investigating Commission (FIC) came into being at the end of June, Smith joined State Senator Robert F. Wagner as cochair. In the course of the commission's four-year life, it heard hundreds of witnesses and compiled thousands of pages of testimony. Its members traveled around the state, visiting factories and other workplaces, viewing for themselves the conditions under which New York's workers toiled.

The FIC was a milestone. First, it proposed and saw passed dozens of new laws governing workplace safety and health issues, as well as wages and hours. Second, it brought elements of Tammany Hall into league with the sort of high-minded social reformers who would never have collaborated with them just a short time earlier. In part, this resulted from a conscious effort by Tammany to shore up its shaky support among Jews and the working class. But it also reflected a personal awakening on the part of Smith and Wagner, both of whom went on, Smith as governor and Wagner as a U.S. senator, to play central roles in the development of the welfare state on both state and national levels. Third, the FIC showed just how central Jews had become to the political life of the city and state. Of the FIC members, publisher and fire buff Simon Brentano and American Federation of Labor chief Samuel Gompers were Jewish, though they had little connection to the Jewish community or culture. But the FIC staff included a number of Jews, some closely identified with either uptown Jewish philanthropic circles or the immigrant labor community. Among the former were the FIC's counsel Abram Elkus, a prominent jurist and member of the American Jewish Committee who later served as U.S. ambassador to Turkey. The investigatory staff was even more bound up with the Jewish labor movement. Its chief, Dr. George Price, an immigrant physician, had authored pamphlets and articles in Russian and Yiddish on Jewish immigrant life in America. Rose Schneiderman, Clara Lemlich, and labor activist Pauline Newman all worked for the FIC, with Newman especially important in guiding Wagner and Smith through the state's industrial netherworlds.[42]

■ 1912

In the wake of the Triangle Fire, the 1912 election pitted a Tammany Hall newly committed to social reform against the new Progressive Party of Theodore Roosevelt, the surging Socialists, and the Republicans. For president, the Republicans renominated President William Howard Taft, who had disappointed many Jews by failing to fulfill his promise to abrogate the 1832 trade treaty with Russia after Russia refused to honor the American passports of Jewish travelers. The Democrats put up the southern-born governor of New Jersey, Woodrow Wilson. Wilson gained some Jewish support with his progressive positions and scholarly approach, as well as his opposition to the Russian policy. The charismatic and saintly Debs bore the Socialist standard for the fourth time.

But former president Theodore Roosevelt, running on the ticket of the breakaway Progressive Party, attracted the most attention in Jewish districts. Roosevelt's welcoming attitude toward the new wave of immigrants, and Jews in particular, had already made him a familiar and popular figure in the immigrant community. A native New Yorker, Roosevelt had appointed a number of Jews to the police department when he was commissioner in the 1890s. And, at Jacob Schiff's recommendation, he had named Oscar Straus the first Jewish cabinet secretary in 1906. Roosevelt advocated that immigrants become good Americans by conforming to Anglo-American culture and had supported measures to weed out the sickly and the politically dangerous. But Jewish voters focused more on his many statements criticizing anti-Semitism and on his opposition to immigration restriction on the grounds that the melting pot should include a healthy dash of Jewish and other new-stock ethnic groups. Likewise, his Progressive Party was just the kind of independent political movement that attracted Jewish support in local elections.[43]

The Progressive Party's state convention tapped Oscar Straus for governor, his nomination seconded by Belle Moskowitz. The German-born Straus had grown up in Georgia, where he for a time attended a Baptist Sunday school. But though his Hebrew was said to be "rudimentary," he expressed his strong Jewish identity by playing a leading role in Jewish philanthropy and communal affairs. As an amateur historian, he specialized in discovering Hebraic roots for America's democratic institutions. More than some others of his social milieu, he was also willing to enter general politics. While his brothers Isidor and Nathan ran the family business, Macy's department store, Oscar Straus served in a number of appointive posts, culminating in his three-year stint as secretary of commerce and labor under Presidents Roosevelt and Taft. Along with Isidor (who died in the sinking of the *Titanic* earlier in the year) and Nathan, Straus was already a popular figure in the immigrant neighborhoods. And although Straus refused to emphasize his Jewishness in the campaign, his party, whose theme song was the Protestant hymn "Onward, Christian Soldiers," did not hesitate to do so.

Ironically, Straus's main opponent, non-Jewish Democratic Congressman William Sulzer, played the ethnic card more enthusiastically in Jewish districts than did Straus. Ruggedly handsome and "one of Tammany Hall's leading orators," Sulzer modeled himself after Henry Clay (with a dash of Lincoln). As representative of an East Side Manhattan district, Sulzer was outspoken in the fight to abrogate the Russian-American trade treaty and had won over many Jewish friends. In fact, Sulzer's nomination partly reflected Tammany's response to the Straus candidacy. Sulzer attacked Straus mercilessly from a Jewish point of view. The former secretary should "tell us what he ever did to aid his race at home or abroad," Sulzer challenged. "Go and ask him how many Jews he sent back to be murdered by the Czar while he was secretary of commerce and labor."[44]

Election results in the Jewish districts once again demonstrated that Jewish voters were willing to split tickets. Though Roosevelt barely edged out Wilson in most of the predominantly Jewish assembly districts in Manhattan and Brooklyn, Straus carried all of them with a healthy plurality. Meanwhile, Tammany Congressman Goldfogle won reelection, but with numbers that did not bode well for the future. In a four-way race, he received only 39.3 percent of the vote, while Socialist Meyer London took 31.2 percent and Progressive Henry Moskowitz took 22.3 percent. It seemed likely that a substantial number of Moskowitz voters would align with the Socialists next time.[45]

Sulzer was elected governor of New York. But he did not remain in office for long. He ran afoul of Tammany boss Charles Murphy, who orchestrated his impeachment. Jews once again played an array of important supporting parts in this unfolding drama. Sulzer's trouble started when he started to think of himself as an independent progressive governor and not the Tammany tool that Murphy had hoped he would be. After Sulzer turned down Murphy's offers of money, dragged his feet on recommended appointments, supported an open primary bill, and started an investigation into corruption that threatened Tammany interests, Murphy decided to get rid of the governor once and for all.

Ironically, Sulzer was impeached for improprieties in campaign financing. The role of prosecutor fell to the majority leader, Ahearn protégé Aaron Jefferson Levy. Interviewed at the start of the process, Levy told a reporter, "If you knew what I do, you would know that Governor Sulzer hasn't a chance."[46] In the course of the trial, it turned out that the uptown Jewish elite had rewarded Sulzer for his work on the Russian issue by tendering him considerable material support. Jacob Schiff, Abram Elkus, and Henry Morgenthau had all given him money. Herbert Lehman was an especially generous backer, testifying that he had given Sulzer $5,000 unconditionally, for whatever purpose he saw fit. As Sulzer's counsel, Louis Marshall tried hard to get the governor off the hook, but in vain. The Jewish elite thus stuck loyally with Sulzer in a way that his Tammany prosecutors should have appreciated.

The vote to remove Sulzer came in October 1913, less than a month before the general election, and Tammany's attack on the governor backfired. The dynamic young reformer John Purroy Mitchel swept into the mayoralty on the Fusion ticket with substantial Jewish support.[47] (Fusion, in New York political parlance, meant an independent reform ticket with support from elements of the Democratic and Republican Parties along with independents.) Sulzer returned to the Lower East Side triumphantly, winning election to the state assembly. Many Tammany men lost their races. Levy barely survived to gain a seat on the municipal court. But as late as 1923, when he sought to move up to the state supreme court, he worried that memory of his role in the Sulzer affair would cost him votes.[48]

■ Socialist Upsurge

Even more disturbing to Tammany was the Socialist surge that began in 1914 with the election of Meyer London to Congress and continued for more than half a decade. The maturation of the Jewish labor movement contributed to London's victory, but so did his personality and willingness to view himself as a representative of an ethnic as well as a class community. In contrast to Hillquit's earlier campaigns for the same seat, London willingly appealed to a constituency beyond the proletariat by portraying himself as the most viable alternative to Tammany. As one shopkeeper who intended to vote for London explained, "The politicians sap the blood of us businessmen," but London would "liberate us from graft." Leftists in the Socialist Party criticized the London campaign's personal and "racial" appeals and muttered about a supposed unofficial "split for London" strategy. But the voters responded, giving London 49.5 percent of the vote to Goldfogle's 41.1 percent.[49]

The following year, Brownsville, Brooklyn, sent Socialist Abraham Shiplacoff to the state assembly, the first of a number of Socialists to represent Jewish districts in the state legislature and the city board of aldermen. For the next several years, the Socialists seriously contested every local election, sometimes as the largest party in the working-class Jewish areas of Manhattan, Brooklyn, and the Bronx. The Socialist movement maintained a lively presence in Jewish neighborhoods. In Brownsville, for example, the Russian-born Shiplacoff, a former shop worker turned teacher, and Barnett Wolff, son of a local grocer, organized the William Morris Educational Club to work among young English speakers. Later, they helped build the Labor Lyceum on Sackman Street, which provided programs in Yiddish and English. The neighborhood home of the Workmen's Circle and the garment unions, the Lyceum offered concerts, lectures, debates, socials, dances, and holiday celebrations. At election time, it was Socialist Party campaign headquarters. The dense network of labor organizations based at the Lyceum sent Shiplacoff, Wolff, and others to the state assembly and board of alderman.[50]

The high point for the Socialists' surge came in 1917, the year that Morris Hillquit mounted a vigorous "peace and milk" campaign for mayor. By that time, the "fighting" reform mayor, John Purroy Mitchel, had worn out his welcome among large swaths of the electorate through his inflexible and impolitic actions. A Catholic and grandson of a hero of Irish nationalism, Mitchel seemed to go out of his way to alienate fellow Catholics by attacking the Church. He lost Jewish support as well by implementing the "Gary Plan," a system designed to enrich the curriculum in the public schools and to cut costs by accommodating more students, but which many people in the community feared would shunt children of immigrant parents into vocational tracks and obstruct their social mobility. While some reformers continued to believe that Mitchel's nonpartisan, expert-driven administration was the best New York ever had, many voters had come to view him as an elitist snob and bigot.

American entry into World War I earlier in the year also became a major bone of contention in the campaign. Attempting to seize the mantle of patriotism, Mitchel called himself a "100 percent American mayor" and attacked his Democratic opponents as allies of the Hohenzollerns and Habsburgs. Unfortunately for Mitchel, large sections of the Irish, German, and Jewish populations in New York harbored antiwar sentiments. The Democrats that year put up John "Red Mike" Hylan, a Brooklyn judge and machine mediocrity. On domestic issues, Hylan took a populist stance, vowing to hold down subway fares and calling for municipal ownership of public utilities. He tried to straddle the war issue, proclaiming his support for the war effort but decrying Mitchel's militarism.[51]

Hillquit, for his part, criticized Mitchel's "cold business administration" and pushed the traditional Socialist program of social transformation. But it was the war issue that really generated the tremendous enthusiasm around the campaign. With Hillquit voicing his party's unambiguous opposition to the war effort, the campaign acquired such momentum that Tammany took fright. It responded by sending in "wrecking crews" to break up Socialist street meetings and soliciting warnings by Jewish Democratic stalwarts that a large Hillquit vote would stir up anti-Semitism. As the election became a referendum on the war, the Socialist Party expanded its support in German and Irish districts, but Hillquit only received a majority of votes in Jewish neighborhoods. In the end, Hylan beat Mitchel decisively. Hillquit finished a strong third in a four-way race, with over 20 percent of the vote. That year, the Socialists sent a delegation of ten to the state assembly and seven to the board of aldermen. Socialist Jacob Panken was elected to the municipal court for a ten-year term.[52]

Although the war helped propel the Socialists to their highest level of support in 1917, it also sowed the seeds of dissension within their ranks and contributed to their subsequent rapid electoral decline. London spoke out against the war, but he took what he saw as a responsible position as a member of Congress. In practice, this meant that he voted against the declaration of war and conscription but supported the sale of Liberty Bonds once the United States had entered the fray. The party's left wing—soon to split to form the Communist Party—excoriated him for his compromises, while prowar groups attacked him as a traitor. In the meantime, London forfeited the support of Labor Zionists when he refused to endorse the British government's Balfour Declaration favoring a Jewish homeland in Palestine. He lost his seat in 1918.

London returned to Congress after the 1920 elections, which also sent five Socialists to the state assembly. This turned out to be the Socialist Party's last hurrah. In addition to internal dissension over the war and the new Soviet government in Russia, the Socialists faced a stepped-up attack from their political opponents. Districts were gerrymandered to dilute Socialist voting strength. The board of aldermen refused to seat the two Socialists elected in 1919 until weeks before the 1920 election, and in a case that became a cause célèbre, the state legislature rejected the five Socialists elected to the assembly in 1920. Finally, the Democrats and Republicans took to running Fusion candidates against the Socialists. In the face of altered districts, fused opposition, state repression, and a dose of old-fashioned Tammany intimidation, the Socialists lost their toe-hold in the electoral system. By 1923, the only remaining Socialist elected official was Judge Jacob Panken, whose ten-year term ended in 1927.[53]

■ Woman Suffrage

In the midst of the political ferment of the late 1910s, Jewish voters provided critical support for the 1917 referendum that gave women the right to vote in New York State. Indeed, the working-class Jewish districts of New York City were among the most prosuffrage. The Jewish labor movement and Socialist Party played a role in this victory, as did a decade of suffragist activity aimed directly at capturing immigrant Jewish votes. The spike in the Jewish and Socialist vote brought about by the Hillquit campaign for mayor helped push the 1917 referendum over the top. It is true that by that time Tammany Hall also favored votes for women, but Tammany's core constituency—Irish Catholic men—remained the least favorably inclined toward female suffrage.[54]

Supporters of suffrage within the Jewish immigrant community stressed its link to the cause of labor. Outspoken labor suffragists such as Lemlich, Schneiderman, and Malkiel emphasized the importance of suffrage to women workers in their efforts to win better conditions in the shops and at home. As Lemlich put it,

> The manufacturer has the vote; the bosses have votes, the foremen have votes, the inspectors have votes. The working girl has no vote. When she asks to have a building in which she must work made clean and safe, the officials do not have to listen. The bosses can say to the officials: "Our votes put you in office. . . . Never mind what they say. . . . They can't do anything." That is true. For until the men in the Legislature at Albany represent her as well as the bosses and foremen, she will not get justice; she will not get fair conditions. That is why the working-woman now says that she must have the vote.

Some suffrage organizations issued Yiddish literature and held street meetings and parades in the immigrant districts. They successfully lobbied the Yiddish press, which, from left to right, supported suffrage by 1917. The ILGWU and the United Hebrew Trades endorsed suffrage. The Women's Suffrage Party systematically canvassed the immigrant neighborhoods, finding widespread support among Jewish men as well as women.[55]

Maud Nathan was one of the few Jewish women to play a leading role in middle-class suffrage circles, but affluent Jews also supported the movement.

The central body of Reform rabbis endorsed votes for women, and Rabbi Stephen Wise was outspoken in his support.

■ Al Smith

New York women voted for the first time in 1918. That year, Al Smith was elected governor with widespread Jewish support. By that time, he had become a hero to many social reformers, who overcame their distaste for his Tammany roots to back his candidacy. His inner circle now included Jews, such as Abram Elkus, the lawyer for the FIC who became Smith's campaign manager, and Elkus's law partner, Joseph Proskauer. Perhaps most surprising, not only for her Jewishness and reform background but also for her gender, Belle Moskowitz emerged as Smith's most trusted and influential adviser. During the campaign, Moskowitz joined a number of progressives who surprised themselves as much as anyone by creating the Independent Citizens' Committee for Al Smith. Moskowitz headed the committee's Women's Division and during the campaign had her first "real personal meeting" with Smith to advise him on women's attitudes toward the issue of prohibition. After the election, she pushed him to initiate a number of social reform projects. She also recruited Robert Moses, of Jewish origin though he did not think of himself as a Jew, to Smith's administration. Smith's embrace of structural governmental reform under the influence of Moses surprised observers even more than his espousal of social policies.[56]

By 1920, Jews were just beginning to make a distinctive mark on New York's politics. In the following decades, Jews provided the most reliable constituency for a politics of social reform that helped make New York City one of the most advanced social democratic polities in the country. In the 1930s and 1940s, Jewish Socialists entered the mainstream first through the American Labor Party and then through the Liberal Party, which backed progressive candidates regardless of their party affiliation and commanded large minorities of the Jewish vote. In the meantime, Al Smith and Franklin Delano Roosevelt transformed the state's Democratic Party into a more consistent advocate of social reform, attracting the bulk of Jewish support. Even the Republican Party in New York had its liberal wing, in which Jews played a prominent role. Herbert Lehman became the first Jewish governor in 1933, but non-Jewish liberals Smith, Roosevelt, and Mayor Fiorello La Guardia also served as important vehicles for Jewish involvement in politics and government. By 1940, Jews' numbers and activism made them one of the city's most important voting blocs. The legacy of Jewish labor and reformist politics thus endured for the better part of the century in New York's political culture.

Bertha Kalich arrived in New York City in the mid-1890s; there her great acting talent landed her prime roles in the Yiddish and, for a time, English-language theater. (American Jewish Historical Society, New York and Newton Centre, MA)

CHAPTER 7

Jews and
New York Culture

On any day in 1905, any number of well-dressed, neatly groomed men—prosperous bankers, businessmen, and professionals—could be found in the sumptuous club rooms at 45 West Forty-Second Street. Depending on the day of the week and time of day, they might be reading in the library, smoking in one of the lounges, playing cards, bowling, or exercising in the well-equipped gymnasium. A few patronized the bar. Sometimes their wives and sisters might join them for dinner in the elegant dining room or for a dance in the palatial ballroom—though of late "stag" evenings, which brought men together for entertainments without the ladies, had become more popular. The men were members of the Harmonie Club, one of the oldest, most exclusive, and best-appointed social clubs in the city, with membership limited to 650 of those able to pay its high initiation fee and annual dues. Prospective members waited for places to open up.

All the men were Jews, though this was seldom noted at Harmonie Club activities or even in the club's official histories. Most were of German descent, and while English had become the club's dominant language by 1905, one could still hear some older members conversing in German. One of the major topics of conversation that year must have been Harmonie's impending move from its thirty-eight-year-old building on Forty-Second Street to new quarters on East Sixtieth Street. The old clubhouse, designed by Henry Fernbach, who was also responsible for Temple Emanu-El and Central Synagogue, had cost over $200,000 to build. In 1867, its three stories, plus basement and attic, and one-hundred-foot front on the street impressed passersby. But as times changed, balls and "large entertainments" had fallen out of fashion. Now members' own residences were so large and opulent that most major family social events took place at home. The new clubhouse, a tall Renaissance palace designed by Stanford White and built at a cost of $875,000, omitted the ballroom and catered mostly to the men alone. It guaranteed that Harmonie remained the leader among the approximately thirteen Jewish social clubs in the city.[1]

The social scene in the heart of the immigrant district downtown differed strikingly. On East Broadway, Jewish men and women, not so elegantly dressed as Harmonie Club members, though perhaps with a certain bohemian flair, might be seen descending the steps to Goodman and Levine's basement cafe. Opening the door, they were assaulted by the "smell of roast herring and cooked fish, sour borsht, fried pancakes, bad coffee, scalded milk, as well as odors so intermingled that it wasn't easy to say which was which." Many cafe patrons had the calloused hands of building-trades workers or factory operatives, but some at Goodman and Levine's knew that they were really something else—literary men and women, members of a new and revolutionary generation of Yiddish poets. Braving "barely endurable" food, a haze of cigarette smoke, the owners' hostile stares when the poets did not spend enough money, kitchen heat in the summer, and icy drafts in the winter, the young writers—and those who liked to be among writers—came night after night to discuss literary theories and gossip.[2]

Goodman and Levine's was one of nearly three hundred Jewish cafes on the Lower East Side. Also known as "coffee and cake parlors" or "coffee saloons," eastern European Jewish immigrant cafes actually served up more tea than coffee, along with food and a lot of talk. These were working-class resorts, but unlike the saloons that traditionally served as American workingmen's "clubs," they offered little alcohol and attracted an intellectual and artistic clientele that established their reputation as vibrant centers of debate on politics, art, and society. Unlike the working-class saloons and the upper-class Harmonie Club, the cafes attracted women as well as men. As one sympathetic if slightly scandalized observer exclaimed, "And where the cigarette smoke is thickest and the denunciation of the present forms of government loudest, there you find women!" Each cafe had its specialty. Radicals congregated at the Monopole on Second Avenue. Theater people met first at Schreiber's on Canal Street and later at the Café Royale on Second Avenue, which eventually became the preeminent cafe of the Yiddish-speaking intelligentsia. Goodman and Levine's set aside several tables for the young poets who came there regularly, disdaining the better-established literary haunt Herrick's (later Sholem's) on Division Street, partly for ideological reasons and partly because Goodman and Levine's was cheaper.[3]

Strikingly different in terms of class, language, customs, and ethos, the Harmonie Club and Goodman and Levine's cafe represent only part of a vast range of Jewish cultural expressions in New York. Such venues contributed to a vibrant, dynamic urban scene that encouraged new ideas and cultural productivity. Indeed, as New York became both the nation's cultural capital and its Jewish capital, Jews came to play a leading role in the production of all sorts of music, literature, drama, and visual art. Viewing art and ideas as vital elements of daily life, New York Jews expressed their earnest respect for cultural expression by becoming crucial consumers of the city's cultural products. As artists, organizers, consumers, and critics, Jews thus produced a rich culture that was Jewish in medium, content, and intended audience. But they also contributed mightily to the *general* culture, not explicitly Jewish, indeed sometimes typically "American." New forms of commercialized culture—popular music and theater, movies, the mass-circulation press—were especially open to immigrant participation. So were modernist movements in the visual arts and music. Significantly, fluid boundaries existed between the Jewish and the general, as well as among various genres. Arriving as these currents emerged and as New York developed into their center, Jewish immigrants and their children took advantage of the city's relative openness to remake themselves, the city, and American culture as a whole.

Even the borders between languages—especially English, German, and Yiddish—were porous. New York Jewry mainly spoke English at the beginning of the nineteenth century, but the subsequent central European immigration put German almost on a par with English as the community's public language. Rabbis extolled its virtues from the pulpit, and organizations kept their minutes in it. Jews also participated in general German singing societies, theater, and newspapers. But a substantial proportion of central European Jewish immigrants were only thinly "Germanized." Nearly half came not from Germany proper but from Bohemia and Moravia, regions of Poland under Prussian or Austrian rule, Hungary, and Alsace, all areas where most Jews still spoke Yiddish. Many of those from small towns in Germany spoke Yiddish into the middle of the century. Immigrants from these regions continued to speak Yiddish, or Yiddish-inflected German, at home and on the street, even when they used standard German in more formal settings. Despite the cultural prestige of German, however, English made steady inroads. The Harmonie Club's linguistic evolution symbolizes this transition.[4]

But before New York Jewry could be thoroughly re-Anglicized, millions of immigrants poured in from the Yiddish-speaking heartland of eastern Europe. Yiddish now became an important language of public and private discourse in the city. Almost immediately, however, it began to absorb English influences. Many loanwords came from the sphere of work and business: *shap* (shop), *payde* (payday, meaning "wages"), *opreyter* (operator, of a sewing machine), *nekst* (next, meaning "turn"), *sharup* (shut up). Hybrid words included *alraytnik* (someone who has worked his way up). English also influenced Yiddish syntax. The effects could be comical, as in Yiddish writer Sholem Aleichem's rendering of his character Motl Peysi's mother's American Yiddish speech (in the following excerpt, words in italics are given in English in the Yiddish original):

> [My mother] says that we earn our bit of bread fair and square, because at dawn, before the *stand* opens, we deliver the morning *paper* to our *customers*. Afterward, we go to *school* (yes, we are already in *school*). And when we come home from *school*, we help *attend* to the *business*. That is what my mother says, in those words. She already speaks half in the local language. She no longer uses the Yiddish words, "hun" and "kikh." She says *chicken* and *kitchen*. So, what then? With her it comes out backward. A kikh is for her a *chicken* and a hun is for her a *kitchen*. "I'm going," she says, "to the *chicken* to salt the *kitchen* . . ." Everyone laughs at her. She laughs too.

German further influenced New York Yiddish, especially in the press and in organizational life, where Yiddish-speaking lodges borrowed terminology from their German counterparts. Newcomers complained that they could barely understand the Yiddish spoken and printed in America, but they soon learned it too.[5]

One wonders whether people would have laughed so hard at Motl's mother if they realized how much people like her were influencing American English, especially in New York. Henry James fretted over the immigrants' propensity to "play, to their heart's content, with the English language [and to] dump their mountain of promiscuous material into the foundation of the American." James's fears were borne out. The influence of Yiddish on American English appeared indirectly at first, via loan words in German in the mid-nineteenth century, partly through underworld speech but also because the German speech of Jewish immigrants was peppered with Yiddish: *ganef* (thief), *kosher* (okay, reliable), *mazuma* (cash, from *mezumen*), *meshugeh* (crazy). H. L. Mencken, for whom Abraham Cahan was an important informant, reported that by the 1920s many New Yorkers, Jewish and non-Jewish, understood dozens of Yiddishisms. Yiddish influenced the New York accent as well, at least in the speech of English-speaking Jews. Just as English entered Yiddish through the shop, so did Yiddish enter English: for example, Mencken lists "schmoosing" as garment workers' slang for "idling around and talking shop." But entertainers did the most to spread Yiddishisms, especially outside the city. (See the Marx brothers: "Hurray for Captain Spalding, the African explorer. Did someone call me *shnorer*?")[6]

▪ From Chatham Street to East Sixtieth Street: Central European Jewish Identity Moves Indoors

The roots of the Harmonie Club lay in the downtown immigrant cultural scene of the mid-nineteenth century, which more resembled its 1905 Yiddish-language successor than Harmonie's current members would have liked to admit. In the early years, the Jewish clubs like Harmonie were very German in that they linked sociability to German *Kultur*. In addition to playing cards and billiards, common activities included attending lectures, musical and dramatic productions, singing circles, balls, libraries, and carnivals, all in German, the club's official language. Founded in 1852 by six German-Jewish immigrants, the Harmonie Gesellschaft for some years rented a succession of modest quarters in and around the downtown immigrant neighborhood. In 1859, the club held a *Mai-Fest* in Conrad's Park.

Only gradually did Harmonie and other Jewish clubs become more purely social, relegating cultural activities to the sidelines in favor of athletics, card playing, and balls. Indeed, the evolution of the Jewish club marked not only the economic rise of the Chatham Street hawkers but also their attempt to establish themselves as socially respectable and culturally mainstream, on a par with the native Protestant elite. Muting their ethnic distinctiveness, Jewish clubs came to have much in common with those clubs of the Protestant upper class that excluded Jews. Indeed, what made a man "clubbable" was a quality of "gentlemanliness" and congeniality that for Jewish clubmen involved being "unobtrusive and discreet" in expressing their Jewishness. In 1893, English

became the official language, and the name was changed officially from Harmonie Gesellschaft to Harmonie Club.[7]

■ New York's Lecture Culture

In moving uptown, Harmonie Club members all but abandoned the democratic, grass-roots network of cultural consumption that extended in the
nineteenth and early twentieth centuries from the educated English-speaking
middle class to German and Yiddish working-class immigrants. Through the
city's myriad of literary societies, dramatic clubs, self-education associations,
political movements, and adult education centers, New York Jews participated
in a vibrant lecture culture that provided "entertainment and instruction" on
everything from popular mechanics to contemporary political controversies.
Jewish interest in public lectures long survived their "golden age" between the
1850s and 1870s.[8]

Indeed, eastern European Jewish immigrants of the late nineteenth and
early twentieth centuries avidly consumed adult education programs produced largely by two sources: elite Americanizers and radical movements.
The New York City Board of Education, for example, began its highly popular
adult education program in 1888 and its Yiddish-language lectures in 1903.
Headed by Henry M. Leipziger, an immigrant born in England to German-
Jewish parents, the Board of Education programs stressed American citizenship, moral development, hygiene, and vocational advancement. Socialist
educational efforts aimed to give workers the tools to understand the world,
the better to change it. Toward this end, in 1913, the Workmen's Circle made
available lectures in "Ancient Greek Drama," "Ibsen's Contribution to Wom-
en's Liberation," and "The Bible, Not as Religion but as Literature," among
other topics. Young people on the Lower East Side and other immigrant Jewish neighborhoods flocked to these lectures in public schools, Labor Lyce-
ums, settlement houses, and other venues. One immigrant, Moyshe Shapiro,
maintained that common intellectual interests would secure a couple's happy
relationship, though his illiterate fiancée's parents sneered, "Lectures, *shmec-
tures*, whoever heard of a young man who likes a girl having lectures on his
mind?" But Shapiro had plenty of company. One study showed that nearly a
third of Russian-Jewish men, aged seventeen to twenty-five, attended at least
one lecture every week.[9] And, despite Shapiro's in-laws' attitude, so did many
young women.

■ Public Education for Children

As important as adult education programs were, the New York City public schools did much of the work of creating several generations of English-speaking Jewish consumers of all the city's cultural offerings. In fact, Jews began their "passionate love affair" with the public schools as early as the 1860s, taking advantage of the free school system while continually chipping away at Christian elements in the curriculum. Secularization of the public schools proceeded in fits and starts and was not completed until well into the twentieth century.[10] But while overtly Christian elements diminished over time, the schools' vaguely Protestant culture persisted because it dovetailed so closely with the educators' conception of what constituted true Americanism. With the influx of immigrant children at the turn of the twentieth century, the public schools redoubled their efforts at Americanization, stressing instruction in the English language, hygiene, etiquette, citizenship, and vocational training. The children's home language of Yiddish was denigrated. Teachers, few of whom were Jewish, served as "model[s] of good [read: "American"] taste [and] deportment."[11]

Influential Jews who played a role in the system backed its mission of Americanization.[12] The most influential Jewish educator was Julia Richman, New York's first Jewish public school principal and district superintendent and also the first woman principal in Manhattan. The daughter of working-class Jewish immigrants from Bohemia, Richman grew up partly in the Long Island countryside and partly in New York City's teeming Kleindeutschland neighborhood. Strong willed and ambitious, she reputedly told a friend at the age of eleven or twelve, "I am not pretty, my father is not rich, and I am not going to marry, but before I die, all New York will know my name!" After graduating in the first class from the Female Normal College (later Hunter College), she became a teacher. In 1903, after years as a principal, she was named superintendent for the districts that included the Jewish Lower East Side.[13]

Richman maintained Jewish involvements as a founder and board member of the YWHA and Educational Alliance. But despite her own immigrant background, Richman was an ardent Americanizer who sometimes found herself in conflict with the community she served. Concerned with raising "a race of worthy citizens," she wrote, "Between the alien of today and the citizen of tomorrow stands the school, and upon the influence exerted by the school depends the kind of citizen the immigrant child will become." This in itself would not have bothered Lower East Side parents, many of whom fully agreed with her sentiments. But a perceived lack of sensitivity to the sensibilities of the Jewish immigrant community sparked several unsuccessful campaigns to remove her from her post. In 1911, the *Forward* opined, "When she visits a school, it is like Yom Kippur." Nevertheless, she retained the friendship and support of Louis Marshall and other uptown Jewish leaders. When she died in 1912, the *New York Times* decried the "cabal" that had opposed her "efforts to reform and purify the district and free its children from degrading influences."[14]

While immigrant parents often shared the schools' Americanization goals, they did not always agree that vocational education was most appropriate for their children. When New York attempted to import the Gary System, so called because it originated in Gary, Indiana, Jewish students and parents rebelled. The Gary System attempted to utilize the public infrastructure as efficiently as possible by organizing the school day in such a way that all facilities were constantly in use. At the same time, it claimed to enrich the pupils' academic experience with shop and laboratory work, physical play, and service to the school community. But as the reform administration of Mayor John Purroy Mitchel implemented the Gary System in New York, it seemed much more concerned with cost savings than educational enhancement. And since the system called for a cut in hours that children spent on strictly academic work, many immigrant parents saw it as a move to shunt their children onto a vocational track. Students and parents demonstrated, and in some cases rioted, in front of schools where the Gary System had been put in place. An issue in the 1917 mayoral election, the plan died with Mitchel's decisive defeat.[15]

Jewish children gained a reputation for intellectual precociousness, even aggressiveness, an image happily burnished in retrospect by American Jews themselves. There is some truth to the image—the *Forward* even found it necessary to warn Jewish parents not to push their children too hard to excel in school and extracurricular studies. But, raised to the level of myth, the image is also greatly exaggerated—for every Jewish youth debating Marxist doctrine or wiling away the hours in the Seward Park branch of the public library, more were wandering the streets, fighting with rival gangs, playing baseball in city sandlots, and swimming in the East River. Most young Jews left school before graduating in order to earn a living and contribute to the family economy.[16]

City College for boys and, to a lesser extent, Hunter College for girls occupy a central place in the myth of Jewish intellectual accomplishment. By the first decades of the twentieth century, Jews did indeed compose more than three-quarters of the student body at City College. Still, with only 112 graduates in 1910, for example, CCNY could not really shape the lives of significant numbers of Jewish youth. This only began to happen in the 1920s and '30s, by which time, despite attempts to limit their numbers, many Jews attended local private institutions such as Columbia and New York University as well.[17]

■ Anglo-Jewish Letters in the Nineteenth Century

The periodical press offered another important outlet for public culture. The first independent Jewish newspaper in New York was probably the *Jew*, which appeared in 1823, but the Jewish press really grew in the middle of the century. The *Asmonean* appeared weekly between 1849 and 1859, published by the London-born Robert Lyon. Styling itself "a family journal of commerce, politics, religion, and literature, devoted to the interests of the American Israelites," the *Asmonean* defended Judaism against incursions by missionaries, opposed nativism, and allied itself with the Democratic Party. It avoided taking sides in controversies between the Orthodox and Reform camps in the Jewish community.[18] Beginning in 1857, on the other hand, Samuel Myers Isaacs's *Jewish Messenger* argued against religious reform even as it fought the exclusion of Jews from the American mainstream and advocated a national body of American Jews.[19] The *American Hebrew*, founded in 1879, raised Anglo-Jewish journalism to a new level. Edited for its first twenty-six years by Philip Cowen, the New York–born son of German-Jewish immigrants, the *American Hebrew* at various times published the writings of Emma Lazarus, Henrietta Szold, Cyrus Adler, Alexander Kohut, Kaufman Kohler, and Israel Zangwill. Sympathetic to tradition, it also advocated religious and cultural modernization and Americanization. It provided a forum for wide-ranging discussions on a broad variety of issues facing American Jewry.[20] These and other periodicals also published the handful of writers who wrote fiction and poetry on Jewish themes in English, including Emma Lazarus, by far the most important American Jewish writer of the nineteenth century.

In some ways, Lazarus's life and career foreshadowed those of important American Jewish literary figures writing in English half a century and more after her death. She was not religiously observant but nevertheless had a strong Jewish cultural identity. Indeed, events in Europe and America strengthened her Jewish commitment in the 1880s. Moreover, Lazarus at once participated in New York's general cultural scene, writing on a variety of topics for magazines with predominantly non-Jewish readerships, *and* she wrote on specifically Jewish issues for Jewish (and non-Jewish) publications. At the same time, however, she faced difficulties that her successors did not, including the fact that she was almost alone as a Jew in a genteel literary set that sometimes harbored subtle anti-Semitic attitudes. Though none of her close friends was Jewish, and her American ancestry extended as far back as most of theirs, she could never forget that her Jewishness set her apart.

Lazarus was born in 1849 into a well-off, illustrious, but nonobservant, old-stock Sephardic family. She received little Jewish education but knew German and French well. Well integrated into New York high society, her family "groomed [her] to be noticed from an early age." [21] In fact, when she was seventeen years old in 1866, her father proudly printed a volume of her poems. The book caught the attention of a number of prominent American writers, most importantly Ralph Waldo Emerson, who praised the young poet and adopted her as a kind of literary protégé. They began a long epistolary relationship, but when Emerson omitted her from his massive poetry anthology, *Parnassus* (1874), she reacted angrily. She may, however, have overreacted, for the good company excluded from the volume included Walt Whitman, Edgar Allan Poe, Herman Melville, and Emerson himself. In any case, Lazarus continued her relationship with Emerson. By the time of his anthological snub, Lazarus was well established as a poet, essayist, translator, and member of New York intellectual society.

The 1881 wave of pogroms in Russia and the subsequent refugee crisis and spike in Jewish immigration to the United States intensified Lazarus's interest in Jewish themes. She had earlier written "In the Jewish Synagogue at Newport" (1867) as a poetic refutation of Longfellow's view of the Jews as a backward-looking and dead nation in "The Jewish Cemetery at Newport" (1854). She had translated Heinrich Heine's work as well as a number of medieval Hebrew hymns (from German translations). But beginning in 1882, she became a proto-Zionist, advocating havens in Palestine and the United States for oppressed Jews. Her book *Songs of a Semite* appeared that year, and a long series of articles in the *American Hebrew* followed. In Jewish publications, she called for Jewish communal solidarity in the face of oppression. In non-Jewish publications, she sought to elicit sympathy for the downtrodden Jews of eastern Europe. On a practical level, she participated in communal efforts to aid Jewish refugees and immigrants. But she did not have much time left, for during an extended stay in Europe, she fell ill. Returning to New York, she died in 1887.

Emma Lazarus's literary reputation suffered after her death, but one poem kept her name alive. Written in 1883 to raise money for a pedestal for the Statue of Liberty to be erected in New York Harbor, Lazarus's poem "The New Colossus" was inscribed on a plaque mounted at the base of the statue in 1903. The statue, a gift from France, had originally been intended as a monument to free government, but Lazarus's poem—with its call to "Give me your tired, your poor / Your huddled masses yearning to breathe free, / The wretched refuse of your teeming shore"—helped turn it into "the mother of exiles," a beacon for the millions of immigrants who now sailed past it into the "golden door" of New York Harbor.[22]

■ Jews and German Culture

A German-language culture thrived alongside New York's English-language Jewish culture in the nineteenth century. The German immigrant community was distinguished by its singing and dramatic societies. Although German Jews formed their own organizations, they also joined leading German singing societies such as the New Yorker Sängerrunde, New Yorker Männerchor, Deutsche Liederkranz, and Arion Glee Club. The talents of writer Max Cohnheim, later a leading local German playwright, and musical director Leopold Damrosch helped make the Arion perhaps the preeminent *Gesangverein* in the city. At least one predominantly Jewish singing society, the Orpheus, participated in the great *Sängerfeste* (singing festivals), which were highlights of the German communal calendar. Tensions sometimes strained relations between German-speaking Jews and non-Jews. For a time, the Arion Glee Club apparently banned Jews and incorporated anti-Semitic ditties into its repertoire. But many of its satirical songs ridiculed a variety of groups, including Yankees, and some were even written by Jews. In any case, by 1895, Jews once again figured on the roster of the Arion club.[23]

German societies also began to stage amateur theatrical productions, starting as early as the 1840s. Plays presented by Jewish clubs sometimes attracted
derision, as in this description in the German-language *Puck*:

> They gave "Camille" the other night at our friend Dinkelspiel's, with disastrous results.
> Almost every young lady with theatrical ambitions yearns to play *Camille*; and Miss
> Rebecca Dinkelspiel was no exception to this rule. Mr. Oppenheimer, her betrothed
> (fancy goods, Grand Street), likewise saw a future before him as *Armand*, and nearly
> all of the members of the Kosher Dramatic Club expressed a willingness to take the
> subordinate parts. The play was presented, after long and careful preparation, at Mr.
> Dinkelspiel's residence, in 73rd Street. [The production was so disastrous that] the Ko-
> sher Club is dissolved; the engagement of Miss Dinkelspiel and Mr. Oppenheimer
> is off.

But despite *Puck*'s emphasis on the distinctive characteristics that differentiated Jews from other Germans (names, trades, residential patterns, dietary
laws), Jewish amateur productions differed little in theme or quality from
those of non-Jews.[24]

The opening of the Stadttheater on September 4, 1854, marked the beginning of the professional German-language stage in New York. Jews contributed to the professional German theater as actors, playwrights, producers,
financiers, and, perhaps above all, audience members. Observers noted that
Jews made up a large part of the audience—as much as 80 percent—and even
attributed the success of New York's theaters relative to those of other places to
the city's large Jewish element. Jewish shop clerks and peddlers loved to attend
theater, especially when plays with Jewish themes were produced. Jewish organizations also helped keep German theaters afloat by buying blocs of tickets
for benefits.[25]

The German stage gave rise to some of the earliest Jewish popular-culture
celebrities. These included Max Cohnheim, whose melodramas and farces often had New York settings. For a time, though, actor Daniel Bandmann shone
as the brightest star of the New York German stage. Born in Cassel, Germany,
in 1840, Bandmann became known for his portrayals of Shakespeare's Hamlet,
Richard III, Othello, and Shylock; the title roles in Karl Gutzkow's *Uriel Acosta*
and Emil Brachvogel's *Narcissus*; and Mephistopheles in Goethe's *Faust*. He
soon crossed over to the English stage, receiving positive reviews, including
one that called him an "artist of strong original genius." (A less friendly critic,

however, saw his fame as the "product of systematic puffery" and his popularity with Jewish audiences.) After several seasons in New York, Bandmann departed for London and Australia, before attempting a less-than-successful comeback in New York. He finished his days as a rancher and farmer in Montana, where he was known to watch visiting troupes with an especially critical eye.[26]

∎ Yiddish Culture

As Emma Lazarus penned "The New Colossus," she knew of the arrival of masses of Yiddish-speaking immigrants. What she did not know was that the newcomers had begun to create the conditions for an American Jewish literature, first in Yiddish and later in English. In fact, New York became one of the main centers where a modern, secular Yiddish literature developed. New York Jews distinguished themselves especially in the areas of Yiddish poetry, journalism, and theater, learning much from American, as well as European, contemporaries and teaching them something as well. In fact, the Yiddish literary scene in New York cannot be seen in isolation from the English-language scene. The cafe devotees of the Lower East Side interacted on a regular basis with those of Greenwich Village, a short walk away. Several individual figures, most prominently Abraham Cahan and Emma Goldman, facilitated the exchange.

A similar direct connection existed between the German theater and its Yiddish counterpart. In 1882, a thirteen-year-old cigarette maker named Boris Thomashefsky teamed up with a Jewish saloon keeper to import a troupe from London and mount the first professional Yiddish theater production in New York. The performance of Abraham Goldfaden's *Koldunye*, at the German Turn Hall on Fourth Street, flopped according to Thomashefsky. But within a decade, Yiddish drama was firmly ensconced in its own theaters on the Bowery, Grand Street, and Second Avenue. Theaters later also appeared in Brooklyn and the Bronx. Rival troupes, led by stars such as Thomashefsky, Jacob Adler, and David Kessler, competed for a growing audience of avid theatergoers.

Popular productions of low artistic quality, known as *shund*, marked early Yiddish theater. Writers such as Joseph Lateiner and "Professor" Moyshe Hurwitz churned out biblical spectaculars, domestic melodramas, and overwrought commentaries on current events. Often they simply plagiarized plays from German or Romanian, transposing the setting to a Jewish venue and giving the characters Yiddish names. In any case, the main attractions of the theater were the performers and the spectacle, not the scripts, which actors seldom followed closely anyway. The boisterous audience was a spectacle in itself, a common characteristic of nineteenth-century popular theaters catering to working-class audiences. Similarly, Yiddish music halls thrived along the Bowery, on Fourteenth Street, and in Coney Island, where for a third the price of the regular theater, whole families could enjoy "songs, dances, sketches, and jokes, usually spiced with double entendres and suggestive gestures."[27]

Gradually, a "better" Yiddish theater emerged. When Jacob Gordin attended his first Yiddish play in 1891, he was astounded and dismayed: "Everything I saw and heard was far from real Jewish life. All was vulgar, immoderate, false and coarse. 'Oy, oy!' I thought to myself, and I went home and sat down to write my first play. . . . I wrote my first play the way a pious man, a scribe, copies out a Torah scroll." Gordin, a highly Russified radical intellectual with deep-set eyes, a shock of curly hair, a full beard, and an aristocratic mien, advocated a "realistic," socially conscious Yiddish drama. Gordin's highly didactic plays offered a modern moralistic take on contemporary burning social and cultural issues. With time, the Yiddish theater outgrew him, but Gordin was an important transitional figure.[28]

Influenced by Russian and European trends, other serious playwrights followed, writing more naturalistic plays with plausible settings. Many dealt with vital issues in immigrant life. A new generation of actors and directors also promoted more sophisticated theater. In 1918, Maurice Schwartz took over the Irving Place Theatre, which had previously housed a German company, and founded the Yiddish Art Theater. Among the actors in the first Yiddish production at the Irving Place Theatre was Celia Adler, daughter of the great Yiddish actor Jacob Adler and one of several siblings (Stella, Luther) who made names for themselves on the English as well as the Yiddish stage. But despite critical acclaim, serious Yiddish plays struggled to find an audience outside small circles of Yiddish-speaking intellectuals.[29] *Shund* retained its popularity.

Some Yiddish actors moved over to the English stage. One of the most successful was Bertha Kalich, the "Yiddish Bernhardt." Strikingly beautiful and regal in her bearing, Kalich began her career in the Polish, Yiddish, Romanian, and German theaters in Europe. Fearing an assassination plot by jealous rivals, she came to the United States sometime in the mid-1890s. A leading advocate of better Yiddish drama, she starred in plays by Gordin, Zalman Libin, and

Dovid Pinsky. She first appeared on the English stage in 1905, in the title role of *Fedora*, by Victorien Sardou. After laboring to correct her foreign accent, she worked with the American dramatist Harrison Grey Fiske. For a time, Kalich received wide acclaim, but soon her emotional style became obsolete, and she found it harder to get roles. She then returned to the Yiddish theater, where her experience on the general American stage gave her more cachet.[30]

Much of the debate over the role of the Yiddish theater occurred in the Yiddish press, which became a major enterprise in the first decades of the twentieth century. The *Yidishe tsaytung*, the first Yiddish periodical in the United States, appeared irregularly between 1870 and 1877. Other Yiddish publications followed but failed to find enough readers to survive.[31] The first giant of Yiddish journalism, Kasriel Zevi Sarasohn, founded the weekly *Yidishe gazeten* in 1874; his *Yidishe tageblat* absorbed the *Gazeten* in 1885, becoming the first commercially successful Yiddish daily. Born in 1835 near Suwalki, in northwest Russian Poland, into a rabbinical family, Sarasohn absorbed much of the spirit of the *haskalah*, the European Jewish Enlightenment, but remained traditionally observant. A portrait of him as an older man reveals a determined gaze and set jaw, with a clipped beard and large round yarmulke. In 1874, he was a thirty-nine-year-old printer, in America just three years. His newspapers, first the *Gazeten* and then the *Tageblat*, were Orthodox in religious orientation and conservative politically. Sarasohn and his chief editor, Johan Paley, a pudgy former yeshiva student rumored to have converted to Christianity as a teenager, pioneered the use of Hearst- and Pulitzer-style yellow journalism in the Yiddish press, making the *Tageblat* an odd mixture of piety and sensationalism. Throughout the 1890s and into the 1900s, the *Tageblat* remained the leading Yiddish daily.[32]

Meanwhile, the immigrant community's radicals gained journalistic experience with a series of their own newspapers, including the *Nyu-Yorker yidishe folkstsaytung*, named for the sheet of the local German Socialists, and the first Yiddish Socialist daily, the *Abendblat*. Finally, in 1897, factional squabbles within the Socialist Labor Party, with which the *Abendblat* was aligned, led one group to break away and form a new newspaper, the *Forverts*, named after the organ of the Social Democratic Party of Germany. The founders of the *Forverts* hoped to create a Socialist newspaper that would appeal to the masses of Yiddish readers and avoid the *Abendblat*'s sectarian and pedantic tone. The new paper's first editor, the by-now-veteran Yiddish Socialist propagandist

Abraham Cahan, left after a few months, frustrated at his comrades' inability to transcend old sectarian habits.[33]

When Cahan returned five years later, he brought with him many journalistic methods he had learned during a sojourn in the world of English-language journalism. Under Cahan's stern, some said dictatorial, editorial control, the *Forverts* became both the premier Yiddish daily in the world and the country's leading Socialist daily. It gained this position with a shrewd mix of political earnestness and sensationalistic reporting on crime and vice. The *Jewish Daily Forward*, as it was known in English, printed Cahan's high-minded realist drama and literary criticism alongside installments of trashy novellas. News analysis by some of the leading Socialist thinkers of Europe appeared alongside local human-interest stories. Cahan's most famous innovation—an advice column called the *bintl brief* (bundle of letters)—featured letters from readers seeking solutions to their problems. Many reflected the peculiar cultural crosscurrents at work in the lives of working-class Jewish immigrants, including shop romances, conflicts between traditional parents and radical or Americanized children, tensions between husbands and wives, and worry about family members left behind. By 1911, the *Forverts* claimed a circulation of 122,532 (compared to the *Tageblat's* 69,000), and the following year it erected its tower on East Broadway.[34]

The *Jewish Communal Register* estimated that between 1872 and 1917, some 150 Yiddish publications had appeared in New York at one time or another. At least twenty-nine still published in 1917, including five daily newspapers, with a combined circulation in New York of over three hundred thousand. The most significant dailies besides the *Forverts* and the *Tageblat* were the *Morgn zhurnal*, which had supplanted the *Tageblat* as the city's leading Orthodox newspaper; the *Varhayt*, founded by former *Forverts* editor Louis Miller; and the *Tog* (Day), founded in 1914. The *Tog* adopted a liberal, Zionist editorial stance and boasted of an impressive array of columnists with a wide range of views. The motto on its masthead read, "The *Tog* is the newspaper for the Jewish intelligentsia." In addition to the dailies were many weekly, monthly, annual, and occasional publications ranging from the Anarchist *Fraye arbeter shtime* (Free Voice of Labor) to the *Vegvayzer in der amerikaner biznes velt* (Guide to the American Business World).[35]

The Yiddish press also provided a stage for the early Yiddish "sweatshop poets," who got their nickname not only because most of them put in time in the shops themselves but also because the travails of the shop worker often provided much of the material for their poetry. Influenced by Russian, German, and American writers, as well as by Anarchist and Socialist ideas, Morris Winchevsky, Dovid Edelshtat, Yoysef Bovshover, and Morris Rosenfeld penned melancholy laments over the plight of sweated workers, stirring calls to revolutionary action, and an occasional anthem of Jewish nationalism. They intended their poems to be declaimed or sung. Many were indeed set to music and became standards at Socialist meetings in the United States and Europe. Edelshtat, who died of tuberculosis at age twenty-six, and Bovshover, who spent his last years in a psychiatric hospital, were viewed as martyrs of sorts to the poverty of the immigrant years as well as to their sensitive artistic natures.

Rosenfeld, on the other hand, became the first Yiddish writer to attract an audience in English. "A man of flamboyant temperament inclined to lapses into depression," Rosenfeld was born in a village near Suwalki and received a traditional Jewish education. He settled permanently in New York in 1886, becoming a presser in the garment industry. A charismatic orator with a fine tenor voice, he became a popular presence at Socialist and union meetings declaiming and singing his own poems, which were printed in the radical Yiddish press. His poems, highly formal in style, expressed his identification with his audience of poor workers:

> The groans of slaves, when they are tired,
> awake my songs;
> it's only then that I'm inspired:
> I reckon up their wrongs.

Rosenfeld struggled until Bialystok-born Harvard professor Leo Wiener "discovered" him and published a volume of translations of Rosenfeld's work, *Songs from the Ghetto* (1898). A success, the book led to translations into German, Polish, Romanian, Czech, and Hungarian. For a time, Rosenfeld earned a living speaking and reading at colleges and settlement houses, while also writing for the Yiddish press. But a series of reverses embittered Rosenfeld, and changing literary styles deepened his isolation. When he died in 1923, thousands turned out for his funeral, but the mainstream of Yiddish literature had passed him by.[36]

In fact, a revolution took place in Yiddish poetry around 1907–1908, led by some of the regulars at Goodman and Levine's. Grouped around the journal *Di yugnt* (Youth), they came to be known as *di yunge*, the young ones. Most of *di yunge* made their livings as manual workers—garment workers, cobblers, and construction workers. Some participated in radical politics. But they sought to separate their art from political engagement, disparaging the older sweat-shop poets as nothing more than "the rhyme department of the Jewish labor movement." Instead of slogans or lamentations over the fate of the proletariat, they sought poetry for poetry's sake. "Poetry was for us young ones the entire content of our lives," recalled one of their leading lights, Mani Leyb. "Poetry illuminated our gray days of hard physical labor at the sewing machine, the scaffolding, or the hatter's block." They found inspiration in Jewish folksong and modern European poetry, especially Russian, German, and French.[37]

"Tall, thin, somewhat slouching and handsome," Mani Leyb (Brahinsky) was perhaps the "most attractive member of the group," not only for his prom-inent chin and high cheekbones but also for his dreamy "poetic personality." Mani Leyb's autobiographical poem "I Am . . ." expresses a sentiment almost exactly opposite that of Rosenfeld's "Teardrop Millionaire." While Rosenfeld denied any aesthetic intention apart from giving voice to the suffering of his class, Mani Leyb, a shoemaker by trade, proclaims that no matter what the ap-pearance, his poet's heart sets him apart from his fellow shoemakers:

> In Brownsville, Yehupets, beyond them, even,
> My name shall ever be known, oh Muse.
> And I'm not a cobbler who writes, thank heaven,
> But a poet who makes shoes.[38]

Di yunge thus strove to create a new kind of literary art in Yiddish, one that depended on an elite audience of refined taste and sophistication. The sophis-ticated milieu that nurtured this new generation of Yiddish writers formed a subculture within the immigrant Jewish community. The Lower East Side remained its hub, but as with the population as a whole, its members increas-ingly lived elsewhere. The Bronx possessed an especially lively cultural scene. Aaron Domnitz recalled that his friend the poet I. J. Schwartz moved to the Bronx to escape the stultifying atmosphere in Brownsville, Brooklyn. Gradu-ally, "circles started to form": "People would go for walks and sit in the park in the evenings dreaming and scheming about how to build a new Yiddish litera-ture. . . . New talents could be found in the Bronx. We looked up to each other and put out for each other, creating an atmosphere of creativity." Domnitz lived in the same apartment house as Joseph Opatovski, a young engineering student who later achieved fame as the novelist Yoysef Opatashu. Some mornings, before Opatashu left for his job as a newspaper deliverer, he would enter Domnitz's room through the fire escape to show his friend his latest draft.[39]

Before 1920, fewer distinguished Yiddish prose writers than poets made their homes in New York. Sholem Aleichem, the folksy Yiddish writer renowned as one of the founders of modern Yiddish literature, arrived at the end of 1914, only to die a year and a half later. Like Rabbi Jacob Joseph, Sholem Aleichem suffered from neglect in America, only to be mourned with a massive funeral procession in May 1916. Altogether, somewhere between 150,000 and 250,000 people took part.[40] Besides Opatashu and Sholem Aleichem, the most important novelist was probably Sholem Asch, who came to New York in 1914 and stayed until 1924 (he later returned). Both Opatashu and Asch treated eastern European and American themes, but Asch became the Yiddish writer most widely read in English since Rosenfeld.

The world of Jewish immigrant letters extended beyond Yiddish to other languages. In the 1870s, a news and literary weekly, *Ha-tsofe ba-arets ha-hadasha*, appeared in Hebrew, and in 1880, a short-lived Hebrew literary society, Shocharei S'fath Eber, counted Jacob Schiff as a member. But only the eastern European migration brought sufficient numbers of committed Hebraists to sustain stable cultural organizations and publications. Beginning in 1902, the Mefitsei Sefat Ever ve'Sifrutah sponsored lectures in and about Hebrew. The lectures "created a veritable sensation," with hundreds of people attending at the Educational Alliance. One member recalled that the society was composed of "students, teachers, workers, merchants, professionals, peddlers": "For people like me, who were slaves all week in factories, the Sunday meetings of Mefitsei Sefat Ever were truly refreshing." A younger cohort of Hebraists founded a second organization, Achiever, in 1909 to use "more aggressive methods" to further the revival of Hebrew as a vehicle of modern cultural expression. This group, in turn, founded *Ha-toren*, a high-quality weekly literary journal, in 1913, and a national organization, the Histadrut Haivrit, three years later. American Hebraists saw America as an important potential center of Hebrew renaissance and sometimes turned to American themes in their writing. The Hebraists never attracted large numbers, but they exerted an influence on American Jewish culture—especially in education—disproportionate to their numbers.[41]

Surrounded by well over a million Ashkenazi Jews, New York's estimated twenty thousand recent Sephardic immigrants lived as a minority within a minority. Most spoke Ladino (Judeo-Spanish), and they too established their own press: the weekly *La Amerika*, founded in 1910, was traditionalist in orientation; *La Boz del Pueblo* (1915) was Socialist. A satirical journal, *El Kirbatch Amerikano*, followed in 1917. The Ladino press had a limited circulation (a total of perhaps fifteen hundred, according to the *Jewish Communal Register*, though this number apparently increased by the late 1920s), but, like the Yiddish press, it guided new immigrants, offered advice columns, and covered communal activities.[42]

Jewish journalists contributed to immigrant publications in non-Jewish languages as well. Most importantly, Jews were responsible for much of New York's Russian-language journalism in the period before World War I. In fact, in the 1880s and 1890s, the local Russian press was mainly produced by Jewish radicals for Jewish readers, and many pioneers of Russian journalism went on to write for and edit Yiddish publications. Jews continued to contribute to later Russian-language newspapers, including the most important, *Novy Mir* (founded as *Russkoye Slovo* in 1910, a daily from 1913).[43]

■ New Jewish Cultural Expressions in English

The new Yiddish bohemia reflected in miniature a larger English-language scene centered in Greenwich Village, in which Jews also participated. The Village had its own cafes, where writers, artists, patrons, and intelligent consumers met to eat cheap food and discuss modernism and social problems. These new bohemians, some of them with impeccable pedigrees and Ivy League educations, were drawn to New York, where, they felt, "something considerable may happen." As the greatest immigrant city in the country, New York seemed exciting and full of promise. In contrast to most of New York society, the bohemians were open to Jews. Some of these Jews, such as Walter Lippmann, Waldo Frank, and James Oppenheim, were American born and hailed from affluent backgrounds. (Frank and Oppenheim helped found the magazine *Seven Arts* in 1916.) Others, such as Ariel Durant and Konrad and Naomi Bercovici, came from immigrant families. Viewing Jews as important carriers of new and vibrant ideas in literature and politics, the bohemians sometimes took a direct interest in the immigrant community and culture. Many visited the Lower East Side, the Yiddish theater, and Jewish cafes, often with a suitable guide, such as Konrad Bercovici or Abraham Cahan.[44]

Indeed, Cahan and Emma Goldman symbolize in different ways the highly politicized connections between the immigrant and native intelligentsias. Cahan in particular mediated between the two cultural worlds, often guiding American intellectuals who wanted to get to know the immigrant quarter. Cahan first met the dean of American letters, William Dean Howells, in 1892, when Howells sought him out as an informant on working conditions and the labor movement on the Lower East Side. The two hit it off, partly because of their shared admiration for Russian realist writers. Later, Cahan shepherded Hutchins Hapgood through the Yiddish cafes when Hapgood was researching his book *Spirit of the Ghetto* (a chapter of which is devoted to Cahan). Cahan played a similar role as a reporter for the *Commercial Advertiser* from 1897 to 1902.

In addition to Cahan's journalism, he wrote realist fiction in English about the immigrant experience. His first story, "A Providential Match," appeared in *Short Stories* magazine in 1895 and caught the eye of Howells, who became Cahan's "discoverer" and sponsor, helping to find a publisher for Cahan's *Yekl: A Tale of the New York Ghetto* (1896). Viewing Cahan as "fully American and fully Russian," Howells introduced Cahan to the New York literary scene in the hope that Cahan would become a "cultural mediator" between foreign-born and native, rich and poor. Cahan happily accepted this assignment—as English-language writer interpreting "the ghetto" to literate native audiences and as Yiddish editor interpreting America to the immigrants. The title of Cahan's English magnum opus, *The Rise of David Levinsky* (1917), echoed that of Howells's *The Rise of Silas Lapham. Levinsky* tells the epic story of Jewish immigration through the eyes of one immigrant who rises to wealth as a garment manufacturer but loses his soul in the process. Many critics have asserted that the character of Levinsky is a thinly veiled stand-in for Cahan himself. But the character was actually the opposite of the author as he saw himself; whereas Levinsky was morally compromised and deficient in culture, Cahan devoted himself to social justice and cultural pursuits.[45]

Fiery and charismatic, the Anarchist Emma Goldman was temperamentally the opposite of the dour social democrat Cahan. Born in Kovno, Lithuania, in 1869, Goldman moved with her family to St. Petersburg at the age of twelve. There she became a factory worker and gained a revolutionary education through reading Russian literature. In constant conflict with her father, disgusted by the oppressive Tsarist system, and facing an arranged marriage, Goldman fled Russia to join a sister in Rochester, New York. But she found Rochester and a brief marriage there stultifying as well, and she once more escaped, this time to New York City. In the meantime, the execution of the Chicago Haymarket martyrs in 1886 had cemented her commitment to Anarchism. When she arrived in the city, she made her way to the Anarchist cafes, Sachs's and Schwab's, where she met the leading Anarchist of the day, Johan Most, and the youthful Alexander Berkman, who became her lifelong friend, comrade, and sometime lover. Though detractors suggested that she was best before "neophyte" audiences, preaching the "a, b, c's" of radicalism, there was no doubt that she was a "mesmerizing speaker," and in 1897 she undertook her first national speaking tour.[46]

Soon Goldman acquired a reputation as "the most dangerous woman in the world," an image enhanced by her implication in Berkman's attempted assassination of steel-industry magnate Henry Clay Frick in 1892 and the confession of President William McKinley's assassin Leon Czolgosz that he had been inspired by Goldman's writings. Her reputation undoubtedly grew through her own "relentless fascination with herself" and knack for self-promotion. Her lectures were as much spectacle as edification, and for a time she even appeared at Oscar Hammerstein's theater, between a dog act and a dance routine. Her physical appearance belied her great energy: "Spectacled and severe, [she] dressed in a simple shirtwaist, tie, and skirt, her hair pulled back in a bun." She reminded Mabel Dodge, the wealthy bohemian and patron of the arts, of a "severe but warm-hearted school teacher." Although she professed a sense of solidarity with the downtrodden masses and espoused a form of stateless collectivism, her Anarchism owed much to an American tradition of individualism. She placed more stock in a spirit of personal rebellion against constraint than in collective class action. She attacked conventional institutions, such as marriage, as particularly oppressive to women and advocated free love and birth control. She viewed suffrage as a trap by which women would become coopted by the state. Cultural issues interested her as much as economic ones. She often lectured on literature and art, and her magazine, *Mother Earth*, combined political commentary with cultural analysis.[47]

Fluent in Russian, German, and Yiddish, in addition to English, Goldman quickly distanced herself from the Lower East Side and its Jewish milieu. She believed that "real social changes could be accomplished only by the natives" and so set out to spread "propaganda in English among the American people." In fact, she expressed contempt for her Jewish comrades, whom she accused of "sell[ing] their Anarchism in real estate, or in playing dominoes in restaurants." Anglo-Americans, by contrast, "live Anarchism and thereby are having a moral influence, of greater [and] more lasting value, than 10 years publication of a F[raye] A[rbeter] S[htime]." She did occasionally return to the immigrant quarter to dance at an Anarchist Yom Kippur ball or to speak in Yiddish, but even then she avoided Jewish or Russian themes.[48]

Like Cahan and Goldman, Anzia Yezierska made a mark on American culture. Like Cahan, she wrote fiction about immigrant life, and since, like him, she often wrote in the first person about characters who at least superficially resembled the author, her work is often taken to be autobiographical. But while her work clearly draws on her own experiences in the tenements and shops, she just as clearly differs from her characters. For example, she graduated from college and spoke educated, unaccented English, whereas her heroines often speak in Yiddish cadences. Indeed, having arrived in the United States as a child, Yezierska was really more of a pioneer second-generation writer than an immigrant one, and her work expressed her generation's sense of alienation from both her old-worldly parents, on the one hand, and the new world's culture, on the other.

Yezierska shrouded her early life in a mist largely of her own creation. Born in Poland sometime between 1880 and 1885, she came to the United States with her family in the early 1890s. Her father is usually described as a traditional scholar too otherworldly to make a living but not too distant to rule over his family despotically. Anzia frequently fought with him, and he often appears in her stories as a misogynistic petty tyrant. Yezierska attended public schools, worked at a variety of menial jobs, and gained a degree in home economics from Teachers College of Columbia University. She taught in the public schools but disliked both the profession and her subject. Charismatic, vivacious, and beautiful, with "thick red hair, prominent blue eyes, and a creamy complexion," she briefly aspired to a stage career. In 1915, *Forum* published her first story, "Free Vacation House," which describes the disappointment and humiliation of a poor Jewish immigrant woman faced with the condescension of charitable do-gooders. The attraction of the young, Jewish, female protagonist to an Anglo-Protestant intellectual mentor/lover is a recurrent theme in her work, though any such liaison is usually stymied by racial and cultural differences. In real life, Yezierska was already a published author when she met the philosopher John Dewey, "the love of her life." Their relationship, though intense, apparently remained platonic and ended after about a year.[49]

Yezierska's stories often depict the tortured ambivalence of the heroine, longing to escape a suffocating Jewish culture but feeling alienated from mainstream America. Her story "Fat of the Land," about the loneliness of an immigrant woman supported by her successful American children, won the 1919 Edward J. O'Brien Award for best short story of the year. The following year, her collection of stories *Hungry Hearts* appeared to generally positive reviews but little commercial success. Still, Samuel Goldwyn not only bought the movie rights for *Hungry Hearts* but also brought Yezierska to Hollywood to help write the screenplay. Repelled by the crass commercialism and mercenary attitudes of the writers in Hollywood, she soon returned to New York. After some continued success in the 1920s, her fame faded, until women's historians rediscovered her in the 1970s.[50]

Jews also influenced New York's mainstream English-language press as it emerged into the twentieth century. A look at three different newspapers—the *New York World*, the *New York Times*, and the *Commercial Advertiser*—illustrates how varied that influence was. Joseph Pulitzer was a thirty-six-year-old immigrant from Hungary with a background in German-language journalism in St. Louis when he purchased the flagging *New York World* in 1883. With the *World*, Pulitzer helped to revolutionize American journalism. The newspaper introduced banner headlines, pictures, color cartoons, and a sports page. Pulitzer wanted punchy language, ran more human-interest stories, and focused his newspaper's attention on the details of violence, scandals, and executions. While it is not even clear whether Pulitzer knew that both his parents were Jews, his adversaries sometimes added a dose of anti-Semitism to their critiques of his journalism, and his immigrant background colored the *World*'s populist approach. With sympathetic writing about the working class and immigrants, the paper played to ethnic tastes and prejudices. By appealing to the first- and second-generation Irish, Germans, and Jews who made up a majority of New York's population, Pulitzer raised his newspaper's daily circulation from 15,000 to 450,000 by 1895.[51]

Adolph Ochs had a different Jewish background and path to journalistic success. Born in Cincinnati to German-Jewish immigrant parents, Ochs moved with his family to Knoxville, Tennessee, in 1865. His father was a poor businessman, and Adolph was forced to leave school to help support the family. He entered journalism as a delivery boy and subsequently worked as a printer's helper, business manager, and (briefly) reporter. By 1878, when he was only twenty years old, Ochs managed to acquire the *Chattanooga Times*, turning it into a respected local newspaper. He married Effie Miriam Wise, the daughter of Rabbi Isaac Mayer Wise, the leading figure in American Reform Judaism, and remained an active Reform Jew the rest of his life.

In 1896, Ochs took over the ailing *New York Times*, with a circulation of just nine thousand and on the brink of bankruptcy. Realizing the futility of competing with Pulitzer's *World* and William Randolph Hearst's *Journal* on their own terms, Ochs decided to rebuild the *Times* as a "high-standard newspaper, clean, dignified and trustworthy" for "thoughtful, pure-minded people." The following year, he introduced the *Times's* now famous motto, "All the news that's fit to print." Conservative and stodgy, serving the educated upper-middle and upper classes, the *Times* kept a studied distance from the urban crucible in the working-class immigrant neighborhoods. Nevertheless, under Ochs, it established itself as the standard for honest, objective reporting, the "newspaper of record." Jewish critics complained that Ochs failed to take strong and open stands on Jewish issues. Indeed, the *Times* carefully avoided taking any stands that would call attention to itself as a Jewish-owned newspaper, refusing, for example, to editorialize in favor of the French Jewish officer Alfred Dreyfus, whose unjust conviction for treason became an international cause célèbre in the late 1890s. The one exception came during the Leo Frank case in 1913–1915. Frank, the Brooklyn-bred co-owner and manager of an Atlanta, Georgia, pencil factory, stood accused of murdering Mary Phagan, a teenage employee. Frank was the president of the local B'nai B'rith chapter, and his arrest and conviction shook southern Jews especially profoundly. Perhaps because of Ochs's own southern roots, he took a personal interest in the case, and the *Times* printed dozens of articles that pointed toward Frank's innocence and the blatant unfairness of the proceedings against him. Ochs went so far as to try to persuade southern newspapers to reprint *Times* editorials, one of which concluded that the trial had been "about everything a murder trial ought not to be." Frank's eventual lynching, and the callous response from southern journalists, disturbed Ochs deeply. He reacted by further distancing the *Times* from subsequent Jewish causes.[52]

Meanwhile, a third newspaper with Jewish influence, the *Commercial Advertiser*, provided an intelligent alternative to both the yellow sensationalism of Pulitzer and Hearst and the stuffy high-mindedness of the *Times*. Under the leadership of the non-Jewish Californian Lincoln Steffens, who became city editor in 1897, the *Commercial Advertiser* strove to bridge the gap between the immigrant working class and the educated middle class. Steffens attracted a coterie of Ivy League graduates with aspirations toward serious writing. They reveled in the "hard, beautiful city" and saw its foreign quarters as the main crucibles of a cosmopolitan urban future. The *Commercial Advertiser*'s reporters penned detailed and sympathetic accounts of immigrant life in an effort to reach the hearts and minds of their educated readers.[53] Their chief guide in this undertaking was Abraham Cahan, the erstwhile and future Yiddish journalist, who joined the staff of the *Advertiser* shortly after Steffens took over. Cahan contributed stories himself, showed his colleagues around the Lower East Side, and in the *Commercial Advertiser* newsroom assumed the role of lecturer, educating the Americans on Russian literary realism and Socialist theory. When Steffens left the *Commercial Advertiser* in 1901, Cahan followed, returning to his perch at the *Forward*, to which he brought his experiences in English-language "new journalism."[54]

■ The Visual Arts

A Jewish presence in the visual arts emerged closely tied to the literary scenes in both Greenwich Village and the Lower East Side. Only a handful of American Jews rose to prominence in the visual arts in the nineteenth century (one of them was Jacob Hart Lazarus, Emma's uncle), but at the beginning of the twentieth, a generation of Jewish painters and sculptors helped to revolutionize American art. Most were either immigrants from eastern Europe or children of immigrants. Their experiences as newcomers and their relationship with the diverse, turbulent city informed their art, leading them away from academic tradition toward modernism in style and subject matter. They found an openness in New York's art scene. Despite complaints of antimodernist and anti-Semitic critics such as Royal Cortissoz of the *New York Herald-Tribune*, who decried "Ellis Island art,"[55] Jewish artists received support from a number of established artists, critics, gallery owners, and teachers who shared their aesthetic sensibilities and interest in urban themes. Some of those mentors were not Jewish, such as Robert Henri and Henry McBride; others, such as Alfred Stieglitz, were second-generation German-Jewish Americans.

New York native Jacob Epstein (1880–1959) achieved artistic acclaim, one of the earliest of this new wave of New York Jewish artists, though he did not stay in the city or a Jewish milieu for long. Hutchins Hapgood, whose sympathetic if romanticized portrait of the Jewish immigrant community Epstein illustrated, discovered Epstein in a shedlike room on top of a "pestiferous and dingy" staircase in "a tumble-down rickety building" at the corner of Hester and Forsyth Streets. The artist told Hapgood that he had tried for a time to paint country scenes but had difficulty: "It was only in the Ghetto . . . that I have ideas for sketches. . . . It is only the minds and souls of my people that fill me with the desire to work." Although Hapgood extolled Epstein as one of a rising generation of vibrant "ghetto" artists, Epstein soon left for Paris and then London. There he became a sculptor of note, seldom touching on Jewish themes in his art or writing. He later recalled a reaction to his early environment quite at odds with what Hapgood had reported: "I saw a great deal of Jewish orthodox life, traditional and narrow. . . . As my thoughts were elsewhere, this did not greatly influence me."[56]

Other New York Jews followed Epstein to Paris but then returned to influence American developments. Abraham Walkowitz, for example, traveled abroad in 1906–1907, and Max Weber did between 1905 and 1909. Walkowitz came back as what one art historian called the "first American modernist," staging a one-man show at Julius Haas's frame shop. Weber, a friend of *di yunge* who in Paris fell under the influence of Cezanne, Matisse, and Picasso, exhibited at Haas's as well. Stieglitz—whom one hostile critic referred to as a "Hoboken Jew without knowledge of, or interest in, the historical American background"—was a pioneering modernist photographer. But he also played an especially important role in introducing European modernist currents to American audiences. At his Photo-Secession Gallery, known as 291, he exhibited Rodin drawings and Matisse paintings for the first time in the United States. He also championed young American modernists. The journal *Seven Arts*, edited by James Oppenheim, Paul Rosenfeld, Waldo Frank, and Van Wyck Brooks—the first three of German-Jewish origin—also promoted the new wave. Walkowitz and others were featured in both the 1913 International

Exhibition of Modern Art—the famous "Armory Show"—and the 1916 Forum Exhibition of Modern American Painting, which highlighted American artists slighted at the Armory Show. That one-third of the organizing committee and nearly a quarter of the artists featured in the Forum show were Jews demonstrated their growing importance in the New York art scene.[57]

An eclectic combination of settlement houses, radical activists, and non-Jewish art teachers nurtured immigrant Jewish artists. In 1892, the Educational Alliance, as part of its mission to Americanize immigrants and improve their "standards of taste," inaugurated a series of annual exhibitions of pieces loaned from private collections. The tremendous response demonstrated a thirst for serious art among the immigrant population—in 1895, attendance topped 106,000 in just under five weeks. That year, the Alliance augmented the exhibitions with art classes. When artist and critic Henry McBride came to the school in 1898, he added life drawing, industrial design, and painting to the curriculum. But the Alliance suspended art classes in 1905, when an increase in the number of immigrants entering the country taxed its resources.[58]

The Anarchist Ferrer Center (also called the Modern School), founded in 1911, stood at the "nexus between radical politics and the artistic avant-garde," as well as between Greenwich Village and the Lower East Side. Most of its teachers and leaders, including prominent Ashcan School members Robert Henri and George Bellows, were not Jewish. Most of the students were Jews. Under Bellows and Henri, instruction was antiacademic and included techniques such as "rapid sketching and the short pose," intended to encourage freedom and discourage academic rigidity. Henri was a brilliant teacher. The artist Moses Soyer, a teenager when he attended Henri's class, recalled that Henri's critique of his work permanently altered his approach—and those of his brothers Raphael and Isaac, whom he told about his experience.[59]

Between 1915 and 1918, a related organization, the People's Art Guild, strove to make art part of the lives of the working classes and to create a market for the work of member artists. Although the Guild held most of its sixty exhibitions at settlement houses, it strenuously objected to the settlement view of art as uplift. Rather than distance the masses from their daily lives, the Guild argued, art should empower workers by bringing them "into closer touch with their own circumstances." The Guild was a Jewish organization, with its constitution printed in Yiddish as well as English, but it opened its activities to non-Jews as well. Its largest undertaking—a 1917 exhibition at the Forward

Building—involved eighty-nine artists. Yiddish writer David Ignatoff remembered, "The crowds who came were so great that it became necessary to call the police to hold back the people who sought to push their way into the hall."[60]

By the time of the Forward Building show, the Educational Alliance had reestablished its art school down the block. The new director was Abbo Ostrowsky, an immigrant from Russia who had studied at the National Academy of Design and taught previously at the University Settlement. Uninterested in avant-garde art, Ostrowsky had radical political leanings. According to artist Louis Lozowick, who taught at the Alliance, the art school fostered a "definite social orientation. [The student] is made to feel his identity with the community of which he is a product by drawing inspiration from its life, reflecting the peculiarities of its environment and embodying in permanent form its cultural heritage." Although conceived as a "community art center," the art school assumed a more professional character under Ostrowsky than it had under McBride. A number of prominent Jewish artists trained there, including Chaim Gross, Elias Newman, Philip Evergood, Ben Shahn, Leonard Baskin, Moses Soyer, Isaac Soyer, Jo Davidson, Dina Melicov, Leo Gottlieb, and Peter Blume.[61]

■ The Performing Arts

By the time Bertha Kalich debuted on the English-language stage, Jews played an enormous role in the New York theater world. Nowhere was this more striking than in vaudeville, the popular form of variety show that featured a mix of singing, dancing, comedic and dramatic sketches, acrobatics and gymnastics, and animal acts, generally performed continuously and for a low price. By the twentieth century, the American vaudeville empire centered in New York's Times Square, where the largest circuits had their offices and the most opulent theaters enticed audiences. In New York, other centers of vaudeville performance developed in the Bronx, at the "hub" around 149th Street; on Fulton Street and in Williamsburg and Coney Island in Brooklyn; on the Lower East Side; and in Queens and Staten Island.[62] A cosmopolitan lot, vaudeville performers arose mainly from working-class backgrounds and ethnic minorities. If in the nineteenth century the Irish dominated, Jews became the most visible group in the early twentieth.

Eddie Cantor, a son of the Jewish Lower East Side, typified the stars emerging out of vaudeville. Born in 1892 and orphaned at the age of two, Cantor flirted as a youth with a life of crime. He entered show business as a performer at weddings and bar mitzvahs but got his first break when he won an amateur contest at Miner's Bowery Theater in 1908. Over the next few months, he toured the circuit, worked as a singing waiter in Coney Island, and sang at weddings. Then he signed on as a valet to one of the top jugglers in vaudeville, gradually working himself into the act. By 1917, he reached the big time, performing with Ziegfeld's Follies.[63]

Sophie Tucker's victory in an amateur contest launched her show-business career as well. Born in Russia in 1884, Tucker grew up in Hartford, Connecticut, where her parents ran a delicatessen and restaurant. Among the customers were some of the biggest names in the Yiddish theater as well as in vaudeville. Tucker impressed them with her singing, and when she decided to enter show business in New York, Jewish vaudevillian Willie Howard gave her a letter of recommendation to top songwriter Howard Von Tilzer. In 1907, she entered Chris Brown's amateur night, where she made a hit singing in blackface. She soon became famous as "a world renowned coon singer." Only after losing her makeup on tour did she jettison the façade and perform as who she was—a Jewish woman. Even without blackface, Tucker continued to be known for her bluesy style and risqué lyrics replete with double entendres. She sometimes sang in Yiddish dialect.[64]

By the 1910s, Jewish performers such as Tucker, as well as composers and lyricists such as Irving Berlin, saw themselves and were seen by others as having a special relationship to African American music. Adopting syncopated rhythms and slangy idioms, Jews played a leading role in injecting them into the mainstream of American popular music. But the relationship was not always free of exploitation. A propensity for singing in blackface was a disturbing aspect of the Jewish rise to success. White American performers had been "blacking up" and performing pseudo–African American music, with varying degrees of grotesquery, since at least the 1830s; Jews joined this well-established tradition, becoming premier blackface performers by the 1910s. In addition to Cantor and Tucker, Jewish performers George Burns and George Jessel painted their faces. But no one surpassed Al Jolson, whom Jessel called "a no-good son-of-a-bitch" but "the greatest entertainer" he had ever seen. Born in Russia and brought as a child to Washington, DC, where his father was a rabbi, Jolson retrieved blackface from low-class variety obscurity and returned it to big-time vaudeville, the legitimate stage, and eventually to the silver screen. Perhaps the most dynamic performer of his generation, Jolson made a career of portraying pseudo-black characters longing for the antebellum Southland and for "mammy."[65]

The Shubert brothers—Sam, Lee, and J.J. (Jacob)—promoted Jolson from the vaudeville circuit to the "legitimate stage," where unified casts presented plays with continuous story lines. Indeed the Shuberts, Polish-Jewish immigrants who had grown up in Syracuse and arrived in New York City around the turn of the century, became the most powerful theatrical producers of their day. To reach that position, they overcame their archrivals in the Theatrical Syndicate, a combination headed by the Jewish Abraham Lincoln Erlanger and the non-Jewish Marc Klaw, which monopolized bookings, and therefore ultimately production, of plays in theaters in and out of town. Erlanger and the Shuberts—along with Oscar Hammerstein, David Belasco, and the team of Joe Weber and Lew Fields—helped define Broadway for the twentieth century, in both drama and musical comedy. In the process, they built Times Square into the city's premier popular entertainment center.[66]

Many of the songs for both vaudeville and the legitimate stage came from the new popular song industry based on West Twenty-Eighth Street and composed mainly of Jewish-owned firms. "Tin Pan Alley" got its start in 1886,

Considered by many people the foremost entertainer of his generation, Al Jolson also brought blackface from vaudeville to the legitimate stage and, eventually, to the silver screen. (Theater Collection, Museum of the City of New York)

when the Jewish-owned printing company specializing in sheet music Witmark and Sons moved to Twenty-Eighth Street. It acquired its nickname from those who likened the disparate sounds emerging from the street's brownstone studios to a cacophony of tin pans. One observer described the Tin Pan Alley songwriters as "a clever group of scoundrels that monopolize the lyric-writing game at present—all Jews." He exaggerated, though Jews did play a disproportionate role. When asked to sum up the secret of Tin Pan Alley success, one of the "scoundrels," Gus Kahn, answered, "Oh, that's a cinch. 'Mother,' 'Sweetheart,' 'Home,' and 'Yearning For You.' All these simple heart tugs have infinite variations." Some songs transcended the formula, becoming classics of American popular culture. Moreover, these themes transferred easily, and a side industry arose translating Tin Pan Alley hits into Yiddish or writing original Yiddish songs in a Tin Pan Alley style.[67]

The most important of the Jewish songwriters to emerge from Tin Pan Alley was Irving Berlin. Called the "Norman Rockwell of melody," Berlin epitomizes the way in which New York Jewish songwriters reached well beyond the boundaries of their own ethnic and geographical origins. Berlin, of course, crafted such patriotic classics as "God Bless America" and such tinselly songs as "White Christmas" and "Easter Parade," both of which portrayed essentially secular visions of their respective, traditionally Christian, holidays. He also wrote "coon songs" for blackface performers, drawing from African American sources (though he sometimes denied the real black influence on his music). But Berlin composed in all sorts of ethnic idioms as well, including Irish songs in brogue, Yiddish-accented Jewish songs, and Italian-themed lyrics. So pervasive was Berlin's influence that his colleague Jerome Kern could plausibly claim that "Irving Berlin has *no* place in American music; HE IS AMERICAN MUSIC."[68]

Young people heard the new music in the numerous dance halls that dotted the city. By 1910, as social worker Belle Moskowitz noted, "The town [was] dance mad." From the working-class immigrant districts of all ethnicities to the poshest precincts, young people flocked to venues ranging from small rented lofts and the backrooms of shady saloons to grand "dance palaces" in Midtown. But however large or small, fancy or plain, dance halls represented a loosening of Victorian morals and an arena for a new public culture of sexually charged freedom that became associated with New York and other large cities. Social dances performed to the syncopated rhythms of ragtime music encouraged close physical contact between the sexes. Since dance halls could be found in many neighborhoods, they became popular and convenient places for young people to meet, flirt, touch, and sometimes engage in more overt sexual activity.[69]

Young women exhibited particular enthusiasm for dancing. One young immigrant, Minnie Goldstein, later recalled the thrill of being singled out by the "professor" of a dance class:

> It always happened that the "professor" of the class . . . took me himself to dance with. Once, the "professor" said to me, "Minnie, we are having a ball in a large hall, and I am going to lead the march. Do you want to go with me?" I could not believe my ears. Such a handsome young man! Many girls considered it an honor when he said a word to them. And he was inviting me—of all people—to lead the march with him! . . . I felt so happy that I could not even think straight.[70]

It was the inability to "think straight" that concerned the guardians of morality, who feared that young women would be led astray by such "professors" or by ordinary young men who plied girls with drink. Immigrant lodges and societies sponsored balls that offered a more respectable venue for young people to meet and dance under the watchful eyes of parents, friends, and *landslayt*. Incidentally, these lodge balls provided employment to immigrant musicians capable of playing both traditional Jewish folk tunes and up-to-date American dances.[71]

While young people of all classes danced, those with more serious musical tastes attended the opera. Here, too, the careers of two impresarios—Heinrich Conried and Oscar Hammerstein—illustrate not only the important role that Jews played in the organization of a cultural enterprise but also links between immigrant and "mainstream," popular and high culture. A native of Silesia, Conried was born in 1855, the son of a Jewish weaver. After beginning a career as an actor, theater director, and stage manager in Vienna and Bremen, he arrived in New York in 1878 to manage and act in the Germania Theatre. In 1893, Conried took over the Irving Place Theater and transformed it into the city's leading German-language venue by introducing a more modern naturalistic style influenced by up-to-date trends in Germany. Finally, in 1903, he became director of the Metropolitan Opera, where he endeavored to improve the quality of productions. He brought Gustav Mahler from Europe to conduct the orchestra and produced the New York premieres of Wagner's *Parsifal* and Strauss's controversial *Salome*. He retired in ill health in 1908 and died the following year.[72]

At the time Conried retired, the Met was locked in battle with the rival Manhattan Opera Company, led by Hammerstein. Also a German immigrant, the colorful and energetic Hammerstein had been a cigar maker, inventor, real estate mogul, composer, playwright, builder of theaters, and theatrical producer before opening the Manhattan Opera in 1906. Hammerstein and Conried hated each other, an enmity apparently stemming from a brief association in the German-language theater. More than Conried, Hammerstein aimed to shake up the opera world by downplaying its association with high society; as he put it, "It is society in the broad sense that I hope to attract and please." With an emphasis on modern works and aggressive marketing, the Manhattan Opera gave the Met a run for its money. In 1910, though, Met president Otto Kahn negotiated a merger of the two companies. Though the period of competition was brief, Hammerstein influenced the Met's development over the long term, partly because Kahn sympathized with Hammerstein's approach.[73]

■ The Movies

In 1905, vaudeville and variety shows still used moving pictures merely to fill the time between acts. But within two or three years, movies became the main attraction themselves in dozens of "nickelodeons," storefront theaters that charged five or ten cents for admission. Hundreds of thousands of people flocked to the movies each day, with Jews and other immigrants the prime audience for this new cheap and thrilling form of entertainment. Of the 123 nickelodeons that operated in Manhattan in 1908, nearly half were located on the Lower East Side or in Jewish East Harlem. The *Forward* reported, "When you go through the streets of our neighborhood you will be amazed by the mass of moving picture houses. Four or more 'shows' can be found on one street. In some streets, there are even two 'shows' on one block, facing each other." The small theaters, each seating between two and three hundred, became neighborhood gathering places, with an informal atmosphere resembling that of the Yiddish theater, which encouraged socializing.[74]

Jewish entrepreneurs quickly stepped into the market. Adolph Zukor was a thirty-year-old immigrant from the Carpathian Mountains and a successful furrier when, with a partner, he opened an arcade on Fourteenth Street with kinetoscopes (very short peep-show films). He later operated conventional nickelodeons as well. Likewise, Marcus Loew, a native New Yorker who had grown up in an immigrant family in the heart of Kleindeutschland, opened his first nickelodeon in 1905. Three years later, he branched out into vaudeville and Brooklyn, and by 1911, Loew owned forty theaters throughout the city. William Fox, born in Hungary and brought to New York as an infant, had already experienced success in the garment industry when he began to renovate dilapidated theaters in Brooklyn.

Zukor, Fox, Loew, and others changed the way movies were made and exhibited, pioneering the production of feature films and showing them in ever larger and more luxurious surroundings. As Zukor later put it, the "nickelodeon had to go, theaters replaced shooting galleries, temples replaced theaters, and cathedrals replaced temples." As early as 1908, Fox's thousand-seat Dewey Theater on Fourteenth Street offered programs of vaudeville and movies for as little as a nickel or a dime, all under the watchful eyes of red-uniformed ushers. At the same time, Loew methodically expanded his chain, which at first showed a combination of vaudeville and movies, until it spread throughout the United States and Canada. Loew's large, luxurious, and conveniently located theaters attracted respectable middle class families. In New York, they dotted the entire city, reaching into outer borough neighborhoods where their patrons increasingly lived.[75]

Zukor and German-Jewish immigrant Carl Laemmle also concluded that audiences would be more than willing to sit through longer movies, especially if drawn by the names of famous stars. Zukor first began importing features from Europe. Then he formed Famous Players Film Company together with the older Jewish American theatrical impresarios Daniel and Charles Frohman and David Belasco to produce their own films, releasing the tremendously successful *Prisoner of Zenda* in 1913. By 1916, Famous Players had merged with Jesse Lasky and Samuel Goldwyn's successful company to create the Famous Players-Lasky Corporation, which in turn took over the distribution company Paramount Pictures Corporation. Enlisting the help of the Jewish Wall Street firm Kuhn Loeb to raise the capital to open a string of first-run movie palaces across the country, the company thereby combined production with marketing and distribution.[76]

As early as 1910, movie production began to shift to Hollywood. Although executive offices remained in New York for a time, by 1922, the city's share of the industry dropped to only 12 percent. Still, New York remained an important factor in American film. Jews contributed to the American film industry's early years, not only as producers and exhibitors but also as audience members. And the city proved a powerful presence in American movies, fully a third of which in the 1920s and '30s featured New York as their setting. Moreover, Hollywood became a sort of colony of Jewish New York, broadcasting New York Jewish style throughout the nation.[77]

In the 1920s and '30s, New York Jewry gradually edged away from its immigrant roots. The community's German-speaking element had faded away almost entirely (to be revived on a smaller scale by refugees in the 1930s and after). The Yiddish sector shrank as well, although it retained some heft and much creativity through the interwar years. The modernists of the *in zikh* (introspectivist) group superseded *di yunge* as the vanguard of Yiddish poetry. And the brothers Israel Joshua and Isaac Bashevis Singer arrived to bolster Yiddish prose. The Yiddish art theater maintained high standards, attracting the admiration of critics from beyond the Yiddish-speaking world. But audiences peaked in this period and then declined. Although the Yiddish press continued to count its readers in the hundreds of thousands, it, too, peaked as early as 1916, as readers deserted to English-language newspapers. Yiddish culture was marginalized as its public contracted. Though American Jewish culture retained a Yiddish substratum, its future lay in English.[78]

Indeed, by the interwar period, the association of Jews with New York culture was so pervasive that for many Americans the two were nearly synonymous. Jewish influence existed on a number of levels: Yinglish slang fused with earlier Irish and German elements in New York speech; Jewish nervous energy contributed to the speed with which events seemed to move in New York compared to the rest of the country; Jews in the New York garment industry set the style for other Americans. Whether cultivated by the Jewish labor movement or the public schools, Jews formed much of the market for both popular and "high" culture: In the 1930s, Jews made up more than half the subscribers to the New York Philharmonic; in the 1960s, they constituted half of Broadway's audiences.[79]

With Hollywood, and later radio and television, helping to broadcast Jews' handiwork to the country and the world, they supplied much of the creative talent as well. A new generation of Jewish songwriters, composers, and performers arose in New York. George Gershwin, whose first hit, "Swanee," sung by Jolson, appeared in 1919, contributed to show, jazz, and classical music. Jerome Kern and Oscar Hammerstein II, grandson of the impresario, collaborated on *Showboat* (based on a story by Edna Ferber), revolutionizing the Broadway musical in 1927. *Showboat*, along with George and Ira Gershwin's musical *Porgy and Bess*, also helped shift Jewish artists' relationship to African American culture away from blackface to a more respectful stance, even injecting explicitly antiracist themes into popular culture. The Jewish presence also grew in American classical music, literature, dance, and the visual arts.[80]

It was not that any of these fields lacked non-Jewish artists or even that there was anything identifiably "Judaic" about the contributions made by individual Jews. But as key players in the arts, New York Jews infused American culture with a range of expressions influenced by their own experiences as immigrants or children of immigrants in the nation's largest, most cosmopolitan, and most multiethnic and multireligious city. As New York became the cultural capital of the United States (with Hollywood its colony), Jews thus brought their sensibilities to bear on American culture in powerful ways.

Raphael Soyer's 1929 "East Side Street Scene" shows the remnants of the once bustling neighborhood. The Yiddish sign at the left announces "corner floor for rent." As transportation lines and upward mobility propelled longtime Jewish residents to Brooklyn and the Bronx, new quota laws vastly reduced the number of newcomers flowing into the neighborhood, leading to its decline as a Jewish population center. (Courtesy of Joseph S. Lieber)

Conclusion: The Jewish Metropolis at the End of the Immigrant Era

By 1920, New York's Jews numbered over 1.6 million, making the city the greatest Jewish metropolis of all time.[1] But New York Jewry's growth had been fueled by a massive, nearly century-long wave of immigration that diminished suddenly to a trickle, at first temporarily when World War I obstructed paths of migration and then permanently as a result of two acts of Congress. The cessation of immigration led to the gradual transformation of New York's Jewish community from one largely working class and immigrant in composition into one with an American-born, middle-class majority. As New York Jews entered the middle class, they developed a range of neighborhoods in Brooklyn and the Bronx, where they expressed their New York Jewish identity in increasingly diverse ways.

■ Closing the Golden Door

In April 1924, Passover sermons in New York synagogues drew parallels not between the Pharaoh and the Tsar as they did on Ellis Island in 1906, but between Pharaoh's oppressive policies and new immigration quotas that were gaining momentum in Congress. At Shearith Israel, the nation's oldest synagogue, now located on Central Park West, Rabbi David de Sola Pool explained, "The opening chapters of Exodus give us the earliest examples of anti-alien legislation on record," and then he warned, "While the measures which Pharaoh took were barbarous, the spirit of the Egypt of his day is not dead." Dr. I. Mortimer Bloom, rabbi of the Hebrew Tabernacle of West 116th Street, was more direct:

The immigration restriction bills are a denial and reversal of long-cherished American ideals and traditions, an affront to the memory of the founders of the Republic, a dagger thrust into the hearts of thousands of human beings who yearn for an opportunity to lead the normal decent life which their own lands deny them and a staggering blow to humanitarians everywhere. . . . Not as a Jew, not as one whose co-religionists happen to be seriously affected by the proposed legislation, but as an American steeped in the best traditions of his land, an American who craves for his country to be true to the high and holy mission for which she was called into being, do I cry against these discriminatory, heartless, un-American bills.[2]

As anti-immigrant sentiment peaked in the form of severely restrictive immigration laws, New York Jewish congressmen, rabbis, and communal leaders joined other New Yorkers to champion a pluralist vision of an American nation made richer by their own and other immigrants' experiences. Though they failed, and Congress ultimately enacted anti-immigrant quotas, their fight speaks of their deep faith in the promise of inclusion and tolerance best fulfilled in New York City. Despite quotas and nativist sentiment, New York Jews continued to fashion American identities rooted in the city's pluralist cosmopolitanism.

The passage of immigration restriction marked the triumph of a nativist movement that had originally arisen in response to the growing European immigration of the 1830s and '40s. The movement had waxed and waned over the decades but emerged from World War I much strengthened. In the atmosphere of supercharged patriotism during the war, German Americans (with whom Jews were sometimes still associated) came under attack, as did radicals who opposed American entry into the war and "hyphenated Americans" who were seen to have loyalties outside the borders of the United States. After the war, many Americans feared that immigrants would spread the revolutionary contagion sweeping Europe. During the "tribal 'twenties," the reemergence of the Ku Klux Klan epitomized the reactionary, antimodern, antiurban, racist, and xenophobic mood of much of the country.[3]

In this atmosphere, an anti-Semitic strand of nativism flourished in certain respectable circles. Madison Grant, a patrician New Yorker and founder of the New York Zoological Society, expressed some of the racial anxieties of the times when he wrote, "The man of the old stock is being crowded out of many country districts by these foreigners, just as he is to-day being literally driven off the streets of New York City by the swarms of Polish Jews. These immigrants adopt the language of the native American; they wear his clothes; they steal his name; and they are beginning to take his women, but they seldom adopt his religion or understand his ideals." In Brooklyn, a group of citizens published the *Anti-Bolshevik*, which described itself as "A Monthly Magazine Devoted to the Defense of American Institutions against the Jewish Bolshevist Doctrine of Morris Hillquit and Leon Trotsky," two Jewish New Yorkers, as Trotsky had lived briefly in the Bronx. The most admired industrialist of the time, Henry Ford, further emphasized the political dangers posed by a secret, international Jewish cabal. Beginning in 1920, Ford's *Dearborn Independent* began a campaign against Jewish influence. Distributed in the hundreds of thousands through his car dealerships throughout the country, it even reprinted an adaptation of the Tsarist forgery *The Protocols of the Elders of Zion*.[4]

The main Jewish defense agency, the American Jewish Committee, was in a quandary about how to deal with this upsurge in anti-Jewish sentiment. It vociferously denied any Jewish link to Communism but hesitated over how to respond to Ford. Although anti-Semitic conspiracy theorists named the AJC's chairman, Louis Marshall, as the chief Jewish conspirator in the United States, the organization ultimately maintained its standard low-key, reasoned approach. Appealing to "enlightened" public opinion, it commissioned and distributed several books and pamphlets rebutting the *Protocols* and highlighting Jewish contributions to American culture and Western civilization. It lobbied former and sitting presidents, with some success in enlisting their support. However, against Marshall's advice, Jewish journalist Herman Bernstein sued Ford for libel after the *Independent* named him as its source for the *Protocols*. Based partly on a 1913 New York State group-libel statute drafted by Marshall, Bernstein's suit went nowhere. But one by California attorney Aaron Sapiro, accused by Ford of dominating American agriculture on behalf of the Jewish conspiracy, forced the industrialist to retreat. Although the matter was settled out of court, Ford issued an apologetic statement in 1927 that had been written for him by Marshall.[5]

But by that time, much legislative damage had been done. Since 1875, Congress had been slowly adding categories to the kinds of people barred from entering the country. By the time of World War I, laws banned convicts, prostitutes, "idiots," "lunatics," contract laborers, polygamists, Anarchists, Chinese laborers, and people deemed likely to need public support. In 1917, Congress added illiterates to the list and created an "Asiatic barred zone" that effectively excluded almost all Asians. The Immigration Act of 1921, sponsored by Representative Albert Johnson of Washington, went further by setting an overall numerical limit of 350,000 immigrants each year. Johnson's concern was not strictly quantitative, however. Afraid that the nation would be polluted by an influx of "abnormally twisted," "unassimilable" Jews, "filthy, un-American and often dangerous in their habits," Johnson also aimed to shape the flow qualitatively. His bill, passed overwhelmingly despite objections by Meyer London and other immigrant and Jewish representatives, established annual quotas for each country equaling 3 percent of the number of individuals from that country present in the United States in 1910.[6]

But when the 1921 law failed to stem immigration to the extent desired, Congress reexamined the issue in 1924. The new proposal, named again for Johnson and for Senator David A. Reed of Pennsylvania, cut national quotas to 2 percent of the number from a given country in the United States as of 1890. This was a blatant attempt to exclude southern and eastern Europeans, along with Asians, who were barred altogether. In the halls of Congress, where the bill's proponents attacked its opponents as a "foreign bloc," the representatives of immigrant districts put up a last-ditch defense. By this time, New York's delegation included four Jewish members—Democrats Samuel Dickstein, Emanuel Celler, and Sol Bloom, and Republican Nathan Perlman. Significantly, Dickstein and Perlman were foreign-born, while Bloom was the son and Celler the grandson of immigrants. Much of the debate centered on the effects that the bill's anti-Asian provisions would have on U.S.-Japanese relations, but New York City's Jewish congressmen joined with most of their New York colleagues, as well as Catholic and Jewish representatives from other states, to defend immigrant contributions and to criticize nativist bigotry. Notably, twenty out of twenty-two of New York State's Democratic house members issued a public statement opposing the Johnson-Reed Act. But they failed to convince their fellow legislators; the bill passed both the House and Senate overwhelmingly.[7]

The nativist triumph after World War I overshadowed persistent alternative visions championed by many New York Jews. Some held on to their faith in the power of the melting pot to Americanize immigrants and their children. Some, such as Horace Kallen, an active Zionist and from 1919 a founding member of the faculty of the New School for Social Research, argued for a more radical notion of cultural pluralism, according to which America should be a nation of diverse ethnic groups that would maintain their distinctiveness. Kallen believed it impossible for an individual to shed his or her inborn ethnic identity. Columbia University anthropology professor Franz Boas, on the other hand, believed environment more important than birth in determining individual and group characteristics. Of Jewish origin, though uninvolved in the Jewish community, Boas attacked the racialist ideas that underpinned the new restrictive laws. But in the anxious times that followed the world war, Americans outside of places like New York were little inclined to heed these more inclusive visions of national identity.[8]

The new laws dramatically affected immigration in general and Jewish immigration in particular. The numbers of new arrivals plummeted, from over 800,000 altogether, including almost 120,000 Jews, in the year before the passage of the 1921 law, to slightly under 295,000 altogether and just over 10,000 Jews in the year after enactment of the Johnson-Reed Act.[9] Without the massive influx that had characterized the previous century, New York Jewry began a slow transition from a Yiddish-speaking immigrant community (German had been largely jettisoned long before) to a native-born and English-speaking one.

Of course, despite the sudden shift in the numbers entering the country, the community's demographic transformation occurred gradually. Not only did a trickle of legal immigrants continue to arrive, but so did smaller numbers of illegals. A predominantly Jewish network of smugglers that until this time had focused its energies on helping migrants sneak *out* of Russia now turned its attention to enabling its clients to *enter* the United States, often through either Cuba or Canada. Minnie Kusnetz, one such illegal immigrant, paid $200 to be driven over the border from Canada. She left Montreal at eight one morning and arrived at her sister's home in Brooklyn twenty-two hours later. New York thus remained a magnet for Jewish immigrants, as much now because of ties with family there as because of economic opportunity. Kusnetz, for example, had thrived in Canada for several years but longed to join her sisters in New York. A few years later, Kusnetz was informed on by a Jewish employer who resented her union activism. Held at Ellis Island for deportation, she enlisted the help of her fiancé and her brother-in-law, both citizens, who in turn hired a lawyer and contacted local politicians with whom they were acquainted. Their efforts helped her legalize her status. Kusnetz's story thus illustrates not only the vulnerability of the undocumented immigrant but the degree to which Jews were integrated into the local power structure, even as they remained politically marginal nationally.[10]

▪ From Chatham Square to Jewish Metropolis

When Minnie Kusnetz crossed the border and arrived in New York City, her smuggler dropped her off, not on the Lower East Side but in Brooklyn, where her eldest sister lived.[11] By that time, Jews had spilled over the edges of their original areas of settlement and lived throughout the city. Whereas mid-nineteenth-century New York Jews had found their niche in and around Chatham Square, in the Five Points neighborhood and Kleindeutschland, interwar-era New York Jews resided in a wide variety of neighborhoods in Manhattan, the Bronx, Brooklyn, and to a much lesser extent Queens. These Jewish neighborhoods included grimy tenement districts, blocks of well-appointed elevator apartment buildings, and leafy streets of single- and two-family homes. Some housed poor Yiddish-speaking immigrants and their children, others a striving middle class, and still others those who had already made their way to the top. Just as these various and variegated Jewish quarters separated out by class, they took on different religious, political, and cultural attributes.

The business streets in these neighborhoods marked them as integrally Jewish. As memoirist Ruth Gay recalled, "The neighborhoods of the Bronx and Brooklyn were lined with little shops minutely divided by specialization, each one just barely supporting a family by offering an indispensable service or selling necessary goods."[12] Delicatessens, "appetizing" stores, cafeterias, and Jewish bakeries catered to Jewish culinary tastes, doubled as local gathering places, and added an ethnic ambiance to the neighborhood. Candy stores—with newsstands and lunch counters—were ubiquitous in New York, usually run by Jews even in non-Jewish neighborhoods. They, too, served as meeting places, especially for young people. Brownsville, Williamsburg, and the East Bronx all had pushcart street markets as well, something that the residents of the Upper West Side and the Grand Concourse happily lacked. Synagogues, of course, clearly marked a district as Jewish. But the specific mix of Orthodox, Conservative, and Reform varieties differentiated Jewish areas from one another; in some sections, Jewish life revolved around the synagogues, and in others, they usually sat empty, while radical fraternal orders dominated the scene. The archipelago of neighborhoods in which Jews were segregated from non-Jews even more thoroughly than they had been in older areas of immigrant settlement thus constituted a kind of city within a city.

By 1920, Manhattan had already begun to decline as the center of Jewish residential life, a process that continued in the 1920s before stalling in the Depression decade. (Most, though not all, of Manhattan's overall demographic decline in the 1920s is attributable to the exodus of Jews.) In 1892, some 75 percent of the city's Jews had lived on the Lower East Side. But by 1930, the old immigrant quarter's share had fallen to one in twenty. In fact, Manhattan's three hundred thousand Jews made up only a little over a quarter of New York's Jewish population, and many of them lived uptown, on the Upper West Side, in Washington Heights, Yorkville, and, in diminishing numbers, Harlem. The Lower East Side remained the seat of much of the Yiddish-speaking sector's communal and cultural life, but only the poorest of the city's Jews resided there. The Upper West Side, whose cavernous streets were lined with elegant apartment buildings, epitomized the "opposite of the Lower East Side." The city's wealthiest Jewish community, it included prosperous manufacturers, professionals, and other businesspeople, with a median family income almost seven times that of the older area.[13]

Brooklyn and the Bronx succeeded Manhattan as centers of Jewish residence. Almost half the city's Jews lived in Brooklyn, almost three times as many as in Manhattan. Brooklyn neighborhoods ran the gamut: Williamsburg, just over the bridge from the Lower East Side, and Brownsville continued to be inhabited by working-class immigrants and their children, the poorest Jews outside of Lower Manhattan. While Williamsburg gained a reputation as a bastion of Orthodoxy, Brownsville harbored a strong radical contingent. Meanwhile, Flatbush and Borough Park, their leafy streets lined with stately one- and two-family houses, and Eastern Parkway, its apartment buildings resembling those of the Upper West Side, attracted more Americanized businesspeople, professionals, and white-collar workers. Borough Park, especially, was a stronghold of Zionism. A typical path of social ascent might take a Jewish family from Brownsville to East Flatbush to Flatbush or Eastern Parkway.[14]

Similarly, in the Bronx, where Jews made up nearly half the population, an upwardly mobile family would move from east to west. In the largely working-class but heterogeneous East Bronx, some areas were "duplications of the ghetto," gritty industrial and tenement districts inhabited by Yiddish-speaking

manual workers and their families. Irving Howe recalled that Fox Street symbolized for his parents the depths to which one might fall during the Great
Depression. "At least we're not on Fox Street," his father would say philosophi-
cally during a crisis. Better-off workers occupied the blocks around Crotona
Park, on the other hand, living in moderately priced modern apartment buildings with all the latest improvements. The East Bronx had a reputation for
radicalism, the Workmen's Circle and garment unions maintaining an active
presence there. To the west lay the Grand Concourse, the Bronx's "Fifth Avenue," though in truth its white-collar residents were more middle class than
wealthy, with average incomes lower than those of Brooklyn's better neighborhoods. As bourgeois and American as the Concourse seemed, moreover, it
was 75 percent Jewish, one of the most solidly Jewish neighborhoods outside
of Brownsville.[15]

Some Jewish families traversed these neighborhoods as they climbed
the socioeconomic ladder. Recall Mary Wasserzug, who arrived from Ver-
belov, Lithuania, in 1876 at the age of thirteen to join her father in the Chatham Square area. When Mary went to work, first as a domestic and then as
a buttonhole maker, the family moved to slightly improved lodgings on East
Broadway. Several years later, neighborhood networks connected her to Sam
Natelson, a young man with a reputation as "a good businessman." The couple moved to tenement rooms on the corner of Orchard Street and Rivington, and while Sam worked as a peddler, Mary kept three boarders. As they
became more rooted in the city, they in turn helped other newcomers settle
in by clothing them, finding them places to live, and getting them jobs. The
Natelsons moved to Williamsburg, while Sam worked as a salesman for the
Singer sewing machine company. When a cutters' strike halted business, Mary
compensated by taking in boarders. She then persuaded Sam to open an office, where they sold sewing machines, coal, insurance, and real estate. Notic-
ing the arrival of new immigrants in need of assistance, Mary organized the
Williamsburg Ladies Aid Society, which negotiated with landlords on behalf
of tenants, made loans, and helped the unemployed find jobs. The business
flourished, and the Natelsons eventually found their way to Borough Park. By
the 1920s, their American born and educated children embarked on successful careers; their son, Nathan, ran a glass business, while all four daughters
became public school teachers. One daughter, Rachel, became "swept up in
Zionist activity under the leadership of Miss Szold, the founder of Hadassah."

As the family achieved stable middle-class status, it thus not only settled in appropriate neighborhoods but joined appropriate organizations.[16]

These neighborhoods gave their residents a sense of being at home within a broader city that often seemed remote, unwelcoming, inaccessible. As Alfred Kazin wrote of the second generation, "We were of the city, but somehow not in it. I saw New York as a foreign city.... New York was what we put last on our address, but first in thinking of the others around us. *They* were New York, the Gentiles, America." Other children of immigrants echoed this sentiment, whether they were from Brownsville, like him, or from the East Bronx. Vivian Gornick recalled that Manhattan was like "Araby," exotic and enticing. This sense of alienation from the city as a whole underlines the fact that Jews remained a minority of New York's population at 29 percent.[17] Wide swaths of the city—most of Queens and Staten Island and pockets of Manhattan, Brooklyn, and even the Bronx—remained the property of others, not just, or even primarily, of established Anglo-American Protestants but of the various Catholic ethnic groups who by this time together constituted the majority.

The Lower East Side remained an island of familiarity. Though Kazin described Manhattan as "foreign," he acknowledged that the East Side, at least, was part of his childhood. From an early age, he attended meetings with his father in the *Jewish Daily Forward* building. Later, when he had become separated from his class on a field trip to Manhattan, he decided to cross the Brooklyn Bridge alone. As he made his way through the crowds, shaken by the traffic and visual stimulation, he noted, "Only the electric sign of the Jewish Daily *Forward*, burning high over the tenements of the East Side, suddenly stilled the riot in my heart." Though Ruth Gay grew up in the Bronx, she also recalled the Forward Building in the 1920s, "its name emblazoned in lights across the sky on East Broadway." No longer the thriving residential neighborhood it had been a quarter century before, the broader Lower East Side still held many of the Jewish institutions—the Educational Alliance, a host of synagogues, and union halls—that had given the second generation's parents a leg up. It also remained a center of Jewish commerce.[18]

Growing older, members of the American-raised generation began to feel impatient with their confining neighborhoods. Eager to claim the cosmopolitan opportunities offered by Manhattan, they discovered that these had been shaped in many ways by the cumulative impact of immigrant Jews. As Kazin and others became "walkers in the city," they could see how generations of immigrant Jews had bequeathed to New Yorkers enduring patterns of association, labor, culture, politics, and religion. Moorish synagogues in Midtown spoke to the way Jewish houses of worship helped cultivate New York's tolerance and cosmopolitanism; Macy's and other department stores showed how Jews had shaped the city's patterns of commerce and consumption; garment factories in the West Thirties attested to the maturity of the industry; rallies in Union Square pointed to the enduring strength of radical and labor movements.

Despite Jewish New Yorkers' feeling that their neighborhoods stood somehow apart from the city as a whole, New York had already become in some senses a "Jewish city." At nearly a third of the population, Jews were New York's largest single ethnic group, and they profoundly influenced the city's culture, politics, and economy. Of course, the city shaped them as well. This was especially true of the second generation, those born or raised in New York, who in the 1920s came into their own as the dominant segment of the community. Jewish immigrants had laid the foundation for the Jewish metropolis. Their American-born children and grandchildren built on that groundwork for the remainder of the twentieth century.

An Introduction to the Visual and Material Culture of New York City Jews, 1840–1920

DIANA L. LINDEN

What can a mass-produced postcard tell us about New York City Jewish life? In the late nineteenth century, concurrent with the great exodus of eastern European Jews to the United States, postcard designers and printers created a niche market targeting Jewish consumers, in particular women, offering a range of illustrated cards for Jewish holidays and life-cycle events. Many of the cards pictured Jewish women, except for scenes set in synagogues. These cards brought Jewish women into "the visual universe of Jewish experience," writes historian Ellen Smith.[1] Women purchased the cards and exchanged them with friends and family, both in America and back in Europe. The cards illustrated Jews—both women and men—of all ages engaged in observing holy days and using modern inventions (including ocean liners and telephones) that bridge distances and create a transnational Jewish world. Communication by postcard with "A Happy New Year" written in Hebrew and English across the front image permitted Jews on either side of the ocean to send inspirational pictures and words of good cheer in observance of their common holidays.

In the postcard on the following page, at left, we see confident New York Jews who had previously made the voyage to America. The men and women wear fine, brightly colored outfits and lack any obvious religious garments or objects, and though they wear hats, some of the men are clean shaven, a sign of their modern Orthodox Jewish practice. The American Jews extend their arms to the eastern European Jews to welcome them. Perhaps, also, they intend to grasp their hands to pull these "greenhorns," whose arms hang limply at their

"A Happy New Year," New Year's postcard, c. 1900. (Alfred
& Elizabeth Bendiner Collection, Prints and Photographs
Division, Library of Congress, Washington, DC)

sides, into the modern world. Holding bundled parcels of their few belongings, wearing weathered hats or scarves, with rounded shoulders and faces cast
slightly toward the ground, the newcomers express stasis rather than motion.

These picturesque holiday cards provide clues into the lives of New York
City Jews and how they represented themselves to other Jews. The images on
the front of the cards—pleasing, fanciful, and picturesque—are equal in value,
despite their mass production, to the handwritten notes on their backs. If we
read the cards and images literally, all was well for Jews in New York. Postcards,

greeting cards, and the like allowed Jewish purchasers to choose how they would be represented. Such mass-produced cards satisfied the group's desire to be seen at its best: without stereotypes, looking healthy and fashionable, aware of holidays and traditions, and making good in the United States. The picture postcard was often prettier than the lives Jewish consumers actually lived, and in a manner served as a note of self-congratulation on their new lives.

Newly arrived New York Jews faced myriad challenges but did not passively accept the status quo. They formed and participated in labor unions, social clubs uninflected by anti-Semitism, and Jewish-focused charities as they strove to maintain their community and heritage while controlling their representation to the larger social world. These nascent New Yorkers published newspapers in Yiddish and Ladino for their own communities. They fought to reform American capitalism with the theories and direct action of Socialism and Communism.

These efforts at building an institutional Jewish culture in New York did not occur in a vacuum. Americans have been shaped by different levels of social, political, and economic institutions. From the moment that Jewish newcomers —and all other New York–bound immigrants—landed at either Castle Garden or Ellis Island, they were scrutinized by health officials, evaluated to see if they could read, and assessed for their possible employability before traveling to the tenements of Brownsville, Brooklyn, and the Lower East Side. Such street names as Orchard and Cherry must have sounded lush and idyllic to the immigrants—until they arrived at their new homes.

The process of Americanization, at times heavy-handed, included mandatory lessons in patriotism for public school children accompanied by saluting the American flag. Working classes and immigrants were often unable to maintain either privacy or respect for the independence of their family units. Social workers, reporters, medical professionals, teachers, and politicians freely entered tenement apartments in order to help and instruct newcomers on correct American household practices. Along with lessons on citizenship and English, public school teachers taught immigrant children about the proper way to brush teeth, dress, and decorate one's home. While many of these lessons improved the health and welfare of the poor, they were often instilled without regard for cultural and religious traditions.

As both established Jews and "greenhorns" strove to become Americans, they worked to accommodate themselves to American social standards.

Christian merchants often closed their stores on Sunday in observance of their Sabbath, for example, but remained open on the Jewish Sabbath. This posed a quandary for Jewish workers. These social norms shaped Jewish aspirations for their new lives in New York.

Often these new Jewish Americans, especially the younger generation, picked up American cultural norms without much coaxing. They clambered onto subway cars to escape the summer heat at Coney Island's beach and amusement park and became avid fans of American sports; men excelled in boxing and basketball. Women heightened their skirt lengths to just above the ankle and became their own political advocates by joining unions. New York's Jews took pains—as shown in the postcard—to represent themselves in particular ways, showing off in many cases their new American identities.

The objects and images that follow offer a visual travelogue of tradition and change, cooperation and conflict, promises fulfilled and broken, as New York's Jewish immigrants refashioned themselves into Americans. They invite close examination of details that enhance our understanding of Jewish New York City during the era of mass immigration. In this key period in the growth of New York as a "Jewish" city, the institutions Jews developed, the reforms they were subjected to and sometimes contested, and the caricatures they battled against all worked together to forge a new Jewish American identity and helped to establish New York as the capital of the Jewish world.

Thousands of German Jews traveled to the United States between 1840 and 1860, driven by political, economic, and social instability in Germany.[2] German Jews left behind or sold most of their worldly goods, sometimes in order to afford the price of their passage. Many brought small personal items such as the miniature book of prayers shown on the facing page. Its cover, written in Hebrew, German, and Yiddish, states, "especially for travelers by sea to the state of America." Upon arrival to New York, many Jewish immigrants struggled to uphold religious traditions and sought out other German Jews for mutual support and familiarity. Small and personal sized, this prayer book traveled easily from Germany to America, providing spiritual and religious continuity in a new land. It helped Jewish immigrants to find their way as they sought to build an urban community in New York.

Artist Samuel B. Waugh's *The Mirror of Italy*, an approximately eight-hundred-foot-long survey of the Grand European Tour, belongs to the era of mass German-Jewish migration. *The Bay and Harbor of New York* (c. 1853–1855)

Top: *Tefilah mi-kol ha-shanah*: *Minhah Ketanah* (Prayers of the Entire Year, Minor Offering) (Fürth, Germany: Zurndoffer & Sommer, 1842). (Library of Congress, Washington, DC)
Bottom: Samuel B. Waugh, *The Bay and Harbor of New York*, c. 1853–1855, watercolor on canvas. (Gift of Mrs. Robert M. Littlejohn, Museum of the City of New York, New York)

259

was the final canvas in Waugh's fifty-scene panorama. Waugh painted the lower left part of the canvas with dark tones to contrast with the foreground at right, which is brightened by sunlight, drawing attention to the wealthy passengers disembarking who will next journey to their well-appointed homes.

But there were others who disembarked from the same ship, including Jews, Lutherans, and Catholics from Germany, as well as Irish immigrants, whose immediate futures were uncertain.[3] The most pronounced ethnic stereotypes Waugh reserved for the newly arrived Irish farm boys, shown in the lower right with apelike faces. As each immigrant group entered American society, it was subjected to a visual hazing by being rendered as the new subject of caricature.[4] Waugh differentiates between social classes and nationalities through the use of light and color, the comportment of individuals' bodies, and the condition of their possessions. America offered its promises to both working class and well-to-do, but Jews figured more prominently in the former category. They faced the challenge of moving from the darkness in which Waugh paints them to a light of their own making.

Alfred Stieglitz later credited *The Steerage* as his first modernist photograph and added, if all his work were lost except for *The Steerage* to represent his career, "I'd be satisfied."[5] In recalling the making of the work in 1942, the German-Jewish photographer stated that at his wife Emily's insistence, the couple, their baby, and their nanny traveled to Paris on a luxury ocean liner. Bored by the nouveaux riche of the first class, he wandered down to the steerage class, where he seems to have noticed the poor for the first time.[6] While Stieglitz and his family enjoyed a pleasure trip, they shared the ship with men and women being repatriated after being turned away from Ellis Island. The title *The Steerage* suggests a historical narrative of the hardships and conditions under which immigrants journeyed to America. Often, the photograph is reproduced in American history textbooks to represent the history of immigration, but this photograph is not a celebration of American immigration. But in truth, the journeys taken by those in steerage and by the Stieglitz family differed enormously. Stieglitz possessed education and wealth that allowed him to create a new modern New York photographic aesthetic; it took several more decades before those Jews who came as newcomers from eastern Europe succeeded in picturing New York on their own.

Alfred Stieglitz, *The Steerage*, 1907, photogravure. (Digital Image © The Museum of Modern Art / Licensed by SCALA / Art Resource, New York)

Frederic Auguste Bartholdi, *Arm of the Statue of Liberty*, 1876, photo, Centennial Exhibition, Philadelphia. (The Granger Collection, New York)

The monumental uplifted hand of the Statue of Liberty is that of a woman, but neither her ethnic heritage nor her cultural roots are apparent. In nineteenth-century America, the artistic vocabulary of the neoclassical was understood as white, European. Yet the poetry of Emma Lazarus, a New York Sephardic Jew descended from one of the oldest Jewish families in America, bonded the monument to American Jewish history. Frederic Auguste Bartholdi intended his sculpture as a gift to America from the people of France to commemorate the enduring friendship of the two countries, as well as France's participation in America's War for Independence.[7] Bartholdi never intended his statue either to celebrate American immigration or to serve as a welcoming figure to America.

Lazarus recast the Statue of Liberty's meaning in a way that endures today. In order to raise funds to build a pedestal and to place the monument in New York Harbor facing out to seaward, a planning committee approached her to write a sonnet. Lazarus wrote her fourteen-line "The New Colossus" in November 1883. Her words, affixed to the statue's base in 1903, transformed the Statue of Liberty into a welcome to "the wretched refuse" to America's "golden door." Despite the sculptor's intentions, Lazarus's words articulated the statue's message. It became a beacon for people seeking self-determination and a new life in America as well as a New York City icon.

Let your eye travel the length of this smooth wooden buttonhook that ends with a steel loop, cold to the touch. Immigrants dreaded the "buttonhook men," as they called the Ellis Island health inspectors who controlled whether they could remain in this promised land. With one deft move, inspectors would slide the metal tip just under the eyelid and with a quick yank flip the eyelid back on itself to check for inflammation. Red swelling indicated trachoma, a highly infectious disease that causes blindness. The use of a buttonhook as a medical device reveals both the haste and misinformation guiding immigration officials, who readily saw "foreign bodies" (immigrants) as the carriers of "foreign bodies" (bacteria and viruses).

Jews were blamed for cholera, tuberculosis (known as "the Jew's disease" or "the tailor's disease"), and trachoma.[8] If trachoma was suspected, the agent would chalk a "CT" on the immigrant's outer garments. Eastern European Jews nicknamed Ellis Island *Trernindzl*, or the "Isle of Tears," to express the strong emotions they felt upon arrival. Suspicion of trachoma resulted in the greatest number of exclusions to entry. If diagnosed with trachoma, an immigrant would spend six months in the trachoma ward on Ellis Island before being repatriated to his or her port of origin, dashing his or her hopes for starting a new, freer life in America. Although Jews traveled to New York's Ellis Island determined to start life anew, they encountered demands of medical officers whose views reflected stereotypes. These challenges required Jews

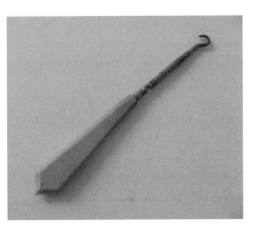

Buttonhook designed to fasten shoes, late nineteenth to early twentieth centuries, wood and metal. (Collection of Carol Hamoy, New York; courtesy of Carol Hamoy)

Carol Hamoy, *Welcome to America: An Installation Documenting Jewish Women's Immigration to America*, 1996, mixed media, Ellis Island Immigration Museum, New York. (Courtesy of the artist)

to respond to Americans' perceptions even as they fashioned new images of themselves as American Jews.[9]

Contemporary artist Carol Hamoy's installation *Welcome to America* (1996) weaves together two strands of American Jewish history: immigration and the garment industry. As had many of the new immigrants, Hamoy's family labored in the needle trades, and as a young girl she played with buttons, lace remnants, and scraps of textiles rich in pattern and texture.[10] In 1996, the Ellis Island Immigration Museum invited Hamoy to participate in an art exhibition on Jewish women's immigration. Hamoy chronicled and celebrated just some of the thousands of Jewish women who made New York their new home and found themselves among the working class in New York's garment center. Hamoy has represented these women's stories and journeys posthumously, bringing back to public attention how women experienced Ellis Island and immigration. Those stories, shaped equally by poverty and aspiration, differed from men's in terms of emotion, financial self-determination, marital status, and motherhood. They let us feel and imagine what it might have been to be a young working-class Jewish immigrant woman entering an utterly new world of experience. Hamoy studied archival documents and oral histories of immigrants to inform her work and carefully crafted garments onto which she affixed gilded text documenting each émigré's personal story. In total, she constructed thirty dresses from fragments of aged lace, flimsy gauze, antique wedding dresses, and table scarves, all considered feminine objects. When walking through the installation, a viewer's slightest movements would stir up air currents, animating the dresses as if reawakening spirits from the past.

For young immigrant Americans, a jaunty escape from the stifling slums to the ocean breezes, wide beaches, and ocean waves of Coney Island with its amusement parks meant a day of freedom and delight. The first sight of the Statue of Liberty was a cherished memory recalled over the years by immigrants, reaching mythic status with each retelling. But immigrants arriving at Coney Island first spied a monumental elephant, from 1885 until 1896, when it burned to the ground. The Colossus of Coney (following page), a gigantic fabricated pachyderm, was a 122-foot-tall seven-floor hotel and brothel that featured thirty-one body-part-themed guest rooms including the Stomach Room and the Shoulder Room.

While the Statue of Liberty stood for political freedom, Coney Island and its jumbo elephant expressed personal freedom and a sense of self-determination. Coney Island offered an escape from oppressive factories and crowded tenements and also from traditional sexual and social mores, which the older, more traditional generation struggled to maintain.[11] On the beach and cuddled together in swan boats, young Jewish Americans could flirt with whomever they fancied, dance with bodies pressed close together, frolic in the ocean waves, and steal kisses on amusement rides.

Some German Jews who had arrived at Castle Garden in the mid-nineteenth century went on to become prestigious, wealthy New Yorkers. Still, the doors of the city's posh Metropolitan Club and other men's clubs remained tightly closed to Jews despite their deep pockets. In 1852, six German Jews established their own club, which they called the Harmonie Club (page 267).[12] Inside, members reveled in their German heritage, hosting boisterous communal singing and declamatory contests in German, the club's official language. By the century's end, such members as financer Joseph Seligman and

James V. Lafferty, *The Colossus of Coney*, 1885–1896, wood and tin covering, 122 feet high, located on Surf Avenue, Coney Island, Brooklyn, New York. (Courtesy of Charles Denson, www.coneyislandhistory.org)

Harmonie Club, established 1852, postcard of the new Dining Room, 10 East Sixtieth Street, designed by architect Stanford White, 1906. (Picture Collection, Astor, Lenox and Tilden Foundations, New York Public Library, New York)

the Lehman brothers felt it time to bring the building in line with the style preferred by high society.

The club members awarded the commission to *the* premier architectural firm of the Gilded Age, McKim, Mead & White, whose patrons included Vanderbilts and Whitneys. In a 1906 article about the new Harmonie Club, architectural critic Herbert D. Croly crowed, "No firm of architects in this country has had anything like the experience which McKim, Mead & White have had in designing club houses."[13] White's interpretation of an Italian palazzo fit for a Medici was lavishly decorated throughout with neoclassical details, such as here in the dining hall. Located at 4 East Sixtieth Street, uptown German Jews distanced themselves by geographic location, class, and money from the newly arriving immigrants on the Lower East Side and sought to represent themselves as firmly belonging among the city's elite.

Top: George Wesley Bellows, *Forty-Two Kids*, 1907, oil on canvas. (Museum purchase, William A. Clark fund, Corcoran Gallery of Art, Washington, DC)
Bottom: Purim Association Fancy Dress Ball, March 15, 1881. (American Jewish Historical Society, New York, NY, and Newton Centre, MA)

Forty-two boys, or "kids," swim in the dirty waters of the East River to escape the stifling heat of ill-ventilated tenement apartments. Where are their parents? Where are their clothes?! Under the dark cover of night at the city's edge, the boys use a modified dog paddle as their stroke to push floating garbage out of their way.[14] George Bellows's brushy, rough application of paint marked the boys' social class onto their bodies, which are nude and scrawny. Bellows did not record any of the forty-two boys' names, but the painterly manner in which he depicted them and what he titled the canvas suggest that none of the boys bore the last name of Morgan, Frick, or Stuyvesant. The term "kid" was popularized by the cartoon *Hogan's Alley*, whose protagonist was "The Yellow Kid," a slum-dwelling hooligan.[15]

Bellows's depiction of city boys diving off splintered piers and reveling in their freedom, coupled with his bravura, painterly style, appalled several New York art critics. One caustically appraised Bellows's canvas, asserting that "most of the boys look more like maggots than humans."[16] Yet while many other critics employed similar derisive words that denigrated poor immigrants, the boys themselves are clearly enjoying their escape from their families' and society's scrutiny as they take control of their own physical comfort and social life.

In 1861, at the start of the Civil War, ten "jovial Hebrew young men," all bachelor sons of Harmonie Club members, formed the Purim Association. Over the decades, the annual ball, such as the one held in 1881, became *the* highlight of the Jewish social calendar.[17] The men designed their Purim Masquerades and Fancy Dress Balls as fund-raisers for Jewish charities, rather than simply youthful bacchanals of dance and drink. Seated at center, Queen Esther directs the proceedings with masked revelers at her side. She raises her richly decorated arm with golden bracelets in the classic "orator's pose," as if to announce the evening's start. Just below the Queen, in the shadows, are plainly dressed children in need of charity. The Punchinello and Esther drop coins their way, and at the composition's left, a girl lifts her skirt to form a basket to catch them. Uptown Jews envisioned the Purim Association's charitable dances as a retort to those who criticized Jewish "extravagance and propriety in public amusement." Myer S. Isaacs, whose father edited the *Jewish Messenger*, cautioned that the Purim Ball must proceed in a "refined way that should fittingly represent the social side of Judaism."[18] Despite America's freedoms, New York Jews remained conscious of their minority position in

NEW YORK CITY. — "DOING THE SLUMS." — A SCENE IN THE FIVE POINTS.
FROM A SKETCH BY A STAFF ARTIST. — SEE PAGE 247.

society as they negotiated the tricky terrain of proper American Jewish forms of socializing.

"Doing the Slums: A Scene in the Five Points" offers a visual commentary on the dramatic social and economic differences that distinguished residents of the Five Points in Lower Manhattan from a group of upper-class New Yorkers partaking in a leisurely "slumming" tour.[19] Small stifling apartments forced immigrant families to live some of their private lives on their doorsteps and out on sidewalks, where voyeuristic uptown women and men were free to observe and pass judgment. *Frank Leslie's Illustrated Newspaper* permitted thousands of Americans to become armchair tourists, to observe the poor without leaving their parlors. While the wealthy voyeurs were able to enter the neighborhoods of the poor, here accompanied by a policeman, it is doubtful that residents of the Five Points were free to promenade Upper Fifth Avenue.

One of the most frequently reproduced photographs by social reformer Jacob Riis is of a Jewish cobbler preparing for the Sabbath in his Ludlow Street coal cellar. The picture has carried different titles over the years. Some focus on the man's poverty, while others highlight his religious observance in a most inhospitable setting; and occasionally his trade as a cobbler is mentioned. Over the decades, the photograph has been cropped, or edited, proving how malleable "realistic" photographs can be.[20] In uncropped versions of this photograph, a second person stands next to the seated man, neutralizing the overwhelming sense of loneliness that Riis wanted to convey. Aided by an assistant, Riis would burst into tenement apartments, shocking his subjects by shooting off a magnesium flash explosion. In a manner, Riis held people's public presentation hostage, denying them the right to control their own representation or even the publication of their photograph.

Riis reproduced this photo for the first time on page 6 of an eight-page special Christmas edition of William Randolph Hearst's *The Journal*, on December 22, 1895,[21] in a photo essay entitled "Where Santa Will Not Go." When the

FACING PAGE:
Top: "Doing the Slums: A Scene in the Five Points from a Sketch by a Staff Artist," *Frank Leslie's Illustrated Newspaper*, December 5, 1885, 243. (Prints and Photographs Division, Library of Congress, Washington, DC)
Bottom: Jacob Riis, "Where the Sound of Church Bells Never Goes," c. 1890, from "Where Santa Will Not Go," *The Journal: Christmas Edition*, December 22, 1895, 6. (Jacob A. Riis Collection, Museum of the City of New York, New York)

photograph was first reproduced, it was titled "Where the Sound of Church Bells Never Goes" and bore the legend "especially for the Journal." The Christmas edition totaled forty pages in all, so almost one-fourth of the newspaper presented Riis's views on those who were excluded from the joys of the Christian holiday. All of the people Riis photographed for this piece, with the exception of the Jewish cobbler, were denied the visit of Santa because of poverty or immoral behavior. Bearing the original title highlighting the man's exclusion from joyous church bells, and focusing only on his image, it is possible that conveying a sense of social isolation due to his Jewishness, rather than loneliness, might have motivated the highly moralist Riis.

In contrast to those who lived in the Five Points or to Riis's subjects, Jewish Freemason Levi Isaacs controlled how he was visually represented, by whom, and for what benefit. A portrait serves both to depict an individual and also to inscribe social identity. A commissioned portrait was a commodity, a luxury good whose patronage itself announced status.[22] Isaacs, who had recently

been appointed as Lodge Master and was also a sexton of congregation Shearith Israel, placed his body a bit on an angle in relation to the camera lens, making his ring, his lapel badge, and the symbolic Masonic apron across his lap easier to view. Calm and composed, Isaacs insists that we look at him, that we admire his accomplishments, and that we recognize him as an important man.

Levi Isaacs in Freemason Regalia, photograph, c. 1895. (American Jewish Historical Society, New York, NY, and Newton Centre, MA)

Bakers and the Big Loaf, New York City, photograph, May 1, 1909. (George Gratham Bain Collection, Prints and Photographs Division, Library of Congress, Washington, DC)

Over the course of the nineteenth century, New York Jews circulated and participated in organizations, many of which were not specific to Jews.[23] American Jewish men saw Freemasonry as "a means for social integration and an ideological system sympathetic to and derived from traditional Judaism," writes Alice M. Greenwald.[24] A family man, a businessman, a sexton at his synagogue, and leader in his Masonic lodge, Isaac took control of his multifaceted identity in America, ensuring that viewers saw him as he wanted to be seen.

From uptown on the East Side to the Lower East Side and from Brownsville to Williamsburg in Brooklyn, workers, including American Jews, marched the wide boulevards of the city and then gathered at Union Square each May 1 to celebrate May Day. This workers' holiday was founded in 1886 in America as part of the labor movement's fight for an eight-hour workday.[25] Approximately thirty to fifty thousand laborers filled the streets of the city each May Day in the early 1900s. In the photograph above stand three bakers as a united entity, on strike to demand a maximum ten-hour day, a minimum wage, recognition of the union, and the right to use the union's label.[26] On their shoulders, the

Customers at the Main Entrance Waiting for Opening, Abraham & Straus, Brooklyn, NY, undated. (Personal collection of Ron Schweiger, Brooklyn Borough Historian, Brooklyn, NY; courtesy of Ronald Schweiger)

men balance a large wooden platform on which rests a gigantic loaf of bread measuring fifteen feet long and five feet wide; you can sense a bit of strain on the face of the man at the left. Rather than industrial workers, these men were artisan bakers fighting to maintain their craft, which included making bagels, which vanished from the city during the strike. In the early twentieth century, New York City acquired prominence as a national center of bread baking. But for the workers, the bread that they held aloft communicated two meanings: first, an example of their extraordinary talents and, second, the bread that they wanted to provide to their families with a decent wage.

A large clock, situated just below the store's name, Abraham & Straus, is forever frozen at 8:30 a.m. in the postcard above, as a crowd of customers— mainly women dressed in long skirts and coats, with large hats on their heads —wait eagerly for the shopping day to begin.[27] For immigrants, consumerism enabled women to buy and announce their status as Americans through purchasing just the right hat, shoes, and handbag to match.[28] Young Jewish women flocked to these Jewish-owned department stores. They, like most young urban women, wanted to purchase the most popular women's garments of the time, shirtwaists. These blouses tucked in at the waist created the much-desired slenderized "wasp waist," with a neat row of buttons down the front and a crisp snap to the shoulders. Although the term *department store* was not in use prior to 1887, by the late 1860s, the concept of a grand shopping emporium had caught on with Americans.[29]

Brooklyn's Abraham & Straus and other magnificent department stores employed young Jewish women as sales help. This particular postcard was sent from one woman to another to share news about Bessie, a friend the women had in common. The first woman wrote along the right side of the card, "This is where Bessie works." Immigrant women, especially those with a good command of English, could hold respectable jobs in stores like A&S, as it came to be known, enabling them to contribute to their family's finances and, perhaps, saving a bit of money for their own clothes and fun.

In speaking with a *New York Times* reporter in 1910, illustrator Charles Dana Gibson explained that the singular beauty of the "Gibson Girl," his idyllic and iconic image of American womanhood, which was widely reproduced on magazine covers, in illustrated newspapers, and even as wallpaper and other decorative and collectable items, derived from her Anglo-Saxon, Protestant,

and white heritage. "The best part of the American girl's beauty will and had always come from our nation of origin, Great Britain."[30] Such standards and sentiments left Jewish women named Lottie, Rose, Margit, and Bessie, who were not of British ancestry and whose bodies and faces differed from the Gibson Girl, outside the markers of both beauty and Americanness.

Charles Dana Gibson, *Patience*, drawing, pen and ink, date created/published 1910? (Cabinet of American Illustration, Prints and Photographs Division, Library of Congress, Washington, DC)

The Gibson Girl, with her pert upturned button nose, alabaster skin, and trim waist, was often pictured wearing a shirtwaist paired with a long skirt that hit just above her ankles. The fictive Gibson Girl inspired the vogue for shirtwaists, which were manufactured by young Jewish and Italian women in sweatshops, such as the Triangle Shirtwaist Factory. Jewish women, including those who sewed in sweatshops, also purchased or sewed their own shirtwaists, as they strove to present themselves as modern Americans. Yet although working-class women's paychecks allowed them some purchasing power, the ideals of Gibson Girl beauty and virtue were not for sale, nor did fashionable wear release the young women from the wage system.

Echoing the rogues' gallery of photographs maintained by the New York Police Department, the "Gallery of Missing Husbands" published by the *Jewish Daily Forward* depicted wanted men. All were Jewish husbands and fathers who had deserted their families, perhaps having gone out for a pack of cigarettes one day and never coming back. In the early twentieth century, New Yorkers' expanding consumer culture was redefining the masculine ideal from producer/laborer to consumer. But in truth, the family system with the husband as the lone breadwinner rarely worked because working-class men either did not earn enough or did not share their wages with their wives and children.[31]

The frequency of desertion became of great concern to the Jewish community and also to social reformers who wanted to protect the "public purse." The National Desertion Bureau (NDB) worked to reunite Jewish families, to secure financial support for abandoned wives and children, and also to push Jewish families to conform to middle-class American standards. Abraham Cahan's *Jewish Daily Forward*, in cooperation with the NDB, started to publish "The Gallery of Missing Husbands" as a weekly column accompanied by photographs of the deserters.[32] The first "Gallery" debuted on March 26, 1911, although it is doubtful that missing men were the Jewish community's primary focus that day. Jewish daughters, most likely, occupied utmost concern, because of the Triangle Shirtwaist Fire that happened one day earlier.

On March 25, 1911, a fire broke out in the Triangle Shirtwaist Factory on the edge of Washington Square Park, which culminated in the worst labor tragedy to that date. The garment factory was littered with inflammable scraps of fabric and rags, so the fire spread like quicksilver. The building's locked exits and inadequate safety measures led to the deaths of 133 young Italian and

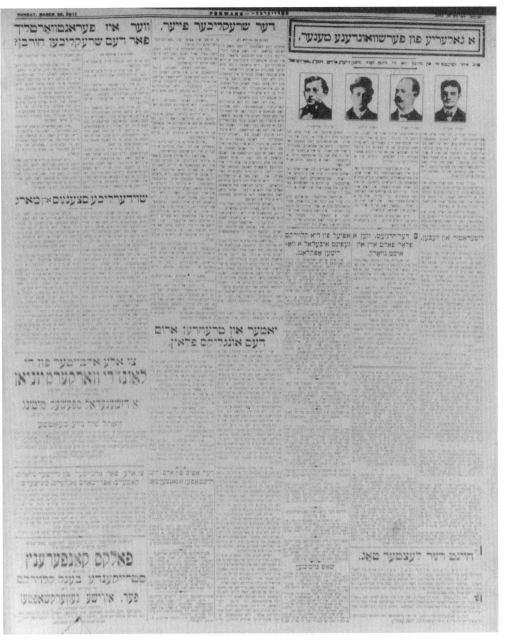

"Gallery of Missing Husbands," *Jewish Daily Forward*, March 26, 1911, 8. (New York Public Library, New York)

Jewish women, including teenagers, and 13 young men—a total of 146 workers. Many jumped from the windows in an attempt to save their lives, only to die upon impact with the sidewalk. The broken and burned corpses were lined up in rows along the sidewalks so that relatives could identify their daughters. Immigrant Jews from Russia and Galicia had previously witnessed mass deaths, as in the Kishinev Pogrom of 1906, which in comparison had killed approximately forty-six Jews. Far from the tsar's army in the United States, immigrant Jews suffered under the oppressive owners of garment factories, who frequently were also Jews who had arrived in the mid-nineteenth century and advanced to middle-class and managerial status.

Responses to the tragedy in New York City sharply divided along class, religious, and geographic lines, with newspapers catering to each group. Anglo-Saxon Protestants, the city's wealthy and powerful, believed that, as with many emotions, grief should be kept private and under control. While they empathized with the mourning families' losses, they also sat in judgment of how they should behave in public. William Randolph Hearst's *New York American* expressed support for the workers; his writers and photographers sensationalized an already sensational event, deploying features of period melodrama.[33] Hearst's staff "preyed on families," as art historian Ellen Wiley Todd writes, staging pictures at the morgue before and after the victims were identified, such as the two photographs shown on the facing page. The papers read by the survivors, such as the *Jewish Daily Forward*, saw no need to sensationalize or criticize the mourners' behavior. As a mouthpiece of Jewish immigrants, it denounced the heartless capitalist Jews whose failure to recognize the Jewish union led to the tragedy. And it mourned openly and sorrowfully the promising innocent lives lost.

Approximately twenty-five thousand Levantine Sephardic Jews entered the United States between 1899 and 1925, and most of them settled in New York. A minority within the Jewish minority, they were less educated and less prepared to succeed in the United States. Many spoke Ladino (Judeo-Spanish); others spoke Greek or Arabic. Even under the umbrella term *Sephardic Jews*, these immigrants came from numerous countries, with different cultural and religious traditions.[34] But the needs of these differing groups were the same: to secure work, to find housing, to practice their religion, to maintain ties with their homelands, and to succeed as Americans. The Ladino press was a key medium that Sephardim used in order to secure recognition as Jews by the

Sole Fire Escape on Shirtwaist Factory Found a Ghastly Joke

STEEP AND NARROW STAIRWAYS WERE OBSTRUCTED BY IRON GATES

AWAITING THEIR TURN TO SEEK LOST RELATIVES—Parents and friends of the victims in front of the improvised morgue on the Charities Pier.

Woman's Suit Demands Building Superintendent's Removal

MILLER'S APPOINTMENT BY M'ANENY ILLEGAL, SAYS GARAGE OWNER

GRIEF STRICKEN RELATIVES LEAVING THE MORGUE—A scene of keen pathos yesterday the departure of those who had found their loved ones among the charred bodies lying on the pier. Some were hysterical, others wept quietly, and others were dumb with despair.

Top: "Awaiting Their Turn to Seek Lost Relatives," *New York American*, March 27, 1911, 2. (New York Public Library, New York)
Bottom: "Grief Stricken Relatives Leaving the Morgue," *New York American*, March 27, 1911, 3. (New York Public Library, New York)

La America   לה אמיריקה   La America

LA AMERICA·ORIENTAL SPANISH-JEWISH JOURNAL

Subscription Rates:	Published Weekly By THE ORIENTAL PRINTING & PUB. CO.	אבונאמיינטוס
United States Foreign	180 Chrystie Street, New York, Telephone 4886 Orchard	...
One Year .... $1.50 10 Francs	פירייודיקו נאסייונאל, ליטיראריו, פוליטיקו אי קומירסיאל.	...
Six Months 0.75 5	אאג'יר א' ל' ב'ירדוס די קאהי סיזאגא.	...
Payable in Advance		

PRICE TWO CENTS   NEW YORK, FRIDAY, MAY 12, 1911   נומירו 11

צו דעם אידישע פאלק

דיא נעכיימיסע (אילדיי) מער־

קישען הויף אדלי "דאס לעבען פון
דעס סון קיטש מלחמה סלאם אברול האמיר־

[Yiddish text columns]

מ' א' ל' יאמולובסקי

BANKING HOUSE OF

M. & L. JARMULOWSKY

165 E. BROADWAY,   NEW YORK

לה באלור דיל זורנאל.

[Ladino text columns]

Moise Gadol, *La America*, May 12, 1911, 1. (New York Public Library, New York) dominant Ashkenazim. The particular issue of *La America* shown on the facing page was written in both Ladino and Yiddish; prominent on the first page is an article, "To the Ashkenazic People," demonstrating Sephardic desire to connect with their coreligionists.[35]

La America was just one of nineteen Judeo-Spanish periodicals published between 1910 and 1948, and its editor was Moise Gadol, a Sephardic Jew from Bulgaria. All but two of the nineteen newspapers were published in New York City. As German Jews and eastern European Jews had also done, these Jews from lands such as Turkey and Syria established self-help charitable organizations, Etz Ha-hayim (Tree of Life) and Rodfei Tsedek (Seekers of the Truth), to help their own. In 1911, the Hebrew Immigrant Aid Society (HIAS) opened its "Oriental Bureau" to serve the needs of the Sephardic Jewish Community.[36]

Look deeply into the composition of the photograph below, a picture documenting a Jewish family doing piecework at home around a table. As background to the scene, Hine has chosen the tenement door, the entry to this family's modest home. Placing the family between him and the locked door

Lewis Hine, *Jewish Family Working on Garters in Kitchen for Tenement Home, NYC,* November 1912. (National Child Labor Committee Collection, Prints and Photographs Division, Library of Congress, Washington, DC)

clarifies that Hine is a welcomed guest of the family, which is working in co-operation with him to create this lasting image.[37] The family members are all neatly, but modestly, dressed; the young boy wears a tie and a yarmulke on his head. Originally from the Midwest, Hine came to New York to teach at Felix Adler's Ethical Culture School. When he started teaching a class in photography, he increasingly found himself drawn to picture immigrants and child laborers. In 1908, he published in *Charities and the Commons* his photograph collection documenting sweatshops and tenements. The same year, Hine went to work for the National Child Labor Committee (NCLC) documenting child labor. This 1912 photograph was commissioned by the NCLC. Discarding the aesthetics of sentimentalism and sensationalism that clouded most photography of the poor, Hine instead encouraged his subjects to express their individualism. He recorded portraits of individuals rather than of anonymous social types.

Kheyders or homers? Which will the young American boy choose in the cartoon on the facing page? Many a Jewish parent and rabbi wrung their hands anxiously over such questions, as the younger generation was seduced by popular and secular culture. The artist Isidore Busatt pokes fun at the separation of generations and the perceived friction between religious orthodoxy and orthodoxy of quite another kind—the secular worship of baseball, America's game. The headline states, "With great pity, in honor of the rabbinical convention held in New York last week, at which hundreds of rabbis wracked their brains over the difficult religious issues as to how to get American youths into *kheyder* [religious school]." Instead of a *Yidisher kop* (an intelligent head), the young boy's head is swelled up into an oversized baseball on which a sporting cap perches. The old rabbi, recoiling at the young boy's power and height, literally cowers in his shadow. The American religion of sports challenged Judaism, enticing boys and men with an appeal that cut across class lines and provided moments of solidarity with other Americans rooting for the same home teams.

"This is a wonderful age we are living in," proclaimed the Jewish American artist Max Weber in 1915. "Surely there will be new numbers, new weights, new colors, and new forms."[38] Weber gave visual form to his passion for the urban and the modern in *Chinese Restaurant* (1915), one of the artist's most heralded and reproduced works. Born in Bialystok, Weber's family settled in Brooklyn when he was ten years old. In his midtwenties, Weber moved to Paris

Isidore Busatt, "A Difficult Path," in the Yiddish humor magazine *Der Groyser Kundes* (The Big Stick), 1914. (Courtesy of Eddy Portnoy)

(1905–1909), where he trained with Matisse and also fraternized with the leading modern artists who formed the School of Paris. For the composition of *Chinese Restaurant*, Weber displays his command of Picasso's Synthetic Cubism in its carefully arranged but seemingly haphazard placement of forms and the manner in which he breaks apart the face of the Chinese waiter, placing facial elements away from each other. The distinct red and gold lacquer that decorated many Chinese restaurants, along with the black-and-white checkered floor linoleum, typifies the many chop suey houses that had sprung up in

Max Weber (1881–1961), *Chinese Restaurant*, oil on canvas, 1915. (Whitney Museum of American Art, New York)

Lower Manhattan. Weber, along with Alfred Stieglitz, was an early champion of modernism and influenced other Jewish New York artists to experiment stylistically. Their works in painting and photography signaled the rise of Jewish involvement in modernism in the city.

For Weber, the exotic and the modern are represented in the restaurant's cuisine and staff. Unlike Stieglitz, both Weber and the waiter he has depicted were immigrants to America. But they were not equal. The Chinese Exclusion Act of 1882 prohibited most Chinese immigration, while Jews remained on the "white" side of the color line.[39] Weber created his work using modernist experimentation within shifting ideas of race, class, and gender.

The elegant calling card on the following page, with italic type on crème paper, passed between women of differing economic situations and, ultimately, became the ticket for a young mother of eight who desperately needed help for her family. Professional settlement-house workers, social reformers, and home economists—all new professions that women dominated—dedicated themselves to helping the ghetto poor. On the reverse of her business card, Harris wrote on behalf of the mother, "the bearer Mrs. J. Goldfarb of 101 Willet Street is absolutely in need of help. She has eight children and no money. Help her with matzos and other things if possible. She is no *shnorer* [beggar]. Yours Ida Harris." The presence or the absence of a father is not noted. Despite the class differences between the social worker and the mother, each was part of a supportive network among Jewish women. Birth-control pioneer Margaret Sanger relied on these same networks of female mutual assistance. Although a non-Jew, Sanger, along with Harris and other social activists, provided much-needed help for Jewish American women.

Business card: Ida Harris, Independent Social Worker of the East Side, 55½ Madison Avenue, New York, n.d. (Archives of the YIVO Institute for Jewish Research, New York)

News photograph, "Margaret Sanger's Brownsville Clinic, 46 Amboy Street, Brownsville, Brooklyn," *New York World-Telegram*, October 27, 1916. (New York World Telegram & Sun Collection, Prints and Photographs Division, Library of Congress, Washington, DC)

In this newspaper photograph, cloth draperies cover each area of glass of this unidentified storefront, which effectively denies the photographer his or her desired shot. This purposeful act of concealment to maintain privacy opposes the purpose of storefront windows to display enticing merchandise. The arrangement of this photograph draws us into the cloistered and nondescript doorway of Margaret Sanger's family-planning clinic, a small two-room curtained store on Amboy Street in Brownsville, Brooklyn.[40] In the days prior its opening on October 16, 1916, Sanger, her sister, and Fania Mandell, a translator, canvassed ghetto neighborhoods with flyers written in Yiddish, Italian, and English that announced, "MOTHERS! Can you afford to have a large family? Do you want any more children? If not, why do you have them?" The three women carefully worded the flyer without ever using terms such as *birth control* or *abortion*. Instead, the activists presented the clinic's services as a way to help women to be better mothers by limiting the number of their children.

What the poster avoids saying is that some women might not want additional children for their own sake; nor is having sex except for reproduction mentioned. Over one hundred women visited the clinic on its first day. An additional four hundred sought Sanger's help until October 26, when police shut down the clinic ten days after it had opened. Consistent with the *Jewish Daily Forward*'s "Gallery of Missing Husbands" and the card of social worker Ida B. Harris (both shown earlier), Sanger's clinic, and the five hundred women she helped, acknowledges the economic burdens that kept immigrants chained to poverty and reflects an organized approach to efforts for social reform.

"A prizefighter you want to be?" Benny Leonard's mother demanded of her son. "Is that a life for a respectable man? For a Jew?" Leonard, who was considered the greatest lightweight champion to ever live, and one of the greatest fighters of any weight class, learned to fight out of necessity. He lived near the public baths on the Lower East Side and recalled, "You had to fight or stay in

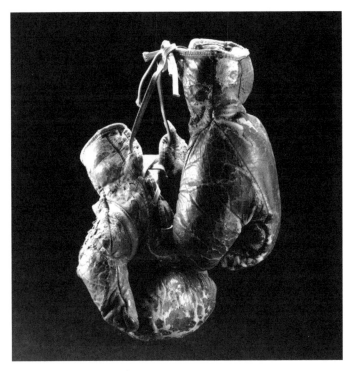

Boxing gloves worn by Benny Leonard in his lightweight title defense against Joe Welling, 1920. (American Jewish Historical Society, New York, NY, and Newton Centre, MA)

the house when the Italian and Irish kids came through on their way to the baths."[41] Jewish fighters had to prove themselves worthy of the sport, given stereotypes of Jewish men as either bookish intellectuals—and therefore passive and feminine—or factory workers whose bodies were weakened by tuberculosis. In Leonard's choice of blue and white boxing trunks decorated with a large Mogen David, he wore his Jewish identity in the ring for all to see. Arthur Brisbane, Hearst's main editor, claimed the boxer had done "more to conquer anti-Semitism than a thousand textbooks." Leonard, through his example and words, asserted the naturalness of being a Jewish boxer. "I believe that the Jew," said the champion, "is especially adapted for the sport of boxing because, in the final analysis, it is the most elemental form of self-defense."[42] Leonard took control of his own representation and also served as a role model, disrupting prevailing ideas about Jewish bodies.

In 1924, the United States closed its borders and ended the mass immigration of European Jews that had begun back in the 1840s. The overwhelming majority of Jewish immigrants, no matter their country of origin, chose to settle in New York City and strove to make a better life for themselves and their families. The city served both as their benefactor, with its free schools, libraries, and parks, and as their demon, due to substandard living and working conditions. In order to maintain control of their lives and their communities, Jews created their own social organizations, cultural institutions, charities, and means of mass communication. At times, they had to relinquish privacy and self-determination to immigration officials, social workers, anti-Semitic club owners, and others, but when they could, they took control of their self-representation. Jews participated in what the city already had to offer while at the same time helping to introduce some of the visual perspectives of modernism in photography and painting. Their creativity also expressed itself in radical politics and communal organizing, in religious innovations, and in print culture, producing a new Jewish capital of the world on the banks of the Hudson and East Rivers.

■ **NOTES TO THE FOREWORD**

1. Milton Lehman, "Veterans Pour into New York to Find That Its Hospitality Far Exceeds Their Dreams," *New York Times*, 8 July 1945, 51.

2. Ira Rosenwaike, *Population History of New York City* (Syracuse: Syracuse University Press, 1972), 98, 101.

3. Robert A. M. Stern, Thomas Mellins, and David Fishman, *New York 1960: Architecture and Urbanism between the Second World War and the Bicentennial* (New York: Monacelli, 1995), 10, 13–19, 27–28.

4. Moses Rischin, *The Promised City: New York's Jews, 1870–1914* (1962; repr., Cambridge: Harvard University Press, 1977), 294.

5. "Levi Strauss," Wikipedia, http://en.wikipedia.org/wiki/Levi_Strauss (accessed July 13, 2011).

6. Rischin, "Preface to the Paperback Edition," in *The Promised City*, vii.

7. Ibid. "City of Ambition" refers to the 1910 photograph by Alfred Stieglitz taken approaching Lower Manhattan from New York Harbor.

8. In this and the following pages, the text draws on the three volumes of City of Promises: A History of the Jews of New York (New York: NYU Press, 2012).

■ **NOTES TO THE INTRODUCTION**

1. Y. Pfeffer, "Pesakh in Nyu York un Elis Ayland: Yetsies mitsrayim dertseylt in onkel sem's hoyz," *Morgen zhurnal*, April 12, 1906.

2. Carol Groneman and David Reimers, "Immigration," in Kenneth Jackson, ed., *Encyclopedia of New York City* (New Haven: Yale University Press, 1995), 581.

3. CastleGarden.org, "Timeline," http://www.castlegarden.org/timeline.php (accessed May 31, 2011). On Castle Garden generally, see Vincent Cannato, *American Passage: The History of Ellis Island* (New York: HarperCollins, 2009), 30–49; George Svejda, "Castle Garden as an Immigrant Depot, 1855–1890," report, Division of History, Office of Archeology and Historic Preservation, National Park Service, U.S. Department of Interior, 1968, especially 34–47, http://www.nps.gov/history/history/online_books/elis/castle_garden.pdf (accessed May 31, 2011); Andrew Dolkart, "Castle Garden," in Jackson, *Encyclopedia of New York City*, 188.

4. *New York Times*, December 23, 1866.

5. Cannato, *American Passage*, 108 (quotes); Barbara Blumberg, "Ellis Island," in Jackson, *Encyclopedia*, 372–373; Virginia Yans-McLaughlin and Marjorie Lightman, *Ellis Island and the Peopling of America: The Official Guide* (New York: New Press, 1997), 64–70.

6. Aaron Domnitz, "Why I Left My Old Home and What I Have Accomplished in America," in Jocelyn Cohen and Daniel Soyer, eds., *My Future Is in America:*

Autobiographies of Eastern European Jewish Immigrants (New York: NYU Press, 2006), 138–139.

7. Minnie Goldstein, "Success or Failure?," in Cohen and Soyer, *My Future Is in America*, 28.

8. Ben Reisman, "Why I Came to America," in Cohen and Soyer, *My Future Is in America*, 66; Domnitz, "Why I Have Left My Old Home," 139, 141–145.

■ **NOTES TO CHAPTER 1**

1. Asa Green, *Travels in America* (New York, 1833), 43, quoted in Rudolf Glanz, *Studies in Judaica Americana* (New York: Ktav, 1970), 127; George G. Foster, *New York in Slices: By an Experienced Carver* (New York, 1849), 14–15, quoted in Egal Feldman, "Jews in the Early Growth of New York City's Men's Clothing Trade," *American Jewish Archives* 12:1 (April 1960): 6–7.

2. Isaac Mayer Wise, *Reminiscences*, ed. David Philipson (Cincinnati: L. Wise, 1901), 17.

3. Cornelius Mathews, *A Pen and Ink Panorama of New York City* (New York, 1853), 164, quoted in Glanz, *Studies in Judaica Americana*, 127.

4. Hyman Grinstein, *The Rise of the Jewish Community of New York, 1654–1860* (Philadelphia: Jewish Publication Society, 1945), 263, 586.

5. Mary Wasserzug Natelson, "The Rabbi's House (Story of a Family)," trans. Rachel Natelson, manuscript in authors' possession.

6. Philip Cowen, *Memories of an American Jew* (New York: International Press, 1932), 24–26.

7. Stanley Nadel, *Little Germany: Ethnicity, Religion, and Class in New York City, 1845–80* (Urbana: University of Illinois Press, 1990), 99.

8. Grinstein, *Rise of the Jewish Community*, 469; Nathan Kantrowitz, "Population," in Kenneth Jackson, ed., *Encyclopedia of New York City* (New Haven: Yale University Press, 1995), 922.

9. Edwin G. Burrows and Mike Wallace, *Gotham: A History of New York City to 1898* (New York: Oxford University Press, 1999), 739.

10. Naomi W. Cohen, *Encounter with Emancipation: The German Jews in the United States, 1830–1914* (Philadelphia: Jewish Publication Society, 1984), 29.

11. Burrows and Wallace, *Gotham*, 1116.

12. Ibid., 456–459.

13. Grinstein, *Rise of the Jewish Community*, 41–49; Jonathan Sarna, *American Judaism: A History* (New Haven: Yale University Press, 2004), 53–55.

14. Edmunt Blunt, *Picture of New York* (New York, 1828), 228, quoted in Glanz, *Studies in Judaica Americana*, 124.

15. Grinstein, *Rise of the Jewish Community*, 48.

16. Burrows and Wallace, *Gotham*, 476.

17. Hasia Diner, *A Time for Gathering: The Second Migration, 1820–1880* (Baltimore: Johns Hopkins University, 1992), 42–49.

18. Cowen, *Memories of an American Jew*, 20–21.

19. Tyler Anbinder, *Five Points: The 19th-Century New York City Neighborhood That*

Invented Tap Dance, Stole Elections, and Became the World's Most Notorious Slum (New York: Free Press, 2001) 17, 45.

20. Ibid., 17–19.

21. Robert Ernst, *Immigrant Life in New York City, 1825–1863* (1949; repr., Syracuse: Syracuse University Press, 1994), 69, 72.

22. Phyllis Dillon and Andrew Godley, "The Evolution of the Jewish Garment Industry, 1840–1940," in Rebecca Kobrin, ed., *Chosen Capital: The Jewish Encounter with American Capitalism* (New Brunswick: Rutgers University Press, 2012), 42–44; Glanz, *Studies in Judaica Americana*, 126; Avraham Barkai, *Branching Out: German Jewish Immigration to the United States, 1820–1924* (New York: Holmes and Meier, 1994), 86; Grinstein, *Rise of the Jewish Community*, 128; Nadel, *Little Germany*, 63.

23. Anbinder, *Five Points*, 47, 98.

24. Dwelling 28, Fourth District, Sixth Ward, 1860 U.S. Census. Also, the Isaacs family was listed as #40 on the Passover matzo distribution list in 1858, "List of 665 Individuals and Institutions," folder 1, Association for Free Distribution of Matsot to the Poor, I-106, American Jewish Historical Society

25. Dwelling 736, Fourth District, Sixth Ward, 1860 U.S Census.

26. "List of 665 Individuals and Institutions," folder 1, Association for Free Distribution of Matsot to the Poor, I-106, American Jewish Historical Society.

27. Dwelling 608, Second District, Sixth Ward, 1860 U.S. Census.

28. Natelson, "The Rabbi's House," 64.

29. Ernst, *Immigrant Life in New York City*, 63–64.

30. Cowen, *Memories of an American Jew*, 24–26.

31. Ibid., 24.

32. Ibid., 36–37.

33. Wise, *Reminiscences*, 18–19, 26.

34. Grinstein, *Rise of the Jewish Community*, 128.

35. Letter from Dr. Waterman, *Asmonean*, May 4, 1855, quoted in Ernst, *Immigrant Life in New York City*, 85.

36. Nadel, *Little Germany*, 44–46; Dorothee Schneider, *Trade Unions and Community: The German Working Class in New York City* (Urbana and Chicago: University of Illinois Press, 1994), 9, 14–16.

37. Cohen, *Encounter with Emancipation*, 29; Feldman, "Jews in the Early Growth," 9; Dillon and Godley, "The Evolution of the Jewish Garment Industry," 6, 8–9.

38. Mathew Hale, *Wonders of a Great City* (Chicago, 1877), 845, quoted in Glanz, *Studies in Judaica Americana*, 126; Cohen, *Encounter with Emancipation*, 29; Jesse Pope, *The Clothing Industry in New York* (Columbia: University of Missouri, 1905), 5–7.

39. Feldman, "Jews in the Early Growth," 5; Barkai, *Branching Out*, 45–46; Nadel, *Little Germany*, 81; Pope, *Clothing Industry in New York*, 7–8.

40. Anbinder, *Five Points*, 242; Grinstein, *Rise of the Jewish Community*, 473.

41. Jay Dolan, *The Immigrant Church: New York's Irish and German Catholics, 1815–1865* (Baltimore: Johns Hopkins University Press, 1975), 58; Grinstein, *Rise of the Jewish Community*, 53–55; Anbinder, *Five Points*, 242–243; Judah Eisenstein, "The History of the

First Russian-American Jewish Congregation: The Beth Hamedrash Hagadol," *Publications of the American Jewish Historical Society* 9 (1901): 63–74.

42. Grinstein, *Rise of the Jewish Community*, 53–55.

43. Ibid., 106–109.

44. Ibid., 306.

45. Ibid., 64, 575; Hasia Diner, "Buying and Selling 'Jewish': The Historical Impact of Commerce on Jewish Communal Life," in Jack Wertheimer, ed., *Imagining the American Jewish Community* (Hanover, NH: University Press of New England / Brandeis University Press, 2007), 29, 32.

46. *Jewish Messenger*, May 18, 1864, 141; Grinstein, *Rise of the Jewish Community*, 470–471.

47. Grinstein, *Rise of the Jewish Community*, x; *Asmonean*, September 27, 1850, and September 28, 1855; *Jewish Messenger*, September 21, 1860. The advertisements were located through a search through the *Asmonean* and *Jewish Messenger* for September 1850, 1855, 1860, 1865, 1870, and 1875.

48. *Jewish Messenger*, September 1860.

49. Burrows and Wallace, *Gotham*, 745.

50. Ernst, *Immigrant Life in New York City*, 96.

51. Mayer Stern and Jacob Abraham were on the list for free matzos in 1858, which included their wives' names and their addresses. Further information about their households was gleaned from the 1860 U.S. Census; for Abraham, Dwelling 23, Second Division, Eleventh Ward; for Stern, Dwelling 116, Fourth District, Eleventh Ward.

52. Nadel, *Little Germany*, 49.

53. Congregation Kahal Adath Jeshurun with Anshe Lubz, Constitution, June 22, 1913, Collection of the Museum at Eldridge Street, Hebrew section.

54. Dolan, *Immigrant Church*, 58; Nadel, *Little Germany*, 91; Grinstein, *Rise of the Jewish Community*, 340–344; Max Lilienthal, letter, *Israelite*, November 17, 1854; Anbinder, *Five Points*, 242–243.

55. Schneider, *Trade Unions and Community*.

56. Harriet Waine McBride, "Fraternal Regalia in America, 1865–1918: Dressing the Lodges; Clothing and the Brotherhood" (Ph.D. diss., Department of History, Ohio State University, 2000).

57. Dale Knobel, "To Be American: Ethnicity, Fraternity and the Improved Order of Red Men," *Journal of American Ethnic History* 4:1 (Fall 1984): 68–69.

58. J. T. Kennedy, "Report of the Eighth Sanitary Inspection District," in Citizen's Association, *Report of the Council of Hygiene and Public Health of the Citizen's Association of New York of the Sanitary Condition of the City* (New York: D. Appleton, 1865).

59. Deborah Dash Moore, *B'nai B'rith and the Challenge of Ethnic Leadership* (Albany: SUNY Press, 1981), 6–7.

60. Ibid., 11.

61. Ibid., 1–10 (quote on 7); Edward Grusd, *B'nai B'rith: The Story of a Covenant* (New York: Appleton-Century, 1966), 12–24.

62. Albert Stevens, *Cyclopedia of Fraternities*, 2nd ed. (1907; repr., Detroit: Gale

Research, 1966), 206–210; Grinstein, *Rise of the Jewish Community*, 112; Daniel Soyer, *Jewish Immigrant Associations and American Identity in New York, 1880–1939* (Cambridge: Harvard University Press, 1997), 38–40; Daniel Soyer, "Entering the 'Tent of Abraham': Fraternal Ritual and American-Jewish Identity, 1880–1920," *Religion and American Culture* 9:2 (Summer 1999): 166.

63. Cornelia Wilhelm, "Independent Order of True Sisters: Friendship, Fraternity, and a Model of Modernity for Nineteenth Century American Jewish Womanhood," *American Jewish Archives* 54:1 (2002): 45; Kehillah (Jewish Community) of New York City, *Jewish Communal Register of New York City, 1917–1918* (New York: Kehillah, 1918), 957.

64. "The Sabbath," *Jewish Messenger*, February 12, 1858, 28; "To Correspondents," *Jewish Messenger*, November 25, 1859, 158.

65. Bernard Drachman, *The Unfailing Light: Memoirs of an American Rabbi* (New York: Rabbinical Council of America, 1948), 227.

66. Alexis McCrossen, *Holy Day, Holiday: The American Sunday* (Ithaca: Cornell University Press, 2000), 41–46.

67. "The Jew Wot Goes Ahead," *Asmonean*, May 19, 1854; Emanuel Brandeis, "Desecration of Sabbath," *Asmonean*, May 22, 1854, 46.

68. "The Jew Wot Goes Ahead"; "Progress and Its Necessity," *Asmonean*, June 1854, 78.

69. Nadel, *Little Germany*, 101; Schneider, *Trade Unions and Community*, 32.

70. Daniel Soyer, "The Rise and Fall of the Garment Industry in New York City," in Daniel Soyer, ed., *A Coat of Many Colors: Immigration, Globalization, and Reform in the New York City Garment Industry* (New York: Fordham University Press, 2005), 4.

71. Pope, *Clothing Industry in New York*, 8.

72. Soyer, "Rise and Fall of the Garment Industry," 8.

73. Natelson, "Rabbi's House, 64.

74. Ibid.

75. Pope, *Clothing Industry in New York*, 106–107.

76. Dillon and Godley, "The Evolution of the Jewish Garment Industry," 21.

77. George R. Adams, National Register of Historic Places Inventory, Nomination Form for R. H. Macy and Company, United States Department of the Interior, National Park Service, 1977.

78. Isaac Markens, *Hebrews in America* (New York: Isaac Markens, 1888), 151.

■ NOTES TO CHAPTER 2

1. Rebekah Kohut, *My Portion* (New York: T. Seltzer, 1925), 121; "Streetscapes: Beekman Place: A Two Block Street by the East Riverside," *New York Times*, November 30, 1997.

2. Kohut, *My Portion*, 179.

3. John S. Billings, *Vital Statistics of the Jews in the United States*, 11th Census, Bulletin No. 19 (Washington DC: U.S. Census Bureau, 1890); Hasia Diner, *A Time for Gathering: The Second Migration, 1820–1880* (Baltimore: Johns Hopkins University Press, 1992), 65. These findings include all American Jews.

4. Hasia Diner, *The Jews of the United States, 1654–2000* (Berkeley: University of California Press, 2004), 100; Tyler Anbinder, *Five Points: The 19th-Century New York City Neighborhood That Invented Tap Dance, Stole Elections, and Became the World's Most Notorious Slum* (New York: Free Press, 2001), 254.

5. Alan M. Kraut and Deborah A. Kraut, *Covenant of Care: Newark Beth Israel and the Jewish Hospital in America* (New Brunswick: Rutgers University Press, 2007), 3.

6. Tina Levitan, *Islands of Compassion: A History of the Jewish Hospitals of New York* (New York: Twayne, 1964), 27; Burrill B. Crohn, "The Centennial Anniversary of the Mount Sinai Hospital (1852–1952)," *American Jewish Historical Society Publications* 42 (September 1952–June 1953): 113–130.

7. Levitan, *Islands of Compassion*, 31–59.

8. Hyman Bogen, *The Luckiest Orphans: A History of the Hebrew Orphan Asylum of New York* (Urbana: University of Illinois Press, 1992); Kehillah (Jewish Community) of New York City, *Jewish Communal Register of New York City, 1917–1918* (New York: Kehillah, 1918), 1057–1058.

9. Edward G. Burrows and Michael Wallace, *Gotham: A History of New York City to 1898* (New York: Oxford University Press, 1999), 845.

10. "Passover and the Poor," *Asmonean*, March 18, 1858.

11. "Matzo Distribution," *Jewish Messenger*, February 26, 1858, 36–37.

12. Hyman Grinstein, *The Rise of the Jewish Community in New York City, 1654–1860* (Philadelphia: Jewish Publication Society, 1945), 119–122.

13. "List of 665 Individuals and Organizations," folder 1, Association for Free Distribution of Matsot to the Poor, 1855–1858, I-106, American Jewish Historical Society; Harris Aaronson, Dwelling 1000, Fourth Division, Ninth Ward, 1860 U.S. Census; Michael Schwab, Dwelling 380, Fourth Division, Thirteenth Ward, 1860 U.S. Census; Zion Bernstein, Dwelling 406, Second District, Fourteenth Ward, 1860 U.S. Census; Judah Jacques Lyons, Dwelling 100, First District, Sixteenth Ward, 1860 U.S. Census; Morris Raphall, New York City Directory, 1859, p. 698; Samuel Myers Isaacs, New York City Directory, 1859, p. 402.

14. "List of 665 Individuals and Organizations."

15. Burrows and Wallace, *Gotham*, 833, 846.

16. "Matzo Distribution," *Jewish Messenger*, February 26, 1858, 36–37.

17. "To the Hebrews of New York," *Jewish Messenger*, March 21, 1858, 46.

18. Burrows and Wallace, *Gotham*, 727.

19. "Passover and the Poor," *Asmonean*, March 18, 1858.

20. "Union of Congregations to Supply the Poor with Matsoth," *Jewish Messenger*, March 21, 1858, 44.

21. "Passover and the Poor."

22. "Agreement with Matzo Baker, March 18, 1858," and "Final Report of the Executive Committee of the Association, April 21, 1858," folder 1, Association for Free Distribution of Matsot to the Poor, I-106, American Jewish Historical Society.

23. Harris Aaronson's passport application, May 26, 1870, U.S. Census, 1860, Fourth Division, Ninth Ward, pp. 261–262; Michael Schwab, U.S. Census, 1860, Thirteenth Ward,

Fourth Division, p. 124; Zion Bernstein, U.S. Census, 1860, Fourteenth Ward, Second District; Judah Jacques Lyons, U.S. Census, 1860, Sixteenth Ward, First District, p. 201; Morris Raphall, *New York City Directory*, 1859, p. 698; Samuel Myers Isaacs, *New York City Directory*, 1859, p. 402.

24. Letters, *Jewish Messenger*, March 25, 1859, 91.

25. Grinstein, *Rise of the Jewish Community*, 406.

26. Diner, *Time for Gathering*, 104; Jacob Rader Marcus, *United States Jewry, 1776–1985*, vol. 2 (Detroit: Wayne State University Press, 1991), 223.

27. Diner, *Time for Gathering*, 104.

28. Philip Goodman, "The Purim Association of the City of New York (1862–1902)," *American Jewish Historical Society Publications* 40 (September 1950–June 1951): 135–172 (quotes on 139, 145).

29. Samuel Myers Isaacs, "New York City," *Jewish Messenger*, April 25, 1862, 120.

30. "The Poor Require Assistance," *Jewish Messenger*, March 31, 1865; March 23, 1866.

31. "Remember the Poor," *Jewish Messenger*, March 23, 1866.

32. Stanley Nadel, *Little Germany: Ethnicity, Religion, and Class in New York City, 1845–80* (Urbana: University of Illinois Press, 1990), 66, 71.

33. Orchard Former Residents/Owners/Shopkeepers, Gumpertz Family, RG 3.6.1, Box 3: 97, Archives of the Lower East Side Tenement Museum.

34. "Shall We Foster Pauperism?," *Jewish Messenger*, March 14, 1873.

35. "Hebrew Benevolent and Orphan Asylum Society," *Jewish Messenger*, March 7, 1873.

36. "Co-operate!," *Jewish Messenger*, February 28, 1873.

37. "True Brotherhood," *Jewish Messenger*, March 21, 1873.

38. Anbinder, *Five Points*, 244.

39. Ibid., 245.

40. *Jewish Messenger*, May 18, 1864, 141.

41. "Our Poor," *Jewish Messenger*, March 27, 1868.

42. "The Hebrew Benevolent Society," *Jewish Messenger*, April 25, 1873; "Remember the Poor!," *Jewish Messenger*, December 19, 1873.

43. "Our Leading Charity," *Jewish Messenger*, May 2, 1873.

44. "Remember the Poor!," *Jewish Messenger*, December 19, 1873.

45. Jewish Social Service Association, *Fifty Years of Social Service: The History of the United Hebrew Charities of the City of New York, Now the Jewish Social Service Association, Inc. New York City* (New York: C. S. Nathan, 1926), 22, 25.

46. *First Annual Report of the Board of Relief of the United Hebrew Charities, 1874–1875*, 4–7.

47. Ibid., 1.

48. Jewish Social Service Association, *Fifty Years of Social Service*.

49. Kehillah, *Jewish Communal Register*, 994–997; Arthur Goren, *New York Jews and the Quest for Community: The Kehillah Experiment, 1908–1922* (New York: Columbia University Press, 1970), 58–59.

50. Kohut, *My Portion*, 173.

51. Sidney Luska (Henry Harland), *The Yoke of the Thorah* (New York: Cassell, 1887), 195.

52. Ibid., 228.

53. Moses Rischin, *The Promised City: New York's Jews, 1870–1914* (Cambridge: Harvard University Press, 1962), 10; Elizabeth Blackmar, "The Congregation and the City," in Arthur Goren and Elizabeth Blackmar, *Congregating and Consecrating at Central Synagogue* (New York: Central Synagogue, 2003), 16.

54. Rischin, *Promised City*, 98–99.

55. Kohut, *My Portion*, 175.

56. Quoted in Jenna Weissman Joselit, "The Special Sphere of the Middle-Class American Jewish Woman: The Synagogue Sisterhood, 1890–1940," in Jack Wertheimer, ed., *The American Synagogue: A Sanctuary Transformed* (Hanover, NH: University Press of New England / Brandeis University Press, 1987), 209.

57. "Souvenir," membership and Summary of Activities, 1895, 106, Women's Organizations, RG 4, Central Synagogue Archives; Blackmar, "Congregation and the City," 16.

58. Hannah B. Einstein, "Sisterhoods of Personal Service," in *The Jewish Encyclopedia* (New York: Funk and Wagnalls, 1901–1906), 398, quoted in Felicia Herman, "From Priestess to Hostess: Sisterhoods of Personal Service in New York City, 1887–1936," in Pamela Nadell and Jonathan Sarna, eds., *Women and American Judaism: Historical Perspectives* (Hanover, NH: University Press of New England / Brandeis University Press, 2001), 154.

59. Hannah Leerburger, "President's Report, 1913," in *Annual Report of the A.C.S.H. Sisterhood of Personal Service, 1913*, 5–8, Women's Organizations, RG 4, Central Synagogue Archives.

60. Hannah B. Einstein, "The Federation of Sisterhoods," in *Twenty-Fifth Annual Report of the United Hebrew Charities of the City of New York* (New York: United Hebrew Charities of the City of New York, 1899), 58.

61. Quoted in Jonathan Sarna, *American Judaism: A History* (New Haven: Yale University Press, 2004), 143.

62. Jewish Social Service Association, *Fifty Years of Social Service*, 50.

63. Leerburger, "President's Report, 1913," 8.

64. Herman, "From Priestess to Hostess," 161.

65. Kohut, *My Portion*, 247.

66. Ibid., 178.

■ NOTES TO CHAPTER 3

1. "Temple Ahawath Chesed," *New York Herald*, December 15, 1870.

2. "Architectural Improvements," *New York Times*, December 3, 1870, 6.

3. *New York Times*, December 15, 1870.

4. Ivan Davidson Kalmar, "Moorish Style: Orientalism, the Jews and Synagogue Architecture," *Jewish Social Studies* 7:3 (Spring–Summer 2001): 84.

5. *New York Times*, April 20, 1920.

6. "Modern Judaism," *New York World*, April 24, 1872.

7. Leon Jick, "The Reform Synagogue," in Jack Wertheimer, ed., *The American Synagogue: A Sanctuary Transformed* (Hanover, NH: University Press of New England / Brandeis University Press, 1987), 89.

8. Uriah Zvi Engelman, "Jewish Statistics in the U.S. Census of Religious Bodies (1850–1936)," *Jewish Social Studies* 9:2 (April 1947): 130–133.

9. Andrew S. Dolkart, *Central Synagogue in Its Changing Neighborhood* (New York: Central Synagogue, 2001), 20.

10. "New City Buildings," *Manufacturer and Builder*, January 7, 1869; "A Synagogue Dedication," *New York Times*, May 12, 1869.

11. Rachel Wischnitzer, *Synagogue Architecture in the United States: History and Interpretation* (Philadelphia: Jewish Publication Society, 1955), 75; Kalmar, "Moorish Style," 72; Dolkart, *Central Synagogue*, 18.

12. The earliest examples of Moorish synagogue architecture were in the 1830s by Friedrich von Gartner in Ingenheim (1832), Binswangen (1835), Kircheimbolanden (1836), and Speyer (1837), and by Gottfried Semper for the interior of the Dresden synagogue (1838–40). Kalmar, "Moorish Style," 69, 72, 84–88; Carol Krinsky, *Synagogues of Europe* (Cambridge: MIT Press, 1985), 82–84.

13. William Henry Bishop, "The House of the Merchant Prince," *Atlantic Monthly*, April 1882, 499.

14. Charles W. Hobbs, *Illustrated New York City and Surroundings* (New York: Charles W. Hobbs, 1889), 53.

15. Jonathan Sarna, *American Judaism: A History* (New Haven: Yale University Press, 2004), 85; Steven Lowenstein, "The 1840s and the Creation of the German-Jewish Religious Reform Movement," in Werner Mosse, ed., *Revolution and Evolution: 1848 in German-Jewish History* (Tübingen: Mohr, 1981); Michael Meyer, *Response to Modernity: A History of the Reform Movement in Judaism* (New York: Oxford University Press, 1988), 225–226.

16. Meyer, *Response to Modernity*, 225; Hyman Grinstein, *The Rise of the Jewish Community of New York, 1654–1860* (Philadelphia: Jewish Publication Society of America, 1945), 333–352; Hasia Diner, *A Time for Gathering: The Second Migration, 1820–1880* (Baltimore: Johns Hopkins University Press, 1992), 114–116; Sarna, *American Judaism*, 73; Jick, "Reform Synagogue," 87.

17. Grinstein, *Rise of the Jewish Community*, 354, 368.

18. Ibid., 355–358.

19. Jonathan Sarna, "Mixed Seating in the American Synagogue," in Wertheimer, *American Synagogue*, 368, 372; Karla Goldman, *Beyond the Synagogue Gallery: Finding a Place for Women in American Judaism* (Cambridge: Harvard University Press, 2000), 8–17.

20. Grinstein, *Rise of the Jewish Community*, 364.

21. Sarna, "Mixed Seating," 374–379.

22. Ibid., 376–377; Grinstein, *Rise of the Jewish Community*, 364, 410–412, 535.

23. Jeffrey Gurock, *American Jewish Orthodoxy in Historical Perspective* (Hoboken, NJ: Ktav, 1996), 71; Jick, "Reform Synagogue," 90–92.

24. Jick, "Reform Synagogue," 91.

25. Grinstein, *Rise of the Jewish Community*, 370.

26. Sarna, *American Judaism*, 132; Meyer, *Response to Modernity*, 266.

27. Arthur Goren, "Public Ceremonies Defining Central Synagogue," in Arthur Goren and Elizabeth Blackmar, *Congregating and Consecrating at Central Synagogue* (New York: Central Synagogue, 2003), 49.

28. Barnett Elzas, "Memoir of Alexander Kohut," in Alexander Kohut, *The Ethics of the Fathers* (New York: Publishers Printing Company, 1920), xxxi.

29. Sarna, *American Judaism*, 147–148.

30. "Orthodoxy and Reform: The Controversy between Rabbis Kohut and Kohler," *New York Times*, June 28, 1885.

31. Rebekah Kohut, *My Portion* (New York: T. Seltzer, 1925), 100–114.

32. Meyer, *Response to Modernity*, 267.

33. Jick, "Reform Synagogue," 90–92.

34. Sarna, *American Judaism*. 150; "More Rabbis Needed," *American Hebrew*, September 23, 1887.

35. Kohut, *My Portion*, 115; Hasia Diner, *The Jews of the United States, 1654–2000* (Berkeley: University of California Press, 2004), 124–127.

36. Allon Schoener, *Portal to America: The Lower East Side, 1870–1925* (New York: Holt, Rinehart, and Winston, 1967), 156.

37. "Tiny Places of Worship: The Humble Synagogues of the Poorer East Side," *New York Daily Tribune*, February 16, 1896.

38. Edward Steiner, "The Russian and Polish Jew in New York," *Outlook*, November 1, 1902, 533.

39. 1887 Seat Contract, signed by L. Matlawsky, secretary, Collection of the Museum at Eldridge Street.

40. "Mi Yodea," *American Israelite*, September 16, 1887, 4.

41. Ibid.

42. "New Jewish Temple," *New York Times*, September 12, 1868; "Mi Yodea."

43. Abraham J. Karp, "New York Chooses a Chief Rabbi," *Publications of the American Jewish Historical Society* 44 (1955): 129–198; Annie Polland, *Landmark of the Spirit: The Eldridge Street Synagogue* (New Haven: Yale University Press, 2009), 41–42.

44. Richard Wheatley, "The Jews in New York," *Century Magazine*, January 1892, 330.

45. Polland, *Landmark of the Spirit*, 12.

46. M. Simons and Sons to Mayor Strong, September 20, 1897, Collection of the Museum at Eldridge Street.

47. "The Jewish New Year," *New York Times*, September 27, 1897, 3.

48. Constitution of the Kahal Adath Jeshurun with Anshe Lubz, 1913, Collection of the Museum at Eldridge Street.

49. "New York on Yom Kippur," *American Hebrew*, October 13, 1905; "Hebrew Use Churches," *New York Daily Tribune*, September 20, 1903; Edward Steiner, "The Russian and Polish Jew in America," *Outlook* November 1, 1902; Kehillah (Jewish Community) of New York City, *Jewish Communal Register of New York City, 1917–1918* (New York:

Kehillah, 1918), 125 (insert); Solomon Foster, *The Workingman and the Synagogue* (Newark, NJ, 1910), 6.

50. Constitution of Kahal Adath Jeshurun.

51. Polland, *Landmark of the Spirit*, 11.

52. Gurock, *American Jewish Orthodoxy*, 82–83.

53. Jeffrey Gurock, *Orthodox Jews in America* (Bloomington: Indiana University Press, 2009), 109–147 (quote on 133).

54. Leonard Dinnerstein, "The Funeral of Rabbi Jacob Joseph," in David A. Gerber, ed., *Anti-Semitism in American History* (Urbana: University of Illinois Press, 1986), 275–301; Edward O'Donnell, "Hibernians versus Hebrews? A New Look at the 1902 Jacob Joseph Funeral Riot," *Journal of the Gilded Age and Progressive Era* 6:2 (April 2007): 209–225; Arthur Goren, *The Politics and Public Culture of American Jews* (Bloomington: Indiana University Press, 1999), 51–56 (quotes on 56).

55. Eldridge Street Synagogue, Minutes, April 27, 1891, Collection of the Museum at Eldridge Street.

56. Kehillah, *Jewish Communal Register*, 368–370, 389–390, 396–398; Zalmen Yefroikin, "Yidishe dertsiung in di fareynikte shtatn," *Algemeyne entsiklopedia: Yidn hey* (New York: Dubnov Fund and Encyclopedia Committee, 1957), 198–199.

57. Kehillah, *Jewish Communal Register*, 394–395, 1201–1202; Jeffrey Gurock, *Men and Women of the Yeshiva: Higher Education, Orthodoxy, and American Judaism* (New York: Columbia University Press, 1988), 11, 16, 52–53; Yefroikin, "Yidishe dertsiung," 172.

■ NOTES TO CHAPTER 4

1. "Frantic Depositors Plead for Their Savings," *New York Times*, December 13, 1901.

2. Ibid.

3. Ibid.

4. "Run on Jarmulowsky's Bank," *The Sun*, December 12, 1901, 2.

5. "Frantic Depositors Plead for Their Savings," *New York Times*, December 13, 1901; "Jarmulowsky's Bank Run is Over," *Evening World*, December 16, 1901, 10.

6. "Banking on the Densely Populated East Side Is a Serious Business, but Has Amusing Features," *New York Tribune*, May 15, 1903, B4.

7. "Latest Dealings in Realty Field," *New York Times*, May 28, 1911, XXI; Michael D. Caratzas, "Research Report," Landmarks Preservation Commission, October 13, 2009, Designation List 419, LP 2363.

8. *Jewish Daily Forward*, October 4, 1912.

9. Quoted in Moses Rischin, *The Promised City: New York's Jews, 1870–1914* (Cambridge: Harvard University Press, 1962), 75.

10. This ad ran in the *Yidishe gazeten* throughout 1887.

11. David Warfield, *Ghetto Silhouettes* (New York: James Pott, 1902), 81–82.

12. Abraham Karp, *Golden Door to America: The Jewish Immigrant Experience* (New York: Viking, 1973), 233.

13. Louis Lipsky, *Memoirs in Profile* (Philadelphia: Jewish Publication Society, 1975), 12–13.

14. "Reb Sender Yarmulowski: Banker and Philanthropist Has Died," *Tageblat*, June 2, 1912.

15. "Run on East Side Bank," *New York Tribune*, February 17, 1912, 11.

16. "Banking on the Densely Populated East Side Is a Serious Business."

17. Jared N. Day, *Urban Castles: Tenement Housing and Landlord Activism in New York City, 1890–1943* (New York: Columbia University Press, 1999), 37.

18. Ibid., 37–41.

19. *New York Tribune*, May 15, 1903.

20. Aaron Domnitz, "Why I Left My Old Home and What I Have Accomplished in America," in Jocelyn Cohen and Daniel Soyer, eds., *My Future Is in America: Autobiographies of Eastern European Jewish Immigrants* (New York: NYU Press, 2006), 143.

21. Ira Katznelson, "On the Margins of Liberalism," in Pierre Birnbaum and Ira Katznelson, eds., *Paths of Emancipation: Jews, States, and Citizenship* (Princeton: Princeton University Press, 1995), 186.

22. Simon Kuznets, "Immigration of Russian Jews to the United States: Background and Structure," *Perspectives in American History* 9 (1975): 94–100.

23. Stanley Nadel, *Little Germany: Ethnicity, Religion, and Class in New York City, 1845–80* (Urbana: University of Illinois Press, 1990), 30–31; Rischin, *Promised City*, 79–80.

24. Katznelson, "On the Margins of Liberalism," 184.

25. Nancy Foner, *From Ellis Island to JFK: New York's Two Great Waves of Immigration* (New Haven: Yale University Press, 2000), 43, 45–47.

26. Andrew Dolkart, *Biography of a Tenement House in New York City: An Architectural History of 97 Orchard Street* (Santa Fe, NM: Center for American Places, 2006), 61.

27. Rose Radin, American Jewish Committee Oral Histories, New York Public Library, I-8–9.

28. Dolkart, *Biography of a Tenement*, 81–84.

29. Quoted in Nancy Green, ed., *Jewish Workers in the Modern Diaspora* (Berkeley: University of California Press, 1998), 17.

30. Jenna Weissman Joselit, "A Set Table: Jewish Domestic Culture in the New World, 1880–1950," in Susan Braunstein and Jenna Weissman Joselit, eds., *Getting Comfortable in New York: The American Jewish Home, 1880–1950* (New York: Jewish Museum, 1990), 27–33; Barbara Kirshenblatt-Gimblett, "Kitchen Judaism," in ibid., 77–105; Joselit, *The Wonders of America: Reinventing Jewish Culture, 1880–1950* (New York: Hill and Wang, 1994), 137–140.

31. Domnitz, "Why I Left My Old Home," 143.

32. Joselit, "A Set Table," 33; Joselit, *Wonders of America*, 148.

33. Andrew Heinze, *Adapting to Abundance: Jewish Immigrants, Mass Consumption, and the Search for American Identity* (New York: Columbia University Press, 1990), 133, 134, 138–140; Joselit, "A Set Table," 35.

34. Domnitz, "Why I Left My Old Home," 144; Heinze, *Adapting to Abundance*, 89–104 (*Tribune* quote on 93).

35. Nan Enstad, *Ladies of Labor, Girls of Adventure: Working Women, Popular Cul-*

ture, and Labor Politics at the Turn of the Twentieth Century (New York: Columbia University Press, 1999), 22–31 (quote, from Bertha Richardson, on 29); Heinze, *Adapting to Abundance.*

36. Charles S. Bernheimer, "The Jewish Immigrant as an Industrial Worker," *Annals of the American Academy of Political and Social Science* 33:2 (March 1909): 177.

37. Eli Lederhendler, *Jewish Immigrants and American Capitalism, 1880–1920: From Caste to Class* (Cambridge: Cambridge University Press, 2009), 41.

38. Domnitz, "Why I Left My Old Home," 142, 145.

39. Isaac M. Rubinow, "Economic and Industrial Condition, New York," in Charles S. Bernheimer, ed., *The Russian Jew in the United States* (Philadelphia: John C. Winston, 1905), 112–113.

40. Daniel Soyer, "Cockroach Capitalists: Jewish Contractors at the Turn of the Twentieth Century," in Daniel Soyer, ed., *A Coat of Many Colors: Immigration, Globalism, and Reform in the New York City Garment Industry* (New York: Fordham University Press, 2005), 92–93.

41. Bernard Weinstein, *Di idishe yunyons in Amerike* (New York: United Hebrew Trades, 1929), 48.

42. Soyer, "Cockroach Capitalists," 98–108.

43. David Von Drehle, *Triangle: The Fire That Changed America* (New York: Grove, 2003), 47.

44. Burton J. Hendricks, "The Jewish Invasion of America," *McClure's Magazine*, March 12, 1912, 126; Jesse Pope, *The Clothing Industry in New York* (Columbia: University of Missouri, 1905), quoted in Karp, *Golden Door to America*, 111; Benjamin Stolberg, *Tailor's Progress: The Story of a Famous Union and the Men Who Made It* (Garden City, NY: Doubleday, Doran, 1944), 9.

45. Alan M. Kraut, "The Butcher, the Baker, the Pushcart Peddler," *Journal of American Culture* 6:4 (Winter 1983): 76.

46. Rischin, *Promised City*, 56.

47. Andrew Heinze, "Jewish Street Merchants and Mass Consumption in New York City, 1880–1914," *American Jewish Archives* 41:2 (Fall–Winter 1989): 206–207.

48. Ibid., 204.

49. Minnie Goldstein, "Success or Failure?," in Cohen and Soyer, *My Future Is in America*, 24–25.

50. Rose Cohen, *Out of the Shadow* (Ithaca: Cornell University Press, 1995), 205.

51. Goldstein, "Success or Failure?," 28.

52. Rose Radin, American Jewish Committee Oral Histories, New York Public Library, I-8–9.

53. Samuel Joseph, *Jewish Immigration to the United States from 1881 to 1910* (New York: Columbia University, 1914), 140, 145.

54. John Bodnar, *The Transplanted: A History of Immigrants in Urban America* (Bloomington: University of Indiana Press, 1986), 57–84; Susan A. Glenn, *Daughters of the Shtetl: Life and Labor in the Immigrant Generation* (Ithaca: Cornell University Press,

1990), 66–67; Judith E. Smith, *Family Connections: A History of Italian and Jewish Lives in Providence, Rhode Island, 1900–1940* (Albany: SUNY Press, 1985), 23–82.

55. Joseph, *Jewish Immigration*, 156–157.

56. Bernheimer, "Jewish Immigrant as an Industrial Worker," 179–180.

57. Foner, *From Ellis Island to JFK*, 189–191.

58. Samuel Chotzinoff, "Life on Stanton Street," in Harold U. Ribalow, ed., *Autobiographies of American Jews* (Philadelphia: Jewish Publication Society, 1968), 264.

59. Glenn, *Daughters of the Shtetl*, 68–69.

60. Ben Reisman, "Why I Came to America," in Cohen and Soyer, *My Future Is in America*, 67; Domnitz, "Why I Left My Old Home," 142–143.

61. Abraham Kokofsky, Lower East Side Oral History Project, NS 33-64, Tamiment Institute.

62. Harry Golden, "East Side Memoir, 1910s," in Ribalow, *Autobiographies of American Jews*, 309.

63. Domnitz, "Why I Left My Old Home," 145.

64. Glenn, *Daughters of the Shtetl*, 133–135, 139; Rischin, *Promised City*, 85–86, 146–147; *Jewish Daily Forward*, February 4, 1906.

65. See the collection of oral interviews housed in the Lower East Side Oral History Project, Tamiment Institute.

66. H. S. Goldstein, *Forty Years of Struggle for a Principle* (New York: Bloch, 1928), 32–33.

67. Harry Golden, "East Side Memoir, 1910s," 307.

68. Chotzinoff, "Life on Stanton Street," 264.

69. Anne Goldman, Lower East Side Oral History Project, NS 33-58, Tamiment Institute.

70. "Layden, layden di kleyne stors," *Jewish Daily Forward*, April 7, 1902; see also the editorial in that issue on the subject: "Unser 'goody-goody' shtot regirung."

71. Rod Glogower, "The Impact of the American Experience on Responsa Literature," *American Jewish History* 69:2 (December 1979): 263.

72. Livia Garfinkel, "Reflections on Other Times, New York, 1881–1931," Brooklyn, 1981, Small Collections 5873, American Jewish Archives.

73. Annie Polland, "May a Free Thinker Help a Pious Man? The Shared World of the 'Religious' and the 'Secular' among Eastern European Jewish Immigrants to America," *American Jewish History* 93:4 (December 2007): 375–407.

74. "Jews Want Closer Sabbath Keeping," *New York Times*, May 31, 1909; "The Jewish Sabbath Association," *American Hebrew*, January 8, 1909, 265, 272; *American Hebrew*, January 15, 1909, 286; "Police Commissioner Bingham and Jewish Sabbath Observers," *Shabes zhurnal*, February 1909; Alexis McCrossen, *Holy Day, Holiday: The American Sunday* (Ithaca: Cornell University Press, 2000), 107.

75. Rischin, *Promised City*, 134; "The Work of the New York Kehillah: Salient Points of the Executive Committee's Report," *American Hebrew*, May 1, 1914, 5.

76. "Non-commercial Employment Bureaus in the Jewish Community of New York," in Kehillah (Jewish Community) of New York City, *Jewish Communal Register of New*

York City, 1917–1918 (New York: Kehillah, 1918), 646; Bernard Drachman, "Jewish Sabbath Association," in ibid., 330.

77. "The Ghetto Market, Hester Street," *New York Times*, November 14, 1897, reprinted in Allon Schoener, ed., *Portal to America: The Lower East Side, 1870–1925* (New York: Holt, Reinhart, Winston, 1967), 55.

78. Bertram Reinitz, "The East Side Looks into Its Future," *New York Times*, March 13, 1932.

79. Edward Steiner, "The Russian and Polish Jew in New York," *Outlook*, November 1, 1902.

80. Richard Wheatley, "The Jews of New York," *Century Magazine*, January 1892, 327.

81. Joseph Benjamin, "The Comforts and Discomforts of East Side Tenements," in *Report of the Year's Work* (New York: University Settlement Society, 1897), 27.

82. Abraham Kokofsky, Lower East Side Oral History Project, NS 33-64, Tamiment Institute.

83. Anne Goldman, Lower East Side Oral History Project, NS 33-58, Tamiment Institute.

84. Helen Rosenfield, Lower East Side Oral History Project, NS 33-75, Tamiment Institute.

85. Helen Harris, Lower East Side Oral History Project, NS 33-60, Tamiment Institute.

86. Joselit, *Wonders of America*, 187–188, 193–195; Heinze, *Adapting to Abundance*, 175–177.

87. Paula E. Hyman, "Immigrant Women and Consumer Protest: The New York City Kosher Meat Boycott of 1902," *American Jewish History* 70:1 (September 1980): 91–105 (quotes on 93).

88. Joselit, *Wonders of America*, 176; Heinze, *Adapting to Abundance*, 177.

89. Christopher Gray, "The Unmaking of a Landmark," *New York Times*, May 26, 1991.

90. Day, *Urban Castles*, 32–33.

91. Abraham Cahan, *Bleter fun mayn lebn*, vol. 3 (New York: Forward Association, 1926), 428.

92. Day, *Urban Castles*, 42–46; Jeffrey Gurock, *When Harlem Was Jewish, 1879–1930* (New York: Columbia University Press, 1979), 45–49.

93. Moses Rischin, "Toward the Onomastics of the Great New York Ghetto: How the Lower East Side Got Its Name," in Hasia Diner, Jeffrey Shandler, and Beth Wenger, eds., *Remembering the Lower East Side: American Jewish Reflections* (Bloomington: Indiana University Press, 2000), 13–24; Deborah Dash Moore, *At Home in America: Second Generation New York Jews* (New York: Columbia University Press, 1981), 8.

94. Moore, *At Home in America*, 19.

95. Cahan, *Bleter fun mayn lebn*, 3:430.

96. Gurock, *When Harlem Was Jewish*, 28, 33.

97. Wendell Pritchet, *Brownsville, Brooklyn: Blacks, Jews, and the Changing Face of the Ghetto* (Chicago: University of Chicago Press, 2002), 11–18; Deborah Dash Moore, "On the Fringes of the City: Jewish Neighborhoods in Three Boroughs," in David Ward and Olivier Zunz, eds., *The Landscape of Modernity: New York City, 1900–1940* (New York:

Russell Sage Foundation, 1992), 256–257; quote from "Brownsville an Example of Rise of Values in Brooklyn Realty," *New York Herald*, undated clipping, A. J. Virginia Scrapbook, Jewish Division, New York Public Library.

98. Alter Landesman, *Brownsville: The Birth, Development and Passing of a Jewish Community in New York* (New York: Bloch, 1971), 58–60.

99. Ibid., 56, 78–79, 86, 88–89, 150; Moore, "On the Fringes of the City."

100. Kehillah, *Jewish Communal Register*, map following p. 80; Domnitz, "Why I Left My Old Home," 149.

101. Hasia Diner, "Buying and Selling 'Jewish': The Historical Impact of Commerce on Jewish Communal Life," in Jack Wertheimer, ed., *Imagining the American Jewish Community* (Hanover, NH: University Press of New England / Brandeis University Press, 2007), 28–41; Moore, *At Home in America*, 20; Gurock, *When Harlem Was Jewish*, 39.

102. Rischin, *Promised City*, 56.

103. Ibid., 57–58; Edmund James, Oscar Flynn, J. Paulding, Mrs. Simon Patton, Walter Scott Andrews, *The Immigrant Jew in America* (New York: B. Buck, 1906), 289; Samuel Chotzinoff, *A Lost Paradise: Early Reminiscences* (1955; repr., New York: Arno, 1975), 182–188; Joselit, *Wonders of America*, 202–203.

104. Joselit, *Wonders of America*, 208–215; James et al., *The Immigrant Jew*, 223; Rischin, *Promised City*, 141.

105. Pritchett, *Brownsville, Brooklyn*, 25; Domnitz, "Why I Left My Old Home," 149–150.

106. Seward Park Branch records, Manuscripts and Archives Division, The New York Public Library, Astor, Lenox, and Tilden Foundations.

■ **NOTES TO CHAPTER 5**

1. Kehillah (Jewish Community) of New York City, *The Jewish Communal Register of New York City, 1917–1918* (New York: Kehillah, 1918), v, 91–98.

2. Jonathan Frankel, *The Damascus Affair: "Ritual Murder," Politics, and the Jews in 1840* (New York: Cambridge University Press, 1997), 225.

3. Hasia Diner, *The Jews of the United States, 1654–2000* (Berkeley: University of California Press, 2004), 176. See also Hyman Grinstein, *The Rise of the Jewish Community of New York City, 1654–1860* (Philadelphia: Jewish Publication Society, 1945), 420–422.

4. Naomi Cohen, "American Jews and the Swiss Treaty: A Case Study in the Indivisibility of Anti-Semitism," in Nathaniel Stampfer, ed., *The Solomon Goldman Lectures: Perspectives in Jewish Learning*, vol. 3 (Chicago: Spertus College of Judaica Press, 1982).

5. David I. Kertzer, *The Kidnapping of Edgardo Mortara* (New York: Vintage Books, 1998), 124–128 (Wise quote on 126); Naomi Cohen, *Encounter with Emancipation: The German Jews in the United States, 1830–1914* (Philadelphia: Jewish Publication Society, 1984), 217; Grinstein, *Rise of the Jewish Community*, 430–432.

6. Alan Tarshish, "The Board of Delegates of American Israelites (1859–1878)," *Publications of the American Jewish Historical Society* 49 (1959): 17–32; Diner, *Jews of the United States*, 190–191; Grinstein, *Rise of the Jewish Community*, 432–436.

7. Leonard Dinnerstein, *Anti-Semitism in America* (New York: Oxford University

Press, 1994), 35–40; John J. Appel, "Jews in American Caricature: 1820–1914," in Jeffrey Gurock, ed., *American Jewish History*, vol. 6, part 1, *Anti-Semitism in America* (New York: Routledge, 1998), 54–62; Hasia Diner, *A Time for Gathering: The Second Migration, 1820–1880* (Baltimore: Johns Hopkins University Press, 1992), 191; John Higham, *Strangers in the Land: Patterns of American Nativism, 1860–1925* (1955; repr., New York: Atheneum, 1981), 26–27.

8. Diner, *Jews of the United States*, 169–170; Higham, *Strangers in the Land*, 43–44, 48–49, 202–204, 340.

9. Quoted in Higham, *Strangers in the Land*, 67.

10. Cohen, *Encounter with Emancipation*, 233.

11. Jacob Rader Marcus, *United States Jewry, 1776–1985*, vol. 2, *The Germanic Period* (Detroit: Wayne State University Press, 1993), 478; Reena Sigman Friedman, "'Send Me My Husband Who Is In New York City': Husband Desertion in the American Jewish Immigrant Community, 1900–1926," *Jewish Social Studies* 44:1 (Winter 1982): 1–18; Abraham Oseroff, "The United Hebrew Charities of the City of New York and Subsidiary Relief Agencies," in Kehillah, *Jewish Communal Register*, 994–996, 1318–1327; Anna R. Igra, *Wives without Husbands: Marriage, Desertion, and Welfare in New York, 1900–1935* (Chapel Hill: University of North Carolina Press, 2007); Peter Romanofsky, "'. . . To Rid Ourselves of the Burden . . .': New York Jewish Charities and the Origins of the Industrial Removal Office, 1890–1901," *American Jewish Historical Quarterly* 64:4 (June 1975): 331.

12. Lillian Wald, *House on Henry Street* (New York: Holt, 1915), 5–7.

13. Marjorie Feld, *Lillian Wald: A Biography* (Chapel Hill: University of North Carolina Press, 2008); Paula Hyman and Deborah Dash Moore, *Jewish Women in America: An Historical Encyclopedia* (New York: Routledge, 1997), 2:1446–1449.

14. Adam Bellow, *The Educational Alliance: A Centennial Celebration* (New York: Educational Alliance, 1990), 41.

15. David Kaufman, *A Shul with a Pool: The "Synagogue Center" in American Jewish History* (Hanover, NH: University Press of New England / Brandeis University Press, 1999), 92; Minutes of a Meeting of the Committee on Religious and Moral Work of the Educational Alliance, May 4, 1916, Records of the Educational Alliance, RG 312, YIVO Institute for Jewish Research.

16. "In a Wide Labor Field," *New York Times*, May 19, 1895.

17. Ibid.

18. Ibid.

19. Minutes of a Meeting of the Committee of Religious and Moral Work of the Educational Alliance, May 4, 1916.

20. "In a Wide Labor Field."

21. Daniel Soyer, "Brownstones and Brownsville: Elite Philanthropists and Immigrant Constituents at the Hebrew Educational Society of Brooklyn, 1899–1929," *American Jewish History* 88:2 (June 2000): 181–207.

22. Faith Rogow, *Gone to Another Meeting: The National Council of Jewish Women, 1893–1993* (Tuscaloosa: University of Alabama Press, 1993), especially 1–35, 225; Hasia Diner and Beryl Lieff Benderly, *Her Works Praise Her: A History of Jewish Women in*

America from Colonial Times to the Present (New York: Basic Books, 2002), 252–253, 255; Martha Katz-Hyman, "American, Sadie," in Hyman and Moore, *Jewish Women in America*, 1:38–39.

23. Rogow, *Gone to Another Meeting*, 231, 232, 233, 234, 236; Carla Goldman, "Kohut, Rebekah Bettelheim," in Hyman and Moore, *Jewish Women in America*, 1: 749–750.

24. Rogow, *Gone to Another Meeting*, 130–142; Diner and Benderly, *Her Works Praise Her*, 256–257.

25. Rogow, *Gone to Another Meeting*, 118; Katz-Hyman, "American, Sadie," in Hyman and Moore, *Jewish Women in America*, 1:38–39.

26. Rogow, *Gone to Another Meeting*, 130–142 (quote on 140); Diner and Benderly, *Her Works Praise Her*, 258.

27. Katz-Hyman, "American, Sadie," in Hyman and Moore, *Jewish Women in America*, 1:39; Rogow, *Gone to Another Meeting*, 118–123.

28. Rogow, *Gone to Another Meeting*, 226; Peggy Pearlstein, "Brenner, Rose," in Hyman and Moore, *Jewish Women in America*, 1:175; Kehillah, *Jewish Communal Register*, 1137, 1232.

29. Daniel Soyer, *Jewish Immigrant Associations and American Identity in New York, 1880–1939* (Cambridge: Harvard University Press, 1997), 61; Kehillah, *Jewish Communal Register*, 888–934.

30. Kehillah, *Jewish Communal Register*, 167–168, 816–817, 881; Isaac Rontch, *Di idishe landsmanshaften fun Nyu York* (New York: IL Peretz Yiddish Writers Union, 1938), 350–351.

31. Jacob Sholtz, autobiography #5, American Jewish Autobiographies, RG 102, YIVO Institute for Jewish Research.

32. Soyer, *Jewish Immigrant Associations*, 117–120 (quote on 118).

33. *Tageblat* and Barondess quoted in ibid., 144.

34. Tina Levitan, *Islands of Compassion: A History of the Jewish Hospitals of New York* (New York: Twayne, 1964), 89–92, 107–149; Kehillah, *Jewish Communal Register*, 119–124, 1014–1015; Soyer, *Jewish Immigrant Associations*, 142–160.

35. Soyer, *Immigrant Associations*, 138–141; Kehillah, *Jewish Communal Register*, 1241, 1243.

36. Steven J. Zipperstein, *Elusive Prophet: Ahad Ha'am and the Origins of Zionism* (Berkeley: University of California Press, 1993), 204–205.

37. Jonathan Frankel, *Prophecy and Politics: Socialism, Nationalism, and the Russian Jews, 1862–1917* (New York: Cambridge University Press, 1981), 473–484 (Cahan quote on 483).

38. Deborah Dash Moore, *B'nai B'rith and the Challenge of Ethnic Leadership* (Albany: SUNY Press, 1981), 74; Monty Noam Penkower, "The Kishinev Pogrom: A Turning Point in Jewish History," *Modern Judaism* 24:3 (October 2004): 191.

39. Frankel, *Prophecy and Politics*, 487–492 (quotes on 487, 488); Penkower, "Kishinev Pogrom," 204.

40. Naomi Cohen, *Not Free to Desist: A History of the American Jewish Committee, 1906–1966* (Philadelphia: Jewish Publication Society, 1972), 8–28 (quotes on 8–9).

41. Ibid., 27; Naomi Cohen, *Jacob Schiff: A Study in American Jewish Leadership* (Hanover, NH: University Press of New England / Brandeis University Press, 1999).

42. Cohen, *Not Free to Desist*, 28.

43. Kehillah, *Jewish Communal Register*, 1415–1422, 1426.

44. Cohen, *Not Free to Desist*, 19–28, 40–48, 57–58; Matthew Silver, "Louis Marshall and the Democratization of Jewish Identity," *American Jewish History* 94:1–2 (March–June 2008): 41–69; Ann E. Healy, "Tsarist Anti-Semitism and Russian-American Relations," *Slavic Review* 42:3 (Autumn 1983): 408–425; Esther Panitz, "In Defense of the Jewish Immigrant (1891–1924)," *American Jewish Historical Quarterly* 55 (1965): 63–64.

45. Diner, *Jews of the United States*, 181; Mark A. Raider, *The Emergence of American Zionism* (New York: NYU Press, 1998), 10–13; Evyatar Friesel, "Brandeis' Role in American Zionism Historically Reconsidered," in Jeffrey Gurock, ed., *American Zionism: Mission and Politics* (New York: Routledge, 1998), 92–96; Naomi Cohen, "The Reaction of Reform Judaism in America to Political Zionism (1897–1922)," in Gurock, *American Zionism*, 31–32; Kehillah, *Jewish Communal Register*, 1340–1342.

46. Raider, *Emergence of American Zionism*, 18–19.

47. Kehillah, *Jewish Communal Register*, 1360–1361, 1370–1371; Hyman and Moore, *Jewish Women in America*, 1:571.

48. Erica B. Simmons, *Hadassah and the Zionist Project* (Lanham, MD: Rowman and Littlefield, 2006), 11; Raider, *Emergence of American Zionism*, 15–16; Hyman and Moore, *Jewish Women in America*, 2:1368–1370; Mary McCune, *"The Whole Wide World without Limits": International Relief, Gender Politics, and American Jewish Women, 1893–1930* (Detroit: Wayne State University Press, 2005), 23–26.

49. Michael Brown, *The Israeli-American Connection: Its Roots in the Yishuv, 1914–1945* (Detroit: Wayne State University Press, 1996), 145; Hyman and Moore, *Jewish Women in America*, 1:572; Simmons, *Hadassah and the Zionist Project*, 18; Kehillah, *Jewish Communal Register*, 1360–1365.

50. Kehillah, *Jewish Communal Register*, 1340–1409.

51. Tony Michels, *A Fire in Their Hearts: Yiddish Socialists in New York* (Cambridge: Harvard University Press, 2005), 125–178 (quotes on 136, 145); Melech Epstein, *Profiles of Eleven: Profiles of Eleven Men Who Guided the Destiny of an Immigrant Society and Stimulated Social Consciousness among the American People* (Detroit: Wayne State University Press, 1965), 297–317 (quote on 298).

52. Michels, *A Fire in Their Hearts*, 179–216 (quote on 179); Frankel, *Prophecy and Politics*, 453–509.

53. Quoted in Arthur Goren, *New York Jews and the Quest for Community: The Kehillah Experiment, 1908–1922* (New York: Columbia University Press, 1970), 25.

54. Jenna Weissman Joselit, *Our Gang: Jewish Crime and the New York Jewish Community* (Bloomington: Indiana University Press, 1983), 2, 5–8; Timothy Gilfoyle, *City of Eros: New York City, Prostitution, and the Commercialization of Sex, 1790–1920* (New York: Norton, 1992), 264–265, 408n. 35.

55. Goren, *New York Jews and the Quest for Community*, 36.

56. Ibid., 36–38; Arthur Goren, introduction to Arthur Goren, ed., *Dissenter in Zion:*

From the Writings of Judah L. Magnes (Cambridge: Harvard University Press, 1982), 1–58; Deborah Dash Moore, "A New American Judaism," in William M. Brinner and Moses Rischin, eds., *Like All Nations? The Life and Legacy of Judah L. Magnes* (Albany: SUNY Press, 1987), 41–42.

57. Goren, *New York Jews and the Quest for Community*, 52–55, 58–59, 82–84, 86–109, 159–213.

58. Samson Benderly, "The Present Status of Jewish Religious Education in New York City," and Bernard Dushkin, "Cheder Instruction," in Kehillah, *Jewish Communal Register*, 349–357, 397.

59. Goren, *New York Jews and the Quest for Community*, 240; Soyer, *Jewish Immigrant Associations*, 124–127.

60. "Di pflikht fun amerikaner iden," *Tageblat*, August 20, 1914.

61. Henry Rosenfelt, *This Thing of Giving: The Record of a Rare Enterprise of Mercy and Brotherhood* (New York: Plymouth, 1924), 22.

62. McCune, "*The Whole Wide World without Limits*," 50.

63. American Jewish Archives, "An Inventory to the Stephen S. Wise Collection," http://www.americanjewisharchives.org/aja/FindingAids/SWise.htm#bio (accessed August 2, 2010); Kehillah, *Jewish Communal Register*, 1460–1461.

64. Frankel, *Prophecy and Politics*, 509–536 (quote on 536); Kehillah, *Jewish Communal Register*, 1429–1440; "Jews Pick Members for Congress Today," *New York Times*, June 10, 1917.

65. Quoted in Cohen, *Not Free to Desist*, 119.

66. Daniel Walkowitz, *Working with Class: Social Workers and the Politics of Middle-Class Identity* (Chapel Hill: University of North Carolina Press, 1999), 71–73; Jonathan Woocher, *Sacred Survival: The Civil Religion of American Jews* (Bloomington: Indiana University Press, 1986), 25; Kehillah, *Jewish Communal Register*, 1281–1313; "Have Plan to Unite All Jewish Charity," *New York Times*, June 24, 1916; Deborah Dash Moore, "From Kehillah to Federation: The Communal Functions of Federated Philanthropy in New York City, 1917–1933," *American Jewish History* 68:2 (December 1978): 134.

■ NOTES TO CHAPTER 6

1. Hillel Rogoff, *Meyer London: A biografye* (New York: Meyer London Memorial Fund, 1930), 78–79; Melech Epstein, *Jewish Labor in the USA*, vol. 1, *1882–1914* (1950; repr., New York: Ktav, 1969), 358–360.

2. Abraham Cahan, *Bleter fun mayn lebn* (New York: Forward Association, 1926–1931), vol. 4 (1928), 606–607; vol. 5 (1931), 25–27, 240–241; Shirley Zavin, Forward Building, Landmarks Preservation Commission Designation, 1986.

3. Tammany Society, or Columbian Order, *150th Anniversary Celebration: 1786–July 4–1936* (New York, Tammany Society, 1936), 65; Gustavus Myers, *The History of Tammany Hall* (New York: G. Myers, 1901), 257–258; Edwin G. Burrows and Mike Wallace, *Gotham: A History of New York City to 1898* (New York: Oxford University Press, 1999), 995, 1145.

4. Hasia Diner, *The Jews of the United States, 1654–2000* (Berkeley: University of

California Press, 2004), 48; Eli Faber, *A Time for Planting: The First Migration, 1654–1820*, The Jewish People in America 1 (Baltimore: Johns Hopkins University Press, 1992), 99, 100–101, 128; Ira Forman, "The Politics of Minority Consciousness: The Historical Voting Behavior of American Jews," in L. Sandy Maisel, ed., *Jews in American Politics* (Lanham, MD: Rowman and Littlefield, 2001), 144; Lawrence H. Fuchs, *Political Behavior of American Jews* (Glencoe, IL: Free Press, 1956), 25–27.

5. "Biographical Profiles," in Maisel, *Jews in American Politics*, 328, 334, 351; Myers, *History of Tammany Hall*, 166–167; Fuchs, *Political Behavior of American Jews*, 29, 32–46; Arthur Silver, "Jews in the Political Life of New York City, 1865–1897" (DHL diss., Yeshiva University, 1954), 7–8, 80, 107–108, 113–120.

6. Andrew Kaufman, *Cardozo* (Cambridge: Harvard University Press, 1998), 6–19 (quote on 15); Alexander Callow, *The Tweed Ring* (New York: Oxford University Press, 1965), 133–134, 138–139, 149, 180; M. R. Werner, *Tammany Hall* (Garden City, NY: Doubleday, Doran, 1928), 103, 112–113, 128–129 (quotes on 128); Oliver Allen, *The Tiger: The Rise and Fall of Tammany Hall* (Reading, MA: Addison-Wesley, 1993), 97–98; Myers, *History of Tammany Hall*, 262–263.

7. Steven Erie, *Rainbow's End: Irish-Americans and the Dilemmas of Urban Machine Politics, 1840–1985* (Berkeley: University of California Press, 1988).

8. Edmund James, Oscar Flynn, J. Paulding, Mrs. Simon Patton, and Walter Scott Andrews, *The Immigrant Jew in America* (New York: B. Buck, 1906), 258–259.

9. Moses Rischin, *The Promised City: New York's Jews, 1870–1914* (Cambridge: Harvard University Press, 1962), 222; Irving Howe, *World of Our Fathers* (New York: Harcourt Brace Jovanovich, 1976), 366; Timothy Gilfoyle, *City of Eros: New York City, Prostitution, and the Commercialization of Sex, 1790–1920* (New York: Norton, 1992), 261; Allen, *The Tiger*, 212–213; "Mr. Engel's New Face," *New York Times*, August 20, 1891; "Engel on the Stand," *New York Times*, December 16, 1897; "Says Tammany Had Big Head," *New York Times*, November 8, 1901; "Martin Engel, Old 'De Ate' Leader, Dies," *New York Times*, July 16, 1915; Nancy Weiss, *Charles Francis Murphy, 1858–1924: Respectability and Responsibility in Tammany Politics* (Northampton, MA: Smith College, 1968), 28.

10. Warner, *Tammany Hall*, 381–382; Rischin, *Promised City*, 223; "Additional Nominations," *New York Times*, October 31, 1888; "An Election Fraud Case," *New York Times*, March 6, 1889; "Smith and Co. Are Arrested," *New York Times*, March 27, 1889 (quote); "O'Brien's Men Were There," *New York Times*, August 6, 1889; "Silver Dollar Smith's Trial," *New York Times*, September 18, 1889; "'Silver Dollar' in a Row," *New York Times*, December 5, 1894; "Charles J. Smith Dies," *New York Times*, December 23, 1899.

11. "Biographical Profiles," in Maisel, *Jews in American Politics*, 344; Louis Eisenstein and Elliot Rosenberg, *A Stripe of Tammany's Tiger* (New York: Robert Speller and Sons, 1966), 29–30; "Russia's Exclusion of Jews," *New York Times*, March 29, 1902; "Goldfogle's Resolution Adopted," *New York Times*, May 1, 1902; "Russia's Exclusion of Jews," *New York Times*, February 19, 1904; "Exclusion of Jews to Go before House," *New York Times*, February 23, 1911; "Literacy Hearing to Be Battle Royal," *New York Times*, January 22, 1915; "Congressman Goldfogle," *New York Times*, October 30, 1920; "H. M. Goldfogle Dies Suddenly," *New York Times*, June 2, 1929; "Eulogies Paid H. M. Goldfogle," *New York*

Times, June 5, 1929; "Birger fun 12ten kongres district," *Tageblat*, October 29, 1912, "A vort vegen kongresman Goldfogl," *Tageblat*, October 31, 1912.

12. Thomas Henderson, *Tammany Hall and the New Immigrants: The Progressive Years* (New York: Arno, 1976), 47–48, 157 (quote).

13. Richard Welch, *King of the Bowery: Big Tim Sullivan, Tammany Hall, and New York City from the Gilded Age to the Progressive Era* (Albany: SUNY Press, 2008), 43–44, 48–49, 66–67, 91, 132 (quote).

14. Eisenstein and Rosenberg, *Stripe of Tammany's Tiger*, 15.

15. Ibid., 5–10, 22–23, 25, 33, 34, 49; Rischin, *Promised City*, 230; Howe, *World of Our Fathers*, 368, 370; Henderson, *Tammany Hall and the New Immigrants*, 167.

16. James et al., *Immigrant Jew in America*, 260.

17. Eisenstein and Rosenberg, *Stripe of Tammany's Tiger*, 56–58; "Samuel S. Koenig, G.O.P. Leader, Dies," *New York Times*, March 18, 1955.

18. Quoted in Tony Michels, *A Fire in Their Hearts: Yiddish Socialists in New York* (Cambridge: Harvard University Press, 2005), 46.

19. Burrows and Wallace, *Gotham*, 1092.

20. Ibid., 1092–1110; Epstein, *Jewish Labor in USA*, 115–116, 144–149; E. Tcherikower, *Geshikhte fun der yidisher arbeter bavegung in di fareynikte shtatn* (New York: Yiddish Scientific Institute—Yivo, 1945), 290–294.

21. Ben Reisman, "Why I Came to America," in Jocelyn Cohen and Daniel Soyer, eds., *My Future Is in America: Autobiographies of Eastern European Jewish Immigrants* (New York: NYU Press, 2006), 67–68.

22. J. S. Hertz, *50 yor arbeter-ring in yidishn lebn* (New York: National Executive Committee of the Workmen's Circle, 1950), 15; A. S. Sachs, *Di geshikhte fun arbayter ring, 1892–1925* (New York: National Executive Committee of the Workmen's Circle, 1925), 3–6; Daniel Soyer, *Jewish Immigrant Associations and American Identity in New York, 1880–1939* (Cambridge: Harvard University Press, 1997), 66–70.

23. Howe, *World of Our Fathers*, 522–543; Melech Epstein, *Profiles of Eleven: Profiles of Eleven Men Who Guided the Destiny of an Immigrant Society and Stimulated Social Consciousness among the American People* (Detroit: Wayne State University Press, 1965), 49–110.

24. Hadassa Kosak, *Cultures of Opposition: Jewish Immigrant Workers, New York City, 1881–1905* (Albany: SUNY Press, 2000).

25. Howe, *World of Our Fathers*, 298.

26. Ibid., 297–299; Annelise Orleck, *Common Sense and a Little Fire: Women and Working-Class Politics in the United States, 1900–1965* (Chapel Hill: University of North Carolina Press, 1995), 39–41, 48–49, 60; Richard Greenwald, *The Triangle Fire, the Protocol of Peace, and Industrial Democracy in Progressive Era New York* (Philadelphia: Temple University Press, 2005), 32–46.

27. Greenwald, *Triangle Fire*, 50–75; Howe, *World of Our Fathers*, 301.

28. James et al., *Immigrant Jew in America*, 261.

29. Irving Howe and Kenneth Libo, eds., *How We Lived: A Documentary History of Immigrant Jews in America, 1880–1930* (New York: Richard Marek, 1979), 190; Epstein,

Profiles of Eleven, 189–232; *Leksikon fun der nayer yiddisher literature*, vol. 3 (New York: Congress for Jewish Culture, 1960), 138–139; Howe, *World of Our Fathers*, 315.

30. Howe, *World of Our Fathers*, 315; Epstein, *Profiles of Eleven*, 159–188 (quotes on 174); Rogoff, *Meyer London*.

31. James et al., *Immigrant Jew in America*, 261.

32. Silver, "Jews in the Political Life of New York City," 35–41; David Hammack, *Power and Society: Greater New York at the Turn of the Century* (1982; repr., New York: Columbia University Press, 1987), 9.

33. Henderson, *Tammany Hall and the New Immigrants*, 103–111, 155–156, 167; James et al., *Immigrant Jew in America*, 257, 264–265; Howe, *World of Our Fathers*, 362; Rischin, *Promised City*, 228; Fuchs, *Political Behavior of American Jews*, 124; Silver, "Jews in the Political Life of New York City," 121–122.

34. S. Sara Monoson, "The Lady and the Tiger: Women's Electoral Activism in New York City before Suffrage," *Journal of Women's History* 2:2 (Fall 1990): 100–134 (Nathan quote on 110).

35. Joyce Antler, *The Journey Home: Jewish Women and the American Century* (New York: Free Press, 1997), 54–61 (quotes on 54–55).

36. Maud Nathan, *The Story of an Epoch-Making Movement* (Garden City, NY: Doubleday, Page, 1926), 89.

37. Elizabeth Israels Perry, *Belle Moskowitz: Feminine Politics and the Exercise of Power in the Age of Al Smith* (1987; repr., Boston: Northeastern University Press, 1992), 118.

38. David Von Drehle, *Triangle: The Fire That Changed America* (New York: Atlantic Monthly Press, 2003); Leon Stein, *The Triangle Fire* (Philadelphia: Lippincott, 1962); Greenwald, *Triangle Fire*, 129–153.

39. *Jewish Daily Forward*, March 26, 1911.

40. Howe and Libo, *How We Lived*, 187.

41. Stein, *Triangle Fire*, 124, 138; Orleck, *Common Sense and a Little Fire*, 36–37, 44–45, 48, 103; Greenwald, *Triangle Fire*, 139–145.

42. Greenwald, *Triangle Fire*, 156–159; Von Drehle, *Triangle*, 209–214; Orleck, *Common Sense and a Little Fire*, 131–132.

43. Rischin, *Promised City*, 228–229; Gary Gerstle, *American Crucible: Race and Nation in the Twentieth Century* (Princeton: Princeton University Press, 2001), 45–56, 72–74; Fuchs, *Political Behavior of American Jews*, 52–59.

44. Warner, *Tammany Hall*, 529–530; Henderson, *Tammany Hall and the New Immigrants*, 116; Naomi Cohen, *Encounter with Emancipation: The German Jews in the United States, 1830–1914* (Philadelphia: Jewish Publication Society, 1984), 144–147, 169–170; "Shtraus shturemt di ist sayd," *Tageblat*, October 29, 1912.

45. Henderson, *Tammany Hall and the New Immigrants*, 118; Melvin Dubofsky, "Success and Failure of Socialism in New York City, 1900–1918: A Case Study," *Labor History* 9:3 (Autumn 1968): 366.

46. "Levy Says Sulzer Coined 'Confession,'" *New York Times*, August 19, 1913.

47. Henderson, *Tammany Hall and the New Immigrants*, 121, 129.

48. Warner, *Tammany Hall*, 532–554; Eisenstein and Rosenberg, *Stripe of Tammany's*

Tiger, 23–24; "Levy Says Sulzer Coined 'Confession'"; "Loyal Few Hear Sulzer Farewell" and "Tammany Dismal, Fear for McCall," *New York Times*, October 19, 1913; "Sulzer Frenzy Hits East Side," *New York Times*, October 23, 1913; "Sulzer Elected to Assembly Two-to-One in Sixth" and "Sulzer Jubilant at Murphy's Defeat," *New York Times*, November 5, 1913; "Aaron J. Levy, 74, Ex-State Justice," *New York Times*, November 22, 1955.

49. Henderson, *Tammany Hall and the New Immigrants*, 177; Howe, *World of Our Fathers*, 313, 315; Dubofsky, "Success and Failure of Socialism," 367–368; Arthur Goren, *The Politics and Public Culture of American Jews* (Bloomington: Indiana University Press, 1999), 84–89, 95–97 (quote on 97).

50. Alter Landesman, *Brownsville: The Birth, Development and Passing of a Jewish Community in New York* (New York: Bloch, 1971), 113–119, 299–302.

51. "Judge Hylan Opens Fight for Ballots," *New York Times*, October 5, 1917.

52. Henderson, *Tammany Hall and the New Immigrants*, 193–219 (quotes on 202, 212); Dubofsky, "Success and Failure of Socialism," 371; Howe, *World of Our Fathers*, 279–280, 319–321; Epstein, *Profiles of Eleven*, 213; "Hylan Victory Is a Tammany Record," *New York Times*, November 8, 1917.

53. Henderson, *Tammany Hall and the New Immigrants*, 222–234; Landesman, *Brownsville*, 304.

54. Elinor Lerner, "Jewish Involvement in the New York City Woman Suffrage Movement," *American Jewish History* 70:4 (June 1981): 442–461, reprinted in Jeffrey Gurock, ed., *American Jewish History*, vol. 3 (New York: Routledge, 1998), 963–982.

55. Orleck, *Common Sense and a Little Fire*, 87–113 (Lemlich quote on 91).

56. Perry, *Belle Moskowitz*, 117–139; Howe, *World of Our Fathers*, 386–391; Dubofsky, "Success and Failure of Socialism," 371.

■ NOTES TO CHAPTER 7

1. Harmonie Club of the City of New York, *One Hundred Years, 1852–1952: The Harmonie Club* (New York: Harmonie Club, 1952); Rudolf Glanz, *Studies in Judaica Americana* (New York: Ktav, 1970), 176, 179, 181.

2. Reuben Iceland, "At Goodman and Levine's," in Irving Howe and Eliezer Greenberg, eds., *Voices from the Yiddish: Essays, Memoirs, Diaries* (1972; repr., New York: Schocken, 1975), 300–303.

3. Irving Howe and Kenneth Libo, eds., *How We Lived: A Documentary History of Immigrant Jews in America, 1880–1930* (New York: Richard Marek, 1979), 288–290; Irving Howe, *World of Our Fathers* (New York: Harcourt Brace Jovanovich, 1976), 235–238; Edmund James, Oscar Flynn, J. Paulding, Mrs. Simon Patton, and Walter Scott Andrews, *The Immigrant Jew in America* (New York: B. Buck, 1906), 222–226.

4. Hasia Diner, *A Time for Gathering: The Second Migration, 1820–1880* (Baltimore: Johns Hopkins University Press, 1992), 8–35, 49–56, 219–226.

5. Sol Steinmetz, *Yiddish and English: A Century of Yiddish in America* (Tuscaloosa: University of Alabama Press, 1986), 30–40; Nancy Green, ed., *Jewish Workers in the Modern Diaspora* (Berkeley: University of California Press, 1998), 193 (Sholem Aleichem quote).

6. Stephen Whitfield, *In Search of American Jewish Culture* (Hanover, NH: University

Press of New England / Brandeis University Press, 1999), 36; Steinmetz, *Yiddish and English*, 41–65; H. L. Mencken, *The American Language: An Inquiry into the Development of English in the United States*, 4th ed. (1936; repr., New York: Knopf, 1962), 368–369, 578, 633–636, and supplements I (1945; 1962), 433–435, and II (1948; 1962), 188–193, 259–262, 754.

7. Jenna Joselit, "Fun and Games: The American Jewish Social Club," in Marc Lee Raphael, ed., *The Columbia History of Jews and Judaism in America* (New York: Columbia University Press, 2008), 246–262; Glanz, *Studies in Judaica Americana*, 169–186; Harmonie Club, *One Hundred Years*.

8. Robert Greef, *Public Lectures in New York, 1851–1878: A Cultural Index of the Times* (Chicago: University of Chicago, 1945), 6 (quote); Sean Wilentz, *Chants Democratic: New York City and the Rise of the American Working Class, 1789–1850* (New York: Oxford University Press, 1984), 181–182, 271–272; Robert Ernst, *Immigrant Life in New York City, 1825–1863* (1949; repr., Syracuse: Syracuse University Press, 1994), 142–144.

9. Tony Michels, *A Fire in Their Hearts: Yiddish Socialists in New York* (Cambridge: Harvard University Press, 2005), 73–91, 189–204; Stephan F. Brumberg, *Going to America, Going to School: The Jewish Immigrant Public School Encounter in Turn-of-the-Century New York City* (New York: Praeger, 1986), 148–174; M. Shapiro (Em.S.), "Why I Came to America and What I Have Accomplished Here," autobiography #34, American Jewish Autobiographies, RG 102, YIVO Institute for Social Research.

10. Diner, *Time for Gathering*, 133–134; Diane Ravitch, *The Great School Wars: A History of the New York City Public Schools* (1974; repr., New York: Basic Books, 1988), 33–76; Naomi Cohen, *Encounter with Emancipation: The German Jews in the United States, 1830–1914* (Philadelphia: Jewish Publication Society, 1984), 92–96.

11. Hyman Grinstein, *Rise of the Jewish Community of New York City, 1654–1860* (Philadelphia: Jewish Publication Society, 1945), 236, 244; Brumberg, *Going to America, Going to School*, 3, 67–69, 74–75, 130–131 138; James et al., *Immigrant Jew in America*, 185–186.

12. Brumberg, *Going to America, Going to School*, 67, 89, 114.

13. Martha Kransdorf, "Julia Richman's Years in the New York City Public Schools, 1872–1912" (Ph.D. diss., University of Michigan, 1979), 58–127 (quote on 58); Paula Hyman and Deborah Dash Moore, eds., *Jewish Women in America: An Historical Encyclopedia* (New York: Routledge, 1997), 2:1148–1149.

14. Kransdorf, "Julia Richman's Years," 66–72, 128–189 (quotes on 66–67, 72, 132–133); Howe, *World of Our Fathers*, 278; "Julia Richman," and "Julia Richman Dies in Paris Hospital," *New York Times*, June 26, 1912.

15. Ravitch, *Great School Wars*, 195–230; David Tyack, *The One Best System: A History of American Urban Education* (Cambridge: Harvard University Press, 1974), 250–251.

16. Howe, *World of Our Fathers*, 256–264, 273; James et al., *Immigrant Jew in America*, 188–191, 194–196.

17. Howe, *World of Our Fathers*, 280–286; James et al., *Immigrant Jew in America*, 191–192; Edwin G. Burrows and Mike Wallace, *Gotham: A History of New York City to 1898* (New York: Oxford University Press, 1999), 781; Morris Raphael Cohen, *A Dreamer's Journey: The Autobiography of Morris Raphael Cohen* (Glencoe, IL: Free Press, 1949), 89.

18. Arthur Goren, "The Jewish Press," in Sally Miller, ed., *The Ethnic Press in the*

United States: A Historical Analysis and Handbook (Westport, CT: Greenwood, 1987), 209; Barbara Straus Reed, "Pioneer Jewish Journalism," in Frankie Hutton and Barbara Straus Reed, eds., *Outsiders in Nineteenth Century Press History: Multicultural Perspectives* (Bowling Green, OH: Bowling Green State University Popular Press, 1995), 41–45; Albert M. Friedenberg, "American Jewish Journalism to the Close of the Civil War," *Publications of the American Jewish Historical Society* 26 (1918): 271; Kenneth Libo, "A History of Jewish Journalism in America," in National Museum of American Jewish History, *A People in Print: Jewish Journalism in America* (Philadelphia: National Museum of American Jewish History, 1987), 34.

19. Jacob Rader Marcus, *United States Jewry, 1776–1985*, vol. 2 (Detroit: Wayne State University Press, 1991), 271. Moshe D. Sherman, *Orthodox Judaism in America: A Biographical Dictionary and Sourcebook* (Westport, CT: Greenwood, 1996), 35.

20. Libo, "History of Jewish Journalism," 36–38; American Jewish Historical Society, "Guide to the Papers of Philip Cowen," http://findingaids.cjh.org/?pID=109145 (accessed December 28, 2011).

21. Bette Roth Young, *Emma Lazarus in Her World: Life and Letters* (Philadelphia: Jewish Publication Society, 1995), 24.

22. Joyce Antler, *The Journey Home: Jewish Women and the American Century* (New York: Free Press, 1997), 10–12; Francis Klagsbrun, foreword to Young, *Emma Lazarus in Her World*, xii–xiii; Esther Schor, *Emma Lazarus* (New York: Nextbook/Schocken, 2006), 17–20, 23–32, 46–49, 51–62, 76–79, 249–250; Young, *Emma Lazarus in Her World*, 3–5, 7–8, 36–57.

23. Glanz, *Studies in Judaica Americana*, 233–236; Stanley Nadel, "Jewish Race and German Soul in Nineteenth Century America," *American Jewish History* 77:1 (September 1987): 14, 25.

24. Quoted in Glanz, *Studies in Judaica Americana*, 243. See also Christa Carvajal, "German-American Theatre," in Maxine Schwartz Seller, ed., *Ethnic Theater in the United States* (Westport, CT: Greenwood, 1983), 177; Nadel, "Jewish Race and German Soul," 10.

25. Carvajal, "German-American Theatre," 181–182; Glanz, *Studies in Judaica Americana*, 239–241; John Koegel, *Music in German Immigrant Theater in New York City, 1840–1940* (Rochester: University of Rochester Press, 2009); Fritz Leuchs, *The Early German Theatre in New York, 1840–1872* (1928; repr., New York: AMS Press, 1966), 82, 86.

26. Leuchs, *Early German Theatre*, 82, 96, 104, 110, 113, 118–119, 134, 145–146, 160–161, 206–207; Glanz, *Studies in Judaica Americana*, 240–241; Isidore Singer and Edgar Meis, "Bandmann, Daniel E.," in *Jewish Encyclopedia* (1901–1906), available online at http://www.jewishencyclopedia.com/view.jsp?artid=202&letter=B&search=bandmann (accessed October 26, 2010); "Daniel Bandmann Dead," *New York Times*, November, 25, 1905; Nadel, "Jewish Race and German Soul," 15.

27. Nadel, "Jewish Race and German Soul," 15–16; Nahma Sandrow, *Vagabond Stars: A World History of the Yiddish Theater* (New York: Harper and Row, 1977), 72–78, 92, 104–109; Nina Warnke, "Immigrant Popular Culture as Contested Space: Yiddish Music Halls, the Yiddish Press, and the Processes of Americanization, 1900–1919," *Theater Journal* 48:3 (October 1996): 326–331; Judith Thissen, "Jewish Immigrant Audiences in

New York City, 1905–1914," in Melvyn Stokes and Richard Maltby, eds., *American Movie Audiences: From the Turn of the Century to the Early Sound Era* (London: BFI, 1999), 18.

28. Sandrow, *Vagabond Stars*, 132.

29. Ibid., 132–163, 169–192, 259–271; Nina Warnke, "Theater as Educational Institution: Jewish Immigrant Intellectuals and Yiddish Theater Reform," in Barbara Kirshenblatt-Gimblett and Jonathan Karp, eds., *The Art of Being Jewish in Modern Times* (Philadelphia: University of Pennsylvania Press, 2008), 23–41.

30. Hyman and Moore, *Jewish Women in America*, 1:715–717.

31. Tony Michels, "'Speaking to Moyshe': The Early Socialist Yiddish Press and Its Readers," *Jewish History* 14:1 (2000): 53; Goren, "Jewish Press," 212.

32. Moses Rischin, *The Promised City: New York's Jews, 1870–1914* (Cambridge: Harvard University Press, 1962), 118; Moyshe Shtarkman, "Vikhtikste momentn in der geshikhte fun der yidisher prese in Amerike," in J. Gladstone, S. Niger, and H. Rogoff, eds., *Finf un zibetsik yor yidishe prese in Amerike, 1870–1945* (New York: Yiddish Writers Union, 1945), 17–19, 25–26; *Leksikon fun der nayer yidisher literature*, vol. 7 (New York: Congress for Jewish Culture, 1968), 88–89.

33. Michels, *Fire in Their Hearts*, 53–56, 95–104.

34. Andrew Heinze, *Adapting to Abundance: Jewish Immigrants, Mass Consumption, and the Search for American Identity* (New York: Columbia University Press, 1990), 150, 153; Goren, "Jewish Press," 215, 217; Michels, "Speaking to Moyshe," 69; Isaac Metzger, *A Bintel Brief: Sixty Years of Letters from the Lower East Side to the Jewish Daily Forward* (New York: Ballantine Books, 1971).

35. S. Margoshes, "The Jewish Press in New York City," in Kehillah (Jewish Community) of New York City, *Jewish Communal Register of New York City, 1917–1918* (New York: Kehillah, 1918), 600–608, 612–632.

36. Irving Howe, Ruth Wisse, and Khone Shmeruk, introduction to Irving Howe, Ruth Wisse, and Khone Shmeruk, eds., *The Penguin Book of Modern Yiddish Verse* (New York: Viking, 1987), 22–25; *Leksikon fun der nayer yidisher literatur* (New York: Congress for Jewish Culture, 1956–1981), vol. 1 (1956), 207–210; vol. 3 (1960), 432–443; vol. 6 (1965), 554–563; vol. 8 (1981), 350–356; Morris Rosenfeld, "The Teardrop Millionaire," in Itche Goldberg and Max Rosenfeld, eds., *Morris Rosenfeld: Selections from His Poetry and Prose* (New York: Yidisher kultur farband, 1964), 29; Sarah Alisa Braun, "Jews, Writing, and the Dynamics of Literary Affiliation, 1880–1940" (Ph.D. diss., University of Michigan, 2007), 72–121.

37. Howe et al., introduction to *Penguin Book*, 28; Mani Leyb, "Ot azoy, azoy, azoy," in Dovid Kazanski, ed., *Zishe Landoy: Zamlbukh aroysgegebn fun khaveyrim* (New York: Farlag Inzl, 1938), 11.

38. Howe et al., introduction to *Penguin Book*, 27–32, Mani Leyb, "I Am . . . / Ikh bin . . . ," in Howe et al., *Penguin Book*, 128–132; Ruth Wisse, *A Little Love in Big Manhattan: Two Yiddish Poets* (Cambridge: Harvard University Press, 1988), 21–44; *Leksikon fun der nayer yidisher literatur*, vol. 5 (1963), 450–456.

39. Aaron Domnitz, "Why I Left My Old Home and What I Have Accomplished in America," in Jocelyn Cohen and Daniel Soyer, eds., *My Future Is in America:*

Autobiographies of Eastern European Jewish Immigrants (New York: NYU Press, 2006), 151–152.

40. Howe, *World of Our Fathers*, 445–451; *Leksikon fun der nayer yidisher literatur*, 8:678–720; 1:83–92; Arthur Goren, *The Politics and Public Culture of American Jews* (Bloomington: Indiana University Press, 1999), 67–71.

41. Margoshes, "Jewish Press," 599; Z'vi Scharfstein, "Hebrew Speaking Clubs in America," in Kehillah, *Jewish Communal Register*, 566–567; Domnitz, "Why I Left My Old Home," 148; Alan Mintz, "Hebrew Literature in America," in Michael Kramer and Hanna Wirth-Nesher, eds., *The Cambridge Companion to Jewish American Literature* (New York: Cambridge University Press, 2003), 92–109; Alan Mintz, "A Sanctuary in the Wilderness: The Beginnings of the Hebrew Movement in America in *Hatoren*," in Alan Mintz, ed., *Hebrew in America: Perspectives and Prospects* (Detroit: Wayne State University Press, 1993), 29–67.

42. Aviva Ben-Ur, "The Ladino (Judeo-Spanish) Press in the United States, 1910–1948," in Werner Sollors, ed., *Multilingual America: Transnationalism, Ethnicity, and the Languages of American Literature* (New York: NYU Press, 1998), 64–79.

43. Rischin, *Promised City*, 128–130; Michels, "Speaking to Moyshe," 67; Nadel, "Jewish Race and German Soul," 16; Nadel, *Little Germany: Ethnicity, Religion, and Class in New York City, 1845–80* (Urbana: University of Illinois Press, 1990), 83.

44. Christine Stansell, *American Moderns: Bohemian New York and the Creation of a New Century* (2000, repr., Princeton: Princeton University Press, 2010); Tony Michels, "Cultural Crossings: Immigrant Jews, Yiddish, and the New York Intellectual Scene" (unpublished paper in authors' possession).

45. Braun, "Jews, Writing, and the Dynamics of Literary Affiliation," 20–67 (quotes on 40–41); Abraham Cahan, *Bleter fun mayn lebn*, vol. 4 (New York: Forward Association, 1928), 21–31; Sanford Marovitz, *Abraham Cahan* (New York: Twayne, 1996), 153–156.

46. Stansell, *American Moderns*, 132, 134.

47. Antler, *Journey Home*, 74; Stansell, *American Moderns*, 121, 134.

48. Antler, *Journey Home*, 73–78, 82–85 (quotes on 85); Stansell, *American Moderns*, 120–144; Hyman and Moore, *Jewish Women in America*, 1:529.

49. Carol Schoen, *Anzia Yezierska* (Boston: Twayne, 1982), 11; Antler, *Journey Home*, 29.

50. Schoen, *Anzia Yezierska*, 1–38; Antler, *Journey Home*, 27–30; Hyman and Moore, *Jewish Women in America*, 2:1521; Alice Kessler Harris, introduction to *Bread Givers*, by Anzia Yezierska (New York: Persea Books, 1975), v–xviii.

51. Burrows and Wallace, *Gotham*, 1151–1154, 1189, 1213; Daniel Pfaff, "Pulitzer, Joseph," *American National Biography Online*, http://www.anb.org.

52. Jacob Rader Marcus, *United States Jewry, 1776–1985*, vol. 3 (Detroit: Wayne State University Press, 1993), 313–314; Susan Barnes, "Ochs, Adolph Simon," *American National Biography Online*, http://www.anb.org; Naomi Cohen, *Not Free to Desist: The American Jewish Committee, 1906–1966* (Philadelphia: Jewish Publication Society, 1972), 74; "Adolph S. Ochs Dead at 77," *New York Times*, April 9, 1935; Harrison Salisbury, "*New*

York Times," in Kenneth Jackson, ed., *Encyclopedia of New York City* (New Haven: Yale University Press, 1995), 846–847; Susan E. Tifft and Alex S. Jones, *The Trust: The Private and Powerful Family Behind the New York Times* (Boston: Little, Brown, 1999), 92–96; "The Frank Case," *New York Times*, May 8, 1914; Deborah Dash Moore, *B'nai B'rith and the Challenge of Ethnic Leadership* (Albany: SUNY Press, 1981), 107–108; Leonard Dinnerstein, *Anti-Semitism in America* (New York: Oxford University Press, 1994), 181–184.

53. Stansell, *American Moderns*, 18–25 (quote on 19).

54. Moses Rischin, introduction to Moses Rischin, ed., *Grandma Never Lived in America: The New Journalism of Abraham Cahan* (Bloomington: Indiana University Press, 1985), xvii–xliv.

55. Norman L. Kleeblatt and Susan Chevlowe, *Painting a Place in America: Jewish Artists in New York, 1900–1945*, exhibition catalogue (New York: Jewish Museum, 1991), 100.

56. Hutchins Hapgood, *The Spirit of the Ghetto* (1902; repr., Cambridge: Harvard University Press, 1967), 254–261; Matthew Baigell, "From Hester Street to Fifty-Seventh Street: Jewish-American Artists in New York," in Kleeblatt and Chevlowe, *Painting a Place in America*, 30–31.

57. Baigell, "From Hester Street to Fifty-Seventh Street," 32; Kleeblatt and Chevlowe, *Painting a Place in America*, 92–93, 198–200; Milton Wolf Brown, *American Painting, from the Armory Show to the Depression* (Princeton: Princeton University Press, 1955), 39–44, 137–138 (quote on 42).

58. Kleeblatt and Chevlowe, *Painting a Place in America*, 94–95, 98.

59. Ibid., 106–109; Paul Avrich, *The Modern School Movement: Anarchism and Education in the United States* (Princeton: Princeton University Press, 1980), 145–153.

60. Kleeblatt and Chevlowe, *Painting a Place in America*, 105–114.

61. Baigell, "From Hester Street to Fifty-Seventh Street," 32; Kleeblatt and Chevlowe, *Painting a Place in America*, 99–100; Adam Bellow, *The Educational Alliance: A Centennial Celebration* (New York: Educational Alliance, 1990), 123.

62. Burrows and Wallace, *Gotham*, 1140–1146; Robert Snyder, *The Voice of the City: Vaudeville and Popular Culture in New York* (New York: Oxford University Press, 1989), 4–37, 82–83, 96–97.

63. Snyder, *Voice of the City*, 42–52.

64. Ibid., 55–56; Hyman and Moore, *Jewish Women in America*, 2:1416–1418.

65. Jonathan Karp, "Of Maestros and Minstrels: American Jewish Composers between Black Vernacular and European Art Music," in Kirshenblatt-Gimblett and Karp, *Art of Being Jewish*, 57–77; Michael Alexander, *Jazz Age Jews* (Princeton: Princeton University Press, 2001), 133–153; Michael Rogin, *Blackface, White Noise: Jewish Immigrants and the Hollywood Melting Pot* (Berkeley: University of California Press, 1996); Whitfield, *In Search of American Jewish Culture*, 149–154.

66. Larry Stempel, *Showtime: A History of the Broadway Musical Theater* (New York: Norton, 2010), 79–84, 124–125, 136; Foster Hirsch, *The Boys from Syracuse: The Shuberts' Theatrical Empire* (1998; repr., New York: Cooper Square Press, 2000).

67. Burrows and Wallace, *Gotham*, 1146–1147; David A. Jasen, *Tin Pan Alley: The*

Golden Age of American Song (New York: Routledge, 2003): ix; Alexander, *Jazz Age Jews*, 156; Heinze, *Adapting to America*, 141; Mark Slobin, *Tenement Songs: The Popular Music of the Jewish Immigrants* (Urbana: University of Illinois Press, 1982), 123; Whitfield, *In Search of American Jewish Culture*, 95.

68. Alexander, *Jazz Age Jews*, 158–163 ("Norman Rockwell" quote on 158); Whitfield, *In Search of American Jewish Culture*, 95–99 (Kern quote on 96); Ann Douglas, *Terrible Honesty: Mongrel Manhattan in the 1920s* (New York: Farrar, Straus and Giroux, 1995), 355–359.

69. David Nasaw, *Going Out: The Rise and Fall of Public Amusements* (New York: Basic Books, 1993), 104–114 (Israels quote on 104).

70. Minnie Goldstein, autobiography #155/155A/267, American Jewish Biographies Collection, RG 102, YIVO Institute for Jewish Research.

71. Kathy Peiss, *Cheap Amusements: Working Women and Leisure in Turn-of-the-Century New York* (Philadelphia: Temple University Press, 1986), 89–99; Heinze, *Adapting to Abundance*, 120; Daniel Soyer, *Jewish Immigrant Associations and American Identity in New York, 1880–1939* (Cambridge: Harvard University Press, 1997), 104–106.

72. "Heinrich Conried Dies in Austria," *New York Times*, April 27, 1909; Carvajal, "German-American Theatre," 182; Nadel, "Jewish Race and German Soul," 15; Joseph Horowitz, *Classical Music in America: A History of Its Rise and Fall* (New York: Norton, 2005), 185–192.

73. Horowitz, *Classical Music in America*, 198–204, 247–255, 364–365; John Frederick Cone, *Oscar Hammerstein's Manhattan Opera Company* (Norman: University of Oklahoma Press, 1966); Jonathan Gill, *Harlem: The Four Hundred Year History from Dutch Village to Capital of Black America* (New York: Grove, 2011), 113–114, 122–125.

74. Ben Singer, "Manhattan Nickelodeons: New Data on Audiences and Exhibitors," *Cinema Journal* 34:3 (Spring 1995): 5; Judith Thissen, "Film and Vaudeville on New York's Lower East Side," in Kirshenblatt-Gimblett and Karp, *Art of Being Jewish*, 45; Heinze, *Adapting to Abundance*, 119, 204; Thissen, "Jewish Immigrant Audiences in New York City," 18–19; Peiss, *Cheap Amusements*, 149.

75. Lary May, *Screening Out the Past: The Birth of Mass Culture and the Motion Picture Industry* (New York: Oxford University Press, 1980), 148 (Zukor quote), 174–175.

76. Heinze, *Adapting to Abundance*, 208–218; Matthew Bernstein, "Zukor, Adolph," *American National Biography Online*, http://www.anb.org; Neal Gabler, *An Empire of Their Own: How the Jews Invented Hollywood* (New York: Crown, 1988), 65–66.

77. Charles Musser and David James, "Filmmaking," in Jackson, *Encyclopedia of New York City*, 404–405; Douglas, *Terrible Honesty*, 61.

78. Howe, *World of Our Fathers*, 485–492; Milton Doroshkin, *Yiddish in America: Social and Cultural Foundations* (Rutherford, NJ: Fairleigh Dickinson University Press, 1969), 218; Whitfield, *In Search of American Jewish Culture*, 30.

79. Horowitz, *Classical Music in America*, 423; Whitfield, *In Search of American Jewish Culture*, 61.

80. Stempel, *Showtime*, 192–194, 250–255; Douglas, *Terrible Honesty*, 102–103; Whitfield, *In Search of American Jewish Culture*, 69–71, 74–77, 155–157.

■ NOTES TO THE CONCLUSION

1. Deborah Dash Moore, *At Home in America: Second Generation New York Jews* (New York: Columbia University Press, 1981), 21.

2. "Likens Alien Bill to Pharaoh's Plan," *New York Times*, April 20, 1924.

3. John Higham, *Strangers in the Land: Patterns of American Nativism, 1860–1925* (New York: Atheneum, 1981), 194–299.

4. Ibid., 270–286; Madison Grant, *The Passing of the Great Race* (New York: Scribner, 1916), 81; Naomi Cohen, *Not Free to Desist: The American Jewish Committee, 1906–1966* (Philadelphia: Jewish Publication Society, 1972), 127.

5. Cohen, *Not Free to Desist*, 124–139; Victoria Saker Woeste, "Insecure Equality: Louis Marshall, Henry Ford, and the Problem of Defamatory Antisemitism, 1920–1929," *Journal of American History* 91:3 (December 2004): 877–905.

6. Roger Daniels, *Guarding the Golden Door: American Immigration Policy and Immigrants since 1882* (New York: Hill and Wang, 2004), 7–49 (quote on 47–48).

7. "Says 'Foreign Bloc' Fights Johnson Bill," *New York Times*, March 2, 1924; Chin Jou, "Contesting Nativism: The New York Congressional Delegation's Case against the Immigration Act of 1924," *Federal History Online* 3 (January 2011): 66–79, http://shfg.org/shfg/wp-content/uploads/2010/07/5%E2%80%93jou_Layout-11-final-2.pdf (accessed May 23, 2011); *Biographical Dictionary of the United States Congress*, http://bioguide.congress.gov (accessed May 23, 2011); House Vote #90 (May 15, 1924), *To Agree to the Report of Conference Committee on H.R. 7995, to Limit the Immigration of Aliens into the United States* (P. 8651-1), GovTrack.com, http://www.govtrack.us/congress/vote.xpd?vote=h68_1-90 (accessed May 23, 2011).

8. John Higham, *Send These to Me: Jews and other Immigrants in Urban America* (New York: Atheneum, 1975), 203–208.

9. Libby Garland, "Not-Quite-Closed Gates: Jewish Alien Smuggling in the Post-Quota Years," *American Jewish History* 94:3 (September 2008): 199.

10. Ibid.; Minnie Kusnetz, "I Haven't Lost Anything by Coming to America," in Jocelyn Cohen and Daniel Soyer, eds., *My Future Is in America: Autobiographies of Eastern European Jewish Immigrants* (New York: NYU Press, 2006), 302, 307–309.

11. Kusnetz, "I Haven't Lost Anything," 302.

12. Ruth Gay, *Unfinished People: Eastern European Jews Encounter America* (New York: Norton, 1996), 124.

13. Moore, *At Home in America*, 19–24, 65–68; Beth Wenger, *New York Jews and the Great Depression: Uncertain Promise* (New Haven: Yale University Press, 1996), 81, 83–84, 94.

14. Moore, *At Home in America*, 23, 66, 71–73, 78–82; Moses Rischin, *The Promised City: New York's Jews, 1870–1914* (Cambridge: Harvard University Press, 1962), 93; Wenger, *New York Jews and the Great Depression*, 85–89.

15. Moore, *At Home in America*, 23, 66, 73–74, 76 (quote on 73); Wenger, *New York Jews and the Great Depression*, 90–93 (Howe quote on 93).

16. Mary Wasserzug Natelson, "The Rabbi's House (Story of a Family)," trans. Rachel Natelson, manuscript in authors' possession.

17. Moore, *At Home in America*, 21, 23, 86 (Kazin quote); Beth Wenger, *New York Jews and the Great Depression*, 81.

18. Alfred Kazin, *A Walker in the City* (1946; repr., San Diego: Harcourt Brace, 1979), 88, 107; Gay, *Unfinished People*, 298.

■ NOTES TO VISUAL ESSAY

I thank Deborah Dash Moore for graciously inviting me to be part of this project, for her support of my work, and for her deep appreciation of objects and images. Jennifer Hammer of New York University Press has worked magic with my writing. It has been a delight to work with all four coauthors: Jeffrey S. Gurock, Annie Polland, Howard Rock, and Daniel Soyer. Danny earns a special thank-you for driving me around New York City to see murals and architecture. I also thank the anonymous readers for their helpful suggestions and advice. Numerous archivists, curators, librarians, collectors, and subscribers to the American Art listserv and the American Jewish History listserv offered valuable information. I appreciate all the living artists who granted me permission to reproduce their work.

Laura Holzman, Nina Liss-Schultz, and Shoshana Olidort were terrific research assistants, and Alexandra Maron was of great help with the illustrations and permissions. Sonja Assouline, Kate Breiger, and Amanda Koire were loving, responsible, and very fun babysitters to Alex and Emily, allowing me to work.

Friends, family, and colleagues have all generously given support, citations, personal stories and photographs, criticism, and beds on which to crash while in New York City. I thank Susanne Hunt for morning walks and for two years of hearing me go on about this book. She makes Claremont, California, home. David Brody finesses the perfect balance between his "amazings" to his "oy gevalts," and I love him for that. Tom Burke, Sarah Cash, Kate Fermoile, George Gorse and Susan Thalmann (both of Pomona College), Martha Grier, Carol Hamoy, Camara Dia Holloway, Russet Lederman, Dr. Erica Rosenfeld, Kerri Steinberg, Craig S. Wilder, and Karen Zukowski—I thank you all. And Carolyn Halpin-Healy is just golden in all regards.

My mom and dad, Joan and David Linden, put a subway map and a subway token in my hands at an early age with the mandate to go learn and love New York City. They are also the world's greatest grandparents. My husband, Peter Ross, offers an unlimited supply of love, humor, understanding, and appreciation; he also holds everything together when I am off to New York on research trips. As my twins, Alex and Emily Linden-Ross, are New York Jews by heritage rather than birth, I am proud that they recognize the Flatiron Building at a distance, love Junior's cheesecake, and hold on tight when the subway sways. I hope that they too will discover the magic of the City of Promises.

1. Ellen Smith, "Greetings from Faith: Early-Twentieth-Century American Jewish New Year Postcards," in David Morgan and Sally M. Promey, eds., *The Visual Culture of American Religions* (Berkeley: University of California Press, 2001), 243–247.

2. Hasia Diner, "A Century of Migration, 1820–1924," in Michael W. Grunberger, ed.,

From Haven to Home: 350 Years of Jewish Life in America (Washington, DC: Library of Congress, 2004), 71.

3. Castle Gardens, the distinctive rounded building in the horizon, was an immigrant processing center from August 1, 1855, until April 18, 1890.

4. Noel Ignatiev, *How the Irish Became White* (New York: Routledge, 1995).

5. Alfred Stieglitz, "How *The Steerage* Happened," in Dorothy Norman, ed., *Twice a Year: A Book of Literature, the Arts and Civil Liberties* 8–9 (1942): 127–131.

6. Ibid., 128.

7. John Higham, *Send These to Me: Immigrants in Urban America*, rev. ed. (Baltimore: Johns Hopkins University Press, 1984), 71–80; Marvin Trachtenberg, *The Statue of Liberty* (New York: Viking Penguin, 1986).

8. Howard Markel, "'The Eyes Have It': Trachoma, the Perception of Disease, the United States Public Health Service, and the American Jewish Immigration Experience, 1897–1924," *Bulletin of the History of Medicine* 74:3 (Fall 2000): 527–529.

9. Alexandra M. Lord, "Advice: An Object Lesson," *Chronicle of Higher Education*, October 1, 2007, http://wiredcampus.chronicle.com/article/An-Object-Lesson/46505 (accessed July 29, 2010).

10. Matthew Baigell, "Sweatshop Images: Jewish History and Memory," *Images* 2 (2009): 81.

11. Kathy Peiss, "The Coney Island Excursion," chap. 5 in *Cheap Amusements: Working Women and Leisure in Turn-of-the-Century New York* (Philadelphia: Temple University Press, 1986), 115–138.

12. Stephen Birmingham, *"Our Crowd": The Great Jewish Families of New York* (New York: Harper and Row, 1967), 132, 148–149.

13. Herbert D. Croly, "The Harmonie Club House," *Architectural Record* 19:4 (1906): 237–243.

14. David Nasaw, *Children of the City: At Work and at Play* (New York: Oxford University Press, 1985).

15. Rebecca Zurier, *Picturing the City: Urban Vision and the Ash Can School* (Berkeley: University of California Press, 2006), 221; Marianne Doezema, *George Bellows and Urban America* (New Haven: Yale University Press, 1992), 147.

16. Joseph Edgar Chamberlin, "An Excellent Academy Show," *New York Evening Mail*, March 14, 1908, quoted by Adam Greenhalgh in Sarah Cash, ed., *Corcoran Gallery of Art: American Paintings to 1945* (Washington, DC: Corcoran Gallery of Art, 2011), 194–195.

17. Jonathan D. Sarna, "American Judaism," in Grunberger, *From Haven to Home*, 142; "Dancing for Charity: The Ball of the Purim Association Was a Grand Success," *New York Times*, March 5, 1890.

18. I. S. Isaacs, "Meyer S. Isaacs," *Publications of the American Jewish Historical Society* 13 (1905): 146.

19. Joshua Brown, *Beyond the Lines: Pictorial Reporting, Everyday Life, and the Crisis of Gilded Age America* (Berkeley: University of California Press, 2006); Tyler Anbinder, *Five Points: The 19th-Century New York City Neighborhood That Invented Tap Dance, Stole Elections, and Became the World's Most Notorious Slum* (New York: Plume, 2002).

20. My interpretation of Riis's photograph draws from the scholarship and input of Riis expert Bonnie Yochelson. I appreciate her enormous generosity in sharing her knowledge of Riis and her research materials.

21. Bonnie Yochelson, *Jacob Riis* (New York: Phaidon, 2001), 118–119.

22. I want to thank decorative arts scholar Karen Zukowski for providing insights into the furniture displayed in the photographer's studio. John Tagg, *The Burden of Representation: Essays on Photographies and Histories* (Minneapolis: University of Minnesota Press, 1988), 37.

23. It is not clear which lodge in New York Levi belonged to, according to Thomas M. Savini, director of the Masonic Library, Grand Lodge, New York (email correspondence with author, September 21, 2010).

24. Alice M. Greenwald, "The Masonic Mizrahi and Lamp: Jewish Ritual Art as a Reflection of Cultural Assimilation," *Journal of Jewish Art* 10 (1984): 101.

25. Donna T. Haverty-Stacke, *America's Forgotten Holiday: May Day and Nationalism, 1867–1960* (New York: NYU Press, 2009), 85–88.

26. Maria Balinska, *The Bagel: The Surprising History of a Modest Bread* (New Haven: Yale University Press, 2008), 115–119. The Jewish bakers' union became famous for adding to their demands something for "which the Jewish labour movement was to become famous: that the bosses allow their workers to give one night's work to unemployed bakers" (ibid., 115).

27. "Big Change in a Big Store Which All Brooklyn Knows," *New York Times*, April 2, 1893; see also Andrew R. Heinze, *Adapting to Abundance: Jewish Immigrants, Mass Consumption, and the Search for American Identity* (New York: Columbia University Press, 1990).

28. See Jenna Weissman Joselit, *A Perfect Fit: Clothes, Character, and the Promise of America* (New York: Holt, 2001).

29. Robert Hendrickson, *The Grand Emporiums: The Illustrated History of America's Great Department Stores* (New York: Stein and Day, 1979), 33.

30. Jennifer A. Greenhill, "Charles Dana Gibson, George du Maurier and the Site of Whiteness in Illustration c. 1900," *Art History* 34 (September 2011): 26; Carolyn Kitch, *The Girl on the Magazine Cover: The Origins of Visual Stereotypes in Mass Media* (Chapel Hill: University of North Carolina Press, 2001), 39–40.

31. A fascinating book on the history of wife desertion is Anna R. Igra, *Wives without Husbands: Marriage, Desertion, and Welfare in New York City, 1900–1935* (Chapel Hill: University of North Carolina Press, 2007), 3–4.

32. Isaac Metzker, introduction to Isaac Metzker, ed., *A Bintel Brief: Sixty Years of Letters from the Lower East Side to the Jewish Daily Forward* (New York: Schocken Books, 1971), 10–15.

33. Ellen Wiley Todd, "Remembering the Unknowns: The Longman Memorial and the 1911 Triangle Shirtwaist Fire," *American Art* 23:3 (Fall 2009): 65.

34. Aviva Ben-Ur, *Sephardic Jews in America: A Diasporic History* (New York: NYU Press, 2009), 111.

35. Marc D. Angel, *La America: The Sephardic Experience in the United States* (Phila-

delphia: Jewish Publication Society of America, 1982). *La America* began publication in 1910 as a national weekly. It continued to be published intermittently until 1925.

36. Helene Schwartz Kenvin, *This Land of Liberty: A History of America's Jews* (New York: Behrman House, 1986), 118–121.

37. Kate Sampsell-Williams, *Lewis Hine: A Social Critic* (Jackson: University of Mississippi Press, 2009), situates Hine within Pragmatism and intellectual history.

38. Quoted in Beth Venn and Adam M. Weinberg, *Frame of Reference: Looking in American Art, 1900–1950* (New York: Whitney Museum of American Art, 1999), 64.

39. Ericka Lee, "The Chinese Exclusion Example," *Journal of American Ethnic History* 21 (Spring 2002): 36–62.

40. Judith Rosenbaum, " 'The Call to Action': Margaret Sanger, the Brownsville Jewish Women, and Political Activism," in Marion A. Kaplan and Deborah Dash Moore, eds., *Gender and Jewish History*, 251–266 (Bloomington: Indiana University Press, 2010); Cathy Moran Hajo, *Birth Control on Main Street: Organizing Clinics in the United States* (Urbana: University of Illinois Press, 2010).

41. "Leonard, Benny," *Jews in Sports Online*, http://www.jewsinsports.org/profile.asp ?sport=boxing&ID=8 (accessed September 27, 2010); see also Stephen H. Norwood, " 'American Jewish Muscle': Forging a New Masculinity in the Streets and in the Ring, 1890–1940," *Modern Judaism* 29:2 (May 2009): 167–193.

42. "Leonard, Benny."

BIBLIOGRAPHY

■ PERIODICALS

American Hebrew
American Israelite
Asmonean
Atlantic Monthly
Century Magazine
Evening World
Forverts (Jewish Daily Forward)
Jewish Messenger
Morgen zhurnal
New York Daily Tribune
New York Herald
New York Times
Occident
Outlook
Shabes zhurnal
Yidishe gazeten
Yidishe tageblat

■ ARCHIVAL COLLECTIONS

American Jewish Archives
    Livia Garfinkel, "Reflections on Other Times, New York, 1881–1931," Brooklyn, 1981,
        Small Collections 5873
American Jewish Historical Society
    Association for Free Distribution of Matsot to the Poor, I-106
Central Synagogue Archives
    Women's Organizations, RG 4
Lower East Side Tenement Museum Archives
Museum at Eldridge Street Collection
New York Public Library
    American Jewish Committee Oral Histories
Tamiment Library, New York University
    Lower East Side Oral History Project, NS 33-64
United States Census, 1860
YIVO Institute for Jewish Research
    American Jewish Autobiographies, RG 102
    Records of the Educational Alliance, RG 312

■ BOOKS, ARTICLES, AND WEBSITES

Alexander, Michael. *Jazz Age Jews*. Princeton: Princeton University Press, 2001.

Allen, Oliver. *The Tiger: The Rise and Fall of Tammany Hall*. Reading, MA: Addison-Wesley, 1993.

American Jewish Archives, "An Inventory to the Stephen S. Wise Collection." http://www.americanjewisharchives.org/aja/FindingAids/SWise.htm#bio (accessed August 2, 2010).

American Jewish Historical Society. "Guide to the Papers of Philip Cowen." http://findingaids.cjh.org/?pID=109145 (accessed December 28, 2011).

American National Biography. http://www.anb.org.avoserv.library.fordham.edu (accessed July 5, 2011).

Anbinder, Tyler. *Five Points: The 19th-Century New York City Neighborhood That Invented Tap Dance, Stole Elections, and Became the World's Most Notorious Slum*. New York: Free Press, 2001.

Antler, Joyce. *The Journey Home: Jewish Women and the American Century*. New York: Free Press, 1997.

Appel, John J. "Jews in American Caricature: 1820–1914." In Jeffrey Gurock, ed., *American Jewish History*, vol. 6, part 1, *Anti-Semitism in America*. New York: Routledge, 1998.

Avrich, Paul. *The Modern School Movement: Anarchism and Education in the United States*. Princeton: Princeton University Press, 1980.

Baigell, Matthew. "From Hester Street to Fifty-Seventh Street: Jewish-American Artists in New York." In Norman L. Kleeblatt and Susan Chevlowe, eds., *Painting a Place in America: Jewish Artists in New York, 1900–1945*. New York: Jewish Museum; Bloomington: Indiana University Press, 1991.

Barkai, Avraham. *Branching Out: German Jewish Immigration to the United States, 1820–1924*. New York: Holmes and Meier, 1994.

Bellow, Adam. *The Educational Alliance: A Centennial Celebration*. New York: Educational Alliance, 1990.

Benjamin, Joseph. "The Comforts and Discomforts of East Side Tenements." In *Report of the Year's Work*. New York: University Settlement Society, 1897.

Ben-Ur, Aviva. "The Ladino (Judeo-Spanish) Press in the United States, 1910–1948." In Werner Sollors, ed., *Multilingual America: Transnationalism, Ethnicity, and the Languages of American Literature*. New York: NYU Press, 1998.

Bernheimer, Charles S. "The Jewish Immigrant as an Industrial Worker." *Annals of the American Academy of Political and Social Science* 33:2 (March 1909): 175–182.

Billings, John S. *Vital Statistics of the Jews in the United States*. 11th Census, Bulletin No. 19. Washington DC: U.S. Census Bureau, 1890.

Birnbaum, Pierre, and Ira Katznelson, eds. *Paths of Emancipation: Jews, States, and Citizenship*. Princeton: Princeton University Press, 1995.

Blackmar, Elizabeth. "The Congregation and the City." In Arthur Goren and Elizabeth Blackmar, *Congregating and Consecrating at Central Synagogue*. New York: Central Synagogue, 2003.

Bodnar, John. *The Transplanted: A History of Immigrants in Urban America*. Bloomington: University of Indiana Press, 1986.

Bogen, Hyman. *The Luckiest Orphans: A History of the Hebrew Orphan Asylum of New York*. Urbana: University of Illinois Press, 1992.

Braun, Sarah Alisa. "Jews, Writing, and the Dynamics of Literary Affiliation, 1880–1940." Ph.D. diss., University of Michigan, 2007.

Brown, Michael. *The Israeli-American Connection: Its Roots in the Yishuv, 1914–1945*. Detroit: Wayne State University Press, 1996.

Brown, Milton Wolf. *American Painting, from the Armory Show to the Depression*. Princeton: Princeton University Press, 1955.

Brumberg, Stephan F. *Going to America, Going to School: The Jewish Immigrant Public School Encounter in Turn-of-the-Century New York City*. New York: Praeger, 1986.

Burrows, Edwin G., and Mike Wallace. *Gotham: A History of New York City to 1898*. New York: Oxford University Press, 1999.

Cahan, Abraham. *Bleter fun mayn lebn*. 5 vols. New York: Forward Association, 1926–1931.

Callow, Alexander. *The Tweed Ring*. New York: Oxford University Press, 1965.

Cannato, Vincent. *American Passage: The History of Ellis Island*. New York: HarperCollins, 2009.

Caratzas, Michael D. "Research Report." Landmarks Preservation Commission, October 13, 2009, Designation List 419, LP 2363.

Carvajal, Christa. "German-American Theatre." In Maxine Schwartz Seller, ed., *Ethnic Theatre in the United States*. Westport, CT: Greenwood, 1983.

Chotzinoff, Samuel. "Life on Stanton Street." In Harold U. Ribalow, ed., *Autobiographies of American Jews*. Philadelphia: Jewish Publication Society, 1968.

———. *A Lost Paradise: Early Reminiscences*. 1955. Reprint, New York: Arno, 1975.

Cohen, Jocelyn, and Daniel Soyer, eds. *My Future Is in America: Autobiographies of Eastern European Jewish Immigrants*. New York: NYU Press, 2006.

Cohen, Morris Raphael. *A Dreamer's Journey: The Autobiography of Morris Raphael Cohen*. Glencoe, IL: Free Press, 1949.

Cohen, Naomi. "American Jews and the Swiss Treaty: A Case Study in the Indivisibility of Anti-Semitism." In Nathaniel Stampfer, ed., *The Solomon Goldman Lectures: Perspectives in Jewish Learning*, vol. 3. Chicago: Spertus College of Judaica Press, 1982.

———. *Encounter with Emancipation: The German Jews in the United States, 1830–1914*. Philadelphia: Jewish Publication Society, 1984.

———. *Jacob Schiff: A Study in American Jewish Leadership*. Hanover, NH: University Press of New England / Brandeis University Press, 1999.

———. *Not Free to Desist: The American Jewish Committee, 1906–1966*. Philadelphia: Jewish Publication Society, 1972.

———. "The Reaction of Reform Judaism in America to Political Zionism (1897–1922)." In Jeffrey Gurock, ed., *American Zionism: Mission and Politics*. New York: Routledge, 1998.

Cohen, Rose. *Out of the Shadow*. Ithaca: Cornell University Press, 1995.

Cone, John Frederick. *Oscar Hammerstein's Manhattan Opera Company*. Norman: University of Oklahoma Press, 1966.

Cowen, Philip. *Memories of an American Jew*. New York: International Press, 1932.

Crohn, Burrill B. "The Centennial Anniversary of the Mount Sinai Hospital (1852–1952)." *American Jewish Historical Society Publications* 42 (September 1952–June 1953): 113–130.

Daniels, Roger. *Guarding the Golden Door: American Immigration Policy and Immigrants since 1882*. New York: Hill and Wang, 2004.

Day, Jared. *Urban Castles: Tenement Housing and Landlord Activism in New York City, 1890–1943*. New York: Columbia University Press, 1999.

Dillon, Phyllis, and Andrew Godley. "The Evolution of the Jewish Garment Industry, 1840–1940." In Rebecca Kobrin, ed., *Chosen Capital: The Jewish Encounter with American Capitalism*. New Brunswick: Rutgers University Press, 2012.

Diner, Hasia. "Buying and Selling 'Jewish': The Historical Impact of Commerce on Jewish Communal Life." In Jack Wertheimer, ed., *Imagining the American Jewish Community*. Hanover, NH: University Press of New England / Brandeis University Press, 2007.

———. *The Jews of the United States, 1654–2000*. Berkeley: University of California Press, 2004.

———. *A Time for Gathering: The Second Migration, 1820–1880*. Baltimore: Johns Hopkins University Press, 1992.

Diner, Hasia, and Beryl Lieff Benderly. *Her Works Praise Her: A History of Jewish Women in America from Colonial Times to the Present*. New York: Basic Books, 2002.

Dinnerstein, Leonard. *Anti-Semitism in America*. New York: Oxford University Press, 1994.

———. "The Funeral of Rabbi Jacob Joseph." In David A. Gerber, ed., *Anti-Semitism in American History*. Urbana: University of Illinois Press, 1986.

Dolan, Jay P. *The Immigrant Church: New York's Irish and German Catholics, 1815–1865*. Baltimore: Johns Hopkins University Press, 1975.

Dolkart, Andrew. *Biography of a Tenement House in New York City: An Architectural History of 97 Orchard Street*. Santa Fe, NM: Center for American Places, 2006.

———. *Central Synagogue in Its Changing Neighborhood*. New York: Central Synagogue, 2001.

Domnitz, Aaron. "Why I Left My Old Home and What I Have Accomplished in America." In Jocelyn Cohen and Daniel Soyer, *My Future Is in America: Autobiographies of Eastern European Jewish Immigrants*. New York: NYU Press, 2006.

Doroshkin, Milton. *Yiddish in America: Social and Cultural Foundations*. Rutherford, NJ: Fairleigh Dickinson University Press, 1969.

Douglas, Ann. *Terrible Honesty: Mongrel Manhattan in the 1920s*. New York: Farrar, Straus and Giroux, 1995.

Drachman, Bernard. *The Unfailing Light: Memoirs of an American Rabbi*. New York: Rabbinical Council of America, 1948.

Dubofsky, Melvyn. "Success and Failure of Socialism in New York City, 1900–1918: A Case Study." *Labor History* 9:3 (Autumn 1968): 361–375.

Eisenstein, Judah. "The History of the First Russian-American Jewish Congregation: The Beth Hamedrash Hagadol." *Publications of the American Jewish Historical Society* 9 (1901): 63–74.

Eisenstein, Louis, and Elliot Rosenberg. *A Stripe of Tammany's Tiger*. New York: Robert Speller and Sons, 1966.

Elzas, Barnett. "Memoir of Alexander Kohut." In Alexander Kohut, *The Ethics of the Fathers*. New York: Publishers Printing Company, 1920.

Engelman, Uriah Zvi. "Jewish Statistics in the U.S. Census of Religious Bodies (1850–1936)." *Jewish Social Studies* 9:2 (April 1947): 127–174.

Enstad, Nan. *Ladies of Labor, Girls of Adventure: Working Women, Popular Culture, and Labor Politics at the Turn of the Twentieth Century*. New York: Columbia University Press, 1999.

Epstein, Melech. *Jewish Labor in the USA*, vol. 1, *1882–1914*. 1950. Reprint, New York: Ktav, 1969.

———. *Profiles of Eleven: Profiles of Eleven Men Who Guided the Destiny of an Immigrant Society and Stimulated Social Consciousness among the American People*. Detroit: Wayne State University Press, 1965.

Erie, Steven. *Rainbow's End: Irish-Americans and the Dilemmas of Urban Machine Politics, 1840–1985*. Berkeley: University of California Press, 1988.

Ernst, Robert. *Immigrant Life in New York City, 1825–1863*. 1949. Reprint, Syracuse: Syracuse University Press, 1994.

Faber, Eli. *A Time for Planting: The First Migration, 1654–1820*. The Jewish People in America 1. Baltimore: Johns Hopkins University Press, 1992.

Feld, Marjorie. *Lillian Wald: A Biography*. Chapel Hill: University of North Carolina Press, 2008.

Feldman, Egal. "Jews in the Early Growth of New York City's Men's Clothing Trade." *American Jewish Archives* 12:1 (April 1960): 3–14.

Foner, Nancy. *From Ellis Island to JFK: New York's Two Great Waves of Immigration*. New Haven: Yale University Press, 2000.

Forman, Ira. "The Politics of Minority Consciousness: The Historical Voting Behavior of American Jews." In L. Sandy Maisel, ed., *Jews in American Politics*. Lanham, MD: Rowman and Littlefield, 2001.

Foster, Solomon. *The Workingman and the Synagogue*. Newark, NJ, 1910.

Frankel, Jonathan. *The Damascus Affair: "Ritual Murder," Politics, and the Jews in 1840*. New York: Cambridge University Press, 1997.

———. *Prophecy and Politics: Socialism, Nationalism, and the Russian Jews, 1862–1917*. New York: Cambridge University Press, 1981.

Friedenberg, Albert. "American Jewish Journalism to the Close of the Civil War." *Publications of the American Jewish Historical Society* 26 (1918): 270–273.

Friedman, Reena Sigman. " 'Send Me My Husband Who Is in New York City': Husband Desertion in the American Jewish Immigrant Community, 1900–1926." *Jewish Social Studies* 44:1 (Winter 1982): 1–18.

Friesel, Evyatar. "Brandeis' Role in American Zionism Historically Reconsidered." In Jeffrey Gurock, ed., *American Zionism: Mission and Politics*. New York: Routledge, 1998.

Fuchs, Lawrence H. *Political Behavior of American Jews*. Glencoe, IL: Free Press, 1956.

Gabler, Neal. *An Empire of Their Own: How the Jews Invented Hollywood.* New York: Crown, 1988.

Garland, Libby, "Not-Quite-Closed Gates: Jewish Alien Smuggling in the Post-Quota Years." *American Jewish History* 94:3 (September 2008): 197–224.

Gay, Ruth. *Unfinished People: Eastern European Jews Encounter America.* New York: Norton, 1996.

Gerstle, Gary. *American Crucible: Race and Nation in the Twentieth Century.* Princeton: Princeton University Press, 2001.

Gilfoyle, Timothy. *City of Eros: New York City, Prostitution, and the Commercialization of Sex, 1790–1920.* New York: Norton, 1992.

Gill, Jonathan. *Harlem: The Four Hundred Year History from Dutch Village to Capital of Black America.* New York: Grove, 2011.

Glanz, Rudolf. *Studies in Judaica Americana.* New York: Ktav, 1970.

Glenn, Susan. *Daughters of the Shtetl: Life and Labor in the Immigrant Generation.* Ithaca: Cornell University Press, 1990.

Glogower, Rod. "The Impact of the American Experience on Responsa Literature." *American Jewish History* 69:2 (December 1979): 257–269.

Goldberg, Itche, and Max Rosenfeld, eds. *Morris Rosenfeld: Selections from His Poetry and Prose.* New York: Yidisher kultur farband, 1964.

Golden, Harry. "East Side Memoir, 1910s." In Harold U. Ribalow, ed., *Autobiographies of American Jews.* Philadelphia: Jewish Publication Society, 1968.

Goldman, Karla. *Beyond the Synagogue Gallery: Finding a Place for Women in American Judaism.* Cambridge: Harvard University Press, 2000.

Goldstein, H. S. *Forty Years of Struggle for a Principle.* New York: Bloch, 1928.

Goldstein, Minnie. "Success or Failure?" In Jocelyn Cohen and Daniel Soyer, *My Future Is in America: Autobiographies of Eastern European Jewish Immigrants.* New York: NYU Press, 2006.

Goodman, Philip. "The Purim Association of the City of New York (1862–1902)." *American Jewish Historical Society Publications* 40 (September 1950–June 1951): 135–172.

Goren, Arthur, ed. *Dissenter in Zion: From the Writings of Judah L. Magnes.* Cambridge: Harvard University Press, 1982.

——. "The Jewish Press." In Sally Miller, ed., *The Ethnic Press in the United States: A Historical Analysis and Handbook.* Westport, CT: Greenwood, 1987.

——. *New York Jews and the Quest for Community: The Kehillah Experiment, 1908–1922.* New York: Columbia University Press, 1970.

——. *The Politics and Public Culture of American Jews.* Bloomington: Indiana University Press, 1999.

——. "Public Ceremonies Defining Central Synagogue." In Arthur Goren and Elizabeth Blackmar, *Congregating and Consecrating at Central Synagogue.* New York: Central Synagogue, 2003.

Goren, Arthur, and Elizabeth Blackmar. *Congregating and Consecrating at Central Synagogue.* New York: Central Synagogue, 2003.

Grant, Madison. *The Passing of the Great Race.* New York: Scribner, 1916.

Greef, Robert. *Public Lectures in New York, 1851–1878: A Cultural Index of the Times.* Chicago: University of Chicago, 1945.

Green, Nancy, ed., *Jewish Workers in the Modern Diaspora.* Berkeley: University of California Press, 1998.

Greenwald, Richard. *The Triangle Fire, the Protocol of Peace, and Industrial Democracy in Progressive Era New York.* Philadelphia: Temple University Press, 2005.

Grinstein, Hyman. *The Rise of the Jewish Community of New York, 1654–1860.* Philadelphia: Jewish Publication Society, 1945.

Grusd, Edward. *B'nai B'rith: The Story of a Covenant.* New York: Appleton-Century, 1966.

Gurock, Jeffrey. *American Jewish Orthodoxy in Historical Perspective.* Hoboken, NJ: Ktav, 1996.

———. *Men and Women of the Yeshiva: Higher Education, Orthodoxy, and American Judaism.* New York: Columbia University Press, 1988.

———. *Orthodox Jews in America.* Bloomington: Indiana University Press, 2009.

———. *When Harlem Was Jewish, 1879–1930.* New York: Columbia University Press, 1979.

Hammack, David. *Power and Society: Greater New York at the Turn of the Century.* 1982. Reprint, New York: Columbia University Press, 1987.

Hapgood, Hutchins. *The Spirit of the Ghetto.* 1902. Reprint, Cambridge: Harvard University Press, 1967.

Harmonie Club of the City of New York. *One Hundred Years, 1852–1952: The Harmonie Club.* New York: Harmonie Club, 1952.

Harris, Alice Kessler. Introduction to *Bread Givers*, by Anzia Yezierska. New York: Persea Books, 1975.

Healy, Ann. "Tsarist Anti-Semitism and Russian-American Relations." *Slavic Review* 42:3 (Autumn 1983): 408–425.

Heinze, Andrew. *Adapting to Abundance: Jewish Immigrants, Mass Consumption, and the Search for American Identity.* New York: Columbia University Press, 1990.

———. "Jewish Street Merchants and Mass Consumption in New York City, 1880–1914." *American Jewish Archives* 41:2 (Fall–Winter 1989): 199–214.

Henderson, Thomas. *Tammany Hall and the New Immigrants: The Progressive Years.* New York: Arno, 1976.

Hendricks, Burton J. "The Jewish Invasion of America." *McClure's Magazine*, March 12, 1912, 125–165.

Herman, Felicia. "From Priestess to Hostess: Sisterhoods of Personal Service in New York City, 1887–1936." In Pamela Nadell and Jonathan Sarna, eds., *Women and American Judaism: Historical Perspectives.* Hanover, NH: University Press of New England / Brandeis University Press, 2001.

Hertz, J. S. *50 yor arbeter-ring in yidishn lebn.* New York: National Executive Committee of the Workmen's Circle, 1950.

Higham, John. *Send These to Me: Jews and Other Immigrants in Urban America.* New York: Atheneum, 1975.

———. *Strangers in the Land: Patterns of American Nativism, 1860–1925.* 1955. Reprint, New York: Atheneum, 1981.

Hirsch, Foster. *The Boys from Syracuse: The Shuberts' Theatrical Empire*. 1998. Reprint, New York: Cooper Square Press, 2000.

Hobbs, Charles W. *Illustrated New York City and Surroundings*. New York: Charles W. Hobbs, 1889.

Horowitz, Joseph. *Classical Music in America: A History of Its Rise and Fall*. New York: Norton, 2005.

Howe, Irving. *World of Our Fathers*. New York: Harcourt Brace Jovanovich, 1976.

Howe, Irving, and Eliezer Greenberg, eds. *Voices from the Yiddish: Essays, Memoirs, Diaries*. 1972. Reprint, New York: Schocken, 1975.

Howe, Irving, and Kenneth Libo, eds. *How We Lived: A Documentary History of Immigrant Jews in America, 1880–1930*. New York: Richard Marek, 1979.

Howe, Irving, Ruth Wisse, and Khone Shmeruk, eds. *The Penguin Book of Modern Yiddish Verse*. New York: Viking, 1987.

Hyman, Paula. "Immigrant Women and Consumer Protest: The New York City Kosher Meat Boycott of 1902." *American Jewish History* 70:1 (September 1980): 91–105

Hyman, Paula, and Deborah Dash Moore. *Jewish Women in America: An Historical Encyclopedia*. 2 vols. New York: Routledge, 1997.

Iceland, Reuben. "At Goodman and Levine's." In Irving Howe and Eliezer Greenberg, eds., *Voices from the Yiddish: Essays, Memoirs, Diaries*. 1972. Reprint, New York: Schocken, 1975.

Igra, Anna R. *Wives without Husbands: Marriage, Desertion, and Welfare in New York, 1900–1935*. Chapel Hill: University of North Carolina Press, 2007.

Jackson, Kenneth, ed. *Encyclopedia of New York City*. New Haven: Yale University Press, 1995.

James, Edmund, Oscar Flynn, J. Paulding, Mrs. Simon Patton, and Walter Scott Andrews. *The Immigrant Jew in America*. New York: B. Buck, 1906.

Jasen, David. *Tin Pan Alley: The Golden Age of American Song*. New York: Routledge, 2003.

Jewish Social Service Association. *Fifty Years of Social Service: The History of the United Hebrew Charities of the City of New York, Now the Jewish Social Service Association, Inc. New York City*. New York: C. S. Nathan, 1926.

Jick, Leon. "The Reform Synagogue." In Jack Wertheimer, ed., *The American Synagogue: A Sanctuary Transformed*. Hanover, NH: University Press of New England / Brandeis University Press, 1987.

Joselit, Jenna Weissman. "Fun and Games: The American Jewish Social Club." In Marc Lee Raphael, ed., *The Columbia History of Jews and Judaism in America*. New York: Columbia University Press, 2008.

———. *Our Gang: Jewish Crime and the New York Jewish Community*. Bloomington: Indiana University Press, 1983.

———. "A Set Table: Jewish Domestic Culture in the New World, 1880–1950." In Susan Braunstein and Jenna Weissman Joselit, eds., *Getting Comfortable in New York: The American Jewish Home, 1880–1950*. New York: Jewish Museum, 1990.

———. "The Special Sphere of the Middle-Class American Jewish Woman: The Synagogue

Sisterhood, 1890–1940." In Jack Wertheimer, ed., *The American Synagogue: A Sanctuary Transformed*. Hanover, NH: University Press of New England / Brandeis University Press, 1987.

——. *The Wonders of America: Reinventing Jewish Culture, 1880–1950*. New York: Hill and Wang, 1994.

Joseph, Samuel. *Jewish Immigration to the United States from 1881 to 1910*. New York: Columbia University, 1914.

Jou, Chin. "Contesting Nativism: The New York Congressional Delegation's Case against the Immigration Act of 1924." *Federal History Online* 3 (January 2011): 66–79. http://shfg.org/shfg/wp-content/uploads/2010/07/5%E2%80%93jou_Layout-11-final-2.pdf (accessed May 23, 2011).

Kalmar, Ivan Davidson. "Moorish Style: Orientalism, the Jews and Synagogue Architecture." *Jewish Social Studies* 7:3 (Spring–Summer 2001): 68–100.

Karp, Abraham. *Golden Door to America: The Jewish Immigrant Experience*. New York: Viking, 1973.

——. "New York Chooses a Chief Rabbi." *Publications of the American Jewish Historical Society* 44 (1955): 129–198.

Karp, Jonathan. "Of Maestros and Minstrels: American Jewish Composers between Black Vernacular and European Art Music." In Barbara Kirshenblatt-Gimblett and Jonathan Karp, eds., *The Art of Being Jewish in Modern Times*, 57–77, Philadelphia: University of Pennsylvania Press, 2008.

Katznelson, Ira. "On the Margins of Liberalism." In Pierre Birnbaum and Ira Katznelson, eds., *Paths of Emancipation: Jews, States, and Citizenship*. Princeton: Princeton University Press, 1995.

Kaufman, Andrew. *Cardozo*. Cambridge: Harvard University Press, 1998.

Kaufman, David. *A Shul with a Pool: The "Synagogue Center" in American Jewish History*. Hanover, NH: University Press of New England / Brandeis University Press, 1999.

Kazin, Alfred. *A Walker in the City*. 1946. Reprint, San Diego: Harcourt Brace, 1979.

Kehillah (Jewish Community) of New York City. *Jewish Communal Register of New York City, 1917–1918*. New York: Kehillah (Jewish Community) of New York City, 1918.

Kennedy, J. T. "Report of the Eighth Sanitary Inspection District." In Citizen's Association, *Report of the Council of Hygiene and Public Health of the Citizen's Association of New York of the Sanitary Condition of the City*. New York: D. Appleton, 1865.

Kertzer, David. *The Kidnapping of Edgardo Mortara*. New York: Vintage Books, 1998.

Kirshenblatt-Gimblett, Barbara. "Kitchen Judaism." In Susan Braunstein and Jenna Weissman Joselit, eds., *Getting Comfortable in New York: The American Jewish Home, 1880–1950*. New York: Jewish Museum, 1990.

Klagsbrun, Francis. Foreword to *Emma Lazarus in Her World: Life and Letters*, by Bette Roth Young. Philadelphia: Jewish Publication Society, 1995.

Kleeblatt, Norman, and Susan Chevlowe. *Painting a Place in America: Jewish Artists in New York, 1900–1945*. Exhibition catalogue. New York: Jewish Museum, 1991.

Knobel, Dale. "To Be American: Ethnicity, Fraternity and the Improved Order of Red Men." *Journal of American Ethnic History* 4:1 (Fall 1984): 62–87.

Koegel, John. *Music in German Immigrant Theater in New York City, 1840–1940*. Rochester: University of Rochester Press, 2009.

Kohut, Rebekah. *My Portion*. New York: T. Seltzer, 1925.

Kosak, Hadassa. *Cultures of Opposition: Jewish Immigrant Workers, New York City, 1881–1905*. Albany: SUNY Press, 2000.

Kransdorf, Martha. "Julia Richman's Years in the New York City Public Schools, 1872–1912." Ph.D. diss., University of Michigan, 1979.

Kraut, Alan M. "The Butcher, the Baker, the Pushcart Peddler." *Journal of American Culture* 6:4 (Winter 1983): 71–83.

Kraut, Alan M., and Deborah A. Kraut. *Covenant of Care: Newark Beth Israel and the Jewish Hospital in America*. New Brunswick: Rutgers University Press, 2007.

Krinsky, Carol. *Synagogues of Europe*. Cambridge: MIT Press, 1985.

Kusnetz, Minnie. "I Haven't Lost Anything by Coming to America." In Jocelyn Cohen and Daniel Soyer, eds., *My Future Is in America: East European Jewish Autobiographies of Eastern European Jewish Immigrants*. New York: NYU Press, 2006.

Kuznets, Simon. "Immigration of Russian Jews to the United States: Background and Structure." *Perspectives in American History* 9 (1975): 35–124.

Landesman, Alter. *Brownsville: The Birth, Development and Passing of a Jewish Community in New York*. New York: Bloch, 1971.

Lederhendler, Eli. *Jewish Immigrants and American Capitalism, 1880–1920: From Caste to Class*. Cambridge: Cambridge University Press, 2009.

Leksikon fun der nayer yiddisher literature. 8 vols. New York: Congress for Jewish Culture, 1956–1981.

Lerner, Elinor. "Jewish Involvement in the New York City Woman Suffrage Movement." *American Jewish History* 70:4 (June 1981): 442–461.

Leuchs, Fritz. *The Early German Theatre in New York, 1840–1872*. 1928. Reprint, New York: AMS Press, 1966.

Levitan, Tina. *Islands of Compassion: A History of the Jewish Hospitals of New York*. New York: Twayne, 1964.

Leyb, Mani. "Ot azoy, azoy, azoy." In Dovid Kazanski, ed., *Zishe Landoy: Zamlbukh aroysgegebn fun khaveyrim*. New York: Farlag Inzl, 1938.

Libo, Kenneth. "A History of Jewish Journalism in America." In National Museum of American Jewish History, *A People in Print: Jewish Journalism in America*. Philadelphia: National Museum of American Jewish History, 1987.

Lipsky, Louis. *Memoirs in Profile*. Philadelphia: Jewish Publication Society, 1975.

Lowenstein, Steven. "The 1840s and the Creation of the German-Jewish Religious Reform Movement." In Werner Mosse, ed., *Revolution and Evolution: 1848 in German-Jewish History*. Tübingen: Mohr, 1981.

Luska, Sidney (Henry Harland). *The Yoke of the Thorah*. New York: Cassell, 1887.

Marcus, Jacob Rader. *United States Jewry, 1776–1985*. 4 vols. Detroit: Wayne State University Press, 1989–1993.

Markens, Isaac. *Hebrews in America*. New York: Isaac Markens, 1888.

Marovitz, Sanford. *Abraham Cahan*. New York: Twayne, 1996.

May, Lary. *Screening Out the Past: The Birth of Mass Culture and the Motion Picture Industry*. New York: Oxford University Press, 1980.

McBride, Harriet Waine. "Fraternal Regalia in America, 1865–1918: Dressing the Lodges; Clothing and the Brotherhood." Ph.D. diss., Department of History, Ohio State University, 2000.

McCrossen, Alexis. *Holy Day, Holiday: The American Sunday*. Ithaca: Cornell University Press, 2000.

McCune, Mary. *"The Whole Wide World without Limits": International Relief, Gender Politics, and American Jewish Women, 1893–1930*. Detroit: Wayne State University Press, 2005.

Mencken, H. L. *The American Language: An Inquiry into the Development of English in the United States*. 4th ed. 1936. Reprint, New York: Knopf, 1962; supplements I (1945; 1962) and II (1948; 1962).

Metzger, Isaac, ed. *A Bintel Brief: Sixty Years of Letters from the Lower East Side to the* Jewish Daily Forward. New York: Ballantine Books, 1971.

Meyer, Michael. *Response to Modernity: A History of the Reform Movement in Judaism*. New York: Oxford University Press, 1988.

Michels, Tony. "Cultural Crossings: Immigrant Jews, Yiddish, and the New York Intellectual Scene." Unpublished paper in authors' possession.

———. *A Fire in Their Hearts: Yiddish Socialists in New York*. Cambridge: Harvard University Press, 2005.

———. " 'Speaking to Moyshe': The Early Socialist Yiddish Press and Its Readers." *Jewish History* 14:1 (2000): 51–82.

Mintz, Alan. "Hebrew Literature in America." In Michael Kramer and Hanna Wirth-Nesher, eds., *The Cambridge Companion to Jewish American Literature*. New York: Cambridge University Press, 2003.

———. "A Sanctuary in the Wilderness: The Beginnings of the Hebrew Movement in America in *Hatoren*." In Alan Mintz, ed., *Hebrew in America: Perspectives and Prospects*. Detroit: Wayne State University Press, 1993.

Monoson, S. Sara. "The Lady and the Tiger: Women's Electoral Activism in New York City before Suffrage." *Journal of Women's History* 2:2 (Fall 1990): 100–134.

Moore, Deborah Dash. *At Home in America: Second Generation New York Jews*. New York: Columbia University Press, 1981.

———. *B'nai B'rith and the Challenge of Ethnic Leadership*. Albany: SUNY Press, 1981.

———. "From Kehillah to Federation: The Communal Functions of Federated Philanthropy in New York City, 1917–1933." *American Jewish History* 68:2 (December 1978): 131–147.

———. "A New American Judaism." In William M. Brinner and Moses Rischin, eds., *Like All Nations? The Life and Legacy of Judah L. Magnes*. Albany: SUNY Press, 1987.

———. "On the Fringes of the City: Jewish Neighborhoods in Three Boroughs." In David Ward and Olivier Zunz, eds., *The Landscape of Modernity: New York City, 1900–1940*. New York: Russell Sage Foundation, 1992.

Myers, Gustavus. *The History of Tammany Hall*. New York: G. Myers, 1901.

Nadel, Stanley. "Jewish Race and German Soul in Nineteenth Century America." *American Jewish History* 77:1 (September 1987): 6–26.

———. *Little Germany: Ethnicity, Religion, and Class in New York City, 1845–80*. Urbana: University of Illinois Press, 1990.

Nasaw, David. *Going Out: The Rise and Fall of Public Amusements*. New York: Basic Books, 1993.

Nathan, Maud. *The Story of an Epoch-Making Movement*. Garden City, NY: Doubleday, Page, 1926.

O'Donnell, Edward. "Hibernians versus Hebrews? A New Look at the 1902 Jacob Joseph Funeral Riot." *Journal of the Gilded Age and Progressive Era* 6:2 (April 2007): 209–225.

Orleck, Annelise. *Common Sense and a Little Fire: Women and Working-Class Politics in the United States, 1900–1965*. Chapel Hill: University of North Carolina Press, 1995.

Panitz, Esther. "In Defense of the Jewish Immigrant (1891–1924)." *American Jewish Historical Quarterly* 55 (1965): 57–98.

Peiss, Kathy. *Cheap Amusements: Working Women and Leisure in Turn-of-the-Century New York*. Philadelphia: Temple University Press, 1986.

Penkower, Monty Noam. "The Kishinev Pogrom: A Turning Point in Jewish History." *Modern Judaism* 24:3 (October 2004): 187–225.

Perry, Elizabeth Israels. *Belle Moskowitz: Feminine Politics and the Exercise of Power in the Age of Al Smith*. 1987. Reprint, Boston: Northeastern University Press, 1992.

Polland, Annie. *Landmark of the Spirit: The Eldridge Street Synagogue*. New Haven: Yale University Press, 2009.

———. "May a Free Thinker Help a Pious Man? The Shared World of the 'Religious' and the 'Secular' among Eastern European Jewish Immigrants to America." *American Jewish History* 93:4 (December 2007): 375–407.

Pope, Jesse. *The Clothing Industry in New York*. Columbia: University of Missouri, 1905.

Pritchet, Wendell. *Brownsville, Brooklyn: Blacks, Jews, and the Changing Face of the Ghetto*. Chicago: University of Chicago Press, 2002.

Raider, Mark A. *The Emergence of American Zionism*. New York: NYU Press, 1998.

Ravitch, Diane. *The Great School Wars: A History of the New York City Public Schools*. 1974. Reprint, New York: Basic Books, 1988.

Reed, Barbara Straus. "Pioneer Jewish Journalism." In Frankie Hutton and Barbara Straus Reed, eds., *Outsiders in Nineteenth Century Press History: Multicultural Perspectives*. Bowling Green, OH: Bowling Green State University Popular Press, 1995.

Reisman, Ben. "Why I Came to America," In Jocelyn Cohen and Daniel Soyer, eds., *My Future Is in America: East European Jewish Autobiographies of Eastern European Jewish Immigrants*. New York: NYU Press, 2006.

Ribalow, Harold U., ed. *Autobiographies of American Jews*. Philadelphia: Jewish Publication Society, 1968.

Rischin, Moses. Introduction to Moses Rischin, ed., *Grandma Never Lived in America: The New Journalism of Abraham Cahan*. Bloomington: Indiana University Press, 1985.

———. *The Promised City: New York's Jews, 1870–1914*. Cambridge: Harvard University Press, 1962.

———. "Toward the Onomastics of the Great New York Ghetto: How the Lower East Side Got Its Name." In Hasia Diner, Jeffrey Shandler, and Beth Wenger, eds., *Remembering the Lower East Side: American Jewish Reflections*. Bloomington: Indiana University Press, 2000.

Rogin, Michael. *Blackface, White Noise: Jewish Immigrants and the Hollywood Melting Pot*. Berkeley: University of California Press, 1996.

Rogoff, Hillel. *Meyer London: A biografye*. New York: Meyer London Memorial Fund, 1930.

Rogow, Faith. *Gone to Another Meeting: The National Council of Jewish Women, 1893–1993*. Tuscaloosa: University of Alabama Press, 1993.

Romanofsky, Peter. "'. . . To Rid Ourselves of the Burden . . .': New York Jewish Charities and the Origins of the Industrial Removal Office, 1890–1901." *American Jewish Historical Quarterly* 64:4 (June 1975): 331–343.

Rontch, Isaac. *Di idishe landsmanshaften fun Nyu York*. New York: IL Peretz Yiddish Writers Union, 1938.

Rosenfeld, Morris. "The Teardrop Millionaire." In Itche Goldberg and Max Rosenfeld, eds., *Morris Rosenfeld: Selections from His Poetry and Prose*. New York: Yidisher kultur farband, 1964.

Rosenfelt, Henry. *This Thing of Giving: The Record of a Rare Enterprise of Mercy and Brotherhood*. New York: Plymouth, 1924.

Rubinow, Isaac M. "Economic and Industrial Condition, New York." In Charles S. Bernheimer, ed., *The Russian Jew in the United States*. Philadelphia: John C. Winston, 1905.

Sachs, A. S. *Di geshikhte fun arbayter ring, 1892–1925*. New York: National Executive Committee of the Workmen's Circle, 1925.

Sandrow, Nahma. *Vagabond Stars: A World History of the Yiddish Theater*. New York: Harper and Row, 1977.

Sarna, Jonathan. *American Judaism: A History*. New Haven: Yale University Press, 2004.

———. "Mixed Seating in the American Synagogue." In Jack Wertheimer, ed., *The American Synagogue: A Sanctuary Transformed*. Hanover, NH: University Press of New England / Brandeis University Press, 1987.

Schneider, Dorothee. *Trade Unions and Community: The German Working Class in New York City, 1870–1900*. Urbana: University of Illinois Press, 1994.

Schoen, Carol. *Anzia Yezierska*. Boston: Twayne, 1982.

Schoener, Allon. *Portal to America: The Lower East Side, 1870–1925*. New York: Holt, Rinehart, and Winston, 1967.

Schor, Esther. *Emma Lazarus*. New York: Nextbook/Schocken, 2006.

Scott, William B., and Peter M. Rutkoff. *New York Modern: The Arts and the City*. Baltimore: Johns Hopkins University Press, 1999.

Sherman, Moshe. *Orthodox Judaism in America: A Biographical Dictionary and Sourcebook*. Westport, CT: Greenwood, 1996.

Shtarkman, Moyshe. "Vikhtikste momentn in der geshikhte fun der yidisher prese in Amerike." In J. Gladstone, S. Niger, and H. Rogoff, eds., *Finf un zibetsik yor yidishe prese in Amerike, 1870–1945*. New York: Yiddish Writers Union, 1945.

Silver, Arthur. "Jews in the Political Life of New York City, 1865–1897." DHL diss., Yeshiva University, 1954.

Silver, Matthew. "Louis Marshall and the Democratization of Jewish Identity." *American Jewish History* 94:1–2 (March–June 2008): 41–69.

Simmons, Erica B. *Hadassah and the Zionist Project.* Lanham, MD: Rowman and Littlefield, 2006.

Singer, Ben. "Manhattan Nickelodeons: New Data on Audiences and Exhibitors." *Cinema Journal* 34:3 (Spring 1995): 5–35.

Slobin, Mark. *Tenement Songs: The Popular Music of the Jewish Immigrants.* Urbana: University of Illinois Press, 1982.

Smith, Judith E. *Family Connections: A History of Italian and Jewish Lives in Providence, Rhode Island, 1900–1940.* Albany: SUNY Press, 1985.

Snyder, Robert. *The Voice of the City: Vaudeville and Popular Culture in New York.* New York: Oxford University Press, 1989.

Soyer, Daniel. "Brownstones and Brownsville: Elite Philanthropists and Immigrant Constituents at the Hebrew Educational Society of Brooklyn, 1899–1929." *American Jewish History* 88:2 (June 2000): 181–207.

———, ed. *A Coat of Many Colors: Immigration, Globalization, and Reform in the New York City Garment Industry.* New York: Fordham University Press, 2005.

———. "Cockroach Capitalists: Jewish Contractors at the Turn of the Twentieth Century." In Soyer, *Coat of Many Colors.*

———. "Entering the 'Tent of Abraham': Fraternal Ritual and American-Jewish Identity, 1880–1920." *Religion and American Culture* 9:2 (Summer 1999): 159–182.

———. *Jewish Immigrant Associations and American Identity in New York, 1880–1939.* Cambridge: Harvard University Press, 1997.

———. "The Rise and Fall of the Garment Industry in New York City." In Soyer, *Coat of Many Colors.*

Stansell, Christine. *American Moderns: Bohemian New York and the Creation of a New Century.* 2000. Reprint, Princeton: Princeton University Press, 2010.

Stein, Leon, *The Triangle Fire.* Philadelphia: Lippincott, 1962.

Steinmetz, Sol. *Yiddish and English: A Century of Yiddish in America.* Tuscaloosa: University of Alabama Press, 1986.

Stempel, Larry. *Showtime: A History of the Broadway Musical Theater.* New York: Norton, 2010.

Stevens, Albert. *Cyclopedia of Fraternities.* 2nd ed. 1907. Reprint, Detroit: Gale Research, 1966.

Stolberg, Benjamin. *Tailor's Progress: The Story of a Famous Union and the Men Who Made It.* Garden City, NY: Doubleday, Doran, 1944.

Svejda, George. "Castle Garden as an Immigrant Depot, 1855–1890." Report, Division of History, Office of Archeology and Historic Preservation, National Park Service, U.S. Department of Interior, 1968. http://www.nps.gov/history/history/online_books/elis/castle_garden.pdf (accessed May 31, 2011).

Tammany Society, or Columbian Order. *150th Anniversary Celebration: 1786–July 4–1936.* New York, Tammany Society, 1936.

Tarshish, Alan. "The Board of Delegates of American Israelites (1859–1878)." *Publications of the American Jewish Historical Society* 49 (1959): 17–32.

Tcherikower, E. *Geshikhte fun der yidisher arbeter bavegung in di fareynikte shtatn.* New York: Yiddish Scientific Institute—Yivo, 1945.

Thissen, Judith. "Film and Vaudeville on New York's Lower East Side." In Barbara Kirshenblatt-Gimblett and Jonathan Karp, eds., *The Art of Being Jewish in Modern Times.* Philadelphia: University of Pennsylvania Press, 2008.

———. "Jewish Immigrant Audiences in New York City, 1905–1914." In Melvyn Stokes and Richard Maltby eds., *American Movie Audiences: From the Turn of the Century to the Early Sound Era.* London: BFI, 1999.

Tifft, Susan, and Alex S. Jones. *The Trust: The Private and Powerful Family behind the New York Times.* Boston: Little, Brown, 1999.

Tyack, David. *The One Best System: A History of American Urban Education.* Cambridge: Harvard University Press, 1974.

Von Drehle, David. *Triangle: The Fire That Changed America.* New York: Atlantic Monthly Press, 2003.

Wald, Lillian. *House on Henry Street.* New York: Holt, 1915.

Walkowitz, Daniel. *Working with Class: Social Workers and the Politics of Middle-Class Identity.* Chapel Hill: University of North Carolina Press, 1999.

Warfield, David. *Ghetto Silhouettes.* New York: James Pott, 1902.

Warner, M. R. *Tammany Hall.* Garden City, NY: Doubleday, Doran, 1928.

Warnke, Nina. "Immigrant Popular Culture as Contested Space: Yiddish Music Halls, the Yiddish Press, and the Processes of Americanization, 1900–1919." *Theater Journal* 48:3 (October 1996): 321–335.

———. "Theater as Educational Institution: Jewish Immigrant Intellectuals and Yiddish Theater Reform." In Barbara Kirshenblatt-Gimblett and Jonathan Karp, eds., *The Art of Being Jewish in Modern Times.* Philadelphia: University of Pennsylvania Press, 2008.

Weinstein, Bernard. *Di idishe yunyons in Amerike.* New York: United Hebrew Trades, 1929.

Weiss, Nancy. *Charles Francis Murphy, 1858–1924: Respectability and Responsibility in Tammany Politics.* Northampton, MA: Smith College, 1968.

Welch, Richard. *King of the Bowery: Big Tim Sullivan, Tammany Hall, and New York City from the Gilded Age to the Progressive Era.* Albany: SUNY Press, 2008.

Wenger, Beth. *New York Jews and the Great Depression: Uncertain Promise.* New Haven: Yale University Press, 1996.

Whitfield, Stephen. *In Search of American Jewish Culture.* Hanover, NH: University Press of New England / Brandeis University Press, 1999.

Wilentz, Sean. *Chants Democratic: New York City and the Rise of the American Working Class, 1789–1850.* New York: Oxford University Press, 1984.

Wilhelm, Cornelia. "Independent Order of True Sisters: Friendship, Fraternity, and a

Model of Modernity for Nineteenth Century American Jewish Womanhood." *American Jewish Archives* 54:1 (2002): 37–63.

Wischnitzer, Rachel. *Synagogue Architecture in the United States: History and Interpretation*. Philadelphia: Jewish Publication Society, 1955.

Wise, Isaac Mayer. *Reminiscences*. Cincinnati: L. Wise, 1901.

Wisse, Ruth. *A Little Love in Big Manhattan: Two Yiddish Poets*. Cambridge: Harvard University Press, 1988.

Woeste, Victoria Saker. "Insecure Equality: Louis Marshall, Henry Ford, and the Problem of Defamatory Antisemitism, 1920–1929." *Journal of American History* 91:3 (December 2004): 877–905.

Woocher, Jonathan. *Sacred Survival: The Civil Religion of American Jews*. Bloomington: Indiana University Press, 1986.

Yans-McLaughlin, Virginia, and Marjorie Lightman. *Ellis Island and the Peopling of America: The Official Guide*. New York: New Press, 1997.

Yefroikin, Zalmen. "Yidishe dertsiung in di fareynikte shtatn." *Algemeyne entsiklopedia: Yidn hey*. New York: Dubnov Fund and Encyclopedia Committee, 1957.

Young, Bette Roth. *Emma Lazarus in Her World: Life and Letters*. Philadelphia: Jewish Publication Society, 1995.

Zipperstein, Steven. *Elusive Prophet: Ahad Ha'am and the Origins of Zionism*. Berkeley: University of California Press, 1993.

INDEX

Page numbers in italics refer to a figure or a caption on the page.

137th Street (Manhattan), 49
149th Street (Bronx), 235
1840s, 23, 43
1850s, 13, 23
1860s, 275
1870–1915, 66
1880–1924, 111–112
1880s, 91
1886 elections, 185
1912 elections, 197–200
1914 elections, 173
1917 mayoral elections, 201–202
1920 elections, 202
1920s and 1930s, 177
1930s and 1940s, 204

A. T. Stewart & Co., 42
Aaronson, Harris, 49, 50, 54–55, 130–131
Abendblat (newspaper), 221
Abraham, Abraham, 147, 153
Abraham, Fanny, 30
Abraham, Jacob, 30–31
Abraham & Straus, 153, 274–275
Academy of Music, 57
Adler, Celia, 220
Adler, Cyrus, 215
Adler, Felix, 85, 95
Adler, Jacob, 219, 220
Adler, Luther, 220
Adler, Samuel, 85
Adler, Stella, 220
Agudath Ha-Rabbannim (Union of Orthodox
  Rabbis of the United States and Canada),
  98
Ahawath Chesed congregation (later Central
  Synagogue): Americanization, 95; Avenue
  C location, 65, 76; Bohemian Jews, 31;
  construction, 73–76; cornerstone laying,
  73–74; dedication, 75–76; facade, 75; Fern-
  bach, Henry, 207; Friday night services, 97;
  German language, 95; German-speaking
  immigrants, 89; Huebsch, Adolph, 85;

Kohut, Alexander, 64, 86, 88; Kohut,
  Rebekah Bettelheim, *64*; Leerburger, Han-
  nah, 68; Moorish architecture, *72, 74, 76,*
  79; Protestant church, remodeling of, 76;
  Reform Judaism, 85–86; seat contracts, 90;
  sisterhood, 68–69; Wise, Isaac Mayer, 75,
  85; women's charitable work, 67
Ahearn, Eddy, 182
Ahearn, John, 182–183, 199
Ahearn Association, 182, 183
Akiva, Rabbi, 53–54
Allen Street (Manhattan), 31, 89, 112
Alliance Israelite Universelle, 154
Allied Conference for Cheap Kosher Meat, 128
Amboy Street (Brooklyn), 286
American, Sadie, 147–148
American Hebrew (magazine): Americaniza-
  tion, 215; Cohn, Max, 86; Cowen, Philip,
  215; cultural modernization, 215; Jewish
  Theological Seminary (JTS), 88; Lazarus,
  Emma, 217; mayoral nomination of Nathan
  Straus, 178; writers published by, 215
American Israelite (newspaper), 92–93
American Jewish Committee (AJC): assimila-
  tion, 160–161; B'nai B'rith, 158; Elkus,
  Abram, 197; Ford, Henry, 247; founding,
  156–158; Jewish immigrants, 157–158;
  Jewish rights and privileges, 157; Kehillah,
  the (The Jewish Community), 164, 165;
  "leading Jews," 158; Magnes, Judah, 163;
  Marshall, Louis, 156, 247; National Liberal
  Immigration League, 158; Roosevelt, Theo-
  dore, 157; United Hebrew Charities (UHC),
  63; Versailles peace talks, 169
American Jewish Congress, 167–169
American Jewish Joint Distribution Commit-
  tee (JDC), 167
American Jewish Relief Committee (AJRC),
  167
American Jewish Year Book (Jewish Publication
  Society), 157
American Labor Party, 204

Annie Polland is Vice President for Programs and Education at the Lower East Side Tenement Museum, where she oversees the development of exhibits and programs. She is the author of *Landmark of the Spirit: The Eldridge Street Synagogue* (Yale University Press, 2009) and teaches at the Eugene Lang College at the New School.

Daniel Soyer is Professor and Chair of the History Department at Fordham University. He is the author or editor of numerous books including *Jewish Immigrant Associations and American Identity in New York, 1880–1939, A Coat of Many Colors: Immigration, Globalization, and Reform in the New York City Garment Industry,* and *My Future Is in America: Autobiographies of Eastern European Jewish Immigrants* (available from NYU Press).